THIS BELL
STILL RINGS

THIS BELL STILL RINGS

My Life of Defiance and Song

BARBARA DANE

Heyday
Berkeley, California

Unless otherwise specified, all images are courtesy of the Barbara Dane Legacy Project. All reasonable attempts were made to locate the copyright holders for the material published in this book. If you believe you may be one of them, please contact Heyday and the publisher will include appropriate acknowledgment in subsequent editions of the book.

Copyright © 2022 by Barbara Dane

All rights reserved. No portion of this work may be reproduced or transmitted in any form or by any means, electronic or mechanical, including photocopying and recording, or by any information storage or retrieval system, without permission in writing from Heyday.

*Library of Congress Cataloging-in-Publication Data
Names: Dane, Barbara, author.
Title: This bell still rings : my life of defiance and song / Barbara Dane.*

*Description: Berkeley, California : Heyday, 2022. | Includes index.
Identifiers: LCCN 2022004475 (print) | LCCN 2022004476 (ebook) | ISBN 9781597145817 (hardcover) | ISBN 9781597145824 (epub)
Subjects: LCSH: Dane, Barbara. | Singers--United States--Biography | Music--Political aspects--United States--History--20th century. | LCGFT: Autobiographies.
Classification: LCC ML420.D1433 A3 2022 (print) | LCC ML420.D1433 (ebook) | DDC 782.42164092 [B]--dc23
LC record available at https://lccn.loc.gov/2022004475
LC ebook record available at https://lccn.loc.gov/2022004476*

*Cover photograph: Barbara Dane with Nina and Paul Menendez, protest against the Vietnam War, San Francisco, 1964. Copyright by Erik Weber. Used by permission.
Cover Design: Archie Ferguson
Interior Design/Typesetting: Ashley Ingram*

*Published by Heyday
P.O. Box 9145, Berkeley, California 94709
(510) 549-3564
heydaybooks.com*

Printed in East Peoria, Illinois, by Versa Press, Inc.

10 9 8 7 6 5 4 3 2 1

Ring the bells that still can ring
Forget your perfect offering
There is a crack in everything
That's how the light gets in.

—Leonard Cohen

CONTENTS

PART ONE: LET MY LITTLE LIGHT SHINE

   1 *Memories Don't Fade* . . . 1
   2 *A Chronic Truant Sings* . . . 10
   3 *The Atomic Age Begins* . . . 24
   4 *Everything Changes* . . . 36
   5 *Postwar Dreams* . . . 48
   6 *From People's Songs to the Home Front* . . . 58
   7 *California, Here It Comes!* . . . 67
   8 *The Party's Over* . . . 81
   9 *Digging Underground* . . . 88
  10 *Byron Dances In* . . . 95
  11 *Gateway Swings to Berkeley* . . . 104
  12 *Yonder Come the Blues* . . . 111
  13 *San Francisco Bay Blues* . . . 119
  14 *Trouble in Mind* . . . 131

PART TWO: ON MY WAY

  15 *From the Alley to the Grove* . . . 141
  16 *From Breakout to Blacklist* . . . 157
  17 *Livin' with the Blues* . . . 167
  18 *Priorities* . . . 179
  19 *Strange Bedfellows* . . . 187
  20 *Riding High on Sugar Hill* . . . 193
  21 *Buzz, Biz, Boom, Blam!* . . . 206
  22 *On the Emes, This Is True* . . . 218
  23 *Wake Up and Sing!* . . . 224
  24 *Do You, Mister Jones?* . . . 229
  25 *Which Side Are You On?* . . . 237
  26 *The Times, They Are a-Changin'* . . . 244

PART THREE: MY AMERICAN DREAM

27 *Irwin Calls, Lightnin' Strikes, Mississippi Beckons* ... 253
28 *Go Tell It on the Mountain* ... 262
29 *Navigating Obstacles Blanketed in Bliss* ... 267
30 *You Don't Know Me* ... 273
31 *Hard Rains Are a-Fallin'* ... 279
32 *Three-Mile Walk of Hope* ... 284
33 *Good Morning Blues* ... 292
34 *Cuba Sí, Yanqui No!* ... 296
35 *Paul Becomes Pablo* ... 311
36 *He's Got the Whole World in His Hands* ... 316
37 *Singers of the World, Unite!* ... 319
38 *Levitate the Pentagon!* ... 325
39 *United We Are Strong* ... 329
40 *Unidentified Flying Object* ... 333
41 *Play Your Guitars, American Friends* ... 340
42 *La Voce dell'altra America* ... 345
43 *Building a Big Wall of Music* ... 353
44 *Free the Army!* ... 356
45 *Solidarity Forever Crossing Borders* ... 370
46 *Wild Women Don't Get the Blues* ... 376
47 *Give Peace a Chance* ... 379

PART FOUR: NOBODY GONNA TURN ME 'ROUND

48 *Pack Up Your Sorrows* ... 391
49 *A Musical Road Trip to Nowhere* ... 398
50 *You Just Can't Make It by Yourself* ... 406
51 *Will the Circle Be Unbroken?* ... 412
52 *Take It Slow and Easy* ... 416
53 *Throw It Away* ... 428

Some Rules for the Road Ahead . . . 443
Gratitude . . . 447
Discography, Key Links, and More . . . 449
Index . . . 455
About the Author . . . 473

PART ONE

LET MY LITTLE LIGHT SHINE

1
MEMORIES DON'T FADE

Blinding blue sparkling skies, immense dark flights of birds slashing the blue from one horizon to the other, high sweet grass as far as I could see: that's what my childhood looks like in memory. My heart swells now to think of how exquisitely, splendidly, bountifully nature spread itself out for us. I loved the smell of the dirt when I dug it with my little tin shovel, and the special damp tang of it when the earthworms surfaced or when I kicked over a rock to see beetles scatter.

Digging a sort of bowl in the dirt and then erecting a bunk over it, a little house made of scraps scrounged from the building sites scattered loosely for blocks around us, and we kids had a hideout. Harvesting dried Queen Anne's lace, thistles, clouds of spirea, teasels, blackberries from thorny thickets, mulberries from underneath an umbrella of branches where we hid, sometimes a few rare wild strawberries, and so many others I can't name—we had us a plentifully stocked pretend kitchen. I was always the head of it.

I mostly gave all that up when my best friend Gloria's big brother Ralphie crawled into the bunk after me once and tried to get inside my panties. No fun anymore, and besides, I was getting older and there was too much else to do, other worlds to explore. And the sense of boundless freedom out in those wide fields was now twisted out of focus. Things *could* go wrong. Also, I think I got my first two-wheel bike about then.

Barbara Dane, mother Dorothy, and sister Julia Anne, c. 1930

Back in 1925, when my parents, Gil and Dorothy, came north from Jonesboro, Arkansas, and first hit Detroit, they barely had a buck between them. But my dad was able to borrow a stake from a local doctor who saw setting him up as a good investment. The idea was that they would both do well if the doctor sent his patients to Gil Spillman at the Biltmore Pharmacy, out there in the far northwest reaches of Detroit. One hand would wash the other. When little Barbara showed up two years later, my cradle was a large cardboard carton that had conveyed Kotex sanitary napkins. With me in that box in the corner, Dorothy could work in the store with Gil and keep me out of trouble at the same time.

The store sat at 16940 W. Six Mile Road, later called McNichols Road, on the side bordering Elmore, a neighborhood with muddy roads and humble little houses, some of them little more than lean-tos with peeling paint. Even though we usually lived on the better side of Six Mile, where the houses were brick, we moved almost every year in search of lower rent.

When I was old enough to count, they set me to work behind a low case with a slanted glass front, waiting on the kids who came in for penny candy. I could see the anxiety on their little faces as they tried hard to find anything that might contain any sort of extra bonus. Crackerjack, the sticky caramel-covered popcorn, had a prize—some little plastic or tin thing—and a paper slip with your fortune, but it cost a nickel, and they mostly had only pennies. Guess What?s were a penny, but they only had two skimpy caramels and a fortune. Poverty is a stern teacher.

It seems as though people got their adult lives started a whole lot younger back then. By the time Mom was twenty-four and Dad was twenty-nine, their lives were defined by three kids and a complicated small business, smack in the middle of the worst Depression this country had yet known. They informed me in no uncertain terms that I was the one who would get a licking if my sister, Julia (two years younger), or my baby brother, Sonny (four years younger), got hurt or broke anything. "You have to set a good example," they insisted.

My dad was in the drugstore from 8:00 a.m. to midnight, seven days a week. When business slowed down later in the evenings, he would be there alone, checking out the cash registers, working on the books, compounding the backed-up prescriptions that only he was licensed to prepare, and going over the items to be restocked after closing. I never heard a word of complaint from him, and only found out years later that he'd often pop a little yellow "dexy" or two to keep going. Every now and then he'd repeat his mantra: "The only reason I'm doing all this is for you kids, so that you can have a better life." That was the motor that drove his generation.

Each of us in turn was enrolled in the grade school that served the affluent Rosedale Park community. This meant that we would have a mile-long walk to Cooke School in the morning, often another mile each way to the drugstore and back for lunch, and then the final mile home in late afternoon. The reasoning was that we would meet a "better class of children" there, and learn to travel in the upscale world beyond Elmore.

Gradually, I was developing an awareness that I was in a whole different category from those Rosedale Park girls. For one thing, they arrived at school in print dresses, starched and ironed, with Shirley Temple sausage curls, carefully combed around their mom's, or maybe the maid's, fingers with black patent-leather Mary Janes on their feet. My sister and I were turned out in woolens with no need for ironing, short Dutch boy haircuts that needed little combing, and sturdy brown Oxfords. I felt that I looked just fine, but couldn't help but notice the difference.

There was a lot of talk then about America being a melting pot, where all people could blend in. But in line at the drinking fountain, we kids would compare notes.

"What are you?"

"I'm Italian, Iranian, Polish, Swiss, French, Greek, etc.," came the replies down the line. When it came to me, all I could say was, "Oh, I'm nothing."

I had no notion of any particular roots, even the southern ones my folks seemed quietly determined to cut loose. I felt adrift among all these kids with seemingly clear identities like anchors. Those exchanges awakened a fierce hunger in my heart, a need to connect with something larger than myself, a lifetime longing to become one with, or at least to know about, everyone and everything on the whole planet. I had become an internationalist by second grade!

My mom was always painfully aware of her occasional southern pronunciations of words, and strove mightily to erase them. She would blush from the shame of saying "UMbrella" instead of "umBRELLa," and would correct us when we slipped into any kind of vernacular language. "Hillbilly" was a term used for anyone vaguely southern and white, and the term was a weapon in the arsenal of the lords of industry, most notably Henry Ford, who looked for every small crack between people in which to lodge his wedges of disunity. The workers sang, "The union makes us strong," but the bosses wanted disunity above all. And a hillbilly was by definition ignorant, poor, and without roots or influence. You wouldn't want to be identified with *him*!

With some effort, recently migrated white folks could pass for long-lost cousins of the upper crust, so my mother signed us up for elocution lessons. This was a win for me because I got to stand up in front of people and demonstrate my comfort, and even delight, in communicating my thoughts and ideas. In short, I was a little show-off.

Mom drove me to school one day in our square black Ford with the running board on the side; incredibly, it had a radio mounted in the dashboard. A man's voice was talking about someone called Roosevelt, and Mom said that she hoped he would be elected president because then things would get better for everyone. Although I had no idea what that really meant, I felt comforted to know she thought about things such as who was making up the rules and taking care of things beyond our neighborhood and family. By then, women had had the vote for only twelve years (and only white women at that point), so I guess she wanted to make her own vote count for something important.

I had a running battle with the Cooke School authorities because the boys were learning to work with wood, while the girls were assigned to a sewing class. I already knew how to sew, but I did not know how to use woodworking tools and had no other access to them, so I kept insisting that they let me cross over to the other class. Finally this was agreed on, and I really did love that place, with its sawdust smells and implements that could make real things, like marble boards, birdhouses, and so much more. But one day the teacher kept me after class and asked me to bring my work over to his desk and stand close, where I could show it to him. I was working on a marionette and needed help figuring out how the joints were going to operate. The teacher gently and gradually moved his hand up under my dress and down to my underwear, where he started stroking me softly between my legs. A wave of heat came over me. Embarrassed and not sure what to do, I twisted out of reach and hurried to the principal's office, where I told someone I needed a ride home. I must have told my mother what happened, because I didn't see that teacher around anymore, and I was sent back to the sewing class without further explanation.

One of the few diversions from the hard-pressed life around us in those deep Depression days was the hope of going to one of the magnificent movie palaces that sprang up around town. In the neighborhood around our drugstore, we saw hungry people every day, saw the difficulties they had just getting food on the table. I remember often seeing this one little boy trudging along to the Kroger store, and noticed that he regularly made his way back home with what looked like a single loaf of bread. I worried about what his family might have to put between the slices, and how many of them would be sharing that loaf. I'd served single-scoop ice cream cones to the neighborhood kids and watched them share it, each taking a lick in turn. I wondered why their lives were so different from mine. I doubted that any of them ever got to go to the picture show.

My mother took my sister, brother, and me to the movies on Dish Night whenever possible. The idea was that you could build up a whole set of nice dinnerware by coming every week and collecting the plates and cups and saucers they gave away free. You got to see a double feature, a cartoon, and the newsreel—covering world events, politics, sports, and fashion.

The newsreels took us to the various hot spots in the world and taught us new words, like *Wehrmacht*, *Luftwaffe*, *Il Duce*, and *der Führer*. We watched Mussolini's Black Shirts marching off to Greece, Albania, Ethiopia, and Libya, and Hitler's thugs, the Brown Shirts, "keeping order" in the streets of Germany while his armies marched into Poland, Austria, Belgium, France, the Netherlands, Norway, the USSR, on and on. Long lines of refugees trudged endlessly toward hope of some sort, dragging their children and pathetic bundles, while terrifying planes strafed them from the sky, causing them to dive into the ditches or underbrush that lined the roads. The visual images of all this turmoil in the world came at us children from huge screens, far bigger than life, in black and white and in two-to-three-minute snips, often blurry and out of focus, with stentorian music and announcers sounding like "the voice of god" interpreting events. By 1936, people had begun to cringe at Hitler's constant ranting about his master race, and the sight of his goose-stepping troops filled the movie house with catcalls.

Movies were important, but my whole life really ran on a parallel track with the rise of the radio, a new and thrilling entertainment that was free for just the click of a knob, and so intimate because everything it gave you was happening inside your own head, no screen needed. The radio console in the living room brought me music from local singers and musicians with their guitars and country-style songs, popular dance tunes, crooners with dreamy lyrics, sometimes live Black church meetings down at the far end of the dial, and late at night even big swing bands from some faraway city.

When I was eight years old, I made a nonnegotiable demand: I need a piano! Since I was such a cooperative and hard-working little kid, my mom found a decent secondhand upright and hired the local teacher, Miss Savery, to give me weekly lessons. I loved to practice, but would never do it when anyone else was in the house. This was *my* thing, and I didn't want to chance any interference. I would ride my bike to the big Woolworth's five-and-dime where they had an ample music counter filled with sheet music and books. Instead of looking for the latest individual songs, I found myself searching for collections of older songs, with piano parts simple enough for me to sight-read. Gradually my practice time found me singing much more than playing piano.

In our Sunday school class at St. James Methodist Church, the teacher was a stout old prune who wore an America First badge prominently on her dress, broadcasting her allegiance to Charles Lindbergh's right-wing isolationist views. I loved to read, and devoured the newspaper scandals from a very young age, so I knew that America First was somehow related to the Black Legion, a white supremacist group connected to those horrifying pictures of lynchings that were turning up in the papers all the time. That made me somewhat afraid of the lady with the badge, but, worse than that, her hypocrisy gave me a pain in the stomach. How can you tell us in one breath to love Jesus because he called all the little children to come unto him, and with the next breath deny the personhood of any child who doesn't look just like us?

By May 1936, the Black Legion, with its Ku Klux Klan (KKK) ties, had nearly thirty thousand members in Michigan. An article in Hearst's *Detroit Times* described the Black Legion like this: "Cults of this nature with their hocus pocus oaths and their 'fe-fi-fo-fum' passwords are throwbacks to medieval times. . . . Unhappily there will always, it seems, be poor dupes to swell the membership rolls of these evil cults. They are invariably of the same stripe: workaday people of limited advantages and intelligence to whom the ceremonials, the silly gibberish, and the spooky trappings promise adventure and romance."

One day I was working at the drugstore when I witnessed a scene so disturbing that it has stayed with me my whole life. Think of the atmosphere on an unbearably humid and blistering midday in a city where no store would permit a Black person and a white person to sit down together for a cool drink of water. Think of my daddy, a young white man striving since his shoeless days on an Arkansas farm to lift himself and his young family up, unremittingly working long hours seven days a week. Think of a cohort of Black men so new to the territory and so desperate for survival that they are working outdoors on this sweltering day in a road-grading gang sponsored by the WPA, the Works Projects Administration created by FDR to keep Americans from starving.

One man steps cautiously inside the door. Softly, he asks the little girl at the soda fountain for a Coke and puts down a nickel. She is hesitant at first, thinking of the training her daddy recently gave her about the exact right way to serve a Coca-Cola: take down one of the special curved glasses with that name on it; open the ribbed, hourglass-shaped bottle; and pour about three-quarters of the way up the glass. Set the bottle and glass down on the counter, side by side.

The man is confused. He doesn't know what is expected of him in this new northern town in the midst of what is clearly "white" territory, so he hesitates. The girl is intent on doing this right, so gives a welcoming smile and indicates that he should sit. He's still not sure, takes a step, and . . .

My daddy comes streaking out of the prescription room, shouting, "Get out of here! You know you can't drink that in here! Get back outside!" The Black man quietly vanishes, but my dad continues to scream at me. "Listen, you can't do that! If we start letting THEM in here, we'll lose all our business. Times are tough enough as it is! Do not EVER do that again!"

I don't remember what I did next, but the scene ended, and my nine-year-old psyche took all of it deep, deep inside. For one thing, my dad had treated me unjustly. He had failed to recognize how well I followed his instructions about how to serve the drink, even screamed at me for doing it. That wasn't fair. More important, my father had refused a thirsty man a drink and had humiliated a grown man before a child. That Black man and I had both been humiliated. He and I had both been refused and denied. Unknowingly, I took him inside my heart and bonded with his hurt, identified with the denial of his personhood.

I identified with the Black man, understanding my white father to be the unjust person in the drama. Unaware of how definitively the die had been cast in those moments, I have spent a lifetime searching for fairness, measuring events by those standards, fighting for justice wherever I could, with whatever tools I could find.

A couple of years later, I spent one glorious summer day sitting under a tree with two neighbor boys, Bob Smock and Bill Hall. We were a small sort of Socratic Society of three, who met now and then to take up serious matters in the manner of eleven- and twelve-year-olds.

Bill Hall was smart and athletic, and today he was all wound up and holding forth. He was carefully explaining about the three ways things were organized in this world.

Number one was capitalism, where only a few people have all the money, make all the rules, and control everyone else. The rest have to work for them and make them richer; things are made for profit, not because they are needed; and working people are bought and sold cheap and thrown away when they got old.

Number two was socialism, where all the people would have a say-so and would work for the betterment of everyone. Things would be made because people needed them, not just for profit, and people would receive the things they needed according to the work they did.

Number three was communism, where as a society we would be able to make or grow everything necessary to live, so everyone could freely access everything they needed.

I decided right then and there that socialism or communism would be a better way to organize things than capitalism, the ruthless effects of which were clear enough everywhere you looked.

2

A CHRONIC TRUANT SINGS

I felt terrible disillusionment at the very beginning of my high school life. I had thought I would be able to choose classes for myself, including music and theater, another of my new interests. But no, said the counselor, there was a prescribed list of classes you had to take, they didn't offer any music except for the Glee Club, and there was no theater for freshmen.

OK, so here I was in the freshman history class at Redford High, with a small group sitting in a circle while the teacher told us that we should now turn to a discussion of the prehistoric—

Wait a minute! I raised my hand eagerly. "If it's prehistoric, doesn't that mean 'before history,' so we actually don't know anything in these books for sure?"

I quickly found myself writing "I will not be impertinent in school again" one hundred times on the huge blackboard, all under the scrutiny of the whole class.

I began a secret life, hoarding my lunch money in order to take the bus randomly to almost anywhere else, spending much of my time standing over tables full of dusty books in used bookstores, reading whatever took my fancy. Most of those bookshops were kept by elderly, run-down intellectuals who didn't seem to know what to make of me. I was voracious and completely without direction, reading something of everything but hardly anything completely, and rarely spending any money. (I remember discovering Oscar Wilde's play *Salome* that way.)

Sometimes I would slip out of class and cross the street to the local diner, where I could drink coffee and smoke cigarettes all afternoon. The jukebox there (one song for a nickel, six for a quarter) had an excellent music menu: Glenn Miller's "String of Pearls," Count Basie's "One O'Clock Jump," Ella Fitzgerald's "A Tisket a Tasket," Duke Ellington with "Do Nothin' Til You Hear from Me," Bing Crosby's "I'll Be Seeing You," both the Bennie Goodman and Andrews Sisters versions of "Bei Mir Bist Du Schoen," and the Andrews Sisters' biggest hit, "Boogie Woogie Bugle Boy from Company B." This was the music that was carried off to war in the hearts of the young draftees, that accompanied the last dances before going overseas. The songs that kept hope and dreams alive in the girls who waited for them to come home.

The counselor at Redford High was constantly scolding me for my truancy, saying that I was just a bum who would never amount to anything and that my parents would never be proud of me. How could she know how much education I was getting from the jukebox, and, for that matter, how could I? My response was to set my jaw, look her directly in the eye, and say, "I'm going to become a teacher. Just wait, you'll see." In my own way, from my platform as a singer, that's exactly what I did.

We had a loose group of girls who we considered our "in" crowd, linked by our love of dark pancake makeup, dark-purple lipstick, lots of black mascara, long baggy sweaters, short pleated skirts (which we made even shorter after leaving for school by rolling up the waistbands), and on our feet thick angora socks and either saddle shoes or huaraches, which we bought from Mexico through magazine ads. We perfected the art of keeping our knees together, distancing ourselves from any of the girls who violated that unwritten law.

As for dating, we thought it best not to get too tight with any particular boy, the better to study these creatures as a species. My friend Sue Jones was always coming up with double dates, which is how I came to go out sometimes with Lothar Witteborg, a guy about six feet five, and other times with Bob Zubick, a guy about five feet six! Bob knew the ropes at a local country club, where a few of us had braved the Michigan winter one night by going out tobogganing down the hills of its frozen golf course. The management allowed us into the clubhouse afterward to warm up, and Zubick ordered the drinks. They weren't shy about selling us the hard stuff, probably because mostly rich kids with influential parents hung out there. We drank a whole lot of Scotch, and I got really sick trying to keep up. I barely made it into the house, and vomited quietly all night long, hoping my parents wouldn't hear me. We had a lot of nice times with other perfectly fine boys, but they all seemed so young, so boring and inarticulate to me that their names and faces have become blurred with time.

I remember waiting for the bus on the way to and from Redford High. Often the men driving by would wave or whistle, or even call out some words of flattery. Now and then one would stop and ask if I wanted a ride, which of course I was shrewd enough to refuse. I had become adept at fending off unwanted touching and ogling too. I affected a cool manner, wore a loose coat that blurred my outlines, and covered my blonde hair with a babushka or a beret. By thirteen or fourteen, I'd learned what most young girls learn sooner or later: the prey can never simply live, but must always exist in relation to a world of hunters.

Barbara Dane, c. 1941

In the summertime, all my high school friends from across Six Mile Road would stop in to get ice cream cones before heading off to Walled Lake for a swim. I credit my smooth cheeks in old age to the fact that I was in there dishing out sodas, sundaes, and milk shakes instead of frying myself into early wrinkles on the beach. It was fun, too, because by now I was old enough to banter with the customers and play the jovial hostess behind the soda fountain, which felt almost like being in the movies. Also, I could wear a little makeup (pancake, the darker the better), and had learned to put my hair up in curlers for that new V-roll hairdo with the curly bangs. (The *V* was for victory, and those bangs can only be seen on poodles nowadays.)

It helped pass the time to invent games in my head, like How many orders could I take without writing them down and still fill them exactly right? You want a pineapple soda with chocolate ice cream? You want a sundae with vanilla ice cream, chocolate syrup, and Spanish peanuts, hold the whipped cream? You'd like a root beer float, two scoops of vanilla? You want a strawberry malt with extra whipped cream? And you, a banana split, three scoops, each a different flavor, with nuts on top? Got it! And, by the way, a banana split with first-class ice cream and syrups, topped with nuts and hand-whipped cream, cost a big fifteen cents when I was a kid. Eat your heart out!

I was becoming acutely conscious of the difference between what people thought I was thinking, what I appeared to be like, and what I was really thinking, what was going on inside my head. In the eternal manner of the young, I was busy constructing my own set of understandings, my own values and motivations. I wasn't ready to display these things at home, and certainly wasn't prepared to defend any of my half-formed opinions. I couldn't risk being teased or belittled on my home turf.

To this day I regret how little I took my mother or father into my confidence about anything I was experiencing or feeling as I sailed through my young teen years. Did they long to be included in my world, and was I cheating them out of their only chances? Did I miss some invaluable counsel, words that would have deepened my understanding and appreciation of life?

I did allow my parents a peek at my singing aspirations from time to time, and one day my father decided to give me some direct encouragement. It seems odd now to realize that my very first paid singing gig was actually set up by my dad. Truthfully, I'm not sure why he did it or how he came to believe I could cut it. I wasn't more than fourteen years old, but there I was, all set to do a few numbers with a real live dance band at the Fireman's Ball. And on one of our only shopping trips together ever, Dad himself took me to pick out a proper dress for the job! I'm sure he much preferred the pink tulle gowns with ruffles like the ones that teenage girls in the magazines wore. But I chose a black taffeta with tiny red pin dots and a red band around the top. It had no sleeves, thin spaghetti straps, and was very plainly cut, making me feel quite stylish, mature, and different. Dad was clearly on a mission to show respect for me, so he went along with my choice.

The first thing that hit me when I got up on the bandstand was that I was mainly meant to be ornamental, and so was told to sit up front the whole time, even when I wasn't singing. The next thing that washed over me was the realization that we had had no rehearsal, that I had no idea which songs the band and I would both know, and that I didn't know my keys to anything. I didn't even have a tune list in my head, let alone on paper. There must have been a few other songs, but the only one I can remember singing, and I had to repeat it a few times, was "Shoo Fly Pie and Apple Pan Dowdy," a popular novelty that Ella Fitzgerald had recorded. Best thing about it was the lyric, which repeated in cycles and didn't mean anything at all!

Well, the people were dancing away, talking and laughing and mingling and drinking all afternoon. I glanced at my dad standing on the sidelines of the dance floor and saw that he was relaxed and smiling, and I noticed some of his fireman friends going over to congratulate him. He never was one to go on and on about his feelings, but we stopped somewhere for a bite to eat on the way home, and he said I had made him feel proud. His eyes had a sparkle I hadn't seen for a while.

My dad kept little file cards in a shoebox where he wrote down the accumulating debts of the many sick neighbors who, out of work during the Depression, had no money for medicine. He spoke very kindly to them and didn't charge them for advice or the small medical services, like removing a splinter or draining a boil. They had come to the druggist hoping for help, since a doctor would have been out of the question for them. Now, with World War II starting up, there was "war work," and Detroit's auto plants began to stir again, converting their assembly lines to turn out military trucks and tanks. Biltmore Pharmacy's customers were now starting to pay their debts with the fruits of their new jobs, and my father was finally able to hire the first nonfamily clerk the drugstore ever had, to take care of the soda fountain and cosmetic counter.

This extra help allowed my mother the chance to experience life beyond the drugstore. Her unspoken dreams of finding fulfillment and recognition in life had been fading fast. Back in Jonesboro, she had sparkled as a peppy blossoming flapper, cutting her hair short into a stylish bob, driving a (borrowed) car, and earning her own spending money by doing odd jobs around town. But these things were moderated by small-town conventions and the inevitable conflicting expectations of parents with nineteenth-century outlooks living in a twentieth-century world. She had grabbed the first opportunity to leave small-town life, but by her mid-twenties she found herself responsible for three little children, with her future cut out as the homemaker and shop assistant that neatly fit into her husband's agenda.

Now, with her youngest off to military school and the wartime prosperity that made it possible to hire help at the drugstore, Dorothy—by now in her mid-thirties—could finally carve out some time for herself, spending some of her afternoons, and some evenings too, downtown among a new crowd of people, one that was entirely unconnected to my father's life.

She began to frequent the Knickerbocker Club, a place that *Sports Illustrated* called "a proper, staid and revered bridge club." Southern girls were traditionally skilled at bridge, but this was a whole new league for Dorothy, who soon was gaining confidence and admiration as she became expert at this competitive, and usually male-dominated, game of contract bridge.

She soon stuck up a friendship with Leo and Olga Friedlander, a Jewish couple who became her cover in case anyone should find it improper for her to be there without her husband. Now and then the Friedlanders came to our house for dinner, or we were invited to their home. They were actually the first identifiable Jews I had ever met, and through them I was introduced to all sorts of new foods and flavors. Food will get me anytime, but the hunger to learn all I could of the world's cultures and peoples was already planted in my gut, and the Friedlanders unwittingly served to pry open one of the first doors. This turned out to be a useful initiation into a world that would come to be as familiar as any culture can be to an outsider. Eventually my mother married two Jewish men in succession, and I married three myself. As my beloved late—and last—husband, Irwin, would have said, go figure!

Detroit had pockets of Jewish life when I was growing up, complete with synagogues and restaurants, family life and customs. But it would be hard to overstate the role of the anti-Jewish sentiment that seeped into everything. As early as 1921, Henry Ford's newspaper, the *Dearborn Independent*, ran prominent ads for Ford's notorious antisemitic publication, *The International Jew*. And the "radio priest," Father Charles Coughlin, now considered to be "the Father of Hate Radio," blasted out his rabidly antisemitic radio program to the nation every Sunday morning from his Shrine of the Little Flower church, located just outside Detroit.

On the other hand, there was the beloved Jewish baseball superstar Hank Greenberg. I've never had much interest in sports, but I remember that when I was seven or eight years old, we were allowed to listen, right in the schoolroom, to the radio broadcast of the Tigers playing an important game and the crowd going crazy for Hammerin' Hank. He was a great hero to the whole town and must have made a lot of Detroiters think about Jews in a new way.

The myth of Henry Ford loomed large over our town, as a beneficent provider of jobs at better pay than other factory work and as the man who made sure that the worker could afford to buy the products he made, bringing the peace and plenty of his dreams to the common man. But his years of fervently promoting antisemitism were rewarded with Hitler's Grand Cross of the German Eagle, the highest decoration given to foreigners sympathetic to Nazism. His relations with the Third Reich were greased by his ideology, and his fortune was greatly enhanced for it. As *Washington Post* reporter Michael Dobbs wrote in 1998, "Hitler was an admirer of American mass production techniques and an avid reader of the antisemitic tracts penned by Ford. 'I regard Henry Ford as my inspiration,' Hitler told a *Detroit News* reporter in 1931, two years before becoming the German Chancellor, explaining why he kept a life-size portrait of the American automaker next to his desk."

By now, I had become a teenager with a wild desire to see live musicians play the music jumping out of the jukeboxes, to see them sweat, to feel those amazing vibes shake my body in person. Most places that brought the bands and singers to town served liquor, which meant you had to be twenty-one years old to get in. I knew my parents would be horrified if they found out where I was going, so I devised a few cover stories, and with Mother spending more and more time playing bridge and Dad still chained to the drugstore, they were not in a position to check up on me. I dolled up in something slipped out of my mother's closet, along with a hat and long gloves, and with a fake ID I could sneak into the place that had some of the greatest bands of the day, Eastwood Gardens. With my long cigarette holder and high heels, I was sure they couldn't tell I was only fifteen. I wasn't really interested in drinking, so I'd order the requisite one-drink minimum, a champagne cocktail, and sip it all evening.

Those may have been hot Detroit nights, but there under the stars at Eastwood Gardens, things were amazingly cool. Over the course of three years, I saw and heard the big bands of Gene Krupa, Woody Herman, Charlie Barnet, Glenn Miller, Jimmy Dorsey, Tommy Dorsey, and Stan Kenton. When they featured a sweet band like Lawrence Welk's, I didn't go. The bands that really interested me were the swinging ones, the hot bands. I'd be crowded down near the bandstand while everybody else was out there dancing. I'd sometimes convince older boys to take me there, but it didn't matter much who they were. I was only in love with the music!

I hadn't noticed that all the bands that played at Eastwood Gardens in those days were white, and wasn't used to noticing things like that. But I had no idea what I was missing. Because I rarely read the papers anymore, let alone the Black press, I would have had no way of knowing that Basie and Ellington, the two hottest bands the world has ever known, were playing right downtown at the Paradise Theater.

By the early 1940s, as more and more migrants from all over the globe began pouring into the city looking for the jobs offered by the booming war industries, they brought their cultures along with their economic desperation. More than four hundred thousand mostly southern Americans, both Black and white, added to the crush, and it wasn't long before it became nearly impossible to find a home in the city.

In 1942, when a hard-won housing project named Sojourner Truth opened, moving Black defense workers and their families into what had been a mostly white neighborhood, the backlash by local whites was intense. Over the following year, tensions continued to grow, with persistent racial discrimination and frequent police brutality against Blacks. On a hot afternoon in June 1943, a fight broke out between Black and white youths on Belle Isle, a park on the edge of Detroit. Unrest quickly expanded into the worst urban confrontation of the wartime era. The "Detroit Riot" caused the destruction of property all over town, but most effectively tore up the Black enclave known as Paradise Valley, one of the city's oldest and most impoverished communities.

Like most youngsters in the mainly white northwest section of the city, I was insulated from any personal knowledge of all this, but the forbidding commands of my parents—"Don't go downtown" and, most particularly, "Don't go to Belle Isle"—made me curious and uneasy when I saw their anxious looks. Clearly the riots must have put Dorothy and Gil on edge about the comings and goings of their adventurous daughter. Ironically, it was only three years later that I found myself living in the notorious Paradise Valley.

At the end of the school year of 1942, I was thrown out of Redford High for chronic truancy and was transferred to Cooley High, which was also practically lily white in those days. I continued to run with Sue Jones and some of the others, although they seemed more feckless and oblivious than ever. It was the height of the war, but my friends and I were affected most personally by the reality of the draft. The girls found it hard to resist young draftees who insisted that it would somehow contribute to the war effort if they were to go "all the way," since after all, going overseas might mean they would not come back, condemned to die a virgin.

Meanwhile, another life was opening up for me in another part of town. I joined the Cooley Glee Club, where I met a girl who became my dearest friend, Virginia Dailey. So different from Sue, who could be quite opinionated and judgmental and whose main goal seemed to be succeeding in her own world, Virginia was open to the world outside, interested in poetry and the exploration of new cultures and scenes. In the Glee Club, we were learning to negotiate "Ballad for Americans," with lyrics by John LaTouche and music by Earl Robinson (who also wrote the labor classic "Joe Hill").

One day another girl in the group invited Virginia and me over to hear a recording her parents had just brought home. It was the first time I heard the unforgettable voice of Paul Robeson—peerless actor, unmatched bass baritone, laureled athlete, multilingual intellectual, one of the greatest American heroes of African descent until Dr. King himself—singing this very same piece of music! Through his indelible interpretation, the deeper meaning of the piece came through to us. It was a message of inclusiveness and true patriotism based on democratic participation, a message the country, and certainly Detroit, desperately needed to hear in those wartime years. A few years later, I went to Washington to take part in a large rally against universal military training, where Robeson sang in person. I was introduced to him as a young singer from Detroit, and he reached out to shake my hand. His sheer physical gravity from across the room could make you tremble, but to actually shake his hand? Electricity personified!

Without thinking much about it, I began to find myself drawn to almost any opportunity to see the inside of what made show business tick, to find out how people got to make a living at it. I signed up right away when I heard that a huge production called *The Oberammergau Passion Play* was looking for "extras." I wasn't the slightest bit interested in the drama of this show. It was the life and behavior of the professional actors offstage that held my interest, and it was a huge disappointment to find that the story didn't matter to any of them either, and that most of them smelled of stale booze and cigarettes and would grab at the flanks of young ladies like me without a care. What a bring-down! All that I had imagined about actors being deep thinkers with creative minds was challenged by observing these third-rate bozos run through their paces for a few weeks.

By the time I was in high school, I had realized that I was never going to become a real piano player, but I wanted more than anything now to find a proper teacher and start working in earnest on whatever it would take to be really good at singing. I convinced my folks to let me ride the bus all the way downtown, an hour's trip, to take lessons at the Conservatory. Finally I could explore the city's heart a little bit, I could do it by myself, and I could do it every week!

The tradition-bound teachers there must have been deaf and blind. They had me singing right away in a thin, high little girl's voice that didn't fit either my type or my temperament, songs like "Ave Maria" and other parent-pleasers. But I began to develop a crush on the glamorous world of opera singers, with their resonant names, like Amelita Galli-Curci, Tito Schipa, and Madame Schumann-Heinke. You could find second-hand records of arias at a shop around the alley from the Conservatory, twelve-inch discs a quarter of an inch thick that played at 78 rpm, as all records did in those days. They only played on one side, scratchy and worn to be sure, but oh what glorious melodies and fearless flights of vocalese!

It wasn't long before I got fed up with the Conservatory lessons, and the novelty of going downtown by myself, an hour-long bus ride, had worn off. But not before I discovered the ten-inch double-sided 78 rpm discs with music like Big Joe Turner's "Goin' to Kansas City" and Lil Green's "Romance in the Dark" and "Why Don't You Do Right?" with Big Bill Broonzy on guitar. At only five cents a copy, I could slip some of these into my room at home. With that discovery I was permanently hooked on the blues, and after a brief decade or two and a few remarkable twists of fate, I actually found myself in Chicago singing with Ransom Knowling, that same great bass player on the record with Lil Green and Broonzy.

One of my only friends in the ongoing classical musical endeavors that made up one of my other private lives was a boy named Lonnie Cothron, who was studying to be a baritone. I loved being in his company because he was kind, a good listener, and good to look at, and didn't try to lay those old moves on me. We could concentrate on our music. It was a while before it dawned on me that, when it came to romance, he secretly preferred boys.

I started looking for a completely different kind of teacher, and Lonnie recommended Mr. Coates, a Welshman who specialized in bel canto. This brilliant man proved to be exactly the one who had the skills to ground my singing abilities and give me the key tool that I would need to sing naturally and with power and confidence: breath control, the foundation for everything.

Here's how he illustrated what that meant. He stood on one side of the room and told me to stand at the other. Then he said that he would begin to sing a tone and that I should run across the room and punch him in his middle, where the diaphragm is located, as hard as I could, listening at the same time to see whether the tone would change at all. His beautiful voice rang out all the way through this onslaught and far beyond, clear and steady, and in tune. So now, the task was to locate that fundamental muscle in myself, learn to use it consciously, and then to become so familiar with how it worked that I could use it unconsciously, freeing my mind for involvement in the song itself.

Mr. Coates gave me some simple exercises, which I practiced infrequently but just enough to show him that I had begun to get the hang of it. First you have to really locate that muscle, and the quickest way is to let your tongue hang out while you pant like a dog. I'm not kidding! You can't do that without the diaphragm playing the leading role. Put your hands on the lower part of your rib cage and feel the diaphragm move in and out as you breathe. Now you breathe in and out for a while, directing your breath to that same place while keeping your chest from moving up and down. Then light a candle and direct a thin stream of air at the flame, just enough to make it turn blue. Continue blowing smoothly, without letting the flame flicker or go out, and never allowing it to turn orange. Just the beautiful blue flame, as steady as possible, for as long as possible. I guarantee to you, dear reader, that if you practice these things a few times, your singing will improve.

Mr. Coates was respectful of my tender young voice, and never insisted that I force it higher or lower, but rather that I learn to locate it in the most comfortable range. Gradually, from week to week, the better my breathing became, the more he could help me increase my range without fear or strain. He showed me how to make the inside of my mouth feel like a large empty space, and to relax my jaw, letting it unhinge and drop from below my ears. Watching singers whose lower jaw quivers lets you know that they are tight back there, and you can see how difficult it is for them to relax that area, which is the only way the throat can open up to let the voice out. He pointed out that singing begins with the feet, that balancing on the balls of the feet with shoulders back and chest lifted was the way to stand for power.

I loved that he had me sing *bergerettes*, melodious little folk-based songs perfectly suited to a young girl. Their French texts were brief, and their music too. I could picture myself as a simple French shepherdess on a hillside, singing to my sheep about the object of my affections. The physical principles of bel canto gave me the strength and endurance that would be required to carry a leading part in a three-act opera, and a secure foundation on which I could build whatever sound I needed. This was one of the most precious things Coates gave me: the confidence to trust myself. The other was the enduring phrase: "First think, then sing."

Around that time, riding on the improved cash flow at the drugstore during the war, my family moved to the edge of Detroit's northwest region, an upscale area known as Franklin Village. Each ranch-style home stood on about five acres. For my father, this house, with its broad green lawn and circular drive, was the realization of a lifetime dream, the perfect setting from which his daughters would marry and his son's future would be launched.

I was to spend my senior year at Baldwin High, an elitist school where they even had fraternities and sororities. When I showed up, the sororities were beginning the annual whirl of parties and rituals that go with the rush season, and I was drawn into its vortex. Young ladies pouring tea from silver tea services and drinking from the thinnest, most delicate china teacups I'd ever seen. Those little triangular sandwiches made of cucumber and white bread with the crusts cut off. Lots of expensive sweater sets, pleated plaid skirts, pretty shoes, hair done up in beauty salons, and natural-looking makeup.

I was looking forward to taking part in the senior play. But when the planning committee decided to mount a minstrel show instead, I groaned with embarrassment and spontaneously withdrew from participation. Then I wrote an essay detailing my objections, which I handed in to the literature teacher who mentored the senior play committee and was also the power behind the sweater girls of the sorority. Suddenly, no more party invitations, no more phone calls or would-be sisters skipping by my side in the halls. I was instantly and silently blackballed from the sorority into which I was being "rushed" only the week before.

I was about ready to relaunch my truancy career, but a sympathetic counselor saved me. "You know your parents will never be satisfied until you have a high school diploma. Here is how many credits you actually need to finish high school. If you just buckle down, attend the classes, and do what you can, you can be out of here in June!" That did it. I behaved as suggested, and while I don't recall actually attending the ceremonies, I may still have that little old diploma, dated June 1945, somewhere in the back of a drawer.

Barbara Spillman, Baldwin High School Graduation Photo. Birmingham, Michigan, c. 1945. © The Arnold Studios

3

THE ATOMIC AGE BEGINS

My old friend Sue's father, O. B. Jones, who ran the Detroit College of Applied Science, sometimes took time to chat with us while smoking his pipe in the evening. One day in mid-August 1945, he was the most serious I had ever seen him. It was a day or two after the US government had dropped two nuclear bombs on Hiroshima and Nagasaki, killing more than two hundred thousand innocent people. "You youngsters are seeing the end of one world and the beginning of another," he said. "The Atomic Age has dawned. The world will never be the same again."

    I understood then that the lives of every living being on the planet had been changed forever with these abominable acts. It seemed to me that the world was being ripped apart and reshaped entirely. What role would our generation play in this new world, where life itself would come to seem so cheap and death so casual? We now had a special responsibility to the world to see that these monstrous weapons were never used again.

With these thoughts, I was about to enter the adult world. But where was I headed? College was at least some sort of destination. My high school experiences had almost killed all interest I may have had in organized education, but I thought I'd give it one more chance. Out of all the possible options, I chose Wayne University. Why? It was in the center of town, what they used to call a "streetcar college," with no exclusive campus atmosphere and none of the fraternity and sorority nonsense. You didn't have the sports rah-rah to deal with, and many of the returning vets would most likely be going there. They would be experienced and responsible men now, as unlike the feckless boys of Redford and Cooley High as one could hope for.

Dad had campaigned hard for a more prestigious college, pointing out that if I were to go to Michigan State, I could meet young men from families whose fathers held managerial jobs in the auto industry, leading to the likelihood of marrying well and settling down to raise a family in one of the nicer parts of Detroit. Dad even arranged for me to meet Clarence Reid, a state senator he must have known from the Lion's Club or the Masonic Lodge, groups that he had joined in recent years to help consolidate his place in the business community of northwest Detroit. He felt that the senator could enlighten me about the benefits of choosing State, or even the more expensive and academically demanding University of Michigan, and I guess he thought I would be impressed.

We drove to the suburbs and up to Reid's house, and there was the old boy himself, in galluses and undershirt, mowing the front lawn in the heat of the day. He invited us inside for a cool glass of iced tea, and began to explain that whenever a vote came up in the legislature to give funds to Wayne, he always went for the "Yes" because, as he put it, "there needed to be a place for all those niggers and kikes"—he actually used those words—to go to school so that they wouldn't wind up trying to go to "the better colleges," which were the places for "nice girls like you." I thanked him politely as we left and, with some considerable effort, restrained myself from spitting in his puffy red face.

In September I started at Wayne University, moving into one of the aging Victorian boardinghouses that stood near the campus. The college catalog seemed as barren of any courses that fit my personal agenda as the high school had been, but I signed up for the class in script writing, one of the few that seemed practical. I had imagined organizing a theater group, but for want of the know-how and money to do it, I began to think that a more direct line to the public, and possibly even an income, would be radio, for which I could probably create a show if I only knew how it was done. After a session or two, I approached the teacher and asked, "Will I be able to write a script at the end of this twenty-week course?"

This teacher was none other than Fran Stryker, then one of radio's most respected script writers, creator of *The Lone Ranger* and *The Green Hornet*. "Well," he replied, "if you already know what you want to do, just start writing some scripts and show them to somebody. This class is really meant for housewives who need some easy credits." I took that as a cue to ask all my other teachers whether the twenty weeks spent in their classes would produce something that seemed useful to me. After hearing their obfuscatory answers, I was becoming pretty disillusioned.

The only other thing in the catalog that seemed relevant at all to my interests was a one-credit elective class called something like Folktales, with an instructor named Thelma James. Maybe it would connect somehow to folk songs? But if I was going to stay at Wayne, I had to find some way of making a little money. Was there a job on campus for someone like me? I looked at the want ads in the school paper, and to my surprise there was Thelma James again, this time offering to hire someone to work in her archives. I immediately made an appointment, and she was soon quizzing me about my interest in folk music.

By this time I had heard about a New York–based singer named Pete Seeger, who played the banjo and sang old folk songs as well as new union organizing songs. This had fired my imagination with other ideas of how whatever gifts I had along those lines might be useful. I had even been in touch with him, and he had mentioned starting a project to publish a sort of newsletter that could help circulate the songs and encourage new ones to be written.

Miss James asked me what made me so eager to work with her collection, and when I mentioned the Seeger name she raised her eyebrows and asked, "Is that the older or the younger Seeger?" Pete, the younger, she pronounced, was not a good model to follow because he sometimes changed the words and otherwise tampered with the true songs. But his father, Charles, the well-known ethnomusicologist, was a very fine scholar, and he'd be the one to investigate and emulate. "He understands the importance of preserving things as they are," she said. When I came to know Charles a few years later, I saw how he would have laughed at Miss James's opinion of him!

"Well, then," she asked, "what are you hoping to get out of working with the archives?"

"Well, I need the pay," I said, "but oh, I can't wait to hear the recordings of the folk songs."

"No, no, my dear, we don't play the recordings," she said. "That might damage them. No, we just catalog them for posterity."

That about did it for me and college, so I went down to the office and demanded my money back.

Dumping Wayne U. made me feel empowered somehow, able to make such important decisions on my own. I hung around the campus for lack of any idea of what else to do or how to explain things to my parents. It was an intense few weeks, because so many new things happened to me all at once, exactly what is meant to happen at college but in a more condensed and unorthodox way.

First of all, I discovered that nobody cared if I sat in a corner of the theater classes and watched the actors exercise and rehearse, and I could even talk to the acting students themselves when they took breaks. These classes were not offered to freshmen, but I could soak up some of what was going on in that way. And witnessing their powerful production of *Oedipus* deepened my regret that I wasn't able to be involved in such engrossing and mysterious matters as making theater.

Then I found a game room in the student building where I could pass the time playing cards, which I did for the first—and last—time in my life. I had always hated the very idea of card games because of my mother's absorption in bridge, but I learned to play pinochle and gin rummy and was occasionally able to make some spending money by gambling, augmenting the small allowance my mother continued to give me until it became clear I was no longer going to college. But there was more for me in that room than games.

An intense young man approached me there and asked me if I wanted to learn to play chess. Looking back on that moment, I doubt that I was the first girl on whom he had tried that gambit. But Rolf Cahn, a veteran just returning to civilian life, was the first grown man who looked me right in the eyes when he spoke instead of sliding his own eyes up and down my body, and who started right off discussing ideas with me instead of a lot of flirty nonsense. An irresistible aphrodisiac!

Rolf was just back from the war, and as he made sure to tell me right up front, he had just been mustered out via the locked ward of the Army psych hospital. *No problem, I can handle that,* I told myself. Then he described arriving back home on the train and being met on the platform by a girl he had married just before going overseas—the one he'd kept thinking of during all his ordeals—who handed him a "Dear John" letter (meaning that she had another guy and that he was now history) and left him standing there alone. That was the last he ever spoke of her.

We took long walks around the campus and around town, talking as we walked. He bought sweet cherries to eat, hanging pairs of them over my ears, the way he remembered the young boys would claim their sweethearts in his long-ago German town of Elberfeld. Rolf was a Jew, and he told me of how all the family he knew had perished in the Holocaust except for his mother and father, who fled the country and brought him to Detroit as a child. He talked about being beaten up regularly by roving gangs of Hitler Youth on the way home from school as a kid in Elberfeld, and that something even more painful than the beatings had been his mother's comment, saying that it was probably his fault anyway, for having a big nose and wearing glasses. I wanted to ease his pain, and I wanted to learn all about his history, his point of view, and his opinions on life, how he saw the future.

He was full of ideas on many subjects, and I came to understand that he had one of those rare minds that can read a book on a particular subject today and teach it with alacrity tomorrow, which made him seem intellectually invincible. At that moment, he was overflowing with his recently acquired knowledge of Marxism and the works of Lenin, Engels, and the rest of the socialist pantheon, and eager to talk about it. Eureka! I had come to Wayne with the idea of finding the communists, and here I was falling in love with one!

Wayne U. was not capable of commanding all my time, not even after meeting Rolf. Owing to my longtime habit of wandering downtown where the used bookstores were clustered and reading for a while, I came across a lot of interesting people, but mostly allowed myself only a brief conversation and then moved on. This day, I felt pretty interesting myself, wearing my hand-embroidered off-the-shoulder peasant blouse with the provocatively untied string closing, a simple cotton skirt that I had made myself gathered at the waist, and my flat ballerina shoes. My hair was naturally a honey blonde, long and straight way before that was the fashion, but for me a symbol of my personal disregard for fashion. No more purple lipstick and dark pancake makeup; my makeup now, if I wore any at all, was light and delicate, au naturel if you please. Actually, I was a knockout, and I knew it, but that was important to me only in that too often it drew undue and unwanted attention. In the bookstores, I usually preferred to cover myself with a roomy old trench coat, to be left alone with my reading, like a serious autodidact.

But this day, while looking through the dusty books, I struck up a conversation with a couple of equally creatively dressed young men, who invited me to their little bohemian digs in an attic somewhere behind the old Wilson Theater, Detroit's number-one legit house. I didn't feel any kind of predatory sex vibe going on, and besides, they seemed so erudite and funny too. We soon became fast friends. They laughed at my jokes and took my ideas seriously; they were artistic and loved interesting music like Satie and Debussy; and on one fragrant spring evening, they introduced me to the magic ritual of drinking May wine with a strawberry in the bottom of the glass. They were gay, of course, but I hadn't yet enough sophistication to put a name on it. They treated me like their adorable mascot, and I loved it! With Dorian and Damon, I could do no wrong.

A few warm spring nights later, I was out walking with Rolf around Grand Circus Park. The air was becoming damp with the greenery erupting all around us and fragrant with blossoms forming in the trees, ready to burst into bloom with the dawn. As we strolled holding hands and talking about intense personal experiences mixed with desperate world affairs in the manner of the young, we were both overcome with an irresistible erotic rush that left me defenseless and dizzy. Got to have it, this is it, this is it, but where can we go? Where could we shelter ourselves with at least the illusion of privacy? Where could we rush forward into this great adventure without causing a scandal? No sense of decision-making entered my mind, only the sure knowledge that I was about to lose that famous virginity, and that this was the right time.

We were just a block or two from their place, so I made for Damon and Dorian's loft behind the theater, Rolf scrambling along with me. It was well after midnight, so I tapped lightly on the door, and then again more insistently. Finally, when it was clear that no one was going to answer, we threw our jackets down on the floor in a small niche next to the door. At least the light was dim, and we were reasonably well hidden from the street view. Eventually the boys came home, found us curled up by their door, and brought us inside, insisting on giving us their bed to allow us a little sleep. As dawn broke, I slipped off to the bus and back to the boardinghouse on Bethune alone, certain that everyone around me on their way to work could tell what had just happened.

Not long after, my folks found out I had dropped out of college, and I had to move back home. I didn't spend much of my time there, though. I was more and more engaged with Rolf and busy making my plans to change the world.

The words *communism* and *socialism* had an exciting ring for millions of people during the Depression of my childhood years. The Communist Party USA, from its founding in 1919 until the latter part of the 1950s, was one of the country's most important leftist organizations. When its membership peaked at eighty-five thousand in 1942, its rallies could fill New York's Madison Square Garden, and the May Day parades that ended in a packed Union Square were legendary. On the other side of the globe, the world's first great socialist experiment was rising from the ashes of serfdom and suffering. Young people worldwide were inspired by talk of a new world where everyone had the right to a job, food, and shelter, and where it was illegal to foment hate between peoples.

Shockingly, just as World War II began, Stalin and Hitler signed a non-aggression pact. Antifascists everywhere were confused and disoriented, and to this day the pact's intentions and effect are debated. But the socialist movement took a hell of a hit, and the various parties around the world lost members in droves.

Eager to get involved in the progressive movements of the day, I began attending events where I hoped to connect with like-minded people. Soon I met Phil Schatz and his wife, Gert. They had been sent from New York by the Communist Party to help expand the Michigan chapter of American Youth for Democracy (AYD), an ambitious new vehicle for young workers and students intended to help build a broad youth movement for the new era of "peaceful coexistence" that, it was anticipated, would flow from the wartime alliances based on opposition to fascism and war. This was just what I was looking for, so I signed up right away.

At age eighteen, I became Michigan state teenage director of the AYD, but since we had slim contacts among Detroit high school kids, there wasn't much action, so I was also made the Michigan state cultural director, a job more suited to my skills. I was able to organize only one event specifically involving teenagers at a high school, after which the Hearst-owned *Detroit Times* sent a reporter to interview me. They published my picture and made me out to be some kind of teenage red menace, which in fact I was.

Looking back at those days, it's clear that my life would have been very different without the astute counsel and kindness of Phil and his wife. Phil was a confident, humorous guy, and Gert was warm and maternal, a wise and kind partner for a man like him. He was the person who would later help me understand what my life's work was going to be, and who helped provide access to the tools I would need to begin it.

Phil was extremely aware of the power of song, and he saw that I was busting to learn more of the kind of songs that could be used in the demonstrations, as opposed to those corny "moon/June" songs. A couple of our comrades, a schoolteacher named Maurie Cooke and his wife, had a collection of 78 rpm records that encompassed just about everything available in this kind of music, which in those days could all fit on a shelf about a yard long. Phil arranged for me to have access to their apartment during the day, when nobody was home, so I had complete privacy and plenty of material to study. These few weeks of intense focus laid the basis for my life's work and meant everything to me.

Now I needed a guitar, so my party club kicked in a couple of bucks each and bought one from somebody's relative's music store. Soon I was tinkering with this shiny new thing, with its f-shaped holes cut out of a curvy top, and six stout bronze and steel strings strung taut across a high bridge. Exactly the wrong kind of guitar for the kind of work I would be doing, meant more for keeping time in a jazz band than for thumping out the rhythms of a picket line or softly supporting the melody of a folk song.

I bought an instruction book, with pictures of little black dots on the strings where you were to place your left-hand fingers as you dragged a pick over the metal strings with your right. I kind of got the hang of that, but it would be nearly two years of "playing" the guitar before I saw anyone else do it up close. I went to the Cookes' place every day for weeks, stuffing my head with as much as it would hold of those songs, and trying to accustom my hands to this guitar beast. Of the music, one singer went straight to my gizzard: Huddie Ledbetter, better known as Lead Belly. I spent hours with my ear up against the speaker, letting his powerfully yearning, insistent voice and that booming twelve-string guitar sound seep right into my bones.

Part of the struggle to play the guitar is getting enough strength into your hands for holding down the strings and thick enough calluses on your left hand to make playing bearable. This means just doing it a lot, and to make it interesting it's better to sing songs as you play, so I learned what I could from Maurie's collection. But gradually, a hunger that had long been sleeping inside me awoke to a craving for the culture of my parents, their parents, and way on back, something of the so-called hillbilly life and music that could help fill the vacuum I had expressed as a child when asked, "What are you?" and I had answered, "I'm nothing."

On a hunch, I headed for the public library, and there discovered the few Library of Congress recordings issued on disc. Now I could hear some of the actual voices of the people from whom I sprang, the accents and attitudes of the culture my parents had found so embarrassing. The culture that Henry Ford's Detroit would use to deny their kind a respectable place at the table while at the same time playing them as pawns in a dangerous racist game of distrust and disunity, fear and hatred that by 1967 would burn the city down.

I had a million ideas, and one of them was to organize regular cabaret nights, evenings that would provide a safe scene for young people to meet and mingle, regardless of race. It was good for recruiting new people, and we could also raise funds. We could sell the *Daily Worker* and other literature there, and of course whatever we presented would have some political content. But where could we do this in a totally segregated town like Detroit? It would have to be in the Black neighborhood, but in a place where the white kids would feel comfortable too. Someone came up with the name of a Black funeral parlor with a large upstairs room, just on the edge of Paradise Valley, and the owner was open to renting it out by the night.

I'd never produced an event before, but I put out the word for talent and soon had a roster of would-be comedians, singers, and dancers who wanted to perform even though there was no pay. I recruited someone to act as the MC and tried to be selective, to never present boring or awkward performers. This was the jitterbug era, so of course we had lots of dancing to the hits. I found myself frequently misunderstood by guys with sweaty palms who assumed the event was mainly arranged so that white girls could meet Black boys, or vice versa. The best defense for this was to start up some political talk and to keep switching partners. Mostly, we had a lot of fun, and I had a place to sharpen my singing skills too, sometimes even with a makeshift band.

I was asked several times to sing for the Jewish People's Fraternal Order, mostly elderly Jewish people, including several German refugees, who met in a bare and modest room that could have been a synagogue or lodge hall. It occurred to me that my learning a couple of songs in Yiddish would please them, and I was deeply touched when I saw how much it meant to them that a young *shiksa* in Detroit, so far from their old homes, had enough respect for their culture to do that. They gave me a lot of love in return, trying to teach me Yiddish phrases and more songs, and even bringing me special food to taste.

Pete Seeger, Barbara Dane, and others, at Ernest Goodman's home in Detroit, c. 1945

One day, a tall young banjo picker named Pete Seeger came to town on a mission. I was too young to have met him when he'd come to Detroit in June 1941 with the Almanac Singers, a group of singing agitators with banjos and guitars that included Woody Guthrie, Sis Cunningham, and Cisco Houston, touring then in support of the CIO (Congress of Industrial Organizations). With the attack on Pearl Harbor in December of that year, Pete had joined the army and Woody and Cisco had joined the merchant marine, but as soon as the war ended in 1945, they regrouped in New York with a few other like-minded friends and comrades to found People's Songs, with its *People's Songs Bulletin*, pledged to "create, promote, and distribute songs of labor and the American people." Pete was in town this time for a handful of performances that included a house party and some union meetings, but also to see what could be done about forming a People's Songs chapter in Detroit.

It must have been Phil Schatz who steered him to me, but I was about as ready for Pete's enthusiasm as anyone could be. He gave me some of the *Bulletins*, and talked about ways of pulling people together, how we might make our activities known and some of the problems we might encounter. During the next few months, I did what I could to scare up some other singers or pickers, but without a lot of success.

Meanwhile, I started to be in demand for singing at picket lines and rallies, spots on the programs at various union meetings, PTA meetings, and so forth, wherever a touch of relevant music was needed to liven up an evening of political speeches, and also for what we called "affairs," the small house parties where funds were raised for our various organizing activities. Rolf liked coming along with me to help with handing out leaflets at the shop-gate rallies and picket lines, and while he was not yet a musician, he was willing to carry my guitar and sometimes to sing harmony. Soon we began calling ourselves the Detroit chapter of People's Songs.

People's Songs picnic. Detroit, c. 1945

4

EVERYTHING CHANGES

Just as all of this was going on, my family experienced a series of devastating changes. In the space of a few months, I left home for good, my mother left my father, and, most shocking of all, my brother, Sonny, suddenly died of bulbar polio. How could anything as seemingly solid and normal as my family suddenly disintegrate altogether? My stunned sister and my traumatized father were left to make sense out of it all.

I was so busy becoming myself, so completely wrapped up in the new life I was piecing together, that I had not paid any attention to my parents' life, and had little sense that it was any of my business. It took me decades to give serious thought as to what led my mother to leave. I can't really know, but her need for self-expression, for a chance to chart her own course and find independence within the almost inescapable boundaries of the narrow path set out for women in those days, certainly played a leading role. How can I know? And while we would always stay in touch and I would always feel sure of her love, she was gone.

This was to have been the time when my father would finally see the fruits of all his years of hard work, presiding over everything with his loving childhood sweetheart, Dorothy, by his side, filling their lovely new home with flowers and music, graduations and weddings, anniversaries and barbeques, laughter and hearty embraces. It wasn't until twenty years later that I slowed down long enough to hear Dad's story of their breakup, watching him come to tears as he sat in his wheelchair after decades of emphysema, heart trouble, and strokes.

My move came not long after I took it upon myself to inspect the deed to Dad's property, only to find that the entire area was covered by what was called a restrictive covenant barring any semitic people from living there. Such things were not at all uncommon in those days, and the subject had come up in a discussion recently among my political friends, so I wanted to know where we stood. This discovery, needless to say, devastated me. I was living in a place where many of my friends would not be accepted, could not buy property, and would be treated with scorn if they tried. I had to confront my family with the fact that I could no longer live there.

The night before, I had stopped by the house in Franklin Village with my close friend and fellow activist Erma Henderson, intent on changing clothes and rushing off to some evening event. Erma, who was Black, said she'd rather wait in the car.

"You know how your dad is. No use getting him upset, because that will only delay us, and we're late already."

A sensible idea, but a crushing blow for me, to see that my friend would not be comfortable even to enter my house. Now it became perfectly clear that I could no longer live in that place. I made arrangements with Bob Purdy, one of our comrades who had a car, to pick me up the next evening. As I carried box after box to Bob's car, my dad began to realize that he had lost me. Wordlessly, he collapsed into a chair in the living room, attempting to conceal his tears behind a handkerchief and sobbing gently.

I was filled with the heat, the adrenalin, the self-righteous zeal of a young person determined to pursue a cleaner path, to walk away from hypocrisy and ignorance, prejudice and injustice. I was filled with a certain kind of madness. I didn't have the words to say good-bye.

Erma's mother had generously invited me to stay with them at their place downtown until I could get settled somewhere. But events were moving fast, and within a few weeks Rolf and I decided to get married so that we could find a place to live together. Yes, that's the way you did it in those days. In that order.

I had shut down all communication with my father, and certainly didn't want to give him notice of my approaching marriage. I knew my choice of partner was beyond Dad's comprehension—it was clear he could find no rational reasons for how I chose my friends or any of my interests. I had long ago given up trying to explain any of this to him. But I did call my mother and asked her to go with us to the judge down at city hall to be our witness. Two of our dearest comrades, Marty Mitchnick and Ann Meyers, would stand up with us too. Mother met us the next day, a warm and pleasant one, and just like that, we were married. I had no wish to be a queen in a white gown, and no desire to put my friends through the stress or expense of wedding showers and gifts and all the fuss of tradition. I was a modern young woman, I knew my mind, and I knew my commitment to the bond, and that was all that mattered. I know my mother was disappointed with this dry practicality, and she probably felt she was betraying my dad by cooperating with it.

This man, who demonstrated with every day of his life that his steadfast commitment to his family was without limit, had been deeply wounded by the fact that his daughter had married without fanfare, without asking his permission, without inviting him or even telling him it was about to take place. The idea of walking his oldest daughter down the aisle was something he had rehearsed in his mind for years. For him, that one perfect day would have been the ultimate proof to himself and all who knew him that he was a successful man of his times, no longer a footloose southern boy scrambling to establish himself in the big city. But his dream of presenting his perfect daughter to a perfect partner in a perfect wedding to be held in a perfect setting was, sadly, not to come true. But for us it was a very happy day, and we were in love.

Here's the way the FBI agent who was hot on our trail described our wedding for the records:

> Wayne County Court records Chancery Division, under Affidavit #[76681] discloses that Barbara Brookfield Spillman married ROLF CAHN, June 11, 1946. CAHN, according to [blank] is an active Communist and American Youth for Democracy leader. The witnesses to the marriage were EMMA MYERS and MARTIN MITCHNICK, who, according to [blank] are also active Communist Party members.

Everything Changes

So here we were, another young postwar couple about to launch our ship on what they used to call "the sea of matrimony." Rolf was on the famous 52-20 tab, the Veterans Administration's promised fifty-two weeks of twenty-dollar checks for every man mustered out of the military. We'd find a cheap place to live; Rolf would continue at Wayne, perhaps teaching a little martial arts on the side; I would get a job; and we'd figure out how to survive. Meanwhile, together we would continue with our party work and keep on looking for ways to change Detroit for the better. Not the world just yet.

Everyone said that it was probably on a swim in the White River, near our grandparents' place in Arkansas, that Sonny caught the virus, but as soon as he returned to Michigan, he went to bed with a raging sore throat. Dad was doing his best to doctor what looked like a flu. I didn't even stop to welcome my brother home, just waved and said hello as I passed his bedroom door. I had moved out, but had come home to get some things. I was in a rush, and besides, I didn't want to catch whatever he had. But I'll never forget Sonny's plaintive voice begging, "Dad, bring me a malted," something he had always loved. Those were the last words I would ever hear from him. Next thing I knew, Mom called and said hurry to the hospital, and it was only hours until bulbar polio, the most virulent and deadly form of the disease, stopped the clock on the poor kid. He was fourteen and otherwise a well-built, healthy, good-looking boy, something of a football star on his team at military school. It was September 8, 1946, and Jonas Salk's vaccine wouldn't come along for another seven years.

I went by the house one last time to gather up a few more belongings, but I didn't stay long. The main reason I came was, of course, to offer what comfort I could. Mother wasn't there, and my sister, Julia, seemed to be grieving in private. Somehow Sonny's dying had brought a sense of finality, certainly an end to my teenage years, even though I was almost a year short of turning twenty. The last thing I saw on my way out was Dad sitting in his den with a hunting rifle across his lap and his head hanging low.

It was left to Julia to bring Dad to his senses. He had called her in and asked her to get him a box from a high shelf in the closet. When it turned out to be filled with shotgun shells, she was so shocked that, in a new and commanding voice, she told him he had to stop and think where it would leave the rest of the family if he were to follow through with his plan. In that moment, something in Julia grew up that could not be denied. Dad didn't leave us that night after all, and he owed his life to the fact that he had another hardheaded daughter, one whose capacity for taking charge, along with her deep well of compassion and love, had been underestimated until then. Father and daughter spent their night in that house in quiet mutual support, with Sonny's body laid out in his coffin in the living room, his unlined pubescent face carefully composed, his last ride ahead of him the following morning.

In those years, Detroit was as segregated as any city in the Deep South. I can't remember a single place outside the Black neighborhoods where a mixed group of friends could even get a cup of coffee together. My close friend and fellow activist Erma Henderson worked as port secretary at the National Maritime Union (NMU), known for its insistence on equality for everyone in its ranks. But there was no place near her job where a Black woman, no matter how beautiful or well groomed, could eat lunch, forcing her to brown-bag it most of the time. To challenge this shameful situation, some of us decided to join with other friends and comrades to organize a test of Michigan's Equal Accommodations Act, enacted in the 1930s but, by the fall of 1946, seldom enforced.

We chose the coffee shop at the Barlum Hotel as our target for two reasons: first, because the hotel was on Cadillac Square, the very place where historic union rallies and demonstrations had taken place, and second, because it was right across the street from the headquarters of the NMU. Erma was a vivacious young woman committed to ending discrimination everywhere, starting with the renowned Barlum Hotel, where only the previous year the great singer, actor, athlete, scholar, and humanitarian Paul Robeson had been refused accommodations.

On Erma's initiative, we pulled together an interracial group of about eight young people, including Rolf and me. To make this foray into such a deluxe environment as the Barlum Hotel, we all did our best to look like solid citizens in our Sunday clothes—the men in suits and the women in dresses, stockings, and heels. Erma looked glamorous in a chic cloth coat with a fox-fur collar framing her glowing brown face and sparkling eyes.

Although the coffee shop was nearly empty when we arrived, we were shown to a couple of tables back near the door where the garbage was taken from the kitchen. A full staff was on hand, but no one came to take our order. Obviously, they had been instructed to stay clear of us. After an hour or so, we were approached by a nervous manager, who firmly informed us that we were never going to be served and must leave the premises immediately.

All right, then we need to speak with the owner of the hotel. Oh, that can't be arranged? Then don't be surprised if your staff has to cross a noisy picket line when they try to go to work here next week. Now maybe he'll see us?

Up a wide marble staircase from the lobby we went to Mr. Barlum's mezzanine office, a salon-like room with tall, coffered ceilings and elaborately framed windows illuminating a long, polished table surrounded by tall-backed side chairs upholstered in red leather, where we sat feeling very small indeed, but steady and ready to declare our intentions. Rolf quoted the Equal Accommodations Act, and pointed out that there were probably a few hundred thousand people in Detroit who would like to see the Barlum policy conform to this law.

With this, the hotel owner started screaming at us and literally chased us back down to the lobby, managing to kick Rolf in the back of the head and knock off his glasses as he descended.

So what was our next move? Several of us rushed to the office of the only Black officer at the district attorney's headquarters and breathlessly described what had just happened. He shook his head sadly and, in essence, advised us to grow up. Nobody ever gets anywhere with this kind of thing, he said. But we youngsters came from a different mind-set. It was justice we were seeking.

Some of our comrades with organizing experience and address books bulging with contacts took over, calling on unions, church groups, and community leaders to support our case. We gathered hundreds of signatures on a petition demanding the end to segregated accommodations. By the following Saturday, we found ourselves at the portals of the Barlum Hotel again, this time accompanied by a couple of hundred more citizens carrying signs, shouting slogans, and briskly

March against fascism and racism. Detroit, 1946

walking in a circle designed to prevent any commerce from entering that lily-white kingdom.

    This was a moment of some historical significance in my hometown of Detroit, and it was, in fact, decisive in determining the road ahead for me personally. It was my first taste of that special excitement that comes from sharing a common purpose with a great many others, a purpose that is clearly on the side of justice. It was my first experience working cooperatively in a well-organized act of defiance. It was also the first opportunity to use my singing voice for something both my heart and my head strongly believed in. It was the dawn of my discovery that I could pitch that voice up and over a crowd of people in a demonstration, helping them raise their own voices to inspire, animate, and coordinate their actions as they thronged up and down in Cadillac Square. I never went back to those little French bergerettes. It was "Solidarity Forever" or "We're Gonna Roll the Union On" from here on out.

One day I went downtown to the Lawyer's Building headquarters, paid my fifty cents, and got myself a Communist Party card at last! According to the FBI informant who was by then keeping a keen eye on me (and, I presume, all the others in the group), I immediately started going to regular meetings of the Joe York Club, one of the neighborhood youth groups that met in one another's homes; ten, fifteen, or even twenty on a good night; earnest young people drawn together by an urgent need to sort out a rapidly changing postwar world, to find ways of ending the nuclear madness, to oppose the festering racial injustice, to master the most effective ways of putting ourselves at the service of this inspiring but daunting mandate.

Our club was named for Joe York, a nineteen-year-old Communist auto worker, killed along with four others by the thugs of Henry Ford's private army in 1932 as they and five thousand marchers organized by the Detroit Unemployed Council crossed into Dearborn, Ford's private fiefdom, carrying the banners of the Hunger March that bore the slogans "Tax the Rich and Feed the Poor," "We Want Bread, not Crumbs," and "Give Us Work." The name gave our club a special reason to support the organizing activities of the United Auto Workers (UAW), and we did what we could to lend our solidarity at their rallies and shop-gate meetings, where I often led the singing, passing out leaflets along with the others.

Here I was, finally allied with people committed to working together to engage with some of these burning issues, and not only with talk. It seemed there was no end of problems confronting our generation, and the Joe York Club was our way of addressing them, of helping create solidarity. We learned how to use the power that comes from uniting five fingers into a fist. The Communist Party gave us the history, the skills, and the forces to make a start.

Rolf continued his studies at Wayne, paid for by the GI Bill and seldom discussed at home. We moved into a garret in the top of one of the old houses near campus. When we took part in a local rent strike, the landlord cut the electricity and heat. Eventually we were kicked out of that place and began moving through a series of room-and-bath rentals as near to Wayne as we could find. Due to lack of funds, we occasionally even skipped out before paying the rent. I contrived many strategies for making our weekly income stretch to cover our needs. Rolf was still on the 52-20 tab, so at least we had that. I would cross the bridge to Canada to find decent cheap meat and sought out recipes for inexpensive things that Rolf liked, such as kidney pie, which he thought of fondly from his European days. I even came to like that one. We even learned to eat horse meat, which was unrationed and cheap, actually sold for use as dog food.

I looked for jobs, but employment was hard to come by with all the men now returning from the war. For a time, I had a filing job at the VA, where I was able to look into Rolf's folder and found his army diagnosis of schizophrenia. He had something going on in his *kopf* all right, but in hindsight I think it was more like his generation's version of posttraumatic stress disorder. He functioned very well most of the time, in his way, and certainly was able to hold his ground in the intense political discussions that went on with his vet friends in our circles. We had passed the "lovers" stage into a fairly good working partnership that didn't require a whole lot of interaction, as it turned out, and our social life together revolved around friends from our party club and the various campaigns we helped to organize.

A factory job came my way through a comrade in the United Electrical Workers Union. The union was beginning an organizing drive at the Detrola plant among the temporary workers, to counter the company's policy of dumping people as soon as they became eligible for permanent positions. I became one of the temps, working first with some older ladies about to be aged out of their jobs, sorting nuts and bolts and other small hardware. Then I was put on the assembly line, poking a red wire into this hole and a green wire into that one and a blue one into that one, all on the metal framework of a small table radio. My next job was to solder these same wires in place, using a hot iron in one hand and a wire containing solder and flux in the other. You had to turn your wrists back and forth to perform this act, a slight motion, but over and over and over and over. I caught myself dreaming of this motion, continuing it in my sleep through the cold winter nights.

Another job was in a mail room, sealing packages with a wide sticky tape that had to be wet with a sponge before applying it to the large shipping cartons. I noticed that people wore work gloves for this, but even then you were sticky all over and stuck together in places you wouldn't believe by the time the day was over. With all this sideways mobility, I was getting a pretty good survey of entry-level jobs, and over the years it has helped me greatly to understand from experience what kinds of hellish, stupid things people go through every day just to keep bread on the table and the rent paid.

We moved to a small but neat two-room ground-floor place in Paradise Valley. It was during this move that my beautiful brand-new orchestra-style guitar was stolen off the back of our friend's pickup truck. That made me feel awful, especially because it was the generosity of my comrades that had put that guitar into my hands. For the next couple of years, I had to make do with a cracked plywood job that had a neck like a baseball bat and wouldn't hold a tuning. You guitar players know what a handicap that was!

Shortly after moving into the new place, I noticed that across the street, one flight up, you could see what looked like a vacant apartment, which was strange given that there were effectively no available rentals in the city in those postwar days. But looking up at the window directly across from our entry door, you could see below a half-raised shade what looked like the lens of a camera permanently pointed in our direction.

Not easily intimidated, we continued going to our party club meetings, and I went on with my life as an outside agitator. Sometimes humor is the best defense, so in this case, to calm my nerves and demonstrate my fake devil-may-care attitude, I took to wearing a red beret cocked over my long blonde locks, combed fetchingly over to one side, that good old pell-mell trench coat from high school days now belted, and a long cigarette holder with which I kept sending out curls of smoke just like Greta Garbo in the flicks.

Years later, someone sent me the few pages they could rescue from the Detroit Red Squad files when the unit was finally folded, entries indicating that even two years after my departure from my father's house in Franklin Village, your tax dollars were still at work supporting their continued surveillance there. So I think it's fair to assume they were doing the same there in the ghetto, capturing images of anyone visiting us, coming or going. Wouldn't I love to have copies of some of those photos, exaggerated poses of nineteen-year-old me vogueing for a couple of unseen nicotine-stained donut addicts!

For years now I had been grabbing every opportunity for sitting in with the occasional band, and though the words always seemed trivial, I acquired a small repertoire of popular songs that all the musicians knew. "Blue Moon," "Embraceable You," "Melancholy Baby," "Stormy Weather," and "Summertime" come to mind. I wasn't taking any of this very seriously, but one day I got a call from a booking agency downtown, and I went for an interview.

"So you wanna be a professional singer? Nice. Now take off your coat and turn around," said the man.

"Don't you want to hear me sing?" I asked. "Nah, they tell me you're pretty good. Now take off your coat."

"Thanks, mister, but I . . . I think I'm in the wrong place. Good-bye."

Still, he called me again a few months later and asked if I wanted to go on tour with Alvino Rey's band, then riding a popularity high and heard on every jukebox. I really could have used the money, but the sense of purpose that came from singing at union rallies and on picket lines just couldn't be matched by putting on a low-cut dress just to be ogled while singing nonsense words in front of a band, even a good one like this. I was on a mission! So I told the booker to please take me off his list.

In the winter of 1946–47, Phil Schatz came up with the idea of presenting me in a concert at the Detroit Institute of Arts, bringing Pete Seeger from New York along with some of his People's Songs coworkers to help draw out an audience and launch me as a professional. The larger objective, of course, was to legitimize this kind of music in order to reach a broader audience for the message of peace, racial harmony, and support for the union organizing going on all over the city. The program consisted of Al Moss, a Black piano man; Tom Glaser, a white union singer; Charlotte Anthony, a woman related to feminist heroine Susan B. Anthony; and of course Pete holding it all together. I was Barbara, the kid from the sticks. That's right, the ingénue. Pete, of course, was kind and supportive, although with his usual shy reserve. He made sure I had whatever musical support I needed in order to feel secure, but I was too green to notice exactly what that might be.

At the time, I was caught up with a very popular bluesy jukebox hit built on a well-known schoolyard song called "Hey! Ba-Ba-Re-Bop," to which I had made up some verses. The street versions had funny verses like these:

> Mama's on the bottom,
> Papa's on the top,
> Sister's in the corner
> Yellin' give it to her, Pop!"
> Shoutin' Hey ba-ba-re-bop,
> hey ba-ba–re-bop,
> yes, your baby knows!"

My version began,

> We're gonna tell old Byrnes,
> like Tilly told Tut,
> If you can't talk peace
> keep your big mouth shut!

James Byrnes was then Truman's hawkish secretary of state, Tilly and Tut mere phantoms of the songwriter's shadow play. I did get everybody shouting and swaying in their seats, and it worked really well at picket lines too!

Tom Glaser, also on the program that night, was known to me mostly as the guy who wrote "A Dollar Bill Don't Buy What It Used To" to the tune of "The Old Gray Mare." He was trying to be encouraging when he said it would be easy for me to go to New York and get into a Broadway show. Secretly, I was terribly insulted by this. How could he not see that my mission was to save the world with my singing, not to become some objectified show-business doll?

5

POSTWAR DREAMS

In 1947, I turned twenty, and looking back it's clear that was my breakout year, the one that indelibly marked and defined my worldview as well as my life's work. Up to this point, my life had been circumscribed by the flat and familiar landscape of Detroit. But there were two events coming into view above that low horizon: the first World Youth Festival, to be held in Prague, Czechoslovakia, in mid-summer, and the first People's Songs convention, which would take place in Chicago as fall was settling in. My first inhalations of any other than that muggy Michigan summer air would be drawn from the fresh sweet winds of peace and justice blowing across the entire postwar world.

In this intense atmosphere of change, young people everywhere were almost delirious with hope and a powerful will to work for rebirth and renewal. You could feel this euphoria everywhere, and even Mother Nature played her part, as young people coupled and planted the seeds of the baby boom, creating an unprecedented surge of new life. I wanted a baby too, but not quite yet.

Most of my generation in the US were touched lightly by the war in comparison to others. The loss of something over four hundred thousand lives was devastating, but no bombs disfigured our cities, and our economy actually thrived. The Brits had a similar number of casualties, but with a population of only forty-eight million, the impact was much more intense and was accompanied by incessant bombing over a period of years, widespread destruction of the infrastructure, families torn apart, and deprivation of every kind. But the Soviets, barely emerging from feudalism and only in the third decade of the world's first large-scale socialist experiment, suffered more than *twenty million* dead, both civilian and military. This meant the alteration of every single remaining life, not to speak of the many cities and towns destroyed. It was the loss of the farms, and the people to restore them, that caused the famine of 1946–47 and brought mass starvation on a scale never seen before. Is it any wonder that something uplifting, positive, and hopeful was desperately needed by those who survived?

I believe now that the idea of a World Youth Festival immediately after the war was a brilliant attempt to connect with the forces of renewal and redemption, the optimism and energy of youth that was sweeping the world, and to build on the hope that they brought. I too was swept up, never questioning whether I had the skills or the equilibrium to represent my town or my country in an international event, mostly because I had no concept of it as any sort of professional opportunity. For me it was the opportunity to be on the right side of history and to see the faces, touch the cultures, of my sisters and brothers who had survived the horrors of war and were dedicating their lives to the proposition of building a lasting peace.

But a sinister undercurrent was about to wash all this over with the icy waters of the Cold War. A cold war. What a concept! The achievement of power through manipulation, deceit, economic and political sleight of hand, quiet assassination, and so forth, instead of using tanks, planes, and armies. Of course the Pentagon went right on planning for the good old-fashioned hot wars, and by the early 1950s the US experienced an unprecedented military buildup, including the testing of a brand-new apocalypse: the hydrogen bomb. But meanwhile, war would be waged on the cultural front.

The State Department wonks of the day decided to demonize the World Youth Festival. They could have mounted a glorious show of postwar American youth culture, bringing an array of our most vibrant artists from every field to the streets of Prague, in the mode of a World's Fair where nations demonstrate their best products for the benefit of commerce, only this time we would be demonstrating our goodwill toward humankind. But no, the American cultural cold warriors canceled the logistical support that had been promised and began to slip hints into the press that the thousands of youth making their way to the celebration were merely puppets in a script written by the Kremlin.

In my town, the lack of newspaper coverage made it nearly impossible to know that the festival was about to take place. I had only the barest notion of what would be happening there. But in New York it was a different story. There, American participation was on track to be drawn from the cream of contemporary artists in various fields. An impressive list of honorary sponsors was drafted, among them major theater figures like Helen Hayes, Judy Holiday, Ingrid Bergman, and Lewis Milestone; modern dancers like José Limón, Doris Humphrey, Pearl Primus, and Ana Sokalow; and writers like Louis Untermeyer, Thomas Mann, Cornelia Otis Skinner, and Arthur Miller.

Ultimately, the State Department's offer to help pay for the US delegation's travel expenses—for what would have been three to five thousand youths—was withdrawn, and in the end only a few hundred were able to make it. The costs involved with getting to Prague were way beyond my resources, so I approached my mother. She was understandably dubious, but she said, "I can come up with a thousand dollars, but you'll have to choose whether to use it for this festival thing or a year of college." I immediately signed up for the festival.

A much-reduced delegation would be heading for Europe on a ship being returned to England as a result of a wartime Lend-Lease arrangement, and we would return via a tramp steamer that belonged to the Yugoslavs. Crossing the ocean? On really big ships? That already sounded like big excitement!

I was the first in my family to apply for a passport. I managed to negotiate the process with a slight case of nerves but no problem, and soon it arrived in the mail bearing a small embossed photo of me with long, stringy blonde hair; an odd combination of smile and smirk on my face; and my unaccustomed married name: Barbara Cahn. The train ticket to New York City cost about forty dollars, but I was covered by my mother's contribution. My excitement was taking over my good sense, and I don't remember what my new husband, Rolf, thought about any of this, or even whether we talked it over much. Next thing I knew I was aboard a train, riding behind a big black steam engine with its reassuring rhythmic clickety-clack, heading straight for New York City and humming every railroad song I'd ever heard in my head.

At Phil Schatz's suggestion, I had written ahead to Pete Seeger and his wife, Toshi, to let them know I was on my way to Prague but would be needing a place to stay for a few days until I could get on the boat to Europe with the delegation. They lived in that same (now legendary) house in Greenwich Village where the loosely organized but storied Almanac Singers came and went, bunking there as needed, as many another itinerant troubadour must have done. The Seegers generously invited me to stay there, and I soon showed up with my little suitcase of clothes and that embarrassing cracked guitar in its crumbling cardboard case.

There I was, actually in "the Village," sitting around their favorite pizza place with Pete and a few of the folk regulars I had just met, trying my best to look like I belonged. Even in those days, any circle of musicians around Pete wanted his recognition more than anything, but these guys seemed to be leaving nothing to chance, sparing little room for a greenhorn like me, a very young female singer with a crappy guitar. For my part, I was determined that the world would take me seriously, but I was clear on the odds. I knew there were not many like me—girls willing to sacrifice the "pretty lady" thing in order to be themselves, to act and not just react, to lead and not just serve, to risk the criticism or the jealousy that moving ahead of the pack can bring. I also understood, though, that this bravery I was able to summon had its own attractions, gave off its own compelling scent.

Next day, I went to the People's Songs office to meet its editor, Irwin Silber, and a few more of the local singing crowd, who immediately invited me to join a picket line together with the seamen and their supporters down at the National Maritime Union Hall. We joined the ranks of the picketers and shouted out some of our songs to encourage the marchers. The crowd joined in, and the air was filled with the raw beauty of voices making harmony out of what could have been chaos. I had experienced this in Detroit demonstrations, but this was my first real understanding of those famous words, "Workers of the World, Unite!" I felt proud and exhilarated to be included, to be needed and useful, especially so far from home. Here was an action with a positive common purpose, and I was seeing it enthusiastically embraced and shared by perfect strangers. Singing together has the amazing age-old ability to wash away our fears and remind us that we can solve almost any problem through the combined power of the many. The very essence of the word *solidarity*!

The day after that, I was on my way to the greatest adventure of my life so far. It was mid-July 1947, and I was on a former troop ship called the SS *Marine Flasher*, steaming out of New York Harbor and bound for Le Havre in France. The ship had a lot of stairs going down, down, deep into the hold where a triple tier of hammocks swung. So this was how our soldiers and marines were sent across the Atlantic to defend democracy? A great many of us were immediately seasick, but we were young and we coped.

This crossing was going to take a couple of weeks, and there would be lots to do during that time. Despite considerable red-baiting in the press and other scare tactics, our delegation was over three hundred strong. Recruited from a wide variety of organizations and cultural groups, each with its own expectations and agendas, coming together from cities and towns scattered across the whole country, we would have to find ways to consolidate ourselves as a group and present ourselves at the festival. Some of the leadership from the World Federation of Democratic Youth was with us, and their skillful guidance helped us discover our common ground.

All of the officers on this ship were British, very white men dressed in very white uniforms with gold braid flashing here and there, and they spoke English in a manner very hard for us to understand. Occasionally they would invite two or three of what they considered the most attractive of us young American girls to have lunch at their tables, but normally we took our meals from a cafeteria line in a large mess hall below decks and had little contact with those who were running the ship, or with any other passengers for that matter.

One night we noticed that a hatch in the floor down there had been cracked open, and eventually a slender, dark-skinned person slipped out and went to collect some water in a tin can at the sink, quickly returning almost soundlessly back down into the hole again. In time, the dark face peered out of the hole once more, shyly asking if we would like to share some chai, and out of curiosity we said we would, although we didn't have the slightest idea what it was. The fragrant, spicy tea drink was delightful, and we invited its bearers to come out and sit with us.

This is how we discovered that a whole colony of Indian and Pakistani workers was being transported in this manner, hidden in the very bottom of the ship, forbidden to come out and show themselves to the other passengers. This led to a hot discussion about how we might be able to rectify this obvious case of racial discrimination. A small delegation of irate young American women now had an important reason to confront those smug gents upstairs in their white suits, those same men who had patronized us and made us feel like objects for their inspection. All we asked was that these people now quarantined in the ship's hold be allowed to share the decks, the fresh air and sunshine, with the rest of us. Or else.

We pressed our case, and we won the day. Soon we had a small band of observers regularly watching us on the rolling decks as we rehearsed a dance routine choreographed for us by the modern dancer Billie Kirpich, who taught it to us in the familiar cadence "1-2-3-4, 1-2-3-4, 5-6-7-8." Some of us got well enough acquainted with them to discuss our families, life back home, and our destination and why we were going there. Then came the day when we were about to reach land and had to face farewells. Our last rehearsal was to be a party, and we found some bits of food and drink to make it special. We went through the last trial run of our simple dance routine. Finally, one of the Indians brought out his dotar, a home-made two-stringed, long-necked Bengali instrument on which he plucked, and sang his parting song for us:

> Won-too-tree-for, Won-too-tree-for, fi-sikh-seven-ate,
> Won-too-tree-for, Won-too-tree-for, fi-sikh-seven-ate.

As we neared the landing in England where the Indians were to disembark, there were tears and hugs, exchanges of trinkets and small photos, and promises not to forget each other. I couldn't tell you their names, but I have never forgotten their faces or their perfect song.

We spent a couple of days in Paris before boarding the train that would take us through war-torn Germany to Prague. The horrific war had ended just two years earlier, and as we looked out the windows, desolation and destroyed buildings gave way here and there to plowed fields and cattle, flocks of chickens or sheep. One enormous railway station had been badly bombed but was limping along anyway, like the population of most of that part of Europe.

At last we reached the legendary city of Prague, well over a thousand years old and still stunningly beautiful even after eight years of Nazis goose-stepping through her streets, and still deeply scarred from a merciless US Air Force bombing only two years before this glorious summer. Now she was waiting in the sunshine for a new invasion, this time by seventeen thousand young people on their way from seventy-one countries, invited to keep her company for nearly a month under the blue flag of the World Federation of Democratic Youth, whose watchword was "Youth Unite, Forward for Lasting Peace."

Prague had been chosen in part to honor the November 1939 uprising of youth and students against the Nazi German occupation, and now young Czech student volunteers were shepherding us into scattered student dormitories and distributing schedules and various coupons for meals and transportation. We poured out into the wide streets, over the ancient flat paving stones, past the watchtowers and over the enormous, broad Charles Bridge, its many graceful arches spanning the famous Moldau of Bedrich Smetana's flowing symphony. Its thirty-odd stone saints still stood tall, looking mutely down through the centuries on other young people passing in review, rain or shine, blizzard or sunburn, ever since it had been built almost six hundred years earlier in 1357. And in 1947, for a solid month, stretching from July 15 to August 15, we would have the run of the city, welcomed and feted wherever we went. It was thrilling to be swept into a circle dancing the hora or singing "Bella Ciao." Here we were, the motley representatives of an exuberant, curious, dedicated, hope-filled new generation, laughing, singing, and dancing as we pledged ourselves to do all we could to stop the wars like those we had just lived through, wars that could destroy a horrific eighty million lives in a few short years. That could never happen again!

But not all of us would go home to a life of peace. One night, I met a young Vietnamese student handing out leaflets to rally support for his country's struggle for independence from French colonial rule. I was overcome as he told us of the bombings and destruction, but his eyes were full of hope as he spoke of their leader Ho Chi Minh.

There were warm speeches of welcome and greeting on opening day from the leaders of the World Federation of Democratic Youth and the Czech officials responsible for hosting us, followed by a jubilant pageant of the many delegations, a spirited introduction to the people of Prague as well as to one another. The bleachers of Strahov Stadium roared with cheering spectators, as young people skipped, marched, and danced their way around the wide oval track, many wearing some version of national dress, many bearing large, billowing banners to indicate their provenance. It occurs to me now that showing up at the festival in their distinctive clothing was a way of expressing the yearning to preserve the old and familiar, the handcrafted versus the ready-made clothing that had begun, since the turn of the century, to replace these expressions of national identity, local pride, and solidarity.

A brass band filled the air, as voices began to ring out:

> Everywhere the youth is singing freedom's song,
> Freedom's song, freedom's song
> We rejoice to show the world that we are strong
> We are strong, we are strong.
> We are the youth,
> And the world acclaims our song of truth
> Everywhere the youth is singing freedom's song,
> Freedom's song, freedom's song

Although it was new to us, it was our anthem and we embraced it, just what was needed to create an instant sense of belonging and unity, a way to rejoice in our oneness and our diversity all at the same time.

The US delegation was mostly made up of individuals, since the State Department's withdrawal of support had sabotaged efforts to bring any of the recognized cultural groups eager to attend. Of the roughly 325 Americans who did attend, we certainly were not officially representing our flag. I guess that's who we were: a bunch of iconoclasts whose main point of unity in addition to resistance to war was resistance to the status quo.

You could sum up the whole experience of this festival with the observations of Joe Sims, a fifteen-year-old kid from Youngstown, Ohio, with a big unruly Afro, who first attended the World Youth Festival in

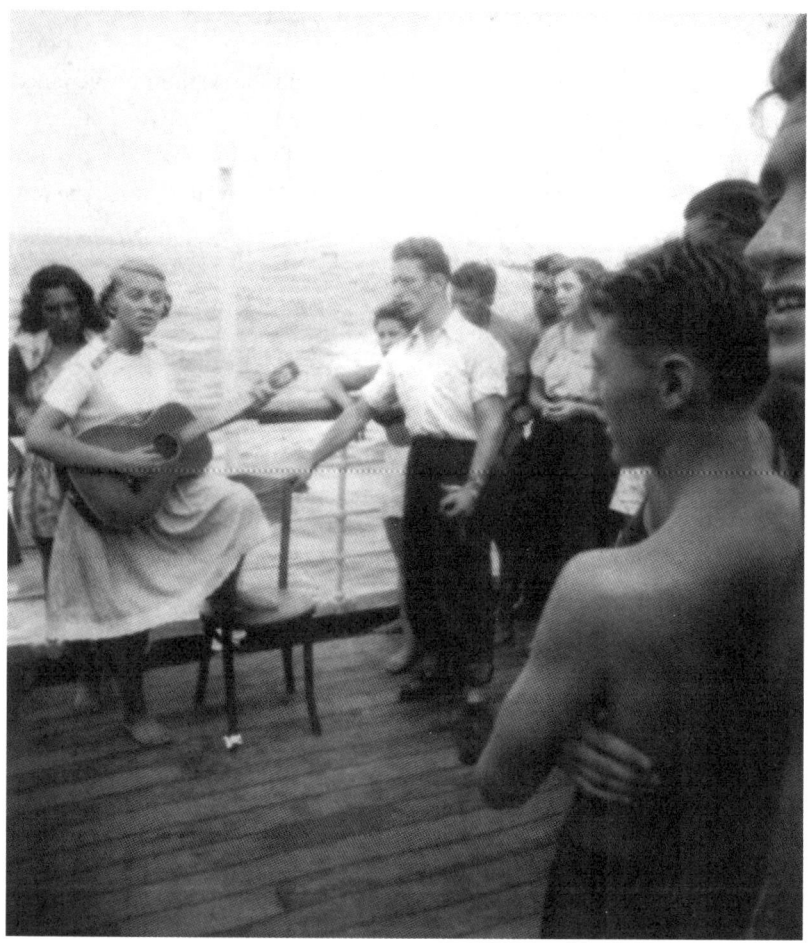

Returning from the World Youth Festival on the *Radnik*, 1947, with Barbara Dane on guitar leading the singing as the ship passed Spain

1951 in Berlin. "The Festival made me an internationalist. It changed my life. . . . Once you attend a Festival, the experience never leaves you." Joe's comments could just as well have been mine; I felt the same sense of transformation while at the 1947 festival, and it has stayed with me all my life.

At the festival's conclusion, we made our way to Yugoslavia (by way of Vienna and Venice) to board the *Radnik*, a Yugoslav tub contracted to bring us all the way to New Jersey. It was a small vessel, without many comforts. A wide open deck was our only gathering place, and there we spent most of our time, in the sun and wind, watching the waves and resting from our travels. But as we passed Spain, a country still under the yoke of fascism, we sang anti-Franco songs as loudly as possible, imagining our defiant voices of solidarity could reach the ears of people on shore.

As we drew at last near the shores of our "good old USA," my sudden eagerness to get home was mingled with reluctance to leave our bubble. But at the sight of the Statue of Liberty, a cheer broke out, and all thoughts turned to family, friends, and the familiarity of home.

In Detroit, where I could understand everyone when they spoke, where I knew what the money was worth and how to work the phones, I was home. I mostly looked the same—though tanned from all that time on the boat deck—but I had a head full of stories and questions and ideas, eager to unload it all on Rolf, my family, my comrades, my friends, anyone who would listen. What about Rolf? Would he want to hear all my stories? Did he still care for me? How had he occupied his time while I was gone? Disgracefully, I'd hardly given him a thought all this time, without a word of communication except for a possible postcard, so anything could have happened. And the summer wasn't over yet.

6

FROM PEOPLE'S SONGS TO THE HOME FRONT

The People's Songs convention in Chicago was calling, and either the time was too short or the travel shock was too strong or the challenges were too overwhelming for me to remember more than a flicker of my arrival from Europe before leaving again for this crucial event. Rolf seemed to be content and glad to welcome me back home, but I don't recall what we might have said or done to reconnect our relationship.

One thing I'll never forget, however, is that my dad made contact with me again and, in his low-key way, took me to visit a music store with him, where I was invited to pick out a guitar! I chose a mahogany Martin, the low-end model, but still, a Martin, and Dad even added a hard case to carry it in. It was like a peace offering, passed to me without flourishes and without speeches. He was proud of me, and this was his way to make me understand that. Mother must have told him how much I needed a decent instrument, knowing that this gesture would allow me to feel his acknowledgment of my commitment to becoming a real musician. But it was Dad, the thwarted and misunderstood father, who held back any judgmental words he might have been thinking, who simply gave his love.

Before long I was stepping off the train in Chicago with my beautiful new guitar, a fledgling ready to take my place in this community of committed artists. A hundred or so singers and musicians, songwriters and organizers, and even some folklorists, made their way from around the country for this event. I suppose we had all heard of one another through the *People's Songs Bulletin*, but this would be our first opportunity to interact and test our possibilities as a group, and it would last over four days in early October.

Irwin Silber, then the twenty-two-year-old executive director of People's Songs, led off with an orientation that helped provide the basis for a couple of days' worth of brisk and fascinating discussion. Pete Seeger, then not yet thirty, gave a keynote speech that, in his special way, filled the occasion, as well as the work that brought us here, with a sense of mission. A Chicago singer, Win Stracke, connected the music with the community, reminding us that we were about organizing as well as making people remember their past through the old songs, and that we could also write new songs to help folks confront new situations. Betty Sanders opened up the subject of the musicians' needs: repertoire, finances, decent working conditions, and most of all an organization like People's Artists to represent them.

Scheduled to appear on the Coast-to-Coast Hootenanny at Orchestra Hall on Friday night was a list of such length, I can't believe everyone actually got on the stage. Pete Seeger, Woody Guthrie, Big Bill Broonzy, Earl Robinson, Betty Sanders, Hally Wood, Alan Lomax, Win Stracke, Bernie Asbel, Ernie Lieberman, Goodson & Vale, and "that ain't all."

My value as a performer at such a concert was largely symbolic. I was a very young female from working-class Detroit, just back from the Youth Festival. What did I sing? A song I learned in Czech, "Na tu svatu, Katerinu, Katerinsku nedyelu..." (or some approximation)—an old song that told the story of a farm boy who was refusing to be dragooned into war by the armies of the Austro-Hungarian empire. I may have gotten in a bit of my "Hey! Ba-Ba-Re-Bop," but everyone was cut short with so many on the program.

After the concert at Orchestra Hall, Broonzy headed quickly off to the South Side of Chicago and his blues club. I was excited to find myself included in a small group of others venturing out to see Bill on his home turf. What happened on the way could very well have put an end to the "folk revival" right then and there! A car pulled up to the stage door, and in the back seat were Pete Seeger, Alan Lomax, and Studs Terkel, leaving the front passenger seat for me, next to Woody Guthrie, who had invited me along. He was at the wheel and in a hurry. As we raced down the highway along the lake, he slowed down and stopped—in the fast lane. "Looks like I missed the exit. But I can fix that!" he said brightly, and proceeded to back up for about a quarter of a mile, still in the fast lane, until he could find the exit again. What would this country look or sound like now if a big old truck had been barreling down the fast lane toward that same exit at that very moment?

As we hit the South Side, we were all eager to find Big Bill's club. But wait, there was one quick stop we had to make. I think it was Studs who said, "Let's poke our heads in that door for a few minutes. We might get lucky and find Memphis Slim at the keyboard." I have to confess that I didn't know who Slim was at the time, but once we got inside the tiny joint, once the special touch of his playing and the piercing but mellow sound of his voice got through to me, I was hooked.

By the time we arrived, Bill had changed clothes and picked up his electric guitar. When playing for white audiences, he tailored his image to their expectations, dressing in overalls and playing an acoustic guitar. Strange, isn't it, that in their search for folky authenticity, these new white audiences were often disappointed when a bluesman expressed connections with modern city life.

Studs and I were probably the only ones among us who were longtime Broonzy fans. I especially loved his "Why Don't You Do Right," his "Romance in the Dark," and his other pop/blues recordings with singer Lil Green and bassist Ransom Knowling that I had listened to so often back home from my secret bedroom record collection. Woody, for his part, spent the whole time sitting in a shadow under the stage honing his blues rhythm skills by keeping time as he quietly played the spoons!

So why was this diverse group of musical activists gathered together, who were they, and what were the stakes? In October 1947, just at the time of our convention, the House Un-American Activities Committee (aka HUAC) subpoenaed more than forty people connected with the film industry, accusing them of communist sympathies and subversive activities. This was a frontal attack on some of the most popular and progressive aspects of American cultural life, swift and brutal. A group of those who defied HUAC, challenging the legitimacy of their investigations, later became known worldwide as the Hollywood Ten and were each sentenced to a year in prison with a thousand-dollar fine. Their universally brilliant careers suffered a complete and thorough blacklisting lasting into the 1960s. This, of course, had a deeply chilling effect on cultural workers in any field, and the more mature ones among us knew that, sooner or later, this was coming to us. Forging a collective effort to nurture the growing movement of singing activists and activist singers was a logical and foresighted thing to do, both for its own sake and for the possible protection there might be in numbers.

Most of the delegates attending our convention had spent their lives collecting music, performing it, composing it, thinking about it. As the Cold War cultural attacks increased and spread, many of these artists had a lot to lose by being identified with a left-leaning organization like this, one with no shortage of obvious connections to the Communist Party, not to mention their own histories of local and international activism. The Library of Congress funding that Alan Lomax depended on to support his song-collecting work had been cut from the budget, an easy way to get rid of him and avoid a fight over blacklisting, causing him to look toward Europe and the Caribbean for most of the 1950s; Earl Robinson was building a solid reputation for his compositions filled with patriotic fervor. His "Ballad for Americans" premiered on radio with Paul Robeson singing, and Frank Sinatra recorded his song "The House I Live In," for which he won an Oscar in 1947. But even Robinson's friendship with Eleanor Roosevelt couldn't save him from the vile Hollywood blacklist that stifled his career when he was "outed" by Elia Kazan in the years just after our convention.

What convictions were strong enough to bring us together in Chicago that fall in spite of the pressures of blacklisting and financial insecurity and possible ruination of reputations?

Woody's famous phrase, which he wore emblazoned on his guitar, "This Machine Kills Fascists," was something any one of us would have been proud to say of our songs. His belief in the power of a song to restore self-respect and inspire a struggle for better days was part of the way most of us felt, and his words here sum that up:

> I am out to sing songs that will prove to you that this
> is your world and that if it has hit you pretty hard and

knocked you for a dozen loops, no matter what color, what size you are, how you are built, I am out to sing the songs that make you take pride in yourself and in your work. And the songs that I sing are made up for the most part by all sorts of folks just about like you.

Pete Seeger, of course, was the conscience of us all. Even at his young age of twenty-eight, he was already better than most at articulating our collective vision, and certainly more skilled at projecting concrete ways of pursuing it, enlisting everyone to find a role. Looking back not long before his death at age ninety-four, he said: "Participation! It's what all my work has been about. . . . Music and poetry can help us teach love and common sense to foolish people who think that money and power are the most important things in life." And in all his life he strove "to sing out in a world where the din of injustice is deafening."

Arriving back in Detroit after months away, I was eager to reconnect with friends and comrades. For young activists, *Daily Worker* sales were always an important part of our efforts to spread the party's views. We sold the paper wherever we could, and where we couldn't sell it, even for its list price of five cents, we gave it away. When the paper launched a drive for new readers, Rolf won the contest for selling the most subscriptions. The prize was a week in Cuba, then in the pre-revolutionary turmoil that filled the years between the end of World War II and the triumph of the revolution in 1959. Neither of us knew much about Cuban politics before his trip, but he came back overflowing with stories about the enthusiastic rallies he had attended, descriptions of ballparks filled with cheering crowds of Cuban workers, and a litany of celebrated leaders.

While he was visiting the island, Rolf had also fallen in love with Cuban dance music, and now went in search of recordings. Soon he found a couple of 78s to put on our rinky-dink turntable, filling our little living room in Detroit's Black ghetto with tropical music. It all felt so exotic and romantic, and there we were, Mr. and Mrs. Young Communist, awkwardly step-slide-step-stepping in time to this unfamiliar but intoxicating beat and doing our best to rekindle our warm feelings toward each other. My German-Jewish husband had stiff, old-fashioned European rhythm in his soul, and I come from a WASP culture that teaches its daughters that it is nasty to move your hips, whether walking or dancing. That's why my mother always made me wear a girdle. No bounce. No jiggle. No fun.

This heady mixture of rumba in the ghetto, *Daily Worker* salesmanship, and lurking FBI shadows was all taking place in 1948, when I was twenty-one, around the time Detroit was just beginning to blossom into one of the biggest economic successes this country has ever seen. How could it have happened that by 2013, it had devolved into the biggest US city ever to declare bankruptcy? What laid the groundwork for the glorious boom? What planted the seeds of the devastating bust? What was it really like as I was growing up? What was I missing as I walked around in my self-absorbed teenage dream? It wouldn't be long before I made my move, leaving it forever to follow that classic American westward migration.

In the early spring of 1948, it became a Communist Party priority to get on the Michigan state ballot by election time. In order to do this, there would have to be petitions gathered from all over the state. I don't recall the actual requirements in terms of numbers of signatures, but the idea of helping gather them seemed like a wonderful way to meet a lot of new people and remind them that the Communists in our country were not only legal but actively pursuing things that the majority of people wanted, like economic and social justice, peace and prosperity. Just as the major parties always advertised, but this was not for show. We Communists were willing to struggle every day to make it real. So I volunteered to go on one of the canvassing trips.

I don't remember the name or exact location of the towns where we worked, but they were a good many hours' drive from Detroit and pretty much undifferentiated. In my mind's eye I see blocks and blocks of flimsy, run-down houses, with broken cars and toys and more mud than plants in the yards. The air feels chilly and unwelcoming, but then this doesn't seem surprising. This is the kind of neighborhood where poverty-stricken young families hunker down while Dad goes out somewhere each day to look for work or any kind of help. If the doorbells were answered, it was mostly by young women clad in rumpled wrappers or what were called housedresses, with curlers in their hair, usually with a cluster of little kids who stared at strangers without animation. Sometimes an ancient pensioner appeared, but they were mostly too wary to communicate. This was not going to be easy.

The work was door-to-door, what is known as cold calling, not so different from a short-term gig I had taken a year or two before, canvassing for a sleazy magazine subscription company. The kind of job you take when you are down to the lint in the bottom of your pocket and too young for a real job. A guy who smelled like too many smokes, in his cheap suit and frayed shirt collar, would meet us at a doughnut shop, where he bought us "coffee and," which we sucked up while he outlined the objectives of the day and reminded us of the sleight-of-hand techniques at our disposal. Get them to sign, whatever the contract says. In those pre-television years, these glossy movie magazines and dream books were a low-rent and welcome distraction, so we emphasized that it cost only a dollar a month to start receiving *House Beautiful* in full color.

But our aesthetic as young communists, our ultimate objective and our entire offering, were as different from those dreams as night is from day. In place of pure escape, we were offering hope. And not only hope but a concrete plan. Simply appearing on your doorstep meant that we had faith in your ability to absorb a new idea. Yes, there are more political choices out there beyond Donkeys and Elephants. And here is a chance to help at least this one alternative organization get on the ballot and therefore become an option. You don't have to agree with, or even understand, what we are working for. This is just to help complete the process of democracy itself, to give another voice a chance to be heard. Will you sign?

To be sure, we had a lot of confused housewives slamming doors in our faces. But we also gave them a free newspaper they could look at in private later, and we poked at least a pinhole in what must have looked to them like the inevitable. A good number were willing to sign the petition once they saw we weren't peddling anything more costly than ideas.

Without realizing it, I was developing a strong attraction to the young man with glowing black skin and kind eyes who was guiding our group. Chris Alston had been a founder of the Southern Negro Youth Congress (SNYC) in the 1930s, a founding member of the UAW, and a leader in the effort to organize African American workers at the Rouge Plant in the early 1940s. As the days went on, I thought about how heroic it was for him to forge right into the middle of this semi-rural all-white world, carrying nothing more lethal than a petition to put the Communist Party on the ballot. He was calm and collected, kind and diplomatic, and he was also in a position to make culturally sensitive decisions that, if unwise, could see us all wind up in serious trouble.

It wasn't until we were back in Detroit that Chris indicated with a subtle sign, perhaps just a lingering look, that he would like to see more of me. His cue was so delicate that I could have missed it, but I was all ears. I agreed to meet him privately even though I knew he was married . . . and oh yes, that's right, so was I.

It didn't enter my mind that I was violating my husband's trust or that I was enabling someone else to do the same. But we were fully aware that this would have to be a matter of great discretion to avoid hurting any of the parties involved, to avoid criticism from the CP comrades, and most especially to make sure that we didn't set off any racial alarms in this city that was so touchy on these matters. So it all came down to a few brief encounters, answering the call of our chemistry and experiencing love in a form uncomplicated by day-to-day concerns, beautiful in its simplicity.

> *Chris, I love you for the precious and rare qualities of your love for the world, so deep that it has made you dedicate your life to your fellow humans, giving your heart and your energy every single day to forging a path toward a place without pain, without loss of dignity, where there is room for joy and beauty. Someone like you should be known and loved by millions the world over.*

By the time summer rolled around, I was all wrapped up in the Henry Wallace presidential campaign. Around then I had begun to experience the telltale signs: I was pregnant! For a minute I wondered whether my baby's skin color would betray my secret love. But even that concern met with a certain "que sera, sera" in me. The child is what mattered; the father in some senses was simply a means to an end. I was overjoyed that I was going to be a mother.

We comrades worked really hard on the Progressive Party campaign with the understanding that the Communist Party's role in the electoral efforts, given the Cold War politics of the day, would mainly be to put forward ideas and help keep the platform on track. The country needed someone with a proven record, who could move things forward with a progressive agenda. We knew chances were slim that a third party could actually win the presidency, but what else could we do but try? So even with my ever-increasing waistline, I climbed up on top of many a sound truck to sing this little ditty that said it all:

> The donkey is tired and thin,
> The elephant thinks he'll move in,
> They fume and they fuss,
> But they ain't foolin' us
> Cause they're brothers right under the skin!
> It's the same, same, merry-go-round,
> Which one will you ride this year?
> The donkey and elephant bob up and down
> On the same merry-go-round.

Wallace had been secretary of agriculture, secretary of commerce, and even vice president under Roosevelt, and the Progressive Party was the only one to campaign against the peacetime draft and to support full voting rights for Blacks and an end to segregation. Critics said that his tolerance of all those Communists in his campaign activities worked against Wallace, with the Red Scare in full gallop as it was. Maybe that was a factor, but more important, the cards were already well stacked against the effective emergence of any third party.

Sometimes I think about what a different world it would be if Wallace had won, if a genuinely pro-peace, anti-racist party had been able to survive and help set the tone for an informed and civil electoral process. I look back on that 1948 election as one of the three times that I had a chance to vote for a presidential candidate that I really wanted to see win the job. (Twenty years later, Eugene McCarthy was the second, and forty years after that, Barack Obama was the third.)

When only a million or so votes were cast for the Progressive Party—even with a candidate as strong as Wallace—a whole lot of wind went out of our sails. For Rolf and me, it was time to move on.

7

CALIFORNIA, HERE IT COMES!

With a baby on the way and no place to live, no job, no money, and now no clear political direction, we decided to take up the suggestion of Rolf's parents and move to Los Angeles, where they were now living.

What kind of fools would travel such a distance on the slim promise that things might be easier for a penniless young couple with a brand-new baby out there in the Golden West? How on earth would we move our few belongings, and where would we put them when we arrived? Rolf definitely possessed an unusual acuity, but no one would mistake him for a captain of practical logistics, so a lot of this planning and decision-making fell to me.

Before I would undertake such a move, at the top of my agenda was seeing a doctor about my pregnancy. The first one I went to groped me during the examination, so I never went back. The second doctor started right off prescribing Miltown, the mood-altering drug du jour for "just in case you have pain." I threw it out. Nobody cautioned me about smoking or drinking alcohol, so of course I did both, although thankfully in moderation. There was very little discussion about nutritional matters and no education about what the birth process itself would involve. Husbands were left out of the discussion, and any preparation for how to handle or nourish the new little critter was accidental. To put it mildly, I was way too short on dependable adult counsel.

The first steps for getting out of Detroit were relatively easy. We asked the party for permission to transfer to another area, and this was easily granted. We determined after some study that the most economical mode of travel would be to drive ourselves and our stuff across the country. The doctor vetoed the idea for me, and plane travel was also not recommended, so I'd have to take the train.

Even I knew it wouldn't be a great idea to travel all alone in my condition, so I approached Virginia, my best friend from high school, to see whether she would be open to such a journey. She already had a beautiful little baby of her own, a girl named Christina, but her marriage was in shambles, and there was a good chance that her husband, Bill Murray, would become violent if she threatened to leave him. She already had plenty of experience with his fists, and she wanted no more of that. All right then, a perfect plan: she would quietly depart westward on the train with me, and he wouldn't have a clue as to where to find her. The obvious problem was money, though. I had been barely able to come up with my own train fare. I thought of asking my mother, but I knew she was struggling to get by. In desperation, I turned to my sister for a loan, hoping she had a little stashed away. She did manage to come up with a couple hundred dollars, most of her savings, out of her unfailing kindness and generosity, and I don't believe she ever saw that money again. So now, how would I solve the problem of getting Rolf and our belongings to California?

I was about to leave my hometown with all my worldly goods, pregnant and broke and even without a forwarding address, when Dad diplomatically, without any lectures or promises, quietly stepped in and saved the day. Through the past couple of years, I had kept my distance from him, firm in my rejection of all of his backward ideas on race and unions and socialism. There is nothing like a teenager with a hard head and a sense of self-righteousness! He didn't try to argue with me or dissuade me anymore; he had seen that this was futile long ago. What mysterious chemistry of fatherhood, what urge to nurture and protect, guided him to find forgiveness within himself instead? How did he find enough love to focus on just exactly the gesture that would assist and even empower me, as I was about to move forever out of his dominion to pursue my youthful and impractical dreams half a continent away?

One day Dad called me and said he had something to show me, so

I met him at the drugstore, and we headed for the nearby Ford franchise run by an acquaintance of his from the Lion's Club. Over to the rear of the showroom in the used-car lot stood a black 1939 sedan, guaranteed to run problem-free, clean and simple and precisely what I needed. Dad put the registration in my name and handed me the keys. No drama, just the keys.

Rolf went about finding a small trailer to haul our books, records, clothing, and so forth to the promised land. He found one typical of its day, a wooden box on wheels, about six by six with a tarp you could tie over it to hold everything down. The price of gas was only twenty-nine cents a gallon then, but without any idea how much would be consumed, or what other expenses might show up along the way, we realized it would cut the risks greatly if Rolf shared the journey with someone else.

We cast about among our comrades and came up with Roselva Rushton and her husband, Ken, who were already planning their own getaway from Detroit. When they showed up in Los Angeles a day or two after my own arrival, my 1939 Ford with its precious burdens looked none the worse for wear, apart from road dust, and had performed like a champ.

My own continent crossing was pleasant, boring, and cozy, up until the train change in Chicago, where the heating system broke down, and it became chilly, unpleasant, and without enough distractions to keep me from growing gradually more apprehensive as I tried to imagine how we would manage once we arrived beneath the blazing blue skies and waving palm trees of California. Virginia and I did our best to keep each other's spirits up with small talk and speculation, and baby Tina managed to divert and amuse us, as babies will.

Along the way, Virginia decided that she wanted a new name with which to begin her new life, and thus became Dee Dee. Somehow, through an agency or a want ad, she had managed to become a sort of mail-order housekeeper for a man in LA who made his living as an independent small-time cement contractor. She would have a small salary along with room and board for herself and baby Tina in exchange for running his simple household, sort of like being married only without the physical relationship part. Or what exactly was the deal? Eddie turned out to be a decent but lonely man, who only wanted his life to run smoothly, a pretty good arrangement. He even offered Rolf a job as his ditch-digging assistant on the modest cement jobs from which he made a living pouring driveways, sidewalks, patios, maybe the occasional foundation.

Rolf, of course, was sure that after four or five of these digging gigs he understood the business and could go out and get his own jobs. He put an ad in the *Los Angeles Times* similar to Eddie's and proceeded to bid on a few contracts, most likely underbidding to get the work. He hadn't reckoned on a margin for error, which would naturally sink the contractor if the costs ran too high, and naturally had no insurance to cover this kind of work. I was distracted by making plans for my fast-approaching motherhood, so I failed to suggest that the rental of a cement mixer, purchase of cement and sand, hiring of manual laborers, wear and tear on vehicles, ads in the newspapers, and other things might run up the costs beyond hope of making a profit.

One dismal afternoon, Rolf stumbled into Eddie's place, where Dee Dee and I were admiring little Tina's efforts to walk. Dropping down into a chair, he let us have the news all in a sentence: "The cement mixer pulled the rear axle and the transmission out of the Ford because it was too heavy for the job, so I had to leave it there." But where? He didn't remember. What part of town? He didn't know anymore. It was the last time we ever spoke about the incident. Rolf—or someone—must have eventually solved the problem, because I do recall having access to a car during the remaining weeks of our life in Los Angeles.

We found a small place near downtown LA on a quiet residential street. Various new friends and acquaintances began giving us gifts of tiny baby clothes, both new and secondhand. Somehow we acquired a baby bassinet and what they call receiving blankets, those small white squares just big enough to wrap around a tiny body. I still had no idea where the baby would be born or how we would pay for the hospitalization, and the delivery date was days away. Rolf's parents suggested that I ask the Jewish Free Loan for the money. Ask for charity? A concept far outside my range of experience, and I was nervous and a little embarrassed, but what choice did I have? In the ancient Jewish spirit of taking care of those in need, I was given a fast hundred dollars and advised that the best place to go for charity medical attention would be Queen of Angels Hospital. The place was famous because they had cared for a lot of big-time movie stars, so I didn't question the choice, but hey, someone might have warned me that it was in fact a profoundly Catholic institution.

The day came when the sharp periodic pains told me that I'd better check in somewhere soon, and I remember distinctly driving myself to the hospital door in a state of mixed fear and bravado. After filling out some papers, a nun in a starched habit held out a box holding a few gold wedding bands. "Better leave it here, honey," she said. "A lot of the girls pull them off and throw them away during labor, and sometimes we can't find them again." I asked her to call somewhere and tell my husband where he could find me, and was taken to a small, dark hospital room where I was to spend fully twenty-seven hours tossing, sweating, and enduring various pokes and prods meant to assess the baby's progress, assaulted by the cries of women that echoed night and day up and down the halls and tearing at my long hair in a useless attempt to keep myself from screaming along with them.

I don't recall ever seeing Rolf during those long hours of labor, but I remember a young nun sitting by my side reading *Life* magazine and occasionally stroking my hands. "Don't worry; God will take care of you," she consoled me, but when I begged for something to ease the terrible pain, an older nurse explained that "it is the belief of the holy Catholic Church that suffering will make you stronger."

After a full day and night of wrenching pains that came and went in shorter and shorter waves, after all those hours with the gathering fear that something could be going wrong that would make this last so long, someone finally made the decision to give me a spinal injection and, by means of an episiotomy, release my baby from his struggle to enter this world.

> *Oh my beautiful boy, or as you know I love to call you, "the man who changed my life"! I cherish your eyes meeting mine, your tiny fingers grasping my long hair or my own fingers, your warm little body nestling into mine, your soft little murmurs convincing me of the reality of you. I know we will work this out together. We will both do the best we can. We're a team now.*

With my baby at home in our tiny apartment, I was in a state of euphoria on the one hand and terror on the other; joy at the very presence of this precious little guy and fear that any way I handled him might harm him, or that by not handling him enough I might be robbing us of the deep wordless communication we both needed. Referring to the dog-eared Dr. Spock book that Dee Dee had given me, I learned that it was foolish to go by the clock to determine his feeding times and that it made much more sense to feed him when he let me know he was hungry. Bit by bit I gained confidence, and with Dr. Spock's encouragement, I allowed myself to take my cues from Nicky. Yes, we gave him a strong and handsome name: Nicholas, for its definition in the baby-naming book, "victory of the people," and, as a middle name, Rolf, to give his dad a sense of continuity and signal his pride in this great gift of a son.

When Nicholas cried, I sometimes sensed that a kind of physical insecurity was causing it, and I visualized a lot of tiny nerve endings trying to connect, trying to become a system. I imagined the kind of tension one would feel before being able to answer, or even ask, these questions: "Who am I? Where am I? What am I to do?" I made the discovery that a gentle stroking over the soft spot on the top of his head seemed to comfort him, and I imagined this creating a sense of center, replacing a painful chaos with the security of repetition, answering the questions with something like, "I am me. I am here. Now I can relax."

But hold on here, Barbara. Did you ever wonder why you found your usually gregarious self feeling so desperately alone at such an important turning point? After all, having this baby, taking this giant step into adult life, was no different from any other social adjustment in a way; one simply cast about for possible allies and then let them know what you need. You weren't without resources. Rolf was circling around trying to be helpful when he saw an opening. There was Dee Dee, of course, but she had a lot on her hands already. In the normal course of things, young women about to give birth made efforts to draw their mother into the action. What made you leave Dorothy out of your plans? And probably there were others who would have been happy to stand by you. Cutting through all the excuses and obfuscations and taking a good hard look at this from the other side of sixty years' time, isn't it just possible that your determination to be a woman who could take care of herself, who could captain her own ship and climb her own mountains, was costing you more than you realized?

Most of the very few people I met in the Los Angeles area were part of the People's Songs chapter we had contacted soon after arriving in town. One of the best songwriters in the LA People's Songs group was a beautiful white-haired woman somewhere near fifty, a schoolteacher from Long Beach by the name of Malvina Reynolds. She had written a great song called "Sing Along" and another one called "Magic Penny," which I loved.

> Love is something if you give it away,
> Give it away, give it away.
> Love is something if you give it away,
> You end up having more.

Malvina, in her motherly way, recognized the look in a young mother's eyes that says, "I need a break!," and soon invited me to bring Rolf and baby Nicky down to visit her family in Long Beach. What a wonderful family she had! There was husband Bud, a carpenter who lived in his overalls and who was generous with his jokes and general charm. There was fourteen-year-old daughter Nancy, who flashed in and out of the house like a hummingbird. And there was Malvina herself, with a way that never condescended, that made us seem like peers in spite of the generation between us. She sang us a few of her new songs, made lots of wholesome and tasty food, including cookies and cupcakes, the kind of thing young people like us seem to constantly crave. Nicky was three months old, and this was his very first visit anywhere. Malvina was among the first to welcome him, with bits of observation, advice, and encouragement. Her approval of how we were handling our new little responsibility meant a great deal to me.

Meanwhile, Dee Dee made a few friends among the local jazz musicians and began to write poetry. I was drawn to the cool modern California-style way they played, and had often wondered how I would manage if I tried singing this way myself. After all, I did it in the car all the time, along with whatever pop tunes were on the radio. She introduced me to a sweet and talented bassist everyone called Creepy, and a gifted piano player friend of his, who offered to cut a few songs on acetate demo discs with me. "Trouble Is a Man," a lesser-known pop song I recorded, had the same old theme as the folk songs. But the doors of my musical world would soon be swinging wider.

For his part, Rolf continued to make fumbling attempts at finding some sort of job, but nothing appeared to work out. Here was this kind and brilliant young man who had, in every phase of his twenty-five years or so, been through enough to break many other men, and as a result struggled with what would now be identified as PTSD. I'm pretty sure it was my usual steadiness and my fondness for him that helped see him through this period, but I was badly in need of rest myself. I needed time to recuperate from the long labor, time to learn how to handle my sweet little Nicky, and a little security for the three of us.

Just as we were about to hit bottom in LA, my mother called and suggested that we come north to San Francisco, where she had recently moved to be with her new husband, Louis Samuels, a fellow bridge player she had known from the Knickerbocker Bridge Club in Detroit. We could stay with them at first, and she would get to meet her first grandchild. Lou had started a new kind of business there, and might even have a job for Rolf. Well, making another move had its scary aspects, but what awaited us sounded like a safe haven. We would have been crazy not to accept Dorothy's offer, so we made our way north.

For Dorothy, the often overworked and sometimes overlooked girl from small-town Arkansas by way of Detroit, the city of San Francisco was a magical place. Lou Samuels wanted nothing more from her than the opportunity to treat her like a princess, to show her off, and to allow her vivacious presence, her sense of joy in everything, to lift him from the dull and colorless life he'd been living. He insisted she shop at Saks Fifth Avenue, wear high-priced shoes, and go to expensive hair stylists; he rented an interesting house on Laidley Street in vibrant Noe Valley where they could learn to live among artists and writers, and took her out many nights to the kind of restaurant that helped make the city famous in those days.

The house on Laidley had open-air decks, which was a new concept to us. The owners lived downstairs, tucked away under them in a small space filled with art and design innovations of their own making, another concept new to me. Margaret De Patta, a jewelry designer who since has been called one of the first American artists to recognize the possibilities for modern design in jewelry, was one of the owners. Her husband, Gene

Bielawski, had contrived a bathroom door that opened up and down riding on ropes and pulleys and even had a stained glass window in it, a table made of slate-like material with hollowed-out spaces instead of plates to hold each diner's food, and lots of other solutions to their space limitations that came from way outside the box.

Margaret and Gene invited us to sit out on their deck in the balmy evening and share the quintessential San Francisco meal: sourdough bread, cracked Dungeness crab with melted butter for dipping, and white wine, all utterly new experiences for us. They also liked my singing, and generously gave a little party so we could meet a few more San Francisco people. My favorite among these was Giacomo Patri, an artist who worked political themes like war and peace in a fierce black-and-white linocut medium. Patri loved to sing old Italian folk songs and was intrigued by my American songs too. He invited me to his studio, where I saw several old handmade instruments on the walls, and where I began to glimpse this amazing San Francisco attention to creativity that seemed to leap out of every corner. Good politics too! Everyone I met seemed to have acquired a set of their own ideas based loosely on the principles of peace and justice, but with a vocabulary and style that was nothing like Detroit.

The first time I needed to find a babysitter, I hit the jackpot of the world. Right across the street and up a million steps lived not one but four young girls, Julie, Karla, Laurie, and Kathy, any one of whom, I was told, could be hired for the job. Even better, their parents turned out to be two of the best to ever walk this planet—and they were bona fide card-carrying Communists! Their mother, Tillie Olsen, was a struggling writer whose first book, *Tell Me a Riddle*, was not to be published until 1960. A novella based on her Russian immigrant mother's last illness and death, it won the O'Henry Prize for best American short story in 1961, and forever after, Tillie has been celebrated as a beloved feminist literary icon. Meanwhile, in 1949, she was working to raise four spirited girls while holding down various office jobs to bring in some cash, and struggling for any quiet moments she could find for her writing.

Tillie's husband, Jack, born Olshansky to his Russian Jewish immigrant parents but known as Olsen most of his life, had cut his political teeth while he was still in high school, circulating petitions to free Sacco and Vanzetti, and by the time the mass unemployment demonstrations of the early 1930s came along, he was ready to join the Young Communist League (YCL). When I met the Olsens, Jack had become an indispensable leader of the International Longshore and Warehouse Union (ILWU). But these were the chilly Cold War years, and while everyone wanted him for his volunteer labor, his income-producing prospects were perpetually shaky.

Since the mid-1930s, the US government had been trying to throw Harry Bridges, the Australian firebrand who led the ILWU, out of the country; now in the late 1940s, they were at it again. The union and all of its militant leadership, including Jack Olsen, were under attack from the FBI, the IRS, and even the CIO, which expelled the ILWU in the red-baiting frenzy that was gripping the nation. But I saw Jack only as this delightful daddy who arrived home nightly to his wife and daughters with embraces and jokes and always an obvious enthusiasm for life. I felt honored and unbelievably fortunate to have been welcomed into this home so full of love and laughter, and hung out there as often as I could.

It was Tillie and Jack who suggested, while brainstorming with us one day, that we apply for public housing, another new concept for me, but one that seemed to be filling a desperate need in the city. We easily met the low-income requirements, and it was only a matter of weeks before we were able to move into a two-room apartment on the south side of Potrero Hill near the shipyards at Hunters Point in the southeast corner of San Francisco. The housing project was basically a series of barracks-like buildings made for the war workers who had flooded the city in the forties and that were designed to be torn down after five years of use. The floor was cold cement painted dark red, scuffed and worn; the shower was a rusty tin box-like affair; the plumbing fixtures were simply galvanized, without the usual chrome; there was no yard; it was on a hill where the stiff wind never seemed to cease. But the rent was only thirty-five dollars a month.

I painted the walls, singing to the baby as I worked, and soon I was able to get us all set up. Our cheesy new green couch/folding bed cost all of a hundred dollars, but even that small amount required a guarantee from one of our parents for the credit we needed to buy it. Scavenged wooden orange crates, bricks, and boards provided shelves and cubbies to hold our few books and belongings. I had a tiny portable Singer sewing machine that had belonged to my mom, so I could make curtains from some cheap remnants of gingham. Later, on that invaluable little machine, I would make Nicky a miniature plaid flannel lumberjack shirt, the first I'd ever seen like it for a baby.

We soon contacted the Bayside chapter of the CP and began to attend its meetings. According to the FBI, Rolf became a member of the executive board of the San Francisco Labor Youth League (LYL) and was soon elected cultural director. Then, they say, Barbara and Rolf organized the Hunters Point branch. Not at all the way I remember this period of our lives, but I do remember taking turns attending meetings until someone suggested that the club could pay the dollar needed to hire a babysitter so that we could both come.

Barbara Dane, Rolf Cahn, and baby Nicky, c. 1948

Lou Samuels's business was something new on the retail scene. You could choose your appliances from catalogs instead of going to a brick-and-mortar store, thus saving the seller the price of rent and warehousing, the hiring of salespeople, and the investment in stock. Then the buyer paid the wholesale price plus 10 percent to the seller. This caught on fast among the many young couples setting up house after the war. It made the seller a bundle, with a minimum of hassle or investment. Lou also had people working on commission who were going door-to-door in low-income places like the very project where we lived, selling sheets and towels, irons and toasters on credit, with installments to be collected by the salesperson, who came by every week. Every time they came to collect, they had the opportunity to sell you something else by adding it to your contract, and of course the housewives' needs were endless. The catch was that if you ever defaulted on your contract, the seller legally could—and probably would—repossess *all* of your purchases.

This is the kind of job that Lou had for Rolf and a revolving series of other desperate young men. There was a tiny weekly guarantee, but the bulk of your income depended on how well you could push the rest of the goods from week to week. I know Rolf hated it, but he made himself do it, until one day he got moved into a new job, one with a desk and a phone. If there was anything more degrading than personally trying to extract a dollar or two from people down on their luck, it was this new thing they called skip tracing—tracking down the people who had skipped out on their contract, taking their purchases with them. The detective-work aspect of it appealed to Rolf, but the pursuit and harassment of very poor and often dysfunctional people embarrassed and tormented him. I had to help him get out of this.

I took a job selling Babee-Tendas door-to-door. This was a very well-built little table, aesthetically pleasing, with a hole in the Formica top where a seat was suspended. The baby could sit in the table, with a sort of harness to restrain him.

Folks in the party club were concerned that we were living in this racially mixed housing project and yet had no Black members in our group. An event was planned, to be held in the community center with music and local celebrities, in the hope of attracting some of the young people who were always looking for something to do in this remote neighborhood. I was given the job of getting the promotional flyers around, and a couple of young Black neighbors were recruited to help me do it. We got together late one afternoon, intending to drive around the projects leaving the flyers wherever we could.

Well, stop-and-frisk wasn't invented yesterday. As soon as we set out on our run, a squad car flashing its red light stopped us, pulled us over, and forced us all to get out of our vehicle and hand over our identification. Next thing I knew I had a mug shot and had been fingerprinted down at the local precinct station, and severely cautioned—more like ordered—to stop hanging around with "these people," meaning Black men. I also had a trunk full of party literature that I was meaning to drop off somewhere later, and they confiscated all of that as well.

In those early days of 1950, I was wholeheartedly dedicated to collecting signatures on the Stockholm Appeal, a worldwide effort calling for a total ban on nuclear weapons that was snowballing into a significant challenge to the war makers, surging up from deeply concerned people everywhere. The appeal was initiated by the famed French Communist physicist Frédéric Joliot-Curie and signed by famous artists like Picasso and Chagall, musicians like Ellington and Shostakovich, writers like Jorge Amado and Thomas Mann, actors like Maurice Chevalier and Simone Signoret, scientists, political figures, and so on, along with an estimated 273,470,566 other citizens of the world. The simple text of the petition read:

> We demand the outlawing of atomic weapons as instruments of intimidation and mass murder of peoples. We demand strict international control to enforce this measure. We believe that any government which first uses atomic weapons against any other country whatsoever will be committing a crime against humanity and should be dealt with as a war criminal. We call on all men and women of good will throughout the world to sign this appeal.

I felt that offering people the chance to sign this petition was a way of empowering them, of giving them a way to express the deep concerns most people were quietly bearing, as well as a great opportunity to discuss the issues with them, so I walked up the hill to the project's rudimentary shopping center, pushing my baby bundled up in his carriage and armed with petitions on a clipboard. But in several days of standing in the relentless chilly wind that assailed this hill in all seasons, I was able to speak with only a handful of people, and most of them seemed more interested in shopping for the evening meal than hearing about efforts to ban the use of atomic bombs. This was not Noe Valley with its artists and writers; it was the Hunters Point Housing Project with its hard-bitten poor. Or maybe I looked too young or too white to be taken seriously, and maybe the wind blew too fiercely.

8

THE PARTY'S OVER

One day a shocking letter came in the mail telling us that both Rolf and I were now summarily expelled from the Communist Party. No discussion, just a list of charges that were enough to choke off all communications with the organization that was by this time at the core of our lives. The letter included a non-association clause: "Cut off from all CP activities."

If you have never had the experience of committing your life to a particular person or group, only to be told that you no longer had any status and were not welcome anymore, you can't understand the sense of shock and even bereavement that sweeps over your heart at first. This is the life you have chosen, often at the expense of family ties and the loss of old friends and even jobs or schooling. These comrades are the people to whom you have declared your intention to fight side by side for a set of values, a series of goals that one assumed were shared by all. Without them, you have no family, no community of shared interests, no ideological home.

Rolf and I didn't handle the situation in the same way. He began to spend more time out of the house, presumably working out or teaching more judo at the Y and hanging out with people who were not my choice of friends, most of whom I had never met. Lots of times I wasn't sure where he was, but I knew he was emotionally shaken, and I didn't want to impose myself on his delicate state. I had little choice but to set about planning my own future. I turned to Tillie and Jack for advice, even though as an expelled person I was not supposed to have social contact with party members. Fortunately they felt secure enough of their own status to ignore that rule. We went over the list of all the charges together and decided that I should write an appeal.

The list of charges was a collection of petty and easily explainable incidents. It ran like this: Rolf was teaching judo to policemen (who happened to have signed up for his class at the Y); Barbara took money from the club (that one dollar per meeting the members had offered to cover the babysitter's fees); Rolf advocated violence at a demonstration (a recent near-eviction where he had revealed his Little League baseball bat); Barbara was a white chauvinist (without any story to illustrate the allegation); and other such unmemorable items.

I wrote up my response, and the Olsens were kind enough to advise me on how to submit this document, a sort of a "knock twice and ask for Joe" situation where I literally handed the appeal through a transom. This was the era when many party leaders had gone underground to avoid prison and when everyone knew that the party was infiltrated with informers and agents provocateurs. I never received any sort of direct response.

We were beginning to be very uncomfortable at Hunters Point, and longed for a yard where Nicky, by now a toddler, could play outdoors and maybe even have a dog. I read in the papers about a new development (as the acres of land newly covered with quickly built houses were called) by the name of Rancho Buri Buri, in South San Francisco, where war veterans could buy a house for only five hundred dollars down. I contacted my mom to see if she could loan me the money, but she tossed the ball to my dad in Detroit, and once again he came through, just at the right moment, and again with no strings attached. Before we knew it, we were moving our few belongings into this brand-new little house with a couple of bedrooms, a nice kitchen, a fireplace, and a bare but fenced backyard. We had no furniture, so we improvised with whatever we could find and even got a German Shepherd from the pound. I think we named him George.

Now I really needed to hustle, knowing that those payments were going to stretch our finances to the maximum. This was the time to get a real job, no more commissions-only work with no security. As a kid in Detroit, I had worked in sales at a few department stores, so this is where I could point to previous experience. With that, and my years at the Biltmore Pharmacy, where I had learned more than my share of the cosmetics okey-doke (jazz musician's slang for scam), and *shazaam*! I was hired! An agency had found me a job as a Rubenstein girl at the City of Paris, one of the most exclusive department stores in San Francisco or, for that matter, in all of America.

This pseudo-prestigious cosmetic line ("Madame" Rubenstein, along with her alternate corporate identity, "Prince" Matchabelli) had its own counter on the main floor near the entrance, ruled over by an older woman who had been "personally trained by the Madame." It was mandatory for me to show up every day fully made up, well groomed in a black dress, and wearing push-up bra, girdle, stockings, and high heels. Madame's "personal representative" owned me for eight hours, and of course was entitled to be the first to chat up any new customers in order to cop the commissions. With at least a few of these leisurely old-style San Francisco dowager shoppers, youth had its appeal, so I did develop a few who only wanted to deal with me, and would even ask for me once we became acquainted. I kind of enjoyed the job in a way, but it was never going to solve all my problems. I was also going to need to be in touch with anyone in my limited support system who might respond in case of trouble.

Meanwhile, my mother's marriage to Lou Samuels had run its course, ending with her lightning departure for New York, where she reunited with another old romance from the bridge world, Ambrose Casner. She confessed to me later that she had been conducting a hot correspondence with Amby for some time, and shared with me a couple of letters where he called her his Magnolia and signed himself her Gaylord (Ravenal), in reference to the two lead characters in the Jerome Kern musical *Showboat*. "We could make-believe . . ." was the theme. Amby looked like no matinee idol, but he was in fact a sort of rough-cut Broadway character. A saxophone player in his youth, he was now a small-time businessman, what was called a jobber. He talked like a Damon Runyon bookie and had a shelf full of silver trophies for his wins at bridge tournaments over the years. I thought she must have been daft; for this guy my mother had vanished from San Francisco into New York

City? But there they were, living out each other's fantasies, right in the place I used to jokingly call "the heart of the throbbing metropolis," only steps from 5th Avenue, Central Park, and Carnegie Hall.

And there I was, in a postwar subdivision called Rancho Buri Buri, squeezed between San Francisco and San Mateo, on a few acres of land—now covered with several hundred quickly and cheaply built houses made to take advantage of the baby boom—land that had originally been stolen by colonizers a couple of centuries ago from the Yelamu tribe of Ohlone people who had once claimed lands to the west all the way to the ocean's shore where its fishing grounds lay. Four years after I had left the restrictive covenants of Franklin Village in Michigan, here I was living on stolen land in California.

I knew not a soul in Rancho Buri Buri, at least two bus rides from my job—three if you count getting from the child-care center where I dropped off baby Nicky for the day, to the City of Paris near Union Square, where I worked. All in reverse again at the end of the day, of course. It damn near broke my heart the first few times I had to watch my baby's face as I headed for the door, leaving him with utter strangers. The kind ladies there assured me that he was content while in their care, but it felt like a vise was gripping my throat as I tried to look as if I was OK with this arrangement so as not to upset the little guy. Each night when I finally made it back to the house carrying my sleeping two-year-old in my arms, I felt physically, emotionally, and mentally exhausted. There had to be a better way.

Rolf required the use of our aging Chevy, bought cheaply from a comrade, for his new "job" of selling insurance on commission. He also had begun to go missing in the evenings since our expulsion from the party, leaving me with little idea of what he was doing. I knew that at least once a week he was teaching judo and that he had made some new friends in the city. One day when I was at work, I received a personal call, something seriously frowned on by management. But it was Rolf, sounding just short of hysterical, saying approximately this: "I'm out here in the Sunset District, and I have a flat tire. I don't have any money, and I don't know what to do." And just what did he imagine I would be able to do?

Remember, I was all of twenty-three years old, and it already seemed that my options had considerably narrowed. My husband was spending more and more time with people I didn't know, and he appeared to need more help than my baby did. He seemed unable to see how much *I* needed *his* help, and incapable of offering it if he did notice. Most of all, I didn't have the counsel and companionship I had imagined a husband would offer as I struggled to get through the disappointments and heartaches of adult life, and he wasn't even available for me just to talk things over. To put the best face on it, maybe he was feeling that life was getting to be too much for him too, and was coping with that feeling by ducking out on it. A couple of wars later, the concept of PTSD would have entered this discussion, but I was beginning to realize that I couldn't continue to carry his load along with so many unexpected burdens of my own.

On a day off, I drove into San Francisco with Nicky in the backseat sleeping in his car bed. I finished my errands and pulled into one of those big popular drive-in restaurants, the kind California was famous for. I was a little too upset for lunch, but I could handle a milk shake—all I could afford anyway. A girl in a short skirt, gliding about on roller skates in the manner of that particular chain, brought it out and put it on a metal tray that hooked onto the driver's-side window. Ahead of me was a high blank wall, newly painted stark white and unblemished. I remember staring at that clueless wall for a long while, thinking about the situation with the party and what it meant for my life.

I probably should have contacted Phil Schatz or someone else back in Michigan who could help me put my world together again, but the problems with communication—not knowing the status of anyone back east and not wanting to "out" anyone who was having to keep their politics quiet, plus my awareness that I was frequently under observation and might cause trouble for someone else if I contacted them, and all sorts of other things having to do with this dark period in American life—held me back from a strong defense of my personal situation. I was enough of a team player to feel that it was of the utmost importance to protect the others even though I may have been sidelined myself.

As I sat there staring at the wall, I heard a voice inside my head speaking clearly. I had thought of the Communist Party as the most effective platform for working toward a day when my country would be free of racism and the constant drumbeat of war, and economic justice would prevail. Just because I had been cast out of that organization didn't mean that my personal goals were any different. I would simply continue as best I could on the same road, only without the support and comradeship of the party. I respected many individuals in it as some of the most principled and decent folks I'd ever known. I would not expose them or disgrace them, but I would not collapse without them either. If I could continue to believe in myself and in my own principles, I'd be OK, and someday it would all get sorted out.

In fact, many years later in 1964, when I was leaving California to start a new life in New York, I ran into Mickey Lima, the highly regarded leader of the Northern California Communist Party who had been indicted under the Smith Act and released by the 9th Circuit Court of Appeals after spending nearly five months in jail during the 1950s. I was not aware that Lima even knew who I was, but he made a point of drawing me aside to a quiet corner where he said, in effect, "I want you to know that we are very grateful for the way you conducted yourself after your unfortunate expulsion from the party, and I just wanted to thank you." I doubt that he could have realized how much he had just eased a heavy heart.

Meanwhile, I urgently needed objective advice about my personal life, and once again turned to Tillie and Jack to ask whether they knew of a party-approved psychologist I could talk to. It was generally frowned on for security reasons to be "telling all" to a shrink. They came up with a trusted name, and I told him up front that I could only afford one session and planned to ask him for an unbiased opinion. After laying out my frustrations with Rolf and his often erratic and unrealistic behavior, he saw clearly what I had to do. "You are the one in the family who is functioning, and you have a child to think of." Before being overcome by the way things were going, he explained, I needed to get out of the relationship. His advice connected immediately with what I already felt in my gut, and maybe all I needed was a neutral appraisal to confirm it. The marriage was over, and Rolf would have to leave.

Reading through copies of FBI files recently released to me from the National Archives, I know now that it was Rolf himself who was "Informant T-1," the person who had supplied them with a copy of my party card, along with some other bits of personal details. According to the file, he informed them of something or other related to me on at least five different occasions in 1952 after we had separated. No harm done, really, because I have never had anything to hide and would have shown the card to them myself if they had asked. It was still a legal party, after all. Perhaps the FBI, knowing I had just left him, saw him as vulnerable at the moment and pursued him. As a soldier, Rolf had been recruited for espionage work by the Office of Strategic Services, a precursor to the CIA, so perhaps he still had some romantic sense of "duty," or perhaps the idea of being an informant seemed exciting to him. Maybe it was out of bitterness. Maybe he needed the money. (Was there money?) Not for me to say. But it wounds my heart to think that he might have gone out of his way to do this. I hope it wasn't like that.

After putting the whole affair into historical perspective, the conclusion I have come to is that there must have been an agent provocateur working to break up that particular party club. It was easy to seize on Rolf and me as the two newest and least-known members of the group, and there really was nothing to be lost by using us as scapegoats. This theory makes more sense than the flimsy list of charges against us. I'm sure we were not the only ones to have felt the sting of this sort of marginalization, and we can only guess at how destructively this kind of thing tore at the network of what were functioning, healthy neighborhood or workplace organizations made up of people who held themselves responsible for trying to make life more bearable for their communities and for working to bring peace and harmony to their neighbors and the world.

Newly single, I realized it would be pointless to hang on to the house in Buri Buri if we were not a family anymore. The City of Paris job wouldn't support living nearer work, even though a young single woman without kids would have considered it a plum job. My only other skill outside of retail sales was my singing, and of course nobody who could offer me a living from that even knew I existed. I began to cast around for clues about how to break into that world.

9

DIGGING UNDERGROUND

Sometimes when all these responsibilities began to overwhelm me; when I felt like I was losing my grip on who I really was, what my real work was supposed to be; when the banality of the daily struggle was beginning to drown me, I would slip off, usually with napping baby in a basket, looking for some corner of the city where music was the reality. I didn't know how to find whatever it was I was looking for, and maybe I wouldn't know it when I found it, but just as when I roamed Detroit as a high school truant, it had to be a place where you didn't need to spend any money. Jack's Record Cellar was just such a place.

Norman Pierce, a middle-aged music junkie who had worked on the docks as a longshoreman, put a few coins together—they say one dollar was the price—and bought the business, probably from one of your standard wealthy music dilettantes glad to be rid of the trouble of running a record store. Jack's Record Cellar became his sinecure. Makeshift shelving covered all the walls, and there were bins on tables in the middle. In fact, you could hardly walk through the place. No advertising signs or decor of any sort distracted the eye from piles and piles and piles of 78 rpm shellac records, and—ever since Columbia records had come out with the first ones in 1948—stacks and stacks and stacks of 33⅓ rpm LP vinyl records. The only place to sit would be a crate of some sort, which you first had to clear of any breakables.

Maybe Pierce found conversations with a questioning young woman toting her sleeping baby in a basket an amusing diversion from having to dust the shelves. He began to play a few of his favorite jazz sides for me and also to hip me to the latest folk song releases. His tastes were as eclectic as mine, playing Bird one minute and Lu Watters the next, followed by Jean Ritchie or Cynthia Gooding. He also began to tell me about the upstairs anarchist with the strong opinions and sexy poetry.

Kenneth Rexroth did come downstairs from time to time, to stretch his legs and try out some new poem or idea on Norman, and I actually chatted with him once or twice. They say he'd come out west from Chicago to help organize maritime workers back before the Depression, and then was a conscientious objector in World War II who assisted Japanese Americans attempting to escape the internment camps. But now he was spending his time in the world of writers and would-be writers, holding a weekly sort of salon right upstairs, where the boys could knock one set of ideas against a few others without breaking any bones. In my imagination they mostly wasted their days in drinking vinegary wine, talking a lot of sticky stuff about women, and smoking endless cigarettes. But given that Rexroth's poetry was said to be pretty widely read and that he had a fair amount of airtime on the recently founded community radio station KPFA, it seems there was more to it than that. His poem "Thou Shalt Not Kill," written when Dylan Thomas died of alcoholism in 1953, was a major influence on Allen Ginsberg's best-known poem, "Howl."

So in this vicarious way, directionless and random, I was picking bits of the Bay Area underground culture out of the air, watching what would later be called the Beat Generation come into its adolescence. Even then, it was clearly a boy's game, but I really didn't care because the whole scene seemed unhealthy to me, self-absorbed and lacking in larger purpose.

I was accustomed to more structured ways, and I yearned for a sense of enormous gears engaging, of big things being broken open, the sound of age-old fetters and chains snapping, and at last a moving forward, causing all kinds of glorious exuberance to burst forth. And in quite a few ways they were, but in unexpected ways and from unexpected quarters. The gears that began to engage were in part the social and cultural rebellions that these very "Beats" helped to unleash, such as the Free

Speech Movement at UC Berkeley. The big things that broke open were the events all over the nation that began with the Freedom Riders and the Montgomery bus boycott. Later, we would see my "glorious exuberance" with the birth of hippie culture and eventually the unprecedented swelling of popular resistance that helped end the Vietnam War.

But at the time, I couldn't see what was in any of this that could lead to a more equitable society. How could this Beat stuff make a single mother on welfare smile or put meat on her table? What would save the life of a teamster falling asleep at the wheel after having driven his truck twenty-four hours straight? How would it get that cop to stop beating a Black teenager bloody because he was simply standing on the corner with his hand in his pocket? Bits of the poetry, the little I actually read, seemed touched by some of that, but when it came to the so-called scene, it was the appearance of self-indulgence and the sense of "dropping out" that pushed me away from what seemed to be a private club of grown men with sadly arrested development.

To be honest, I seldom had any direct evidence of this. As I had blossomed into my later teens, I had become pretty used to the feeling that in any room full of people that included men there would be a subtle parting of the waters as I entered, that someone would offer me a chair, and that at least a few would fasten on my every word. Perhaps most other young women were receiving that same treatment, and maybe each of us was inadvertently being trained to be queen of our own private frog pond. But among gatherings of these burgeoning philosophers and poets, young girls such as I had little fantasy value. Most of these dreamers—unbeknownst to me—were far more interested in boys, something that would pass unremarked today but that could be read by women in those days as at least disregard and at most disdain for anyone outside their "elite" circle. And since I was all about wanting people to be regarded for their ideas, generally genderless, I took offense at the heavily male bias and called it misogynist, therefore to be abjured. In those days I was pretty good at forming quick judgments and being unfettered in my pronouncements, an unfortunate but not uncommon quality in one so young.

The commercial media, as usual, had far too much to do with shaping the general understanding of the "Beat Generation." They focused on "cats" with berets and goatees, "chicks" with kohl-rimmed eyes and black tights, or drugged-out kids with bongo drums and weed for sale. All that did exist, but it was overemphasized in order to trivialize what was growing into a genuine cultural upheaval in the face of the pressure, in this Eisenhower era, to conform, to blend in.

There was much to hide from: Joseph McCarthy's rabid attacks on anyone he could paint as a communist, the rampant union busting that was one of the central reasons for these attacks, the undisputed increase in lynchings of African Americans, hysteria over the imagined theft of atomic secrets that went so far as to justify the execution of a humble Jewish couple named Rosenberg. All this and so much more by way of the inexorable dismantling of fundamental social advances won as far back as the FDR–New Deal days.

Given my own assumptions about the misogyny of the Beats, I was surprised years later when reading Rexroth's comments in a piece he wrote for the *SF Bay Guardian* in 1970 called "Kenneth Rexroth: Comrade." He was certainly speaking to me, as he ripped the mask from the media characterization of the women's movement then capturing national attention: "The debauching of women's liberation is of the greatest significance; freedom and equality of women is the measure of the health and even the economic efficiency of a modern, as of a primitive, society," and more, saying things I'd never dreamed might have been discussed in the rooms over Jack's Record Cellar.

With time, a better understanding of the meaning of the Beats emerged from the piles of nonsense—what Rexroth called *hallucination publicitaire*—that was used to sell magazines in the 1950s.

A few years back I ran into an old musician friend, and as I was rambling on about some of the thoughts I'd been having as I revised my assessment of the Beats, he said something like, "Well, weren't you practically the mother of the Beats?" I went into my "No, no never!" routine, recalling my discomfort with the way any performance of mine seemed to have been linked in those days to the opening of some new "Beat" venue. But as I cooled down, I had to admit that what I was resisting was the media definition of Beat, which implied something like surrender, like giving up or dropping out. I realize now how proud I should have been to be called a daughter of Rexroth, even though he couldn't stand the "father of the Beats" idea and never stopped being the very model of a modern major iconoclast.

I started looking around for like-minded musicians. In Berkeley, someone told me about the San Francisco Labor School, where I might find others who were looking for ways to put their music at the service of progressive causes. There I joined a group working on a sort of living newspaper, incorporating songs with educational skits on current issues. I met Lou Gottlieb, later of the well-known Limeliters but then a UC student working on a music degree, who had a gift for comedy and an easy acquaintance with classical piano as well as pop songs and even bebop. Lou was currently making his living by playing at a piano bar. His delightful renditions casting Mozart as a young hipster and his suggestions that Charlie Parker tunes should be given lyrics like "The boss don't give a damn about your wages" opened up my head a lot and went a long way to bump me off the purist stump I had been standing on.

Someone tipped me off that KGO-TV was about to present its version of Miss America, awarding the title Miss US Television to the winner. What did I have to lose? This was the main TV station in San Francisco, and it seemed like an ideal way to get involved in this new medium. I showed up for the tryouts and was sent to the front of the line. Requirements for the show would be the same as the tired old Miss America formula: (1) a bathing suit lineup, (2) a little speech about your goals in life, and (3) a demonstration of your "talent." I was pretty sure that number 1 would knock me out of the race, considering that like most young women of those days, I never exercised and was slightly overweight as usual. The very definition of *zaftig*. But maybe that's what they liked? I could talk all day about my goals, but would these particular goals please the judges or scare them? The "talent" seemed like the easy part, even though I still had only minimal guitar skills and no real idea of how I needed to present myself.

I searched the racks at City of Paris, where I had a discount but normally never shopped because of the prices. I found a kind of compromise dress for the talent part, one with a fairly low neckline and full skirt that were vaguely folkish but made of a modern no-iron fabric in pale blue, with a gold wash that swirled around on it. I'd have to strut across the stage clad only in their standard strapless black velvet bathing suit with matching high heels, off the rack and the same for every girl,

Miss US Television pageant, 1951

and that part would require nerves of steel for me, wondering if my post-baby blubber would be obvious. I wrote a little statement about my dedication to peace and justice, soft-pedaling the activism related to it that was in my heart. I had my hair done in a beauty salon and plunged into the scenario. Before I knew it, I was "crowned" Miss US Television, though the title was misleading since this was only a local contest.

In addition to a corny little silver compact with this legend printed on it, the real prize was a sixteen-week series that ran from October 1951 to February 1952, making mine (*Folksville, USA*) the first "folk music" show anywhere on TV. The advertising agency Byrne and Grill began to bug me about what name I was going to use, a question that hadn't occurred to me. Thinking it over, I realized that I wasn't going to be Cahn forever and that I didn't want to take back my father's name, mostly because he was embarrassed by my politics. It was time to have a name of my own, one that belonged to no man in my life. I would have to give it meaning through whatever I did for myself. The day before the deadline, I was skipping up Dana Street in Berkeley when I glanced up at the sign: Barbara Dana? Sounds a bit too made up. How about Dane, short and easy to spell, near the top of the alphabet too. OK, let's go with that. I phoned the PR guy, and the die was cast.

Great. I was free as a bird; I had a new name, a television series, and now an agenda. Each week I had to spend hours lining up my (unpaid) guest, selecting and arranging for the borrowing of my wardrobe (provided by certain vendors for a mention in the credits), preparing my songs and whatever would be the framework for the next show. Each week I had to drive alone to the very top of San Francisco, up the barely lit and spooky winding road into Sutro Forest where the station was located, and get there early enough to do my own makeup, a much more exacting job than putting on an ordinary street face. I even recorded the theme song for the sponsor, a used-car dealer: "Low are the prices at Ken's, Low are the prices at Ken's." And all this for the fat weekly paycheck of sixteen dollars. Not enough to quit the City of Paris, but enough to get me fired. The C of P thought, and not incorrectly, that perhaps my full attention would no longer be lavished on my role as its Rubenstein Girl.

10

BYRON DANCES IN

My social life in those days was pretty well limited to the nights when a few of us from the San Francisco Folk Music Club would meet at Vesuvio, a Bohemian bar on Columbus Avenue across the alley from City Lights bookstore, where the owners let us hang out and jam in the back room as long as we liked. I could even put baby Nicky to sleep in his car bed over in a corner.

My musical tastes had begun to be more adventurous, and I developed an interest in hearing more Latin music, drawn in by what sounded to me like deep jazz influences. One night at a meeting of the club, I threw out an idea: "Would anybody like to go with me to hear Perez Prado's band next week? He's got the Cuban percussionist Armando Peraza with him on this tour, and they say it's gonna be hot!" Blank looks, no interest from this bunch of old-timey hillbilly wannabes. A tall, dark-haired man I hadn't noticed before spoke up. We exchanged numbers and made a date for me to pick him up where he lived in Berkeley so we could drive together to Sweet's Ballroom in Oakland's funky downtown.

I'm not a believer in luck or fate or astrology, but I do believe in Mother Nature and her clever ways with the pheromones of males and females. It was almost inevitable that we would discover an irresistible attraction. The moment Byron Menendez pressed against me as I stood in the group close to the bandstand, I knew there was going to be a lot more to the story. He was a superb dancer, and I have always been a clumsy one, but this didn't seem to be a deal breaker. I had no problem with watching while he danced with someone more adept, as long as we were leaving together. It wasn't long before I was making regular trips to Berkeley and we were making plans for the future.

This man with the low, soft voice and graceful way of moving was born in the Bronx to immigrant parents from Spain and Latvia, both labor activists who worked in New York's garment district. He had married a girl named Phyllis, a fellow member of Margot Mayo's American Square Dance Group, not long after coming home from the war. The making of handwrought silver jewelry was something he had learned as a part of the physical therapy given to him by the Veterans Administration because of a shrapnel wound still troubling his arm. Byron had coached Phyllis in some of its techniques, and together they ran a tiny hole-in-the-wall shop near the UC campus in Berkeley. But it was barely paying for itself, and functioned more as a workshop than as a place where you would spend your money on jewelry. By the time of our Perez Prado adventure, he and Phyllis had split for good, Phyllis had moved back to New York alone, and I was newly single.

Byron had discovered a love of dance at a young age, and even studied the work of groundbreaking modern dancers like Sophie Maslow, Jane Dudley, and Pearl Primus. But, leaving aside what might have become a brilliant career as a dancer, he enlisted in the army, determined to do whatever he could to help defeat fascism. He was immediately thrust into the three most horrific battles of World War II: the Battle of the Bulge, the Battle of Normandy, and finally the Battle of Hurtgen Forest, which was so mishandled and murderous that it has been largely effaced by Pentagon historians, costing the US alone thirty-three thousand casualties. Byron was captured at Hurtgen and sent to a Nazi prison camp in Germany. He was subjected to starvation and forced labor.

Is it surprising that all of the trauma from the war was locked up inside him, or that I was unable to gain any knowledge of it during our sixteen years of marriage? This remarkably musical man developed a strategy for avoiding any such talk. He would start picking out tunes on his mandolin or finding melodies on his ever-present harmonica to create a sound barrier. In his late seventies, when he finally did begin to recount his war stories, he would start to shake all over as he relived those terrible days. The concept of PTSD was only developed during the Vietnam conflict of the 1960s, but many who lived through the World War II era can tell stories of how it has affected the lives of everyone close to the returning veterans, and how relentlessly their war memories have invaded their own lives and continue to haunt their dreams. There is nothing good about war.

I think it was a surprise to Byron that an innate sense of design had been awakened in him as he developed his jewelry-making skills. The clean, strong, and graceful lines he created began to evolve into an original style, and his work, using simple hand tools, often made the leap from the level of craft to that of art. He found much satisfaction in his ability to make beautiful things, objects with a degree of permanence that would mean something to people over time: wedding rings that would be worn for decades, brooches meant to mark some special occasion, earrings chosen to wear daily for the way they framed the face and made the wearer feel beautiful. But it was obvious that Byron had no intention of becoming any sort of businessman, and his style of operating "off the grid" was not likely to produce a comfortable or even secure lifestyle any time soon.

About that time, my TV series came to an end, and along with it my paltry but useful sixteen-dollar weekly salary. A while back I had begun helping spruce up Byron's shop and getting to know the ins and outs of discussing the jewelry with customers so that I could help sell the things Byron was making. For his part, Byron was beginning to know my little boy Nicky, and as the implications of moving in together were becoming clearer, we began looking for an apartment.

Byron found a two-room place in the ramshackle building in Berkeley that still hangs over the corner of Adeline and Ashby, borrowed a trailer for the day, and moved us up the long stairs and into our first home together. One of the best things about it was that you could go up on the roof to hang out your laundry. I remember sitting up there together, a gentle breeze and the late afternoon sun adding to the pleasure of being in each other's arms, trying to sort out our new life. Oh, and by the way, now I was pregnant, so we needed to talk and take a good hard look at our future.

Byron, for his part, seemed dazed. He didn't say much, so I wasn't sure how to read his mood, but I guessed that he was staring ahead into a pretty terrifying future and wondering how we would all survive. I imagined he may have felt trapped, too, not necessarily by me but by life moving so fast and bringing circumstances that seemed to be spinning out of control. I felt a little dizzy too, but when I was aching for some sort of expression of love, support, and agreement, he was mute. To be honest, he could have simply left, as many men in his shoes before him have done once they got the picture. But he wasn't that kind of person. Instead, he set about looking for solutions, in his own particular way.

In addition to the jewelry making, he took a job as a nighttime taxi driver for a while, but this proved to be a slow and tiring way of bringing in cash. One night he said he'd finally made eight dollars and was all excited because he had used it to buy some arrows for his hunting bow. Weren't they beautiful? For days I had been worrying about how we were going to cover all the expenses related to the baby, whose arrival was fast approaching. I guess the arrows might have been my cue to become hysterical, but to my way of thinking, that would only make things worse.

I came to make peace with the knowledge that Byron was one of a kind, by turns surprisingly generous or wrenchingly disappointing, sometimes enigmatic and other times instructive and illuminating. He did have a way of expecting people to know what he had on his mind without his having to say anything, and seemed to feel insulted if you couldn't figure it out for yourself.

I was soon pretty pregnant-looking, and still stuck with the quaint old-fashioned idea that my baby should have a real family from the start—parents married with a license guaranteeing his or her place in the world. You have no idea what weight the word *bastard* still had in those days! However, there were two sizable obstacles: each of us was, inconveniently, still married to someone else. So we started making plans to go to Reno for divorces, just as soon as our Christmas business provided the wherewithal for the trip. We could drive there in a few hours, but the rules were that you had to live at least six weeks at the same Nevada address in order to obtain the divorce papers. We'd have to find temporary work to get us through that.

Byron was checking the car out to make sure we would have a safe trip. I was getting Nicky's clothes ready along with my own, not planning to take much because a lot of them didn't fit at that point anyway. Then the news came. The "Mother of All Storms" had hit, making it impossible to cross the notorious Donner Pass. Clearly, there was no way we could get through to Reno, yet we needed to get this show on the road right now. Forced to choose a different destination, we figured that Las Vegas was our best chance. We would need more cash than we had accumulated for this, and I felt uncomfortable letting my mother know, by asking her for a loan, that I had kind of painted myself into a box this time. Byron wasn't eager to ask his family either, since most of them thought he'd done the same, seduced by this unknown and headstrong young woman. In the end, it was my mom's former husband Lou Samuels, the same guy who rescued me when I was on the mat down in LA, who simply offered me a modest grubstake, probably at her suggestion. So off we rolled to Sin City with our little boy and a few belongings.

The old would-be boomtown that was Las Vegas, one long, dusty main drag with a handful of intersections nailed down with hotels sporting two or three stories of rooms, large businesslike gaming saloons, and the occasional wistfully magical showroom, had begun to blossom after 1938 when gambling was banned in California. The Last Frontier, the Golden Nugget, Bugsy Siegel's Flamingo, the El Cortez, and other unlikely excrescences disturbed the desert breezes as they rose during the war years of the 1940s, topped by the Desert Inn's opening in 1950. It wasn't until 1952, the year we arrived, that Del Webb, a well-known speculator, opened the Sahara, soon followed by the Sands, on the former Highway 91, that prime real estate now known worldwide as "the strip." And lavished over everything, in the interest of blinding visitors to all shortcomings, snares, and scams, enough neon to choke a wizard.

After a false start at some blatantly rip-off accommodations, we found a livable place a mile or so out into the desert, and began to look for night jobs, anything with staggered working hours. I was five months pregnant, which in those days would keep most women at home behind closed doors, so a sales job was out, but then I got hired as a shill, a person of any description at all who stands at the crap table playing the game, although secretly with house money. There was a well-worn superstition about playing any table alone, so every house had at least one of these shills around at all times, to keep the jinx away from the game.

The five or six blocks still dominated by the old hotels tapered quickly down to some one- or two-story dives, and the old-fashioned low-rent saloon at the end was where I worked. I have two permanently imprinted memories of the job: I was once given more than a night's pay by a lone man who happened to catch some good luck by betting on the dice I was rolling, a twenty-dollar bill and a "Thank you, ma'am." The other was of a surreal moment in the ladies' room where I saw one woman forget her wallet on the counter momentarily, and before her coattails had disappeared, saw another woman grasping it with the glee of having finally won something in the horse race of life.

Byron got a job cleaning up the local Moose Lodge, or whatever fraternal drinking dive it was, and discovered that when you moved the slot machines in order to sweep, you could also find just the right angle to make coins fall out! Eureka! So this found money and my tips were what we used for our own entertainment, once we discovered a ten-cent crap table in another low-rent joint down one of the dusty side streets.

The divorces came through in a routine way and we were outta there, making it back home early in March. I felt fine with the pregnancy, even after all the driving, but my head and heart were troubled by the sense of having been swimming in a sea of irreversible corruption and moral decay, and I was very happy to get back to my home in Berkeley, where people still seemed to view each other as brothers and sisters rather than as predators and victims. Again I ask those questions: Did I miss something? Am I wrong? Am I asking too much?

A glance at the yellow pages yielded the number of a Lutheran pastor, Reverend Estrum, who would marry us for only a couple of dollars, so I booked him for March 21—the first day of spring—and off we went with our witness, the trusty *éminence grise* Lou Samuels, who even seemed pleased to be invited and glad to be of use to someone. Well, after all, he had staked us to the divorces, so I guess he had skin in the game.

"Greetings," the pastor said, showing us into a small living room thoughtfully decked out with a number of small glass crosses filled with colored bubbling water. "Before we start, I'm going to offer you something that you can never buy anywhere, can never duplicate, that your family will cherish forever. I will make you a recording of this momentous event, and it will cost you only two dollars more. OK, here we go!"

And with that, he reared back and unleashed a stupendous stammer, which gave a colorful and distinctive quality to our nuptials, and before you know it we were "M-m-m-Mr. and M-m-Mrs. M-m-Menendez." We signed the license along with our certificate, and split, eyes scrunched with suppressed laughter, while Lou hung back to pay the piper.

A last word about Lou Samuels. He had known my mother and loved her from afar ever since her days playing bridge at the Knickerbocker in Detroit. His admiration held firm, and after she became single again he persuaded her to follow him to San Francisco, where he had just started that newfangled kind of business generically known as a "cost plus." A kind and generous man who, at the same time, could rip off hundreds of hungry slum dwellers for a few bucks without flinching. Or did he flinch? I have to admit I almost never had more than an exchange of formalities with him by way of conversation. But like my dad, he came through with help at crucial moments, and exacted no exchange in the form of affectionate gestures (I made none) or expressions of regret for being in a pickle (I offered none). My only explanation for the support he regularly extended to me, a young woman who was not blood related or even emotionally related, without looking for something in return was that he must have been making up for something he lost in his first family's life. Or maybe Mom had given him such a gentle letdown when she divorced him that he felt grateful? At any rate, I deeply appreciated his help.

My official marriage to Byron Menendez lasted from 1952 to 1964, and for me it was worth every bit of the trouble it took to make that dream boat float. Any woman would have been lucky to have had all those years with Byron. He did his best to be a stepdad to Nicky, although his own father had left his mother when he was small and so was only a part-time weekend role model. He managed his PTSD so carefully that it has taken years for me to realize what a feat this was. I wouldn't trade anything for the two children we share, and I know he feels the same way. And we did make such an interesting and beautiful couple, don't you think?

Exactly three months to the day after our wedding, around dinnertime, my water broke. We headed straight for Kaiser Hospital in Oakland, maybe fifteen minutes away, a modern secular place where we subscribed to what then was a low-cost medical plan. What a difference three years or so had made! This time I wasn't alone. I had my team, with

Barbara Dane and Byron Menendez, c. 1952

Byron and little Nicky not far away. In just a few short and relatively painless hours, another beautiful baby boy was in my arms, and in my heart. Without skipping a beat, we named him Paul for the great Paul Robeson, who in our times had set the bar as high as it can go. I wanted my little one to aim high too.

Unplanned as he was, Paul was born in 1952 exactly on the summer solstice! He was a vibrant, curious, funny, loving companion right from the start. We were too poor to afford any sort of help in those days, so I simply carried the little guy with me wherever I went, in a homemade contraption of some bright fabric that enabled me to sling him onto my shoulder. From there, he could be a part of every interaction, watching both parties in any conversation, studying their faces and catching the nuances of their moods and inflections with ease. I was in a kind of enchanted motherhood world for a while, contained within our few blocks of Berkeley and a circle of kind and interesting friends, where it seemed that everyone was creative and everyone was interested in us, in my children, and in our various survival hustles. If only the world could always be like this.

While his daddy Byron was busy at his workbench making the handsome, almost sculptural silver jewelry that brought our bread and butter, I was taking care of the rest of the little shop as best I could, talking with the potential clients who would occasionally wander in, telling them about the exquisite craftsmanship and Byron's willingness to create a memorable personal design for weddings, graduations, and other special occasions. The shop consisted of his workbench, a small second-hand display case and counter, and some wall boards Byron had contrived for displaying a few earrings. When the little bundle on my shoulder got too heavy or too active, he was deposited into a large cardboard carton in the corner of the shop, or later, into a second-hand playpen.

I found a wonderful child-care center for Nicky, situated a few blocks away from the shop in a former private home with a large, tree-filled yard. Left over from a wartime system created to make it possible for mothers to go to work, the center was run by several kind and capable women and was subsidized so that if you were eligible, the cost was thankfully within one's possibilities.

Nicky loved his days there, but he had a poetic way of telling me about how one kid felt about having to stay there. "That boy was so sad, with his little mother-wanting face," he said. Perhaps he was also thinking of himself, often the last kid to be picked up in the evening, an unfortunate result of the fact that customers seemed to pop into the jewelry shop at the last minute after what had been a painfully unprofitable day. Coloring with crayons, waiting for me to arrive, three-year-old Nicky would do his best to capture the beauty of the red and purple sunsets he could see through the western window. I probably still have them in a drawer.

11

GATEWAY SWINGS TO BERKELEY

But what about my professional musical work? The prescient producer of my *Folksville, USA* show had insisted that, once I was ready to get going again, I should form a quartet with a repertoire of folk songs like the Greenwich Village–based group called the Weavers. The group was founded in 1948 by Pete Seeger and Lee Hayes, and, with the expert management of Harold Leventhal, they had become instantly popular with their rendition of Lead Belly's "Goodnight Irene," which became a number-one hit in 1950. Shortly after, they were targeted by McCarthy's Red Scare for their ties to left and liberal causes, and were individually surveilled and collectively blacklisted from the media, forcing them to disband by 1952. But they had accomplished something that nobody could have stopped. Their mixture of vernacular music and a pop sensibility had become a part of American life on a broad canvas, and the doors were opened for much that came after—the Kingston Trio; Peter, Paul and Mary; the Brothers Four; the New Christy Minstrels, and others. One such group emerged from a Bay Area confluence of musicians, called the Gateway Singers.

Most of the principals are gone now, so it's left to me to set this group's story straight. Most versions of the origins of the Gateway Singers in circulation today are complete fiction. The truth is that it was I who recruited the group members and led it in its early days, with Lou

Gottlieb's input. Up until this point in 1952, I had always been a solo singer with a mission, not giving much thought to the idea of building a full-time career. But now I needed to figure out how to make this music thing provide my family with a living, and quickly. The fastest way, so I had been told, was to form a vocal quartet, which could accompany itself singing folk songs. I began by enlisting Lou Gottlieb, by this time a good friend from the San Francisco Labor School, partly because of his arranging abilities and partly owing to his sophisticated sense of humor. Lou really liked the idea, and in analyzing what the group would need musically, he got himself a bass and quickly learned to play it. He even got a book on the theory of humor and began to study that too.

The name was Lou's idea, meant to give us the panache of San Francisco, with its reference to our area's most recognizable geographical feature, the Golden Gate. The concept also indicated that we were opening up the musical gates, and the minds of our audiences, to new ideas. He loved to jokingly refer to us as the Re-Weavers. Like those of the Weavers, our shared goals and ideas were firmly planted in the left. We had the expectation of becoming a professional group, one that would play the top nightclubs, tour when the time came, or take a Las Vegas engagement. We would also remain available for benefits and other movement events as befitting our political origins and general agreement on the issues.

Finally, after a year of rehearsing, in mid-1953, we were ready to demonstrate what the Gateway Singers were about and what we could do. We accepted a request to sing at a rather important benefit, where a sizable left-wing audience would give us the feedback we needed. Things went very well, and the audience seemed ecstatic. But a few days later I received a call from Lou saying we had to have a meeting. Fine, but what was the big deal? Lou took the lead, giving me the goods straight and unadulterated.

"Barbara," he said, "we are really sorry to have to say this, but you can't be in the group anymore. We've only now been informed that you were expelled from the CP a couple of years ago, and it just won't work for us to be associated with you now. You will have to be replaced."

Did I scream and faint or even try to argue with them? You know me better than that by now. I simply thanked them for being honest, and headed for the door, getting ready to walk on. As I turned to leave, someone had the—shall we call it presence of mind?—to ask me, "Do you . . . do you happen to know of anyone who might make a good replacement?" And of course I did know exactly the right person, a woman for whose voice I had great admiration, who knew a lot of the repertoire (some of which I had given her), who seemed to be a very decent and intelligent person, one that I personally would gladly have had in my group . . . if I only had one.

I have to admit that as I scrounged through my purse for my address book to give them her phone number, it occurred to me that there was a sort of cosmic joke taking place, and that probably I would be the only one to ever catch it: her origins, combined with their politics, would make it impossible for them *not* to invite her into the group. Elmerlee Thomas was decidedly and indisputably Black. Well, if it wasn't going to be me singing those songs, at least it would be someone who could represent women with force and integrity in that folk scene, which was basically a white boys' club. Also, for the first time there would be an integrated group making music together on the stages of America.

Byron found a brown-shingled former farmhouse for rent only a couple of doors west of where he had his little shop on Dwight Way. He built a small display case for the jewelry, positioned near the sidewalk, that invited the curious to come inside, and we turned the living room into the new shop. The large dining room became our living room, and the large farmhouse-style kitchen had room for a big table in the middle. This was going to be a great spot for our family's musical life to flourish.

Best of all, the rent was a pittance, since it was owned by the University of California and scheduled for demolition "sometime soon," meaning that there were no plans for fixing it up. This didn't worry us, since the university was notorious for stalling on its expansion plans while snapping up titles to all the available property in sight. In fact, the house wasn't torn down until after the People's Park demonstrations in 1969.

Right around the corner, on Telegraph Avenue, the first coffeehouse in Berkeley, Il Piccolo, soon opened. It featured a huge copper espresso machine on the counter, the kind with a flying eagle on top. It hissed and roared on cue, and the adventurous townsfolk began to be drawn to it by the unfamiliar exquisite and complex redolence it released.

Nobody, except maybe those peregrinators who had "done" Europe, had tasted coffee that you couldn't see through before this, but it wasn't long before the word got out: this stuff is good! The corrupted offerings of the ubiquitous Starbucks were way off in the future, and here we were, falling in love with the dense, bitter espresso or the foamy cappuccino that could jack you up pretty good for a few hours of desk work while offering a sociable break in the day. After a year or so, the name was changed to the Mediterraneum, or "the Med" for short, and by that time it was already the hub of street politics as well as a good place to play chess in public or meet a friend for a little gossip. Legend has it that Allen Ginsberg wrote "Howl" in there, stoked by the air, so darkly fragrant, and by whatever he brought in himself.

One day while I went out to pick up Nicky from nursery school, a pair of trench-coated FBI men in the usual fedoras showed up at our house. They began asking Byron if he knew that his wife's name was not really Dane (gasp!), that this was an alias and that she was really named Cahn, Spillman, or possibly Menendez. Mostly they wanted him to know that she was a no-good communist, et cetera. Byron simply told them that if he wanted to know about any of these things, he would ask his wife, and that they should get the hell out now. Then he shut the door in their faces. These FBI visits, which were repeated every few months, were, often transparently, less in pursuit of information than meant to intimidate and terrify anyone willing to stand against an increasingly repressive system. Maybe Byron's years as a prisoner of war and the horrors of World War II had taught him that a submissive soul could not survive. Maybe that is what made him absolutely fearless in the face of these incidents. His quiet and dependable support, and his courage, meant the world to me.

I look back at the years on Dwight Way as a rich time for me and my little family. There we were in this easily accessible big house about to fall down, near Telegraph Avenue in the heart of Berkeley, at the time when Berkeley was building its legend, and we were part of it. We functioned as a sort of folk locus where we held a continuous open house, partly because of the jewelry shop now located in the former living room. We had a well-used upright piano in the former dining room where impromptu rehearsals, jams, and even the occasional lesson came and went.

Byron was almost as big a music junkie as I was, so there was hardly a quiet moment in our lives. Our mornings got off to an irresistible start with bagpipe marching music, or Kid Ory's traditional jazz band swinging hard, or the famous Bulgarian women's choir whose voices could blister the paint on the wall, or the seductive Caribbean rhythms of any number of Calypsonians—Lord Invader or Wilmoth Houdini or Mighty Sparrow—or Bahamian guitar master Joseph Spence, or the extraordinary mellow and simultaneously rough sound of the young Mavis Staples with Pops and the rest of her family singing "Uncloudy Day." The rest of our day and evening went on about like that, often interrupted by musicians dropping around to show me something new or just jawbone a while. It didn't hurt that we often had my famous minestrone or some lamb stew with lentils on the stove to share.

Right next door, a Kentucky grandmother named Bessie Mercer became a source of interesting songs new to me as well as versions of old ones from the Carter Family repertoire. Bessie's grandson Shawn and my son Nicky came from a similar culture clash: a Jewish father married to a nonreligious mother with small-town southern roots. Shawn was just the right age to become friends with Nicky, and his dad was a cantor, so I grabbed the opportunity to allow my little one at least a peek at the religious culture his father was born into. I fondly remember unzipping him from his little green leather jacket when he returned from the service, and the exact words of his five-year-old review of the proceedings: "Well, first you stand up, then you sit down, then you stand up, then you sit down. It was dog-gone disgusting!"

Around that time, two earnest young women came to Berkeley in pursuit of unusual folk-song material. They were doing the field work for their theses, with large notebooks and small tape recorders near at hand. Someone had directed them to me, so I obligingly sang them a couple of Bessie Mercer's twists on familiar tunes like "When the Cold, Cold Clay Is Laid around Me" or "Little Liza Jane" as a lead-up to having them meet the woman from Lincoln and Giles Counties, Kentucky, herself. I sent Nicky over to fetch Bessie, but instead, her daughter Marcia came, eager to record for them a song she explained was a long-lost ballad her mother had but recently remembered. The two students were thrilled; perhaps this is the way they would become famous, through their discovery of a cryptic, exciting, and well-crafted ancient murder ballad that no one had ever recorded before! Only after they had long moved on, Marcia, unable to restrain her pride any longer, confessed to me that she herself had written the song.

One day, a loose-limbed, curly-headed guy from Brooklyn wearing a cowboy hat dropped in unannounced with his girlfriend June on their way to Europe. Jack and June had devised a clever gimmick to collect money for their trip without the baskety air of the busker; June had this large spool of adhesive tape to which folks were invited to stick any loose change that might be weighing them down, and it was beginning to fill up. People seemed to like the idea of joining their spare cash with others to help sponsor somebody's dream; she had yards and yards already stuck with quarters, nickels, and dimes. A bank teller's nightmare!

Jack had a bad cough, but they insisted on sleeping on the floor of our dining room and no, wouldn't be any trouble. I was really busy, so I said it would be OK, but ignored them until late evening when I heard him begin to finger the guitar and spin out some words about Railroad Bill. Well, I had long been a pushover for collecting these verses, so I joined him in a sort of "can you top this," only to find that Jack Elliott was in possession of many more adventures of Railroad Bill than any other human, and he sang them so fast that it was impossible to write them down. I've seldom spoken personally to Jack since then, due to traveling in different directions on the same track, but recently, when we ran into each other backstage at a Dylan concert in Berkeley, he confirmed with a twinkle that although fifty or sixty years had passed, he was still singin' "Railroad Bill," only longer.

Now and then, on his way home from his shoeshine stand on College Avenue, the great one-man band from Georgia known as Jesse "Lone Cat" Fuller would drop by with his twelve-string guitar. My kids loved him because he was always just radiating music and had all these instruments that he could play all by himself. As his big old twelve-string filled the room with sound, they would fly around in that creatively silly way kids can dance, and this would make Jesse grin like a kid himself. He'd keep his "fotdella" thumping and his guitar jumping until his foot just about wore out, just to see them having so much fun. The fotdella was his own invention, a bass-like wooden body that lay on the floor horizontally in front of him, with a series of crude "keys" that his right big toe could strike to make the right notes.

I once managed to get Jesse a job playing intermission music while the traditional jazz band I was singing with took its break. The gig was down in Visalia, about 220 miles south of Oakland, below Fresno, and about a three-and-a-half-hour drive for a normal driver. But Jesse found it safer to drive on the right shoulder lane, the one put there for broken-down cars and other disasters. He had insisted on leaving a lot earlier than I thought necessary, and now I was finding out why. In Jesse's opinion, the freeway speed was way too fast in general, so we traveled in that "slow" lane, at a top speed of about forty-five miles per hour, all the way to Visalia.

Later, I had the great honor of introducing Jesse Fuller to the Ash Grove audience, bringing him down to LA as my opening act, understanding that this was an audience tailor-made for him and predicting that by his next trip south, I would be lucky to be opening for him. And that's exactly what happened.

One day, Jesse quietly told me that when he was a small boy back in Georgia, his mother, unable to provide a home or even food for him, gave him to a prosperous white farmer so that at least he wouldn't starve to death. Even though he was only eight or nine, he was expected to work as hard as anyone else, and to be satisfied with only scraps to eat. One day, when he was achingly hungry, he couldn't resist slipping his finger into a bucket of lard and swallowing what he could scoop out. Caught in the act, he was taken out to the smokehouse, his hands tied together, and hung up with the smoking meats, where he almost died. From the way he told the story, it was the absence of control over his own life that marked him almost more than the physical pain. He would spend the rest of his days developing strategies for surviving on his own, never counting on others to provide for his needs. He called himself Lone Cat Fuller to make that clear.

12

YONDER COME THE BLUES

Long before I realized it myself, people were noticing that I was adding more and more blues, gospel songs, and early jazz to my bag of tunes and soaking up all the sounds, the poetry, and the images of the blues that I could find. Sam Charters, who would one day put together some of the first serious books about country blues as well as a number of important blues recordings, took to dropping by in his tennis whites, a racket in one hand and a couple of scratchy old 78 rpm records in the other, looking for help in teasing out the meaning of some blues lyrics. I loved the challenge, and it came relatively easy for me, maybe because of growing up with southern parents.

Berkeley was also broadening its musical outlook. In 1949 the Pacifica Foundation, venerable innovator of listener-sponsored radio, launched its first station, KPFA. Almost all the music it played was classical and European, with a strong preference for what was termed "Early Music." If not that, it was experimental music, Harry Partch with his strange instruments or Conlon Nancarrow's prepared piano. I had a hard time relating to that stuff emotionally, but I liked knowing about its existence. For a short while, I had a half-hour show there called *People on the Move*, where I played lots of songs about people on boats, trains, and cars and just plain walking to get somewhere else. It was billed as a "folk music" program, one of the first in the West, and I played things from as many Folkways records as I could get my hands on—Pete Seeger of course, but also his younger sister Peggy's first recordings, Lead Belly, Sonny Terry, Woody Guthrie, and so forth. I liked to stretch the definitions, and played Sidney Bechet and George Lewis as examples of jazz still close to its folk origins, those Bulgarian women's choral groups I mentioned a while back, and certainly the Calypsonians, like Lord Invader and Mighty Sparrow, the real ones whose charm seduced the pop market and opened the road for Harry Belafonte.

I was often hired to sing at the Bear's Lair on the UC campus, sponsored by the Associated Students of the University of California. One of the first off-campus folk places to open, probably illegally, was the Blind Lemon, a hole-in-the-wall operated by my former husband, Rolf, now established in Berkeley, along with a couple who prepared and served the first piroshkies in town.

Rolf hired me as one of the early icebreakers. I was having a great time, feeling right at home, when along came that soon-to-be legendary combination postman-jazzman Dick Oxtot, then playing banjo with trombonist Bob Mielke's Bearcats at the Lark's Club a few blocks away. He chatted me up after my second set, insisting that, to his ears, the blues and gospel had been the songs I did best, and inviting me to come on over to the Lark's Club later to try them out in front of a real live traditional jazz band. He didn't know that this was something I'd been waiting all my life to do!

Once I stepped in front of the Bearcats and felt the incredible rush that comes with making music with a half dozen musicians really committed to what they were playing, there was no turning back. I remember the exact songs I sang that first night: "River of Jordan" and "Good Morning Blues." That blues is one I still do almost every time I get up to sing, especially because of its last line: "If I can't be your woman, I ain't gonna be your dog!" It kinda sets the tone, don't you think?

Taking turns with the horns felt like a cosmic conversation, and the rhythmic kick of bass, banjo, and drums filled me with confidence. Here was a safety net that made it possible to take chances with the music and just let the words fly out, carrying all my pent-up feelings with them. I started sitting in regularly with the Bearcats, loving the solid rhythm of Pete Allen's bass, Dick Oxtot's banjo, Don Marchant's drums, and Bill Erickson's piano. The quirky and evocative cornet of P. T. Stanton and Bill Napier's creative clarinet brought a constant surprise, and all of it was woven together by the spirited and skillful leader, Bob Mielke, with his trombone. So effortless, so free, and so strong, all because of the combined intentions that lifted the spirits and raised the roof!

Before these guys came into my life, I thought of the folk music world as the center of the universe and never paid much attention to the traditional jazz revival that had emerged in the Bay Area beginning back in the postwar days of the 1940s. But now it became central to my musical life. As I built up a good tune list and found the best keys to sing them in with brass instruments, I ventured down to the San Francisco Embarcadero, where I could hear the bands making history there, hoping that I might be allowed to sit in with them now and then. I was usually by myself—we couldn't afford babysitters, so Byron had to stay with the children. This wasn't always easy. People made assumptions about a young woman alone traveling in and out of bars and clubs, so I would make a beeline for any musicians I knew, just to make sure I became known as a singer who was there for musical reasons, not to pick up men or play them for a free drink.

Musically, this was a very special time in the history of traditional jazz, or what we alternatively called New Orleans jazz. Many of the last of the originators came to play right there in my home territory. One of the musicians who moved me most deeply was George Lewis, the lyrical and profound clarinetist who for years had made his daily bread as a stevedore slinging bags of coffee beans on the docks of New Orleans. He brought with him Lawrence Marrero on banjo, Alcide "Slow Drag" Pavageau on bass, trombonist Big Jim Robinson, Kid Howard on cornet, Jim Robichaux or Alton Purnell on piano, and Joe Watkins on drums. Together they embodied the bridge between jazz as the folk music of a community and jazz as a concert-style presentation.

The pieces they played had a significance beyond the music. These were the same sad songs they played to accompany a fallen neighbor to the burying ground, as well as the joyful ones to dance their community back home with spirits uplifted. Lewis's masterpiece, "Burgundy Street," was composed as he lay recovering from an accident on the docks that nearly killed him, and it would move you to tears even if you didn't know that. Kid Howard could do the same with his tender rendition of "Just a Closer Walk with Thee" just before they ramped up the tempo to play

Barbara Dane onstage with George Lewis (center) and "Big Jim" Robinson (left). San Francisco, c. 1955

"Ice Cream" and "Panama." This was the music of their lives, not just their way to make a living, and I couldn't get enough of it.

I showed up so often that George began letting me get up to sing a couple of songs with them. When the Kid Ory band would come to town I did the same thing. When no New Orleans bands were around, I'd go to hear the Turk Murphy band, which was a completely different thing, further from the folkloric roots but strengthened by the formal training many of the musicians had. Turk came out of the legendary Lu Watters band and the gang of local white guys dedicated to the survival of the music of King Oliver and Jelly Roll Morton, whose music soon swept the

Bay Area and far beyond. I loved the occasional chance to sit in with this band, but it felt much more formal, and they played a different repertoire, although to the fans it was all probably "Dixieland" as long as the format was more or less the same. I hated that term for its racist connotations and the way it seemed to trivialize the music. I always deflected it by saying that "Dixieland is a state of mind, and I don't live in it!"

Bob Scobey's band was looser, although he was the famous second trumpet in the Watters band for years before starting his own. The band was excellent, but I went to hear them mainly because Scobey had the brilliant idea of bringing Lizzie Miles to San Francisco. Lizzie was a Creole beauty in her day, and although now she was getting on, she brought a subtle exotic aura to the stage, and an incredibly powerful, energetic, and creative singing style that still reverberates in my head.

One night I went to Chinatown to hear her in person, a rare opportunity. I was walking up the Grant Avenue hill toward the club when, to my surprise, there was Lizzie herself several yards ahead, a heavy woman in her mid-sixties wearing nondescript street clothes but unmistakable all the same, struggling up the hill and then up the long flight of stairs over the restaurant to the club. I kept a discreet distance, and soon was inside and seated, listening to the great Tiny Crump play his intermission piano set. I knew that Crump had accompanied Ida Cox, one of my idols, on the Theatre Owners Booking Association circuit, and at one time he was even her husband and manager. He could still work his piano magic. Then the band opened their set with several instrumentals while I anxiously wondered how and when Lizzie would appear. Finally the band struck up "Tiger Rag" and out she strode, elegantly dressed in a custom-made chiffon gown that could have been from Paris as easily as from New Orleans, her hair piled high on her head and held there with a large tortoiseshell comb, Spanish style. "Hold that tiger, hold that tiger" she sang out, "hold that tiger, don't you let him get away!" Looking like a perfect lady but stamping her feet and punching the air with a power and energy that was unstoppable and unforgettable.

Before the night was over, I had a chance to meet her, and we exchanged addresses. I received two or three Christmas cards from Lizzie after she retired—one where she urged me to take a gig that had been offered her, touring Europe with Art Hodes—and since she passed away, I've thought about how much we've lost. Through her, I was able to witness the kind of commitment to the song, to the human history embedded in it, to the human act of singing, that we don't find very often anymore. If you ever get to see the 2013 Woody Allen film *Blue Jasmine*, toward the end you will hear Lizzie's unforgettable singing, in English and French, "A Good Man Is Hard to Find." The film sound wizards were able to bring out the brilliance and warmth of her voice, almost as if she were there.

Dick Oxtot and I apparently had the same reverence for the depth and beauty of George Lewis's clarinet playing. I was surprised and humbled by the news that Oxtot had arranged a recording date with him. Dick would be playing banjo with bassist Lee Sharpton, and wanted me to sing a couple of songs with them. It would be my first recording date, and looking back now at my work, I was embarrassingly green at it. Trying too hard to get it "right" and still suffering from what I call the "pretty lady" curse, the desire to be liked, instead of being driven by the need to communicate. Well, you have to start somewhere, and I'm grateful for what I learned from the experience. These two tunes have subsequently been included in a couple of currently available collections. If the labels had asked me for permission, I would have declined.

Two vital things were growing in me during those days: my love for this marvelous music along with my knowledge of it, and my beautiful daughter, Nina. One night I went down to the Lark's Club, only a few blocks from my home, to sit in with the Bearcats, even though I'd never seen or heard of an obviously pregnant woman getting up on the bandstand before. Most of the steady audience were friends by now, so I didn't find it odd, but apparently it did make some of the guys nervous. I was singing some spirited tune when, just as we were charging full on into an ensemble out-chorus, the neck of Pete Allen's bass sprung off, creating a loud bang. Musicians and listeners rushed over to the bandstand, somehow sure that I was about to have the baby on the spot! Well, not yet. Nina didn't make her debut until Christmas, and this night was only sometime around Halloween.

Speaking of babies and music, I am convinced that their hearing music so intimately while they were still inside the womb has contributed fundamentally to the musicality of all three of my children. Music has

Barbara Dane with husband Byron Menendez and three children, Paul (left), Nina (center), and Nicky (right)

remained a constant in our lives—when they were babes in arms, then little kids dancing around the living room banging on pots or humming into kazoos, and now as adults, each one with their own particular musical focus that has taken them in all directions. I will always be grateful to the fates for making me a singer in the first place, and for saturating my heart and soul with music. No matter what the genre, music has remained a common language through which we all manage to understand each other. Music has enriched and livened our days, has allowed us to express far more than speech about our hopes and dreams, given us the basis for working together at special moments, and provided a platform from which we could develop our common love for humanity, with all its abundance of creativity and capacity for joy. Music rules!

As the end of 1955 drew near, we were eagerly awaiting the arrival of the daughter I so dearly wished for. (Yes, I was certain this baby was a girl, even in those days before ultrasound.) I was very anxious to be with the boys on Christmas Day, the very day she was scheduled to arrive, just to make sure they didn't feel overshadowed by this new little person about to become the center of our world. I phoned the doctor and asked whether it was possible and safe to move the delivery date up a couple of days, and he said, "No problem at all. In fact I'd like to be home with my family too. Get some castor oil and take it exactly as I tell you, and you will be here delivering nice and easy on December 22." And so it was that, just as Paul had arrived on the summer solstice, my little sunshine Nina arrived on the winter solstice, bringing great joy to us all. We brought her home on Christmas Day, topping anything Santa Claus could possibly have invented.

13

SAN FRANCISCO BAY BLUES

Almost as if on cue, I was finally hired for my first professional job as a singer of the classic blues. The Tin Angel in San Francisco, right across from Pier 23 where the legendary Burt Bales held court playing his rags and blues on the piano, was where I had done a lot of my informal singing. Now Peggy Tolk-Watkins, the notoriously unpredictable owner, was gearing up for the big business she expected when the 1956 Republican Party Convention hit town. Turk Murphy's band would be the attraction, since he was the local guy with the national reputation. I would be the surprise, a woman who was singing in a style that was old and classic, almost forgotten, but suddenly emerging with a new sensibility. Not a Sophie Tucker–like "red hot mama," but singing the deep blues of Bessie Smith, Ida Cox, and Ma Rainey. Perhaps Turk or Peggy would have preferred the pseudosexy stuff, more like the vaudeville side of Bessie and Ma's work, especially for a convention crowd. But I was probably the only woman in the area singing this material in those days and had already begun to have a following for my own take on the blues.

Peggy was an artist and poet who was seldom seen without a cigarette in one hand and a martini in the other. When she decided to open a club that could ride the wave of traditional jazz that was then fascinating postwar San Francisco, she found a deserted warehouse on the Embarcadero and filled it with the odds and ends of furniture and bric-a-brac that were flooding the second-hand stores at that time due to the tearing down of many grand old mansions to make way for urban renewal. This was an unusual style of decorating a club in the mid-1950s, but it proved to be so culturally perceptive that it is still seen as hip and widely copied.

Peggy's partner in the Tin Angel venture was one of her girlfriends, and as the jazz crowds began filling up the Embarcadero location, they opened another club in the elegant, but by then defunct, Nob Hill bordello belonging to Sally Stanford, the town's most infamous former madam. Peggy came up with a cleverly apt name, the Fallen Angel, and it was there that singer Johnny Mathis got his start with his romantic jazzy pop style. From that large, cozy living room with a piano trio and soft lights, Johnny went on to become one of the biggest-selling album artists of his day. Eventually Peggy sold the Tin Angel to Kid Ory, who dumped the funky decor and pared it down to plain whitewashed walls, which pretty much destroyed the colorful atmosphere Peggy had created. Just as the trad jazz fad began to fade, the Embarcadero freeway came along, bypassing the club, and that was that.

Ah, but not for me. After being paid decently for one week at the fabled Tin Angel, I went on to work for two years straight at one of the grimy little dives along the Embarcadero, aptly called Jack's Waterfront Hangout. In 1956, the pay was twenty-five dollars a night, but I had three nights, Friday, Saturday, and Sunday, to strut and fret on that tiny stage for my couple of hours. Maybe I was hired because the owners had seen publicity about the Tin Angel gig, or perhaps some influential jazz fan who liked to drink at Jack's put in the word, or maybe they just wanted someone who could give a little more down-to-earth feeling to an evening spent among slumming socialites and dockside drunks. Whatever the reason, I could never have found a better school for my performer's life ahead. My three goals at Jack's were to build myself an audience base, keep expanding both my folk song and hot jazz chops along with those classic blues, and bring home a handful of those much-needed good-old *Yankee dollahs*.

I insisted that the owner hire my choice of piano player: Bill Erickson, who knew his way around the traditional jazz repertoire and could play the blues songs I kept digging up. My good friend and mentor Dick Oxtot played banjo or cornet as needed, and unearthed jazz tunes he thought

I might like to do. Dick made Bill wear a black-and-white-striped shirt just like his, and called their duo the Polecats. I continued to play rhythm guitar with the occasional finger picking on the folk songs, although I knew I was not a real guitar player and probably never would be.

As was common in this type of establishment, the customers took pleasure in setting up drinks for the entertainers, and expected you to drink them. I was not well acquainted with the hard stuff, had never owned a bottle of whiskey or gin, and yet there it was, and the club owners of course encouraged these poor guys to spend like their money meant nothing to them. Wine was not popular in those days even in fine restaurants, and was rarely seen in clubs like this. And beer was out of the question if I was going to sing anytime soon. Miss Jeanne de Leuze, who'd work at Jack's for years, explained that I could have a little talk with the bartender, who would make sure I didn't get

Barbara Dane with Dick Oxtot (center) and Bill Erickson (right)

overloaded. I took to ordering Scotch and milk, partly because it tasted nice, also because it soothed my throat, and mainly because it disguised the scarcity of booze in the glass. Thank you, Jeanne. Now if you only could have taught me how to banish the thick fog of cigarette smoke that clung to my clothing and hair, wreaking havoc with my vocal cords and nearly driving my husband out of the bedroom when I'd undress at home after work.

Meanwhile, I was learning the craft of holding a disparate audience together, carrying on with the show even if a drunk staggered through the door and fell just in front of the stage. And I was learning to make eye contact with the drinkers all down the long bar, one end of which was across from me on the right, while doing my best to focus mainly on the room full of actual music fans who sat at the six or eight tables to my left.

At first I felt alien and strange, struggling to keep some semblance of authenticity and balance in this new atmosphere, but it wasn't long before I found my feet and even began to broaden my understanding of human nature. My initial disdain was for what seemed a continual hustle being laid on the customers, something I guess I should have expected. But the hustle seemed to be spilling over onto my coworkers and the friends who came around, and like a bad wind, it was almost overwhelming. It seemed to be the modus operandi though, here in this world of night people. To the relatively guileless girl that I was, it felt as though just about everyone around me was trying to figure out ways to "get over."

With time, things somehow softened into rituals as natural as watching the cops slip weekly into the dusty, unused kitchen where they picked up their envelope from the refrigerator otherwise containing a few wilted celery sticks and an aging jar of olives. Even the pathetic guys continually hitting on me and blowing their salaries buying me drinks became fraternally familiar after the tenth time I heard their interchangeable stories of pain and disappointment. It turned out that their wives still didn't understand them even after all those years. Not trying to get over, just trying to stay standing.

I knew that I was unbelievably lucky to be able to go home each night to three beautiful, interesting, and healthy children and a wonderful man who loved them as much as I did. Byron was certainly moody and often hard to read, but I completely trusted him, and it was this trust that made it possible for me to move ahead with my own work. There must have been many nights when he felt lonely or confused by my lifestyle, but I felt sure he trusted me too, even when I would show up as the sky was already beginning to lighten, with my clothes stinking of cigarette smoke and my breath probably reeking of scotch. In one way, I was enduring this lifestyle; in another, I was enjoying it. Either way, I was bringing in some steady money.

In my determination never to drink too much and never to get involved in any sexual monkey business, I would sometimes deflect the enthusiasm of an insistent fellow by agreeing to have "breakfast" after work. I was usually famished by then, having rushed off from home after feeding the kids but leaving myself no time for dinner. I also thought of it as rewarding a lonely heart with a brief bit of innocent companionship, someone willing to listen to his stories and let him feel like a man about town for an hour or so. I don't remember the name or face of a single one of them, except that they were more than happy to buy me a steak or a lobster, indulgences I certainly couldn't dream of on my pay. More to the point, they allowed me to feel like a woman who moved in this storied San Francisco nightlife with ease and sophistication, always in control and always a sort of spy, a secret student of modern human behavior.

I do remember a conversation with one of the nameless men who escorted me to Vanessi's on Broadway one night, my favorite all-night restaurant. It was one of the earliest places in town to feature an open kitchen where you could watch the food being cooked, and the only place I knew that served osso buco, spaghetti carbonara, chicken cacciatore, and even Tuscan-style rabbit. But again, I digress. Someone mentioned food?

Anyhow, this guy claimed that he was one of the writers on the Bob Hope show and had even helped create the always-topical lyrics to Hope's signature opening song, "Thanks for the Memories." Over the shrimp cocktails, while waiting for my Tuscan rabbit, he began to weave a picture of how he would make a guaranteed star out of me overnight.

"First, maybe we should change your name to Barbara Allen, you know, like the folk song. So where are you from? Detroit? Nah, then where are your folks from? Arkansas? Fine . . . You'll be the little girl from Little Rock! They'll eat it up! Say, here's a tip for milking that applause when you finish. It never fails. Just bow deeply to the audience and hold it there, count to five, look up and smile at them and then put your head down again and just stay there ... stay there ... hold it ... As long as you do, they'll keep that applause going!"

The abject cynicism of this way of looking at it made me think about some of the deeper implications of this "show business" life. It always really made my heart ache to see the surrender that the mediocre performers at Jack's seemed to have accommodated, drowning their aspirations of doing anything meaningful with small talk, cigarettes, and booze. What dreams had been left behind? How did they find their footing when the inadequacy of their talents hit them in the face? And how did they find the courage to go on at all? How did they construct their defenses against frustration, disappointment, or grief over lost opportunities?

At first I didn't really want to know any of these people personally. But if things went badly, any of this could be my own lot someday, or that of my lover, or any one of my children. I had better learn ways to open my heart, as well as my eyes and my mind. As time went on, I would have to learn to let more of these wounded travelers in.

What I did in my own shows was haphazard. I didn't like making a set list, preferring to take my cue from the loyal folks who sat in that room on my left. Sometimes Oxtot or Ericson made a request, so of course we'd play that. But my little handful of regulars seemed to like most anything I chose to sing, with a growing emphasis on those classic blues that had grabbed my gizzard and begun to make me understand how cathartic it could be to sing those words, strung together by some long-gone women with the same damn heartaches that I was feeling.

My man had not left me, but the frozen part of Byron's emotional state was starving me for the kind of intimacy I craved and often left me feeling lonely in a crowd of two. On top of that, he seemed incapable of putting any kind of stable economic floor under our lives together. My kids were my greatest joy, but also my biggest worry. Would I be able to keep everything together and give them a sense of security with so much tension in the house? Would I be able to "bring home the bacon" without giving up too much mothering time? As my own mother wisely summed things up so many times: "Don't worry, *something* will happen."

Well, as they say, the beat goes on. I was getting deeper and deeper into the blues, and looking for contact with any of the creators of this music that moved me so. My connection with Brownie McGhee and Sonny Terry, the amazing duo that became such an important part of the folk music world, began when they came to San Francisco in 1957 as part of the cast of *Cat on a Hot Tin Roof*, directed by Elia Kazan and starring Barbara Bel Geddes, Ben Gazzara, and Burl Ives.

Brownie and Sonny were called "Brightie" and "Small" in the playbill, and were assigned to create a plantation-like ambience for the production by passing back and forth occasionally at the back of the set while playing or singing softly, with no spoken lines and no spotlights either. I had known they were coming to town, and thought I'd try to give them some sort of friendly welcome, although we hadn't yet met. When I saw how sketchily they were used on the set, I knew my instincts were right: they would be happy to know that at least some people in this town appreciated them for the amazing musicians they were, so I contrived to get myself backstage. I seized the time and asked whether they would like to play a little house party on their night off if I could arrange it.

They were quick to agree, and I managed to borrow a house with plenty of floor space in the hills above the campus and spread the news to local folk fans and UC students that a great blues duo called Brownie McGhee and Sonny Terry would be playing for several hours there. The house was soon packed with grateful listeners who kept dropping dollars and coins into a cigar box long into the evening. The musicians were clearly grateful for this concrete appreciation they were receiving, as well as for the spellbound young faces sitting in the circle at their feet. Personally, I was just about floored with the endless supply of great lyrics and faultless guitar improvisations Brownie produced that night. Of course Sonny had been haunting my head with his "Fox Chase" for years, and he blew us all away with his blues harp and singing too, so masterful and personal. In short, this impromptu house concert was a huge success, and since we had no overhead, all the proceeds went to the musicians. On the strength of their triumph, I got up the courage to ask Brownie whether he would give me a guitar lesson. He said sure, gladly, for only five dollars.

Next day I met up with him at his hotel in San Francisco, where I was thrilled to receive one of the only guitar lessons I would ever have, providing me with a lasting touch of variety for my simplistic playing. But hanging out with the two of them that day, it dawned on me that although there were a few 78s to be found featuring each man separately, there were practically no recordings of the two of them together, unadorned and well recorded. On an impulse, I picked up the phone and called Max Weiss, partner in what was then a little local label called Fantasy, starting to make waves with their red-and-yellow vinyl LPs starring Dave Brubeck and Cal Tjader, two relatively new artists.

I knew Max from the jazz scene and got right to the point: "So how would you like to record the greatest duo in blues history, Max?" And thus it was that we gathered in Oakland at Jenny Lind Hall, today a Buddhist temple but then a place prized by sound engineers for its perfect acoustics and cherished by musicians lucky enough to play there. Welcoming us was Stan Page, a man deeply appreciated by local jazz musicians, who was to be our engineer. He began methodically setting up his mics and connecting them to his big old rolling Ampex console recorder.

Once the team started, there was no stopping them, not even to eat. I don't recall anything, alcoholic or otherwise, to drink. Maybe some water. In about a day and a half, they had ripped through enough great material for three sparkling albums. No second takes, and no mistakes. Max Weiss and Brownie made a quick deal about publishing rights and such, and Brownie walked off with a big smile and a pretty nice pocketful of cash, which I presume he split with Sonny. He didn't ask whether I needed any. Neither did Weiss, who also neglected to credit my role as producer of the project. As for me, I felt richly rewarded by having been part of such a valuable musical experience, and too naïve to realize that the record business was strictly male turf, with any females on the scene being counted as bystanders at best. Anyhow, those Fantasy recordings still stand as testimony to the spontaneous musicality and creativity, joy and determination of these two musical giants.

As the years rolled by and I got better at my craft, I wound up sharing the stage with Brownie and Sonny on dozens of occasions after that, and got to know each of them a little better each time. I thought they had come to know me better too. Near the end of his life, when I stopped by Brownie's home in Oakland, we finally had a chance to reminisce about old times. In recent months, I had brought several people to his house who wanted to interview Brownie. Some of them even paid him what he asked for the privilege. But this was different, just a relaxed digging up of old memories between two old friends. He talked about how now and then the FBI would come around to question him about why he performed for these "red" events all the time. His answer, he said, was simply, "Because I needed the money." Maybe he was just telling me how he had deflected those questions, not giving me his own feelings. No more political discussion, though.

I wondered whether Brownie remembered the time I was invited to go with the blues duo on their State Department–sponsored tour of India. Did he have any idea why I didn't end up included on the junket? State had been using the promises of racial harmony implied by the unharnessed and free-flowing sound of American jazz in a cynical effort to counter the increasing awareness of US institutionalized racism abroad. When word got to the suits that I was to be the white half of this bill, they must have figured that this big-mouthed commie girl would blow their pretty picture in every interview. The booker soon let me know that I would have to stay home.

The National Council of Arts, Sciences and Professions (NCASP or ASP) arose in the early part of the decade, with the encouragement and participation of W. E. B. Du Bois and others, to gather intellectual, antiracist, and peace activists in an organization with a socialist orientation. I joined, although the others were professors, writers, classical musicians, and artists and mostly older by a decade or two. I wanted to do whatever I could to help maintain a progressive current in those precarious mid-fifties times. After I hosted a party at my house to raise funds for the defense of Julius and Ethel Rosenberg, the FBI came sniffing around again, but when they attempted to interview me, I invited them to kiss my backside once more. Don't you think they would get tired of trying? But yeah, it's their gig.

The so-called McCarthy period was slowly winding down by the mid-fifties, but its bitter dregs still discolor and distort American life today. It had destroyed many lives through blacklisting and accomplished the destruction of most of the Communist Party's influence and leadership in the various social movements of the time, turning the words *socialist* and *communist* into buzzwords filled with fear. Khrushchev's famous "Secret Speech" delivered to the 20th Party Congress in February 1956 made a searing critique of Stalin, revealing decades of repressive policies. This dealt a body blow to Communists throughout the world, while the bloody suppression of Hungary's popular uprising in the fall of 1956, ordered by Khrushchev, was the knockout punch for thousands of Communists worldwide. The great disillusionment that followed was deeply demoralizing, and many old-timers are still inconsolable in their grief. CPUSA membership dropped from its pre–World War II heyday in 1942, when it counted a full 85,000 nationally, down to about 10,000 in 1957, of which at least 1,500 were known to be FBI infiltrators.

The events of 1956 had sucked away all sense of a solid global movement that was united in its dedication to the pursuit of peace and justice. It was on this unity that we hung our hopes for a future where there would be no economic inequality, along with our dreams for the human kindness and decency this would bring. These were the hopes and dreams, this was the commitment, that was so centrally located in the mentality of rank-and-file communists everywhere, and in my own heart. And in my heart they remain.

That first noble experiment called the Union of Soviet Socialist Republics (USSR), built by millions of mostly illiterate former serfs on the ashes of the corrupt and seemingly indestructible Tsarist regime, was dedicated to building a society based on the needs of the people rather than the demands of capital. And against all odds, it was sustained for an incredible sixty years, despite suffering over twenty million casualties, mostly civilian, in World War II. In the end, that first experiment may have collapsed in the face of insurmountable challenges both from within and without, but the goal of someday achieving a world built on genuine socialism is still alive. This vision has never been abandoned. Not by me, and not by millions of others. Call me crazy, but that's the fountain where I still drink from the waters of hope.

B.B. King sings it with all his heart and soul, in the words of that great Doc Pomus blues that cries out,

> Sometimes I wonder just what am I fighting for?
> I may win some battles, but I always lose the war
> I keep right on stumblin' in this no-man's land out here

But I know, mmmmmm, yes, I know
There must be a better world somewhere.

The CPUSA may have been on the wane, but movements for racial justice, and opposition to weapons testing and all things nuclear were springing up all over the country. Many of the old party comrades were pretty much baffled and left behind, but individually they were there, ranks and ranks of them, their familiar faces bringing a strength and validation of their own to every manifestation. One had to love them in their very dedication and consistency, regardless of disconnects in style. The substance was right and true, and they were there. They were there, they were there.

My children were always game to go along with me to movement events. They liked helping paint signs for any picket line about to take place, this time in solidarity with nine Black students being "buked and scorned" as they tried to integrate Central High School in Little Rock. The infamous governor, Orval Faubus, had tried to stop them by calling out the Arkansas National Guard, thinking of it as his private army

Paul and Nina Menendez, antiwar demonstration. San Francisco, 1964

for defending what the good-old boys called "pure-dee" whiteness at a school that he also thought of as belonging only to him and his own kind. Kids usually know what *fair* means, and was it fair to stop someone from going to school? Was it fair for truckloads of uniformed and armed men to stand between these students and their classrooms and teachers? And for that matter, what could be fair about trying to stop the students from coming into school just because their skin color didn't match his? After having helped make the signs, of course my little ones wanted to march with us in the picket line and carry them too.

The people who organize and pull off these demos are the best, and it is always a joy to be among souls who have the will and the guts to walk their talk. We sang, we chanted, we hugged each other in mutual thanks for showing up, we acknowledged one another's solidarity and commitment with our smiles. In the end, because of public pressure like this all over the country, President Eisenhower was forced to send in the 101st Airborne to make sure the students were safe, and the case of the Little Rock Nine was victorious. My own children may have only dimly understood all this at the time, but they had the chance to taste these victories in their own way, as part of their own experience. They got to see how simple citizen actions could actually change things. And even if a particular campaign had ended on a sad note, the experience was always worth it.

Here are some respectful words of advice to young parents: please don't cheat your children out of seeing real life firsthand by shutting them up at home with babysitters. Save that for New Year's Eve or second honeymoons, don't you think?

14

TROUBLE IN MIND

One night in 1957, a fan showed up at Jack's Waterfront Hangout with a man named Al Leavitt, introducing him to me as the owner of San Francisco Records, a new label dedicated to the hi-fi concept to which those voguish creatures known as "audiophiles" subscribed. Al began by saying that he was interested in documenting traditional jazz in the area, starting with me! This was all a complete surprise, but I tried to hide it. Who is this guy, and is he crazy or what? Is this just another hustle? But soon we had signed a contract, fixed a date, and with some brief discussion had settled on the number of backup musicians. To my mind, all that those great singers whose songs I was learning had seemed to need was a piano, one or two horns, and a great bass player, and that would be enough for me.

In those early days of recording they used tubas, because they could be heard on the primitive recording equipment through the hisses and pops. But I wanted a "real" bass, and a real bass man to play it. I knew the name "Pops" Foster from several of the records he had made, and I knew he'd played with Kid Ory, Louis Armstrong, Sidney Bechet, Art Hodes, Jelly Roll Morton, Fats Waller, and many other musicians I admired. I had also heard that he was currently playing with Earl Hines at Doc Dougherty's Club Hangover right here in San Francisco. Foster was considered the number-one traditional jazz bass man in the world, and I never would have presumed that he would play on the first album of an unknown white girl just learning to sing the blues. But Al Leavitt had no such reservations. He simply called him and booked him for the date.

I finally met Pops, but not until the recording date itself, and apart from his great playing, he contributed another unexpected, indispensable, and irreplaceable element to that session, and to my blues work over the rest of my life. That day at the studio during a break, Pops pulled me aside and said, in his candid way of speaking, that I should never doubt what I was doing. He said he could see that I was respectful of my sources, and it made him happy to see that a blue-eyed blonde like me could care enough to be making the blues a part of my own life too. He ended by saying that in his estimation, I was singing those classic blues as well as anyone around at the time, and that if anybody objected or tried to discourage me from getting deep into it, I should simply pay them no mind. It was these words, coming from a musician as respected as George "Pops" Foster, that gave me a license to go on with this work. Any reservations I might have hidden in my heart about whether my identification with the blues would be scorned or welcomed were washed away by his generous words. Maybe that's one of the reasons everyone called him Pops. He knew, without asking, how important it would be for a young girl like me to feel welcomed and respected by the people whose culture I was doing my best to honor, and by virtue of his own life he knew a lot about the endless twists and turns of mind that go with relations between the races in America. He was offering me understanding, the way a good father would.

The piano chair on the date would be filled by Don Ewell, a brilliant choice, because he knew how to play subtly as well as how to provide plenty of meat, with an exquisite sense of dynamics and great taste in his chord choices. All this was crucial, because I was too green to know how to give any guidance to what were basically head arrangements. Don, in partnership with Pops, gave us the perfect foundation.

P. T. Stanton, the cornet man, was a local legend with a sound you would recognize anywhere. He was known as the "least commercial and most original" horn player on the scene. This was one of the few recordings he ever made, along with the George Lewis date we had recently done with Oxtot.

The reed man on the recording was Darnell Howard, and his fat, liquid tones on the clarinet were the perfect foil for brass instruments. At the age of twenty-three he had recorded in New York with W. C. Handy, playing the violin, and that was only 1917. Throughout the 1920s he played with the likes of King Oliver and James P. Johnson, touring in Europe and the Far East. In the 1930s, he held down a long tenure with the Earl Hines band in his Chicago hometown and, lucky for me, had joined Hines again in the 1950s during the band's long run right here in San Francisco at Club Hangover, where Pops was also playing.

My musical brother, Bob Mielke of the Bearcats, was the only logical choice for the trombone chair. His skill and imagination were well respected, and his approach to the genre left an indelible signature on the West Coast jazz revival.

LP cover, *Trouble in Mind*, San Francisco Records, 1957

The LP was titled *Trouble in Mind*, and blazoned across the front cover was the exclamation "A voice like this hasn't been recorded in 30 years!" Jazz journalist Leonard Feather dubbed it "Bessie Smith in stereo." And C. H. Garrigues, jazz columnist for the *San Francisco Examiner*, dug it too, calling it "one of the great blues albums of the era" and declaring that the discovery of "a great new blues voice" was "an occasion for dancing in the streets." He even claimed that if you "play it against any set of Columbia's great 'Bessie Smith Story' I think you will agree that the Dane performances compare favorably with the best that Bessie did." Well, I don't know about the hyperbole of that last part. I nearly fainted when I read it. But of course it felt like a strong welcome and a validation from an important critical voice, even if he had a tendency to get carried away like a schoolboy with his first crush.

With all the media attention, I started to get calls for bookings, mostly at colleges and coffeehouses, which were now ubiquitous in San Francisco. The audiences were actually listening, the lyrics mattered to them, and the social commentary with which I framed each song seemed to be welcome.

One day toward the end of 1957, a small "delegation" from the alternative underside of life in Hollywood showed up in Berkeley. Herbie Cohen (behind his back called "Poison") and a couple of sidekicks were scouting around for pieces of Bay Area hipness they could import for their new venture. They were going to bring the first real "Beat" coffeehouse to Hollywood, and someone had steered them to me, the "Beat" blues and folk singer currently masquerading as a Berkeley housewife. Herbie offered me a long-term gig, four nights a week for at least a year, with whatever accompaniment I chose, if I would move down south and accept their modest but regular wages. How could I resist?

Sometime before this seductive offer came along, I had a kind of crisis with Byron about our day-to-day arrangements. I don't recall just what set it off, but I do remember that I had built up a good deal of frustration because of the load I was carrying as I struggled to (1) be a conscientious wife and mom, (2) help stabilize his jewelry business, and (3) continue growing in my musical work and build some kind of career that could help support our family. The music was both my joy and at the core of my identity, often enabling me to follow my activist heart, but also the most efficient way I could visualize to create an income stream that would allow me to continue doing the first two things as well as possible.

My attempt to hold a serious discussion about all these things seemed to be falling on deaf ears. I was desperate to grasp what was left of me before it vanished in the crush of daily demands. Suddenly something snapped inside. I must have been holding the small metal file box containing the mailing list of potential jewelry customers that I had been painfully assembling over the past few months, together with any accounts receivable information. I ran out of the house, down the steps, and out into the middle of Dwight Way, where I flung the box into the wind and watched the contents blow away under the wheels of the oncoming cars.

PART TWO

ON MY WAY

15

FROM THE ALLEY TO THE GROVE

It was time for me to refocus my life by moving the music to a position of greater importance. I accepted Herbie Cohen's offer and announced that we were moving to LA.

It should be noted here, for those who weren't alive then, that it was not common in those days for a family to follow the mother's work needs. In fact, just about any economic activity on her part would have to be fitted in and around the father's role as "breadwinner." Byron was taking a huge leap into a future with no guarantees, and this required drawing on his great hidden reserves of courage. He was being pulled into a world that would center on the needs of my so-called career from that point forward. Just as so much of our Berkeley life had been focused on his needs, now it was my needs that required both of us to head on down to La La Land and make it work.

We located a nondescript three-bedroom flat that we could barely afford in a low-rent neighborhood where the cultures of larger LA and Hollywood overlapped. I had to plunge right into the Cosmo Alley scene. The owners, Ben Shapiro and Herbie Cohen, wanted those Bessie Smith and Ma Rainey classic blues they had heard on my recording. I needed a piano player who knew the trad jazz repertoire and could play the classic blues with authority. By now I had worked with Don Ewell, one of the best, and that made me pretty hard to satisfy. I tried several players, but there wasn't really anyone I knew in LA who could do what I needed. I would have to count on the fact that this was not really a crowd that dug this particular music very deeply anyway. Mostly, the house was full of people from the movie industry, from the lowliest grips to the biggest stars, looking for some late-night relaxation and a dip into this new-style bohemian, or Beat, life. This we could give them.

To my astonishment, one night Langston Hughes stopped in at Cosmo Alley, and in spite of my near-reverence for his work, it wasn't hard at all to meet and talk with him. Easygoing and sociable, he went right to the subject of my revival of these old Bessie Smith and Ma Rainey songs that he had feared were in danger of being forgotten. He deeply loved that whole genre we now call the "classic blues" and was quite familiar with it. He wanted me to know that he loved my record *Trouble in Mind* and could see that my heart was in the right place in relation to the tradition. In the years to come, he would make many kind gestures to demonstrate his words. He sent postcards frequently, and now and then I would receive a dedicated copy of his latest book in the mail. Once he even sent me a telegram on an opening night, wishing me good luck!

Other musicians and artists would fall by Cosmo Alley just to dig the scene, and in case you notice my current choice of vocabulary, you are now stepping into Barbara's working world of the Hollywood night crawlers. In fact, for years I was addicted to the words *hip* and *cool* and *dig* to the exclusion of everyday English. To get you started, I'll translate a bit. Don't worry, it won't last forever. Anyway, we would see great jazz musicians dropping in just to get up there and *lay down* (play) whatever they wanted after their earlier paid *gigs* (jobs). Folks like Buddy Collette, Chico Hamilton, Don Cherry, Ornette Coleman, Billy Higgins, a whole stream of the *hippest* (most knowledgeable) West Coast jazz players rolled out their creativity at Cosmo Alley *on their own dime* (unpaid) after hours, having a very *cool* (wonderful) time while they *dug* (explored) new ways of bringing their various influences together. Hmmm, now I think I've given the impression that I think you are *square* (uninformed). *On the emes* (truly), I don't.

After all the actors and musicians and listeners faded and went home from their late-night Cosmo Alley ramble, Ben and his wife, Mickey Shapiro, would often sit down for a glass of wine and, in their case, a little weed as dawn was approaching. I was always conscious of the fact that once I got home, my other life as a mother would begin, and that made me wary of the weed, so I only tried a hit or two. Besides, I had usually just experienced that extraordinary high, that exhilarating feeling of release that singing always gave me. Who needed more?

At these times, we would each be quietly hoping that one of the hippest, funniest, and most interesting cats we knew would show up, a young comedian named Lenny Bruce, then doing bits in small San Fernando Valley dives where his wife, Honey Harlow, was stripping, or on the burlesque house stages where his mother, Sally Marr, was likely to be doing her own comedy thing.

Lenny needed a place to jam just like the musicians did, trying out some of his ideas for a new kind of comedy on this safe little audience of three as he slashed away at the social strictures this uptight society has always used to mask its extraordinarily kinky mind-set. More than dancing on the surface, he was showing us how to scrutinize our fellow humans stripped of their conventional costumes, and it was for a serious reason. If you really listened, you could dig that it was Lenny's way of bringing himself, along with the rest of us, closer to our authentic selves. After the shock of his assault on all those foolish pretensions, you couldn't help but feel his tender appreciation of the all-too-human fragility that lay underneath. He was preparing himself for the dangerous job of exposing the weirdness of a world where even life itself has been reduced to a commodity, some kind of object for sale. No, he wasn't foolin' around. He was conjuring up a way to rise above the garbage of modern life by wading right through it to higher ground. And he was funny as hell.

Lenny was always hungry at that late hour, so we would make our way through the alley (yes, Cosmo Alley had one right out back) and into the back door of an all-night Hollywood diner where the burgers were actually pretty tasty and not too expensive. The management owned a large mynah bird, which was kept in a cage adjacent to the cashier's post, and whenever Lenny passed this bird he'd whisper one persistent phrase, "The Pope sucks!" These birds are famous for their ability to copy human speech, so it wasn't long before it was repeating this provocative statement for the benefit of the 4:00 a.m. patrons of this place. The phrase, and the practice it describes, was not in the common vernacular as it is today, as in "my job sucks."

Cosmo Alley was a kind of school for me, at the same time that it was providing me a way of bringing home the ineluctable bacon. The situation wasn't so great for Byron, however, since he was having to take some major responsibility for the children on a daily basis and hadn't yet been able to figure out how to make a few dollars to add to the pot. But things were going along at home reasonably well, until one day I got the word from Herbie that I was being terminated overnight because the main money backer of the place, New York–based actor and singer Theodore Bikel, was coming west for a role in the film *The Defiant Ones* with Tony Curtis and Sidney Poitier and wanted Anita Sheer, his flamenco guitarist girlfriend, to have the feature spot at Cosmo Alley. I'm sure it hadn't occurred to Theo that this would put anyone else out of work; just as sure as I am that Herbie wouldn't have bothered to remind him of that. So here we are, fait accompli. And the house rent meter was ticking fast.

Byron managed to work out an arrangement with Cohen to sell paperback books in a vacant storefront opposite the alley. The new phenomenon of publishing an inexpensive volume—small enough to fit in a pocket and fitted out with innovative new cover designs for the hip new literature as well as some cult classics and other favorites—was exciting the interest of the public and encouraging the publishing world. The press was writing about it, but the books were not yet widely distributed, giving them a slightly underground air. Stocking them across the street from Cosmo Alley was brilliant, adding to the trendy coolness of the area, except that now it fell to Byron to take care of the acquisition and transportation of many heavy boxes of books, as well as organizing and selling them while also keeping track of it all. This soon turned into a daily drag for Byron, but in the end, the place became Herbie's bookstore, because our future was about to connect with a healthier culture in the Hollywood heartland.

Just in time, a man walked into our lives who grew to be one of this country's most dedicated producers in the world of folk and vernacular music. Ed Pearl was about to launch a venue that would present the kind of music for which a whole generation was hungering, music with authenticity in a world overfed on artifice. Ed had bravely leased a former furniture factory in Hollywood, on Melrose Avenue near Fairfax, and named it the Ash Grove after an old English folk song. He was very young, and to say "inexperienced" would be an understatement. But he had the right idea, the financial backing of his wife, dancer Kate Hoyt-Hughes, and the support as well as hands-on volunteer help of a number of friends who shared his vision. Before long, Ed was discovered by an enthusiastic press, which meant that the Ash Grove was soon discovered by a rapidly growing following. In a few short months, the Ash Grove became the place to go for a cultural experience deeper and more meaningful than the celluloid and glitter of mainstream Hollywood. It seemed that in 1958, even in Beverly Hills and Los Angeles, there were audiences who craved the touch of authenticity provided by the kind of artists Ed was bringing to his stage on Melrose Avenue.

Ed was putting together his first few shows and wanted to know whether I would like to take part. I felt honored by his interest, and of course I said yes. I was scheduled for the opening event, a three-day folk festival to take place on July 25, 26, and 27. Ed's first leaflets were posted in Byron's temporary shop window and were passed out to the people who walked through the alley. Next day, Byron arrived to find the shop window had been covered with black paint. Herbie didn't like anything not under his control.

For me, the best way to deal with people like Herbie Cohen and the chaos they like to create has always been to walk on, simply pass them by, and try to do my own thing bigger and better down the road. Any thoughts of revenge are usually too costly in the gut as well as in the pocketbook, so I gave those nasty incidents no room to grow, even though at the time they meant the difference between a certain shaky financial security and whether we would have gas money or food for the kids.

Ed then booked me for every weekend in August, along with Brownie McGhee and Stan Wilson, and there would be more to come, so I was able to stave off panic and begin to see new possibilities.

Herbie wound up sticking around the music's industrial side of Hollywood for most of his life, managing Frank Zappa and even Linda Ronstadt, among others, but I never personally ran into any more mischief from him. At least, none of which I was aware. One day I ran into Herbie's sidekick Vic Maymudes, who later became Bob Dylan's dogsbody, and asked him how he could stand working for a guy like Cohen. His reply was telling: "Oh, I only have to eat a little shit." It sounded as though he'd decided to eat his ethics too, a long time ago.

If Cosmo Alley was a school for me, the Ash Grove was where I got my doctorate. From 1958 to 1974, I was privileged to sing on that stage with some of the greatest living figures of the blues revival. The list included the incomparable musical genius and street preacher Reverend Gary Davis; the amazing duo of songwriter–super-guitarist–singer Brownie McGhee partnered with the soul-wrenching blues harp of Sonny Terry; the Texas sharecropper turned deep professional songster Mance Lipscomb; Big Joe Williams, who roamed from town to town with his nine-string guitar ripping our hearts out; Little Brother Montgomery bringing his indelible touch to the blues piano; and Lightnin' Hopkins creating his own special aura with his unmistakable single-string licks.

For his part, Ed Pearl seemed to trust the artists to bring the best parts of themselves to the platform, and never, to my knowledge, tried to force or censor anything. In fact, his mission seemed to be to make a safe place for open dialog between performer and audience, designing the shows through his choice of artists who could be combined in a way that enabled one act to reveal something about the other. Because he always kept his ears and heart open to new sounds and new ideas, because he was able to draw people from every walk of life into his circle, and because he actually listened to them and considered their insights, Ed's ability to find the right combinations of artists to present became legendary.

Wonderful people came to listen, too. I began to feel that I could say or sing almost anything that came into my story, regardless of style or rhythm, and that none of it would faze this knowing crowd. Now and then I did wonder whether my audiences shared my conviction that the blues fit under the folk music roof and made up a vital part of it. At first I thought I should make the emphasis on blues one night and folk songs the next, but you could never tell what the audiences' expectations were in the abstract. All those definitions meant little in the end. I began to answer, when asked what style was mine, by saying, "Whatever it takes to get the message across!" And right there, my "purist" hang-ups died, quietly and unnoticed. I would come onstage without a set list, leaving myself open to the vibe and learning to go with the proverbial flow. After a while it had become second nature to trust the audience by saying, or singing, anything that was in my heart. In this place, and with these open-minded, open-hearted listeners, I felt as free as I had ever been. They never let me down.

Free as a bird! But some other eyes were on this sparrow, unlike those of the song. My FBI files from this period inexplicably describe me in some detail, all wrong:

> Sex: F; Race W; Age: B. Detroit, Mich, 5-12-27; Residence: 5628 Mirada Ave, LA; Height: 5′2″; Weight: 110; Build: small; Hair: blond; Eyes: blue; Complexion: fair; Occupation: Freelance Entertainer; Marital Status: Married

Well hey, take a look at any photo from those days, and it's plain to see that I have anything but a small build. My sturdy milkmaid bones haven't weighed 110 lbs. since I was about twelve years old, and my medical records show that in my thirties I was then about five feet seven. Eyes look blue or green, depending on what I'm wearing, complexion would probably be fair if I took better care of it, and my hair, well, what day is it? Oh, come on boys, you can do better than that!

I don't know where the money came from, but Kate Hoyt-Hughes's underwriting for the Ash Grove had given Ed Pearl the freedom to follow his vision. On rare occasions, she offered the gift of her own dancing too, beautiful and tender movement descended from an Isadora Duncan–like vision of freedom. She seemed completely clear about the Ash Grove mission. Since we arrived in LA, Byron and I had been having a hellish time trying to rent a decent place to live that we could afford. One day, Ed brought us the unexpected suggestion that, with the aid of a down payment from Kate, we buy a house instead. In a flash, we embarked on a search for something that would accommodate our three children as they grew, easy to reach from the Ash Grove, easy to pay for on our budget, and as interesting as possible, given our taste for the original, if not the exotic. This was our big chance!

Little preschooler Nina went with us as we dashed around Hollywood looking at houses with the real estate lady, and of course we consulted her opinion after each trip. One day, after an ascent from Highland Avenue up Camrose to Rockledge Road, we visited a place that charmed us all, with Nina insisting that this was the house she wanted more than any. You entered by way of a very large reception space, with a stained-glass ceiling, a koi pond in one corner, a red concrete open staircase leading to enough bedrooms at the top, a round Rapunzel-type tower of a dining room with many windows off to the other side, and oddly, a small rudimentary kitchen in which the rough undersides of cupboards and the insides of drawers had never been painted. This led us to speculate that it had been built for a Hollywood starlet who needed a spectacular entry but could not afford that and a fancy kitchen too. The location was perfect, the space was sufficient, and the price was breathtakingly low, so we quickly made the deal.

I began to get occasional bookings out of town. Since it was clear that I would be traveling more, and Byron was now involved with several projects at the Ash Grove, we decided to hire a live-in nanny. We lucked onto a lively young girl from Rochdale, England, by the name of Pearl Kelly, who proved to be reliable, honest, creative, and affectionate.

On one of my first working trips to Chicago, as I was facing new professional challenges, unfamiliar and uncomfortable weather, and almost inconsolable loneliness for my children, I received a poignant letter from my oldest boy. Nicky had often overheard Byron and me discussing our financial difficulties, and on his own, at age twelve, had taken on two paper routes in a manly effort to help out. This would have been a daunting task for anyone and, as it turned out, not a very safe one for a little boy. First, there was the treacherous traffic down Highland Avenue that one small boy on a bike would have had to navigate, in an era long before bikes were often seen on main avenues. The seedy Hollywood Boulevard residential area was, not surprisingly, full of deadbeats who were perfectly capable of simply stiffing the paperboy, leaving him holding the bag for the money owed the distributor. Even worse, a few resident pedophiles had already tried to lure the boy inside their rooms.

Byron took to driving Nicky around, at least on collection days, rather than leaving him to his bicycle and whatever problems he might encounter alone, but this could not have been pleasant for either of them. A letter Nicky later carefully penciled to me in Chicago read, "I have been thinking that two paper routes is too much responsibility for a boy my age, so I decided to quit them." I was pierced to the heart and thought of catching the next plane home. Unfortunately, I had to fulfill my various professional obligations, in part to keep from being branded as unreliable—in the music world a sure way to lose a lot of future work. But I left for Hollywood as quickly as I could.

Byron picked me up at the airport, and as soon as we reached home a serious discussion broke out as I tried to begin a description of my experiences, with the music and the other musicians, with the unfamiliar press attention, with my sadness at having missed so much at home. I needed badly to unpack all this emotion with my partner, longed for understanding and appreciation, longed for a familiar and dear embrace. Byron, for his part, had apparently been holding a load of frustration too, and needed to speak his own piece. But he never was able to elaborate on things like that. He seemed to have the idea that if I really understood him I would already know what he was feeling, that spelling it out would be redundant. What I remember most was his attitude. I had caught glimpses of it building along the way as my career became more demanding, but this night he expressed it pretty clearly: "All you care about is your career. You're never around when we need you." And its opposite: "You can make more money in a shorter while than I can, so why don't you dig up some more jobs?" A classic case of being damned if you do and damned if you don't.

It was around that time that he took to sharing himself with other women, and who could blame him? Again classic behavior, something many men, and most likely some women too, turn to when their ego is at stake. I would have preferred for him to have pursued these activities discreetly, somewhere outside our mutual circles, not simply sleeping with one or another waitress from the same scene where his wife was a leading performer. I decided that the best way to hang on to my dignity was to stay out of it, stay blind to it.

Meanwhile, I was still searching for the piano player who could bring what I longed for, a like-minded thinker with a solid blues beat and the ability to take chances. I needed someone whose musical instincts would be like the other half of a trapeze act, catching me as I leaped from one genre to another, pulling songs out of my memory bank that, quite possibly, the other musicians had never heard before, daring enough to have a go at inventing on the spot. Was I asking for too much? Probably, but one night the exact right person showed up, bringing all those skills and some I had never dreamed of.

I was in the dressing room preparing to make a hasty exit after a late-evening set when one of the regulars stuck his head in the door and said, "I've got your piano player outside." I heard the syncopation in the beat, heard the artfully rambling phrases being improvised, and like the needle in a compass, I was irresistibly pulled back toward the stage area, and there in the darkened showroom we slid into an easy exchange of blues verses, each feeling the other out.

I could barely contain myself. Joy and a sweet relief welled up in me, and I wanted to jump and shout! But it was too dark and too quiet except for his relaxed, direct, and expressive playing. To tell the truth, it was clear from those first few bars that Kenny Whitson's musical motors ran in sync with mine, and right there he became my blues brother and my friend forever. It was a totally unexpected bonus that he also played one of the most tasteful and hot cornets I had ever heard, and did it while maintaining that impeccable beat with his left hand!

My Ash Grove bookings provided a sense of being at the center of an important scene developing in the small town of Hollywood, a place where one could get the feeling that everyone was, in one way or another, all part of a huge creative community. So many of my professional opportunities over the next few years flowed from casual encounters with people who sat in my audiences, people I might not meet personally for weeks or months, people who often knew more about me than I could have imagined.

I was being called by other clubs too, and sang at places around town that featured a variety of styles. One memorable week, I sang trad jazz for two nights, mainstream jazz for two nights, and folk songs for another two nights. Only problem is, this display of versatility is not the way hotcakes are sold. The public wants to know exactly what it is buying, and the merchants want a clear, consistent image that they can easily market. At least that's the way it is in the mainstream auction house.

At the Ash Grove, I was still playing my utilitarian guitar, pulling things out of the folk bag in my head at random. Kenny could keep up with anything I did, and the audience would have no way of knowing we hadn't rehearsed and discussed it for hours beforehand. This is how things stayed fresh, and we could maintain the direct communication we had with the listeners. For me, a performance was always a two-way street, an unspoken dialogue in which I strove to catch the nuances coming from the other side of the lights so that I could speak to the human heart out there striving to catch mine. Someone once said after a show, "I loved your act!" and without missing a beat I replied, "It's not an act—it's real!" And I meant it.

It was during the first days of the Ash Grove in Hollywood that I met Carroll Peery, whose paid work there, I believe, was managing the kitchen. But his most valuable work was managing the cultural misunderstandings and confusions that might arise. Often the white country performers had little experience with things like, for example, sharing a dressing room with a Black person. Some of the southern Black folk needed advice about where to get a haircut or which restaurants were welcoming enough or economical enough to patronize. His sensitivity to all these issues had been developed growing up in rural Minnesota, in the town's only Black family, as the son of a postal worker.

Often, when my night of singing was done, Carroll would offer to join me when I went to Canter's Delicatessen, nearby on Fairfax, and over a corned beef sandwich or maybe a bowl of matzo ball soup he would share his insights while the work was still fresh in my mind. With a few gentle pokes, he helped steer me away from any insecurities or pretensions I might have acquired in my work, heading me toward a deeper acceptance of the value of what I was doing. On a political level too, we understood each other.

One night after a show, a tall, slender woman approached me in the dressing room, telling me how much she loved what I had done and, in all innocence, saying that to her I was "like a white Odetta." It would be a while before I could point out the *gaucherie* of this remark to her, but I recognized that she was searching for a way to give me what she considered a great compliment. Before I knew it, I had invited Noël to our house for a drink. She showed up with a set of six of the thinnest, most elegant wine glasses I had ever seen, half a pound of pâté de foie gras, and a bottle of Pouilly Fuissé, not realizing that the "star" from the Ash Grove bought her wine in generic gallon jugs and drank it out of Welch's Grape Jelly jars. Well, I may have only had a beer purse, but I sure did appreciate the switch to fine wines.

Elegant treats aside, some kind of chemistry soon emerged between us, and even Byron seemed to enjoy the company of this effervescent and lovely woman who became bent on hanging around whenever possible, helping with the kids' bedtime or offering to stay with the children so that we could go to a movie, or maybe even cooking our dinner. She adored thinking of useful small gifts, books, records, trinkets for the kids, and more of those welcome edible extravagances like fancy pâté or some good steaks, and always something choice to drink with them. As time went on, she became like an auntie for the children and a third member of our adult family. We often agreed, with much laughter, that Noël was our fairy godmother.

Noël began acting as my de facto manager. It pained her at first that I was not interested in turning myself out in a more "professional" look, but eventually she saw the value in going my own way, sticking with my own instincts instead of trying to follow the mob. We both realized that I needed a national audience if I was to pursue a meaningful professional career. I was doing the occasional national TV turn, such as Bobby Troup's *Stars of Jazz* (ABC), but at the time, it was the press that created the bridge from local to national, and although I had accumulated a lot of wonderful press in the cities where I had performed most, I didn't have access to that elusive hook on which the national press thrives.

I did start working more in jazz venues out of town, and the first "big-time" place was the Cloister Inn in Chicago. It was considered one of the swankiest joints in town, and even Duke Ellington, Lenny Bruce, and Bill Cosby had performed there. "The World's Greatest Authority," aka Professor Irwin Corey, one of the funniest men alive and one of the kindest, convinced the Cloister booker that I was a rising jazz star and that the owner would be able to claim that he had discovered me if he acted quickly.

It turned out to be one of the coldest weeks in Chicago history, with temperatures ranging well below zero and howling winds ceaselessly blowing from the lake at near-hurricane speed. I attempted to walk the block or so from my hotel to the club without being blown down on the slick sidewalks of the Windy City, literally crawling part of the way, all dressed for work too. The even swankier Black Orchid nearby was featuring no less than Ella Fitzgerald. I don't think either club could have made the nut in that week of arctic weather, but if any jazz vocalist fans ventured out at all, it was certainly for Ella. And that included me. On my night off, I made a point to head over to the club where she was appearing; and after the show I went backstage, introduced myself, and gave her a copy of my LP, *Trouble in Mind*. Astonishingly, a few days after I got back to LA, I received a personal handwritten letter from Ella, with these words: "Thank you for sharing the spirit of the 'old blues' with Chicago. Your style of singing is refreshingly different and I'm confident that you'll reach the zenith of success within a very short time." Ella had been a major part of the soundtrack of my teenage years, with the creativity, ease, and swing she brought to even the tritest lyrics, making them come alive with meaning. This generous and unexpected gesture of encouragement from her was deeply meaningful for me.

Noël would focus on my professional career, but, as a friend, she also tried to keep an eye on my personal life. She insisted I take on a "financial manager" who would receive all my income and dole it out according to a budget, but she never planned into my budget any money for herself. She actually earned a decent living with relatively little time commitment, working as private secretary for a producer who had other staff handling his professional life, leaving Noël with a fairly flexible schedule.

Generously, she often spent afternoons or evenings taking dictation from me and turning out my varied correspondence in great style as well. On top of that, she would watch the children if needed or cook something simple for a family dinner or pick somebody up at school or at the airport—any way she could make herself useful. Everybody needs a friend like Noël, and in many ways it came down to that: we each had found a best girlfriend to share our stories, hear our troubles, and have a lot of just plain fun together. Byron appeared to approve, and in some ways it took a load off of him too. He came to assume that she was part of our team.

Various people suggested that if I slicked up my act a bit, I could be making x amount of big bucks singing in the more upscale hotel venues and concerts, and Noël was quietly frustrated at my seeming indifference to that life. Yes, Miss So-and-So was making quite a lot of money doing that, but then she had to keep her musicians on salary all year round; spend money for arrangements, management, booking agents, publicity, hotel rooms, and transportation for the whole group; hairdressers and makeup people; and a custom-made wardrobe from some name-brand couturier. Then to keep it all rolling, she had to work all year round, traveling most of the time, just to keep her band together. I figured that

Backstage at the Ash Grove. Los Angeles, 1958

I probably took home more in the end, without having to spend such a large part of my life away from my precious children and husband. Guess they'll just have to take me as I am.

In those years, I was always broke, so I made most of the dresses I wore onstage myself, using a simple strategy that didn't require much fitting, and fabrics that could be found on the remnants table for half price. I didn't have money for the usual showbiz glitzy stuff, and anyway, I preferred wearing things that were not in the stores. With these eccentric dresses, Byron's original jewelry, and the interesting but inexpensive shoes Noël helped me choose, I had developed my own "look" to go with the uncurled, uncoiffed short bobbed hair that seemed to me the best way to avoid beauty salons with their expensive and time-consuming appointments. To get by with that, I bleached my ash-blonde hair myself to a pretty horrid yellowish platinum with a paste made of Lux flakes and a bottle of peroxide from the drugstore. That seemed to satisfy the people who wanted me to look like "showbiz."

In its early years, the Ash Grove was going through some difficult growing pains. But there were some helpful things that happened as well. The *Los Angeles Times* published an extensive write-up about the emerging coffeehouse scene, which featured the Ash Grove, with a large and excellent photo of me and my guitar, along with some listeners and a large painting on the wall, a photo that managed to present the place in a very welcoming way. Then there was the arrival of an LP produced by Ed Michel, later a highly regarded jazz recording producer, but in those days my occasional bass player and a huge fan of the whole Ash Grove venture. *A Night at the Ash Grove* was one of the earliest recorded collections of West Coast coffeehouse folksingers (including me), and it made quite a splash in our little puddle.

That LP was a delightful breakthrough, but Ed Pearl's golden dream was soon threatened by a shutdown order by the Los Angeles Police Department. "No permit!" said they. "I didn't know I needed such a thing," said Ed. The fact is they probably invented the whole permit idea in order to shut down the place. Too much interracial activity there, too many peace demonstrations being planned there. Too much glorious genuine people's culture for some Tinseltown bigot or other. Luckily, my friend Noël had recently introduced a newly minted lawyer named Stephen Reinhardt to the place, and he fell in love with it. He took on the Ash Grove license case as his very first, and he won it! Reinhardt, who died in 2018, went on to be one of the most respected federal judges in California, on the 9th Circuit US Court of Appeals. Meanwhile, Noël undertook to open some of the show business doors I didn't even know were available to me.

16

FROM BREAKOUT TO BLACKLIST

Cut to a scene in a chic little dimly lit New York club called the Den in the Duane. I loved the intimate size of the place, located in the area now known as Tribeca, and it seemed that a pretty hip crowd made a point of checking out the new arrivals on its tiny stage. This was currently one of those New York hot spots for launching new talent, and the main show business periodicals of the time covered the action. I was no exception: "Den in the Duane has a winner in singer Barbara Dane . . . a savvy performer . . . she belts out a flock of numbers in a husky, expressive voice that's perfect for the selections offered" (*Variety*). And "Miss Dane's forte is the blues. She has a genuine feeling for this type of song. . . . Her phrasing is excellent, and her sultry alto is effectively used. . . . [This] versatile thrush also does folk numbers and pop tunes . . . her first New York stint, and she's certain to gain a following" (*Billboard*).

One night in the middle of a song, I peered through the darkness to see the sweetly beaming face of William James "Count" Basie in the shadows of the back row. I was deeply touched, and of course very excited that he had taken the trouble to look me up. We had developed a quiet friendship over the previous couple of years. We first met in person when I had the privilege of visiting a band rehearsal in the ballroom of a large hotel in LA where they would be performing later. When they finished, Bill—having noticed my overflowing enthusiasm—invited me to his room for a drink, where we passed a couple of hours in deep conversation.

I opened by telling him how much I respected him as a bandleader. I'm sure he knew it, but I had to say how much it showed that all his musicians respected and loved him, and what a master of diplomacy he must have been to keep the band personnel consistent for so many years. I wanted to say how much he has always inspired people with his ability to steer a path through the treacherous waters of show business with all its ups and downs, especially with the intensified racism that continued to grip the country in these postwar years. I also wanted to ask how he personally was dealing with the quiet daily drumbeat of indignities and slights, but this might not have been the right time.

Bill sat across from me in a big chair, sipping something over rocks, and inspected my face through the half-closed lids of his soft eyes as I spoke. Then he asked me about my life, my career, and my plans for the future. He was notoriously a man of few words and seemed to prefer listening rather than speaking, or maybe that was just his way with women. I've always been one who spilled out whatever I needed most to say, without much prudence or caution, and it had been a long time since a wise and sympathetic man had indicated a willingness to listen. I talked about my uneasy marriage, my love for my kids, my own problems with confronting a world that seemed to see female singers as glorified groupies at best and as party girls at worst. I talked about important things I was learning about survival from listening carefully to what the Black women of the blues had to say in these songs I was singing, and how sometimes I wondered whether it was right for me, a white woman, to use these songs they had created out of their particular pain and joy to express my own feelings.

It was a great gift to have someone like Bill actually listen to my stories and hear my questions, and his gentle touch as we momentarily embraced, his soft, kind voice, and the subtle but spicy fragrance that clung about him will stay with me forever. We managed a couple of other brief talks in other meetings, in other towns, but never again with the time and space for a conversation like that one. Those things only happen when the stars are right.

They must have lined up right again for me just before Basie showed up at the Den in New York. That very night I had unexpectedly received a telegram from the promoters of a jazz festival to take place right away in the Pasadena Civic Auditorium, asking if I would open the show singing with the Firehouse Five, opposite Louis Armstrong and His All-Stars. But this would mean flying to California and then flying right back to fulfill my dates at the Den in the Duane. No way I could afford that, since neither job was paying more than beginner's money. And although I could save on lodging in New York by staying at my mother's place, the bills back home were mounting fast. I mentioned my good luck and my excitement, along with my dilemma, to Bill and asked for his advice. The way he spoke was, like his unmistakable piano style, minimal in the extreme, but with each note carrying its load of meaning: "You have to do this. I got you covered."

Next day, I swung by the Basie office in the Brill Building as he had instructed, where a secretary handed me an envelope containing a plane ticket and a few dollars for cab money. I arrived in LA in top form, full of confidence and energy for the occasion. My performance went very well, and Louis was more than kind in his appreciation. In fact, the November 24 issue of *Time* magazine ran a little review and a picture of me with this quote: "After Barbara appeared with Louis Armstrong at the Pasadena Jazz Festival last month, the master called an agent cross continent and gave his own estimate: 'Did you get that chick? She's a gasser!'"

Back in New York to finish my run at the Den, I was astonished to receive a call from Joe Glaser, Louis's manager, saying that Louis was going on a State Department–sponsored tour to Europe in the spring of 1959 and wanted me to appear with his band as his new singer!

This would mark the pinnacle of her career for any singer of traditional blues. For me it was the beginning of a whole new life as a woman in the music business with enough of a reputation for the quality of her work to move beyond the "band chick" assumptions and all the other traditional tawdry images and low estimations. With Louis in charge of the music, I could free my mind to think more like a musician, part of that marvelous collective spirit that always lifted me up, liberated me, and made me want to fly! When the Den gig ended, I arrived back in California with only a brief few weeks to prepare my home and family for an absence that could run into months.

Louis's manager, Joe Glaser, sent me a contract, and for a variety of reasons I was nervous about signing it. So many musicians had passed around horror stories about this guy. The main speculation was that all of Louis's income was sent straight to Glaser, who had him on a stipend providing enough to live well but far from grandly, even in the days when the Armstrong name on anything meant huge sales. A musician I knew who was an old New Orleans friend of Louis's said Glaser had been a stolen car fence in Mexico in his younger days. It has been well documented that Glaser was on Al Capone's payroll because he ran the Sunset Cafe, where Louis had been the most famous headliner. I was definitely going to sit on that written contract Glaser sent me until I could get some legal advice. But we did start off with a verbal contract, witnessed by others, for a three-year "exclusive agent" relationship.

His first strategic idea for showcasing me was to have me appear on a national TV show with Louis, scheduled for the cold January 7, 1959, in New York City. This was to be one of four specials sponsored by Timex, makers of inexpensive but fairly reliable watches.

The host for this particular show was Jackie Gleason, then at the peak of his popularity, and the show I was booked for had a lineup that was no less than encyclopedic: Duke Ellington and his Orchestra; the George Shearing Quintet; the Dizzy Gillespie Quintet; the Dukes of Dixieland; Louis Armstrong and His All-Stars . . . Then there were special guests Gene Krupa, Bobby Hackett, Roy Eldridge, and my other sax god, Coleman Hawkins, among others.

All this was to take place within one single hour of airtime. Videotape was not yet in general use, meaning that the show would go out over the airwaves in real time, just as we performed it. This type of production required a full week of rehearsal, with the first day dedicated to, for example, determining the marks (positioning) for the artists. Then there was a day for the lighting, another day for the sound, and so on.

I wanted to fly to New York on the weekend to be rested and ready and on time for the big week of rehearsal, but it turned out that it was also the weekend when the Rose Bowl in Pasadena was ending. Not for love, bribery, or trickery was a seat available on any planes heading east to New York during those particular days. Glaser's office had managed to book me on that impossibly crowded show, but had not counted on this logistical nightmare. At the very last moment, one of his minions decided to spring for a first-class ticket.

Cross-country jet flights didn't even exist until later that year, and as I recall, the propeller planes took more than eight hours. I did my best to sleep on the plane, and took a taxi straight to the TV studio, arriving just in time to watch Louis's band packing up their instruments to leave after their final rehearsal. George Simon, the writer and producer of the show, literally blanched when he saw me hurrying in, and made clear that it would be impossible at this late date for me to be included in the show.

All I could do was stand my ground, explain to him why it was impossible for me *not* to be on the show at this point, while trying my best to make eye contact with Louis, who was sitting at the edge of the stage with his shoes off and rubbing his feet. Simon withdrew his gaze from me for a moment, glanced at the stage, started shuffling his papers, and motioned the band to hang on, and when he raised his head, he asked whether I had a song I could do in sixty seconds. First I sputtered, "Hey, I'm a blues singer, and it takes a little longer to develop a theme in the blues . . ." Then better judgment overtook me and I quickly added, "but I could sing 'Old Fashioned Love' in that much time." I knew the exact time of one chorus of that song because I had just done it a few weeks prior on the Bobby Troup show with the Firehouse Five.

Meanwhile, Louis stood up and beckoned me to come to the bandstand. The band unpacked again, ran once through a very snappy chorus with me, quickly packed up again, and split without looking back. Louis put away his horn and sat down on the edge of the stage once more, resumed rubbing his feet in their white athletic socks, and looked up at me. "It was too fast, right?" he half whispered in that unforgettable rasp. "We'll have Gene switch up the tempo after his solo . . . Don't worry." All praises to the music muses for creating a man like Louis, with a heart as big as his talent. Relieved, I headed off to my mom's apartment for a good night's sleep.

The next day in the studio, the stage was a dazzling sight, with so many musical giants it was head-spinning. My sixty seconds with Louis's band was like a rocket to moon and back, leaving me feeling completely validated and full of joy. I had to laugh when I was told that I had made a certain kind of impression on the host, Jackie Gleason, who was overheard inquiring of an acolyte, "Who was that broad with the fabulous ass?"

Coming off the set, I found my mom waiting for me in my dressing room, which happened to be right next to Duke Ellington's. I knew how excited she would be to meet him, so when I saw him standing in the hall,

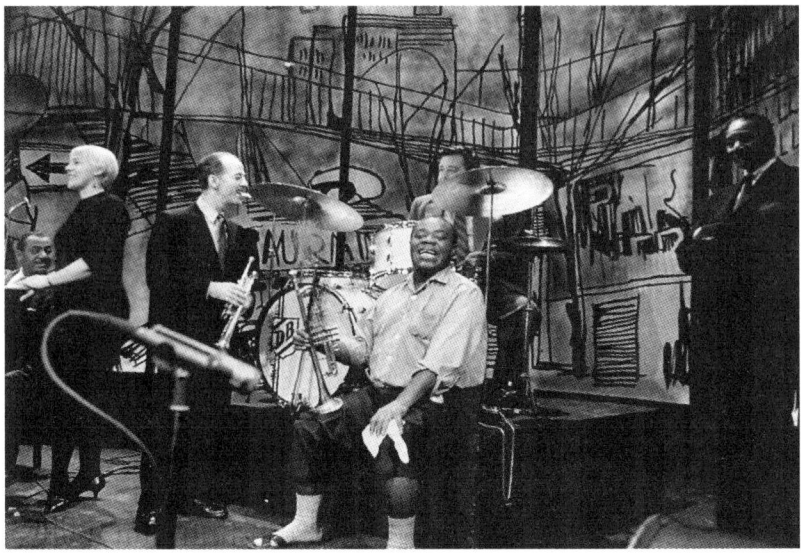

At rehearsal for the *Timex All-Star Jazz Show* with Louis Armstrong, Jackie Gleason, and others. New York City, 1959. © The Milton J. Hinton Photographic Collection

I beckoned to him. "I'd like you to meet my mother, Dorothy Casner." I was thirty-two, but I said it with girlish politeness. Edward Kennedy Ellington gently took her hand and held it between his as he looked long and deeply into her eyes, taking in her middle-aged loveliness as she stood there in her cherished long gray mink coat and her most flattering hairdo. Then he turned to me and said, "See how beautiful you will be when you grow up?" This was a man who understood women.

After the show was over and the musicians began to file out the stage door, a sizeable crowd stood waiting, bearing little notebooks or small scraps of paper and pens, eagerly searching each face as it appeared. I happened to be right behind Louis as we left the building. I watched a man smoothly slip a joint into his palm as he warmly wished him well, and saw Louis slap him on the shoulder in a brotherly gesture, just before a dozen other people pounced at him begging for his autograph. Louis generously began to oblige the crowd. Then, scanning my face, someone on the side hesitantly held up his little book toward me and said, "Are you anybody?" I shook my head and walked on.

Well, maybe I was nobody in New York City, but back in San Francisco, music critic Hal Schaefer's column in the *Chronicle* exclaimed,

"The whole town is Dane Conscious!" I was booked for a two-week engagement with Wally Rose, leading his own band at a new club opened by Turk Murphy called Easy Street, which was a precursor of his later joint, Earthquake McGoon's. No matter how hard I tried, I could not make that band swing. Sometimes you can feel like a mule hitched to a wagon that just won't roll, and this was one of those times. Maybe singing one song with Louis spoils a singer for any other band, but despite the high marks these guys deserved as individual musicians, as a collective things just didn't work out. And as the song says, "It don't mean a thing if it ain't got that swing!"

I guess Glaser wanted to make sure that I was "somebody" for the coming European tour, because his office had started booking some dates for me. I was first sent off to Dallas to sing at the pseudo-swanky but definitely shady 3525 Club, a haven for the overly famous and a showcase for the overly rich. Whatever else was going on there, I didn't want to know.

That March when I opened there, it was strictly business with the club manager, who had all the charm and grace of a B-movie gangster front man. After my opening-night performance, he stomped into my dressing room and growled, "Get yourself some low-cut outfits and sing something happy—you know, more upbeat. People come here for a good time, and they don't want to hear all them gloomy old blues."

Regardless of my discomfort and unsuitability at the 3525 Club, the Dallas press did have interesting things to say. The coolly discerning writer Tony Zoppi said in the *Morning News* that I "seemed a bit out of place" and that, while his comment was no criticism of my interpretative abilities, he wanted folks to know that I was "just crying in the wrong pew." The *Dallas Times Herald* writer Don Safran said I had "a disarming throw-away style in this era of intense girl singers. She doesn't coo, gush or prattle. Her job is singing, and she does it!" And he didn't even comment on how I was dressed or my décolletage. How refreshing!

I finished my gig in Dallas to find that Glaser had suddenly gone silent about the European tour with Louis. Finally, he wrote claiming that he had not been able to convince the bookers to hire a singer about whom they knew nothing, which meant that my participation in the tour was now officially off. He even began to demand the return of a five-hundred-dollar advance he had given me to prepare for the tour.

But his excuse was clearly disingenuous. It's an exceedingly common practice to place a new artist in a package with already well-established ones, and since I was to be presented as Louis's latest discovery, this would have become a huge selling point. If Glaser had followed through with what he started, he would probably have created in me another easily saleable item for his roster once I had made the tour. Clearly, he had commitments he would now have to cancel, so he also loses there. And for hard cash evidence, no agent in the volatile world of show business puts out an advance unless the artist's performance is guaranteed. So this story he concocted made no sense, and one would have to take a good look behind the curtain to find out why I was removed from the tour.

Having an extended time to work with and learn from the man who virtually invented jazz, to be surrounded with the life-giving creative power of his collective of superb musicians, would have made for one of the greatest experiences of my lifetime. But there was even more to it. I'm guessing that from Louis's standpoint, having a white woman up there onstage with him whose singing projected so much respect for his people's music was a statement he wanted to make.

It wasn't until early 2003, watching a great TV documentary about Louis's life for the *American Masters* series on PBS, when something finally pierced the veil I had drawn in my mind across the whole sorry situation. Almost fifty years after the fact, it finally occurred to me that the State Department had probably determined that it would never do to have a loudmouth blonde girl doing interviews all across Europe with Ambassador Satch on the subject of race in America, especially in 1959 when our country's racial strife was inflaming TV screens all over the world, with pictures of lynchings on front pages everywhere. After all, these tours were designed to give a rosy view of race relations in the US. So some shrewd functionary hoping to save his own ass must have passed a memo down the line to dump me off the tour. But how could I know for sure? I discovered that it was the jazz writer Gary Giddins who was responsible for the unusually thorough research on Louis that formed the basis for the PBS documentary, and I was determined to have a conversation with him about my suspicions.

Not long after, on a trip to New York, I contacted Giddins and asked to make a lunch date with him. To my relief, it turned out that this guy, correctly described by *Esquire* as "the best jazz writer in the country," was a straightforward person, unpretentious and easy to talk with. So I cut to the chase, and asked what he thought of my conjecture that the icy hand of the US State Department had pulled the rug from under my tour with Louis.

Giddins acknowledged that Louis was having a lot of trouble with his own urgent desire to throw the weight of his celebrity into the civil rights movement then convulsing the nation. Louis's relations with Joe Glaser were notoriously complicated, and the way he had positioned himself meant that Glaser had little to do with his musical or personal life, but the business side of his career was entirely in Glaser's hands. Any kind of public controversy would be seen, in the mind of a hardcore hustler like Glaser, as a serious threat to his business, a muddying of the carefully cultivated image of his most valuable property. In September 1957, when Louis finally blew his cool and threw his opinions in the face of no less than President Dwight D. Eisenhower, Glaser laid down the law to his main moneymaker in no uncertain terms: no more of that, or else. "Do you dig me when I say, 'I have a right to blow my top over injustice?'" was Louis's question to the press. For Glaser, the answer was simply no.

After talking with Giddins, I remembered another situation that had come about the year before the Glaser episode. Would-be folk czar Albert Grossman had approached me with a proposal for touring India with Brownie McGee and Sonny Terry as part of one of those US State Department junkets. I was flattered to be asked and readily agreed to go, but at the last minute I was pulled off that tour, replaced by another white female singer whose name was unknown then and remains unknown now. Albert was good enough to tell me what had happened, but he offered no clarification as to why the State Department had decided to change horses. At the time, I was too busy running with my work commitments, my family, and the fast-moving events of the times to connect the dots. Now it began to show up as a pattern.

The United States Information Agency Jazz Ambassador program sent many artists abroad during this time, and Dizzy Gillespie and Dave Brubeck led the way. Certain ironies implicit in this work led to the creation in 1961 of a brilliant piece of musical theater by Dave and his wife, Iola, called *The Real Ambassadors*, enlisting Louis Armstrong and Trummy Young, Carmen McRae, and Lambert, Hendricks, and Ross, along with all their side musicians, to tell the tale. Here is a sample of the lyrics from this fascinating piece, inspired by a pep talk routinely delivered to the musicians by the State Department handlers before they set off on the tours:

> Remember who you are, and what you represent.
> Always be a credit to your government!
> No matter what you say, or what you do
> The eyes of the world are watching you
> Remember who you are, and what you represent
> Represent, represent . . .

Apart from my personal disappointment, the collapse of my projected tour with Louis did not create any negative impact on my career. In fact, 1959 shaped up to be one of my most intense traveling years so far. One of the first dates was a return to Chicago's Cloister Inn, when Tony Weitzel of the *Daily News* said they were "standing three feet deep" to get into my show, while Will Leonard at the *Tribune* gushed, "When Barbara sings, Bessie lives!" His column was jammed with quotable lines:

> She looks like Carol Channing, sounds like Bessie Smith, comes across with the impact of the two combined. A lot of feminine power to get in one package . . . an old-time shouter attuned to today's microphones, a primitive with just enough sophistication for Rush Street, a hipster who knows the clientele of the Cloister. . . . She sounds like old times, she sounds like tonight, she sounds like good times coming.

No, I didn't have him on my payroll. I didn't even have a payroll.

17

LIVIN' WITH THE BLUES

This next development might have sprung from a suggestion from Armstrong himself, to soften the blow of the canceled tour. One day, soon after it had become clear that I wouldn't be going to Europe with Louis, I got a call that seemed to come from out of nowhere. Addie Teagarden, wife and manager of one of the jazz musicians I most admired, was offering me a tour with Jack's band that would include several dates on the Eastern Seaboard. Jack Teagarden had been one of Louis's closest friends and associates since the early days. One of the first white musicians to tour with a Black band, "Big T," as he was often called, was considered the father of the jazz trombone, as well as one of the most inventive pre-bop players on the instrument. And I had always loved his singing, which was easily as great as his playing.

    I'd never met Jack, but he lived in Hollywood not far from me, so when Addie invited me over to get acquainted, I was out the door and on my way. I was welcomed into their home warmly and without ceremony, just the way Jack's music seemed to promise, and I couldn't have been more thrilled just to meet this easygoing sweetheart of a man.

    Earlier in the year, Teagarden had returned from an exhausting tour in the Far East, where he had caught the attention of the press when he jammed with the King of Siam, a genuine old-style monarch who played saxophone and fancied himself a jazz musician. For Jack's Eastern

Seaboard tour this June, we would be sharing the bill with Red Nichols and his Five Pennies. A popular film based loosely on Red's life had just come out, starring Danny Kaye, and the publicity surrounding it would help guarantee some big audiences wanting to see the band live. Jack's band would include Don Ewell, who had recorded with me in 1957 on the *Trouble in Mind* album, which gave me a sense of musical security. We traveled all the way down the East Coast, the two bands in one bus, presenting concerts in every major theater along the way and playing for a crowd of over ten thousand people at a jazz festival in Detroit. It was midsummer, and the weather was perfect. I was the only female in the entourage, and it felt as though I was living in a movie from the 1940s. The reviews were great, and I was often singled out for special kudos. Hey, this is the life!!

The only downside was how much I was missing my kids. I called home to wish my little son Paul a happy seventh birthday, and asked him what he would like me to bring for a present. "My trombone!" was his gleeful and spontaneous response. Ever since he was a tiny boy he

Barbara Dane with Jack Teagarden, 1959

had been sitting on the floor looking up at Bob Mielke's golden horn as we rehearsed, and had often talked of wanting to play one himself, but I had always cautioned him that it wouldn't be practical until he had his grown-up front teeth. Now he reminded me that seven is when you get them and that his were all ready to go. I asked Jack if he could help me pick out a horn for my son, and the next day he said that he had decided to give himself a new horn and wanted to pass on the one he was playing now to little Paul. Yes, the same horn he had played on with the King of Siam, and he wouldn't let me pay him anything for it.

If those elusive angels of musical serendipity had come around one day to offer me the customary three wishes, I would have used them to call up the greatest musicians in the history of early jazz. Louis Armstrong would have, quite naturally, been the first; then Jack Teagarden, king of the slide trombone; and third, without the slightest hesitation, the father of hot jazz piano, Earl Hines. Even today I can hardly believe that, one by one, these musicians did, in fact, show up. Possibilities that would have seemed too unrealistic to even wish for actually materialized in this one momentous year of 1959, and really without any plan of my own.

So how did Earl "Fatha" Hines come into the picture? Tom Mack, a jazz producer of some note, was working for the Dot label for a time, and one day his secretary put him on the line. He explained that he had heard me sing several times, and understood why I was always being billed as a folksinger or a blues singer. However, he felt that I was really a jazz singer, and he wanted to be the one to produce a record demonstrating that he was right.

Well, of course! Why not try, and why not get the best available musicians into the studio with me? Mack made it clear that there would be no promotion budget because the label itself was not really backing the venture. We would be using studio time he had basically hoarded on the books when it wasn't used up from several other dates. But this could be a plus because it meant that we would be free to design the date as we saw fit. The idea occurred to me then that we ought to bring together other musicians who were either not currently working their strongest musical muscles or who just might be feeling like stepping into less familiar waters. Perhaps that would intrigue them sufficiently

Barbara Dane with Earl Hines. Oakland, 1959

to overlook the fact that the gig would probably pay only scale. It would not be anything very difficult or time-consuming; we'd be working from head arrangements and basically just having a good old time.

I knew that Hines had been heading up a trad jazz group at the Hangover in San Francisco at the time. Whenever I had heard him there, I felt disappointed that he wasn't really free to display his groundbreaking hot piano playing, so I was guessing he would dig the chance to play the kind of material we had in mind. Why not call and ask whether he'd be willing to play on this date? To my amazement, he readily agreed.

Tom Mack came up with the idea of asking Benny Carter to play trumpet, since he knew how much Benny enjoyed that horn, even though his daily bread came from his storied studio work on the sax. Since the date was going to be in Hollywood, everybody's favorite bassist, Leroy Vinnegar, came to mind. Because I rarely worked with drums, the only drummer I could think of was Shelly Manne. He was more identified with cool jazz, but I knew he was a tasty player who would not overwhelm me and definitely could swing. Mack chose the final components, an excellent valve trombonist named Herbie Harper and an astonishing sax man by the name of Plas Johnson, a revelation to me, playing tenor smoothly and with plenty of grit, just right.

I was well aware that I had this important date at a studio not far from my house, down in central Hollywood, but I had just returned from some really hard traveling and needed to relax in a nice hot bath first. I set the alarm clock, but I didn't hear it ring, and suddenly I realized that I had fallen asleep in the bathtub and was already late for the session! When I arrived, damp and breathless, all those great jazzmen were already tuned up and waiting, and Tom Mack was biting his nails. I had grabbed my little notebook with songs and keys in it as I flew out the door, but had no idea what I was going to sing.

I guess somewhere in that special closet of my mind where the music lives I must have been making lists, and just to get started I called out a title. Of course, I had no charts, but these super-pros had probably already played on every song you can think of during their lifetimes. Earl and Benny needed only a minute or two to put their heads together and organize an intro and an ending. Then we just jumped right in and recorded the tune. I realized that we were going to have to make an entire album within a four-hour studio session that I had already managed to cut short. We couldn't waste time on playbacks unless someone had real doubts about the take. And I have never been a fan of second takes anyhow. I like to throw all my emotion into the first take instead of looking for perfection by tinkering and splicing or trying to relive the feeling over and over. And what is perfection, anyway?

I actually enjoy that way of working, high-wire without a net, and we turned out some pretty fine music, although I will admit that, with a chance to relax together, with a nice leisurely rehearsal or two and unlimited studio time, we could have made a sensational album instead of just a good one.

About this time, Albert Grossman came back into my life. He was once dubbed by Rory O'Conner, writing for *Musician* magazine, "The Citizen Kane of Rock and Roll," although most would say his roots were in the folk scene, which I guess has all to do with how you define the genres. He had become a mover in that world in 1956 with the founding of the Gate of Horn, Chicago's first folk club, in the funky basement of the old

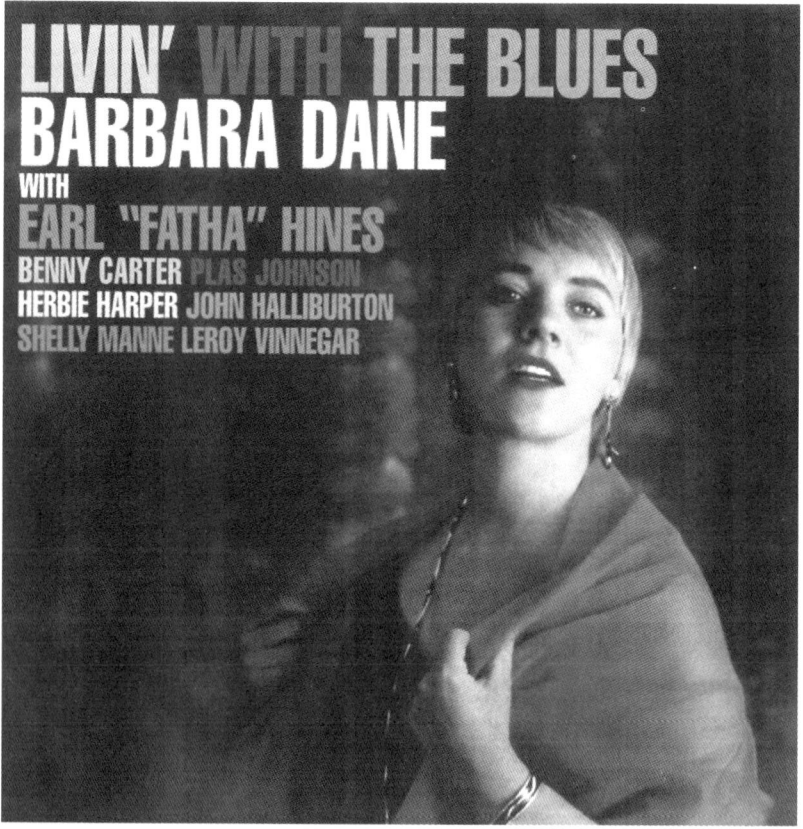

LP cover, *Livin' with the Blues*, Dot Records, 1959

Rice Hotel on the Near North Side. This is where he first featured Big Bill Broonzy and later Bob Gibson and Hamilton Camp, Odetta, and others. By 1959, he had enough credibility in that world to convince George Wein that he should be part of the inner circle as they prepared to launch the Newport Folk Festival, one of the first—and largest—of its kind. This would be the latest addition, and more important, the nonprofit wing, of Wein's operation, which now included the jazz festival and the opera festival at Newport, with backing from the Lorillard tobacco fortune.

Grossman was also quietly building up resources for what was to be the most powerhouse management stable in folk music, and I was high on his wish list. As a way of exploring my potential, he brought me to Chicago and the Gate.

When I first arrived in town, Grossman had asked who I would like to have as my piano man. I must have swallowed twice before I dared to say, "Well, do you know anything about Memphis Slim?" Before you could shake a swizzle stick, I was on my way down to a formerly grand—but now super-sleazy—hotel where I was to meet Slim for a rehearsal. The hotel was worn down and neglected, with that certain smell of vice and mayhem. As I walked through the lobby on my way to the elevators, I felt the weight of the glances of what seemed like a hundred pairs of eyes, searching my style, checking to measure whether my services might be too expensive, would I be worth the money, or whether I was occupied already.

I knocked lightly on the door of Slim's room, and soon it cracked open. There stood the legendary blues man, in his boxer shorts, rumpled T-shirt, and do-rag, waving me to a nearby chair while he slid back under the bedcovers next to his girlfriend, who sat filing her nails, just like in the movies. It was clear that they spent most of their time in that bed, lounging, drinking, eating, watching TV, whatever, anything to kill their boredom. I felt like I was no more than a possibly interesting break in their bleak day, so I quickly launched into a description of what I would be doing at the Gate.

Slim languidly rose and began to run his fingers up and down the keys of a small electric piano he had set up permanently over by the grime-covered window, and I sang a few verses that fit with the twelve-bar form he was playing. Fine—this was going to work, and I was going to love it. But how about the Bessie Smith and Ma Rainey songs? Most of these had a verse first, often followed by a creative chord structure. I laid out one of my simple chord charts for him to see, but that didn't seem to help. The great Memphis Slim he certainly was, and his vertical command of the limited number of keys he played in went deeper than almost any other blues piano I'd ever heard. But outside his domain, what you might call his horizontal grasp of blues styles was apparently barely existent. The problem was that these "classic blues" masterpieces really were the songs I was planning to feature as part of my one-woman campaign to revive what I had come to understand as "women's blues."

Slim broke into my bemused silence by asking if there was a chance the club owner would go for adding a bass player. He had a guy he said was great, had been a member of the Big Three Trio, was a recording artist with Chess, and was well known in Chicago. He had played on Muddy Waters's recording of "Hootchie Cootchie Man" and Chuck Berry's "Maybelline" too, but right now he could use the work. I picked up the phone and soon had Albert's OK to add Willie Dixon. I had no idea who this man was, and only later did I come to understand his centrality to the whole Chicago blues scene. But all right, world, here we come.

Things went a lot better than I expected once we had started the job, but I was uncomfortable not being able to perform the main part of what I had come to do. Luckily, a trick of memory thrust the name of Urreal "Little Brother" Montgomery into my head. It wasn't hard to find him. By asking Dixon, I found out that he was still alive and kicking, and living in Chicago too! Soon I had arranged to have Brother play three nights and Slim play the other three nights, keeping Willie for all six. This was wonderful for me, allowing me to further explore both the eight- and twelve-bar blues with Slim and the classic women's blues with Brother, and those patrons who wanted to hear both styles had to come to the Gate twice in a week!

The line in the song goes, "Bet your bottom dollar you'll lose the blues in Chicago." But actually that is where I found, or certainly matured, my internalization of the blues. The opportunity to sing night after night with masters Memphis Slim and Willie Dixon half the week and with Little Brother Montgomery and Willie the other half was priceless. If the Ash Grove in LA had been my PhD, then working at the Gate of Horn and jamming later at Smitty's Corner was the equivalent of my postdoc. In fact, after I returned to sing at the Ash Grove, Ed Pearl took

Barbara Dane onstage with Memphis Slim (center) and Willie Dixon (right). The Gate of Horn, Chicago, 1958

me aside to tell me that he saw something completely new in my work, that I had acquired more depth in my delivery, and had seemed to have absorbed some new rhythmic sensibility up through the floorboards of those Chicago stages.

Many a night, as soon as my Gate gig was finished, I would jump into my battered ragtop beetle and hightail it to the South Side and Smitty's Corner, where Muddy Waters was holding forth. The possibility of driving myself to places like Smitty's was the reason I drove my third-hand VW all the way to Chicago, and the effort was paying off big-time for me in terms of experience. At that particular time, Muddy's band was one of the all-time greatest in the blues, with Otis Spann on piano, James Cotton on blues harp, Francis Clay on the drums, Andrew Stephenson on bass, plus Pat Hare on second guitar, and of course Muddy. But the days of the good blues gigs were gone now, Black audiences having moved on to what they saw as music more befitting their modern lives in the big cities. White audiences were still stuck in the Mississippi mud. Not until a few years later, when the blues revival took hold, would musicians like these begin to play the festivals and other venues worthy of their talents.

It would be late by the time I could finish with my Gate shows and get to Smitty's. Muddy would have been drinking steadily and, by this time of night, sitting off to the side relaxing. He was happy to see me coming because now he could tell me to go ahead, get up there onstage, and take over for as long as I liked. That way he could concentrate on whatever was making him happy, and I could have what thrilled me out of my mind. His crowd, already slim, would have thinned down by that time to a handful of people, mostly interested in the same thing as Muddy. I didn't have to feel too challenged because mostly they weren't paying any attention anyhow, busy figuring out who they were going to roll with later. And I didn't mind at all because I was lost in my own reverie up there, mining the resources of my twelve-bar repertoire with the greatest blues band imaginable. Not only that, I couldn't be fired if things turned out badly, because it wasn't my gig and I wasn't getting paid anyway.

I realized that a natural thing for people in that overwhelmingly Black world would be to think that this blue-eyed blondie showing up alone late at night in a club was a member of that oldest of professions, otherwise known as a hooker. My way of coping was to make it clear that I was a professional singer, not interested in any diversions. Even Muddy respected that, although he may not have completely understood where I

Barbara Dane onstage with Muddy Waters's band. Smitty's Corner, Chicago, 1959. © *Ebony* magazine

drew the line. One night when he was pretty juiced, he took a chance and half-whispered, half-mumbled in my ear, "Next time you come, bring me some white pussy!" I fell back on the timeless female soft chuckle that says something like, "In your dreams!"

For some time, I had been eager to meet Mama Yancey, widow of pianist Jimmy Yancey and a wonderful singer in her own right. She was known to have provided a haven for musicians at their legendary house rent parties, central to the Chicago blues scene for decades. I asked Little Brother whether he knew her, and would he invite her down to the club. She showed up with her best friend, Eleonora, and I set them up at a table close to the stage with an open tab for that Old Granddad. I joined them after the first set, and the camaraderie was instant. It was clear she was ready to sing, and I was eager to hear her. The power coming out of that little woman was almost shocking to witness! I would ask her about the old-timers who might still be around, and she introduced me to several, including Tampa Red. We had formed a bond that would last forever, and from then on out, she would be the first friend I would call whenever I hit town.

There were after-hours hangs at the Gate as well. Like when Big Joe Williams would stay after closing and play an hour or so just for me and a couple of others, improvising and reminiscing. I had held a soft spot for Joe ever since I had rescued him off of Melrose Avenue in Hollywood, drunk and trudging down the dark street at 2:00 a.m. dragging his guitar case, barely able to stand. I had just finished my own gig at the Ash Grove, where he had played earlier, and although I was exhausted, I managed to get him to where he was staying. Joe never seemed to have a regular place, like the true rolling stone of the blues, on the road to somewhere on his own and bravely facing whatever came along.

On one particular Chicago night, after he had tired of playing that wild nine-string guitar, Joe was ready for a good meal, so I drove him and Mama downtown to that soul-food heaven called Gladys's, where they stayed open most of the night to accommodate hungry musicians and late revelers with the greatest smothered pork chops or fried chicken or greens or cornbread or mac and cheese that ever passed lips. As we waited for our vittles (victuals, to you), Joe spun out a long, only partly intelligible story that climaxed as he very surreptitiously reached into his pocket and, after glancing to the right and left to make sure no stranger was observing, showed us his Conqueroo. This knotty root symbolized the power of High John the Conqueror, a shape-shifting African prince who was sold into slavery but never broken. I was astonished at his courage and honored by his trust. This was not something you shared casually with anyone. It was the strongest spiritual defense in his arsenal. In the words of Zora Neal Hurston, "No matter how bad things look now, it will be worse for those who seek to oppress us. . . . White America, take a laugh from out of our black mouths! . . . We give you High John de Conquer."

Albert Grossman was setting the stage for his next moves in my direction. He made sure I was on the main stage at the first Newport Folk Festival in 1959, right along with other so-called acts that were making a stir. So I was in Newport that July for a weekend in the sun by the sea, surrounded by some of the richest examples of American vernacular music available, right along with those musicians and singer-songwriters like my old friend Pete Seeger who were cutting a new path through the nation's musical and cultural life. Pete helped me arrange for Memphis Slim and Willie Dixon to be invited so that they could play with me on my blues set, as well as do their own thing. I asked Frank Hamilton to play with me on the folk songs, along with Bill Lee, "the people's bass man" (and Spike Lee's father), so I was well set for accompaniment in either style. Now if I could just decide what to sing!

As soon as I stepped out on the stage, a veritable torrent of summer rain began to fall. But instead of running for shelter, most of the audience opted for standing their ground and allowed themselves to be thoroughly soaked as they listened, caught in the spell of this dream of music that was the festival. Luckily, I was standing under an overhang and not playing an electrified instrument, so I kept right on, starting to improvise blues verses about the downpour. I went on and on, inspired by the sea of drenched faces before me, unwilling to surrender the feeling of being in the same boat with a few thousand fellow humans, with all of us rescued by music together. Afterward, Sidney Finklestein, jazz critic and author of *Jazz: A People's Music*, wrote that I had been the only performer really singing folk music that day. Maybe so, if you define it as an expression of real life as it was unfolding right around the singer.

18

PRIORITIES

Chicago publicist Barbara Siegel was a highly regarded and very hip young woman whose work had been responsible for putting the Gate on the map. When she called one day to say that Era Bell Thompson, the formidable managing editor of *Ebony* magazine, would like me to visit her office, I was mildly stunned. *Ebony*, the Black world's answer to *Life* magazine? What do you suppose they wanted with me?

Ms. Thompson came straight to the point: they would like to run an article on my work in the blues. This would be *Ebony*'s first-ever feature story about a white woman, and it couldn't have been easy for her to sell the idea to her fellow editors. But Thompson moved ahead after easily securing my agreement, assigning a photographer and writer to follow me around for several days.

When I first saw *Ebony*'s lead line, though, I had to wince. It was something about a blue-eyed blonde who was keeping the blues alive! Nice rhetoric, but I felt that a certain lack of context there made me look like some kind of crusader at best, or vampire at worst. However, the article was coming out at a time when the people who had brought the blues with them during the great Black migration northward were busy adapting to urban centers like Chicago and Detroit, where they began to reject the old musical styles as backward and old-fashioned, "handkerchief-head music" as some folks called it, as they turned toward new forms. This did, in fact, present the possibility that the blues would become moribund; and actually, until the Rolling Stones and the British Invasion, this was the direction toward which things were headed. I couldn't stand to see that happen. To me, "the blues" was not just a musical form. It represented living human beings, people whose music could bring inspiration to others like them who are struggling to survive. If I could just help remind the world of that, it would be enough.

I'm guessing that another reason for Ms. Thompson's championing of the article had to do with my emphasis on the women's blues of Ma Rainey, Bessie Smith, Ida Cox, Lizzie Miles, and others who had been largely forgotten in the years following World War II. These blueswomen had long ago made it clear that they were to be treated with respect. They also seemed to feel free to express their sexuality, something nice white girls didn't discuss. They had swing, humor, and a strong sense of self-esteem, an obvious conviction that a woman could stand up for herself. I found the bold attitudes of these blueswomen to be mightily liberating and empowering. Ms. Thompson must have seen how I hadn't hesitated to try them for myself. She also might have heard about my habit of talking about this power from the stage night after night.

On the whole, I was more than pleased at the dignified and ample treatment *Ebony* had given the piece, with seven or eight pages, including some nice photos showing me with the musicians I was working with and other people I had come to love and admire. Memphis and Willie were right up front, followed by a couple of beautiful photos of Little Brother Montgomery, one where he's teaching me a blues, one of Mama Yancey and me onstage, and another where I'm chatting with the great gospel singer Clara Ward. There's one with me sitting in with Muddy's band and even a sweet shot of me with my husband Byron, who had come to visit me in Chicago, sitting at a table in Smitty's Corner with Muddy showing us the size of his famous hands.

The article spoke about my refusal to compromise when it came to working with Black musicians, and I think it was meant to show that artists could say no to Jim Crow and still survive. It also showed that there was plenty of audience to support them in this. After all, the *Ebony* story would never have happened if the audiences were not coming out to hear us at the Gate of Horn. But at that time most producers and bookers were still reluctant to take a chance on combining Black and white artists in the same program or on the same tour, with the rare exceptions of certain jazz figures with well-established and high-profile careers.

In the piece, they made a reference to an earlier run-in I had had with the former bandleader Charlie Barnet, a white sax player, now a booking agent in Hollywood. Unexpectedly, and just when I needed it, he had called me to his office to offer me a long-term booking in Las Vegas, fronting my own band. But when I began to list the names of players I would want to include, he cut me off, insisting there would be no way I could hire any Black musicians. In his day, Barnet had been noteworthy for having hired Black musicians including the likes of Billie Holiday to tour with him, so I was angry when he blindsided me by taking this position. His reasoning was that the club owners thought that the Texas high rollers who frequented the casino wouldn't be happy to see a white singer "with Negroes in her band." I stood up, told him he could put his offer "where the sun don't shine," and slammed out the door. Was I really supposed to let some crazed drunken gamblers dictate who would play music with me?

I had good reason to rejoice when I was asked to tour Europe by Louis Armstrong and was able to make recordings with Earl Hines and other Black artists, and the acknowledgment of the *Ebony* story was validating. But I was faced over and over with the fact that racism still permeated the business. Each new time I had to confront these ugly situations, it seemed clearer that I would have to make my own road forward, to find ways to avoid dependence on the music merchants. But you know what? Every time I had to say no, it made me stronger, and I owe a lot of that to the blues.

As 1960 rolled into view, I was invited to appear on Hugh Hefner's nationally syndicated late-night TV hour *Playboy's Penthouse*.

Although my memory of the experience was that I looked terrible and felt no connection to the audience (actors standing around holding cigarettes and drinks), the reality was that I looked great, was fully in command of the three songs I performed, and was clearly enjoying every minute of it. During a comedic number, "The Salvation Army Song," I had everyone singing the chorus ("Away, away with rum, by gum") and

On set, *Playboy's Penthouse*, 1960

even handed a mallet to Hef and asked him to beat the big bass drum, which required him to, yes, get down on his knees.

Shortly after, I was nominated as one of the outstanding jazz artists of the year in the 1960 *Playboy* magazine All-Star Jazz Poll. Nominees were chosen by a board composed of jazz critics, representatives of America's major recording studios, and winners of the 1959 Playboy All-Star Jazz Poll. It felt good to get that kind of recognition, and I didn't even have to take a nude photo to get it!

So with all this media attention, Albert finally popped the question. It went something like this: "Well, Barbara, I know you have a lot going on in your life. You have your family, you have your political activity, and you have your career. So when you have your priorities straight, I want to talk to you about . . ." Hold it right there, Al. I have had my priorities straight for a lot longer than you can imagine, so I guess there isn't much to talk about. Grossman, of course, could never admit to being turned down, and so it was that from then on, if my name should happen to come up among the folk business mandarins, the word was that the Dane girl was not really serious about a career, so why bother with her.

Al certainly knew which horses to choose for this race. He went on to build what Dylan biographer Robert Shelton described as "the most impressive line-up of artists in folk music." It was to include Bob; Peter, Paul and Mary; Janis Joplin; Odetta; the Band; Richie Havens; and other widely recognizable faces.

Regardless of his ultimate motivations, Albert was completely dedicated to his work, taking on way too many artists to be able to sustain his intense involvement with each career. Things began falling apart for him as the 1960s wore on, and when one of his biggest stars, Janis Joplin, overdosed and died in 1970, Al was devastated. According to writer Rory O'Connor, Joplin's biographer Myra Friedman regretted that Albert had been "unwilling to give Janis the kind of direction that could have made the difference in saving her life," and perhaps this was part of his intense distress.

As for me, I was never booked for another major folk or jazz festival in the US, although I did appear at many others, in Cuba, Spain, Italy, Mexico, West Germany, the DDR, and even the USSR. Not much appears in the US press about those festivals, almost as if we were in two different universes, but some of them were huge, and significant on a world scale. They paid only a token fee as a rule, plus airfare and hotels, but the experience, the chance to know some of the great cultural warriors of our time, and the sense of connection with something larger than myself was worth far more than money. No manager has ever owned me or told me where I had to sing or what to sing or even how to sing it. I have no regrets, and, more important, this has taught me a fundamental truth: that every time an artist refuses to do something or become something that violates their ethics or integrity, the more free that artist becomes. And in the words of Ho Chi Minh, "Nothing is more precious than independence and freedom!"

It was around this time that I began introducing more overt social references in my performances. I was in good company when I shared the bill in Chicago with comedian Mort Sahl. For columnist Sam Lesner of the *Chicago Daily News*, "Sahl's fame as an 'intellectual' comedian rests upon his talent to analyze local, national and international news events and extract their humorous overtones." I was surprised and delighted when Lesner later wrote of me, "an exceptional vocal entertainer whose introductions to her songs are priceless musical commentaries. Barbara easily qualifies as the 'Mort Sahl' of a new crop of quick-witted vocalists." My focus was actually different than Sahl's. I was bringing the attitude of the old-time blueswomen and their practical ways of dealing with life—with all the emotions involved, sexy to serious—but at the same time I was pushing the audiences to use their brains, keep on the edge of today's events, and put themselves in that context.

In the summer of 1960, I shared a Colorado bill with TV host and comedian Steve Allen on a benefit for antinuclear activists. I knew that Allen had hosted a meeting in LA several months earlier for the purpose of founding Hollywood for SANE, the Committee for a Sane Nuclear Policy, bringing together Marlon Brando, Henry Fonda, Arthur Miller, Marilyn Monroe, Harry Belafonte, and Ossie Davis, among others. Since its inception in New York in 1957, the organization could count on high-profile supporters like Eleanor Roosevelt, Walter Reuther, and A. Philip Randolph, but other than student chapters, this would be the first Southern California base for promoting a new and powerful message of opposition to war and demanding disarmament through a "sane" nuclear policy.

After the show in Denver, I had the chance to talk to Steve and get to know him a bit. I discovered that he had been covering the cost of building the SANE group mostly out of his own pocket. I volunteered to stage a benefit once we got back home, saying I was sure it could be done at the Ash Grove.

Ed Pearl generously gave us a night, which happened to be during a week when I was appearing there on a bill with Brownie McGhee and Sonny Terry, so of course I invited them to take part. Steve drafted many of his regulars: Don Knotts, Louis Nye, vibist Terry Gibbs, and others. He also drafted Mort Sahl, who did a comedy turn that segued into the fundraising pitch. The house was packed, a lot of Hollywood heavy hitters included, but a bigger surprise was waiting for me just outside.

Lenny Bruce was out there, tapping on the lobby window to be let in, dressed in a striking new look. It was something nobody had tried before. He had hired a tailor to shape a pair of white Levis with a matching jacket, way before designer jeans were a fashion statement, and on him it was a knockout. He was on a mission. Would I mind if he took a few minutes on the program? Most certainly not . . . but I would introduce him as soon as Mort winds up his pitch, a polite one that hadn't created much action. Now Lenny took the mic and began to tell it like it was: "You folks are getting a million-dollar show here after paying the usual two dollars at the door. If you really want to see a *sane* nuclear policy, you need to go home to Beverly Hills and sell your house. You need to give the money to this group, you need to join Hollywood for SANE and help raise the issues yourself." We sent the baskets around again, and the result was worth the audacity. I love you, Lenny, wherever you are.

Ed Pearl had never been less than generous and kind to me and my family, but something happened that year that tested our relationship. As you have seen, we were usually pretty hard pressed for money. This must have been what made Byron take his first—and, as far as I recall, his only—stab at producing. I was quietly astonished to come back from one of my trips to Chicago to find that he had contracted a two-week booking for me and Jesse Fuller across the street from the Ash Grove at the more commercially oriented Troubadour. I certainly didn't want to discourage his efforts to keep me working, and perhaps he saw this as a step up in career terms, but it was an unexpected and embarrassing development in light of Ed Pearl's long-standing support and friendship. I wasn't quite sure how to square it with Ed.

Performers in those days were expected to take an active role in promoting their dates, and the custom was to send out a notice to your fan base via the US Post Office. We had little experience with this end of things, so we asked Ben Shapiro for advice, thinking maybe he had a mailing list for promoting the Renaissance, his new club over on a low-rent stretch of Sunset Boulevard. Well, said Ben, you have access to the Ash Grove office, so why not just slip in one night and use Ed's list? And I am ashamed to say that, without a word in advance to Ed, we actually did just that. This was soon discovered, of course, but Ed's reaction was stunningly simple. No drama, no vengeful acts or words or even looks. Ed just quietly said that everyone is entitled to at least one mistake, so forget it and move on. Even today, I am touched and humbled by his spirit of generosity, which has served as a life lesson for me.

On the musical side, something fundamental began for us at the Troubadour, when the great bassist Wellman Braud came out of retirement to join Kenny Whitson and me, providing that solid bottom beat we both craved. Kenny and I had discussed the idea of adding a bass for some time, but given our shared finely tuned rhythmic awareness, we were hard to please. My rhythm on the guitar was steady, but I wanted Kenny to be freed up so that he could blow those exhilarating cornet solos more often. He always said that even the best bass players we tried had only given him a pain in the gut.

But one day, Kenny discovered that Braud, one of the most respected bassists of the older generation in jazz, had retired from the Ellington band some time before and was living on the outskirts of LA. Kenny began to visit him regularly, checking out Wellman's famous gumbo recipe and his special way with black-eyed peas while encouraging him to tell stories about the old days, a way of slyly tempting him to consider music again. Now in his early seventies, Wellman had even given away his bass, and once he decided to jump back into the game with us, he actually had to buy himself a new one.

For the first couple of days, I was afraid he wasn't going to cut it. His notoriously hot and insistent beat no longer seemed as strong and steady. But by midweek his muscle memory began to kick in, and the old power had begun to show. By the end of the two weeks, we were more than proud that Wellman had agreed to work with us for the long haul. The man inside him who brought that irresistible hot beat to everything he touched had awakened!

19

STRANGE BEDFELLOWS

In 1960, I recorded a 45 rpm single for the Trey label, one of those Hollywood start-ups whose proliferating offices were "in the glove boxes of their cars," as people in the industry joked. But the two partners, Lester Sill and Lee Hazlewood, were far from pretenders, already very deeply enmeshed in the music industry. In fact, American pop music would have been very different without the two of them. Sill was an all-round music executive who actually brokered the partnership between songwriters Jerry Lieber and Mike Stoller and managed the Coasters, one of the most popular West Coast R&B groups of the day. He also survived a long, involved relationship with the legendary, and now infamous, Phil Spector. His partner in Trey Records, Lee Hazlewood, was a singer, songwriter, and producer who made his biggest marks working with Nancy Sinatra.

The day I cut "I'm on My Way" and "Go 'Way from My Window" for Trey Records, I thought, well, that was fun; I earned a little recording fee, and that was that. It was interesting to work with the great Red Mitchell on bass and the fine piano player Hazlewood had provided, but without hearing the finished product, I wasn't expecting it to go any further than home to my living room. Then, without consulting me, Lee overdubbed some horns on the last part of the recording, stepping up its polished radio sound quite a bit. Next thing I knew, Tom Donahue, the Big Daddy of free-form radio whose KSAN programming was shaking up Bay Area music fans, was playing "I'm on My Way" to the point of what the industry calls a "breakout," and the super-commercial DJ, Casey Kasem, was lauding the performance of "the blonde bombshell."

Although it didn't get much further than the San Francisco breakout on any charts back then, in the twenty-first century it has found a whole new life. It seems that the lovers of Northern Soul, a phenomenon in England whose group passion is dancing to 45 rpm discs from the 1960s, consider it perfect for their style. And so it developed a cult following, pirate versions showed up, and it circulates there to this day. Because of that, the Trey version of "I'm on My Way" was featured in a European Samsung commercial in 2015, with scenes of a daring young woman riding her bicycle and listening to it on ear buds. Finally, some money from that little session in 1960! I don't think Sill and Hazlewood had ever paid any royalties, at least nothing worth mentioning.

But the local San Francisco success of the recording in 1960 did have some important repercussions. For one, it caught the attention of the suits at both Capitol and Atlantic Records. Suddenly I found myself being romanced by both companies, invited to "take a lunch" with one of the Ertegun brothers at the Brown Derby on one day and someone from upstairs at Capitol on another day. Without any professional management, I was a little bit confounded, and unsure about what to do next.

I had always admired the work of Atlantic, the respect with which it was known to treat its artists, and the obvious love the Erteguns had for the strains of gospel and blues that saturated the performances of Ray Charles, Solomon Burke, Mose Allison, and others on the label. It was a dream to even be noticed by them, and if I had followed my instincts, my musical life most certainly would have played out entirely differently. But I was living literally within view of the iconic Capitol tower, while Atlantic's operational center was back east somewhere. I made my decision to go with Capitol, based on the fact that I envisioned a scenario where I would do my recording without leaving the children for weeks at a time.

Critic Leonard Feather devoted a whole column to this, pointing out that there could hardly have been a label and an artist further apart in style and intention. In his syndicated column, "Life with Feather," he concluded: "Ironically, Miss Dane has just signed a contract with a jazz-starved company long opposed to everything she stands for in music, the ultra-conservative Capitol Records. If she can budge this monolith one millimeter in her own sincere, unpretentious direction she will have justified another strange contradiction in her altogether unique career."

In those days, General Artists was the second-largest talent agency in the world, just then in the process of launching the career of a new young comedian who had recently made an enormous hit with his first comedy record, *The Button-Down Mind of Bob Newhart,* winning Album of the Year at the 1960 Grammys and becoming a worldwide best seller, topping even Elvis Presley on the charts! To my surprise, his agent, Jerry Perenchio (early in a career that would make him a multi-billionaire), summoned me to meet about the idea of touring with Bob as the musical costar of the show, to be presented in the premiere theaters of many major Canadian cities and down the California coast as far as San Diego.

A meeting with Newhart was arranged so that we could talk about the show itself. I arrived with my piano man Kenny Whitson and performed for them the song with which I planned to close my half of the show, a deep song about a man on his way to being hung after a frame-up, an old, nearly forgotten song by the great Ida Cox called "Last Mile Blues." Capital punishment was being challenged from all sides in California at that time, and the legislature would be voting on this issue in a few weeks. I was using the song to drive home the barbarity of the practice as well as the ever-present possibility of murdering an innocent person because of racism and the many other defects in our legal system. Newhart just about blew his habitual cool when he heard the song, insisting that it would be impossible to follow something that heavy with comedy. But Perenchio intervened. No, you need to let her do it. This is one of her strongest songs. All right, a small victory here.

But the next issue was harder to win. Perenchio was adamant that it wouldn't be possible for me to bring Wellman Braud as part of my backup group. It seems that the last time they had toured a mixed group, they had run into too many problems booking hotel rooms, and the agency just wasn't going to put itself through that again. I took a big risk and explained that I would have to think about this for a day or two. After the Charlie Barnet Las Vegas incident, I was building up a heap of anger inside around this issue. But my bills at home were mounting dangerously, and I had already brushed off one good job. Would I begin to find myself unemployable in the eyes of these big-time agents if I refused to cooperate again? I called a little meeting with Kenny and Wellman, who were waiting to know how long this tour would run and when we were to be ready for departure. All of us needed the opportunity of regular work, and they were holding off other offers of jobs in order to continue our work together. I laid out the story and declared that we wouldn't be doing the tour after all because of this ugly twist in the plan. They already knew that my lifetime commitment to myself was never to cooperate with any discriminatory practices. It was Wellman who looked me in the eye like a stern but respectful father and said, "I think you should go ahead and do the tour this time. You have three children, you and Kenny both need the work badly, and when they see what you both can do, it will move you many notches up the scale of available talent in their book. That will make it possible for you to make your own terms next time. I'll be here when you get back, so don't worry about me."

This was not the only time Wellman Braud demonstrated his loyalty to the music the three of us had been creating together, and the kind of integrity that had earned him the respect of so many others. I found out many years later that he had refused offers from both Louis and Duke to return to work with their bands in order to stick with Kenny and me. I am still humbled by the knowledge that he would quietly do a thing like that, without even mentioning it to us.

Kenny reluctantly agreed with Wellman's strategy about the Newhart tour. We decided to look for a musician who could play a good strong bass for the blues, but also augment the folk song part of my chosen repertoire, especially since the audiences at that time were beginning to look for that sound. We settled on a young instrumentalist from Greenwich Village by the name of Dick Rosmini, later best known for his twelve-string guitar work, but then playing five-string banjo. The three of us packed up all the instruments and a few clothes and set off for the Canadian north.

As far as I can remember it, the tour began in Winnipeg and made its way west from there through Regina, Edmonton, Calgary, and Vancouver, then south to Seattle, Portland, Sacramento, San Francisco, Berkeley, Los Angeles, and finally San Diego. We drove all of it because

Newhart had a phobia about flying and refused to travel that way. This put us in different vehicles, so we saw almost nothing of Bob during the whole trip, but that was fine with us. We prized our independence, and didn't mind sharing the driving in order to enjoy it.

Every theater we played was the biggest one in town, cavernous and jammed with people, and the figures show that ours was the highest-grossing concert package for a tour like ours ever to hit these venues. The crowds seemed to love everything they experienced, and I felt they had a genuine appreciation for the folk songs and, somewhat surprisingly, for the unfamiliar classic blues we were presenting too. I seldom went out into the house after our show to check out what Newhart was doing, but one night I heard him crack an impromptu "joke" that made me upset and angry.

His usual schtick was to feign talking to someone on the phone, often about his fear of flying, especially on the Mrs. J. L. Ferguson Storm Door and Airline Company plane. It was mildly funny. But on this night, at some point he is "interrupted" by an unseen messenger who is bringing him a news flash. "What did you say? Oh, well, I am sorry to have to announce that Patrice Lumumba has been killed. By the way, who was she?" Polite laughter.

I was stunned by the callous ignorance demonstrated by this remark. It would not be surprising if most of the audience didn't know who Patrice Lumumba was, because the same people who arranged for his assassination in person had also arranged for his invisibility in the American press. It was Malcolm X who pointed that out: "You can't understand what's going on in Mississippi if you can't understand what's going on in the Congo"; so we Americans were clearly not meant to grasp the intention or the significance of Patrice Lumumba's life—or his death.

Quite simply, Lumumba was none other than the first legally elected prime minister of the Democratic Republic of Congo after independence from Belgium was declared on June 30, 1960, the rare person capable of uniting the many contending factions in this newly formed nation. Lumumba was assassinated on January 17, 1961, by a combination of Congolese and Belgian assassins funded and encouraged by the US government. Belgian writer Ludo De Witte, author of the most complete book on the subject, called it "the most important assassination of the twentieth century," and history places Lumumba in the hallowed company of Malcolm X, Medgar Evers, and Martin Luther King Jr., all Black men of towering leadership abilities cut down in their prime, just when the world needed them most.

After Newhart's unforgivable belittling remark, I found it impossible to watch any of his many successful TV series in the years that followed, but a large part of the American public seems to have invited his stammering everyman character into their homes, probably because they could identify with his "clueless nice guy" persona. A safer, whiter comedian on US television would be hard to find.

As our tour made its way closer to home, down the Pacific Coast to California, I was becoming more than eager to see my children and husband again. Only four more cities to go, and now we were pulling into Sacramento, the capital of California, where the legislature would soon be voting on yet another attempt to shut down the death penalty in my state. The night of our concert, I had already been introduced and was striding toward the stage when I was intercepted by an unexpectedly agitated Newhart. Dramatically, he threw himself down on his knees and began to implore me, "Please, please don't sing that 'Last Mile Blues' . . . I'll do anything you want. How can I get you to drop that song tonight?"

I might have been shocked by this behavior, but my brain went click, click, quickly reviewing the idea that even though this legislation, at this time, in this place, had been my main target for this powerful song, realistically it was not going to affect the vote one way or the other if I substituted something else. "Well, do you really mean *anything*?"

"Yes, yes, what is it?"

"All right, I want my regular bass man Wellman Braud back with me by tomorrow night at the Masonic in San Francisco." Done! Another victory over stupidity.

20

RIDING HIGH ON SUGAR HILL

While the Newhart tour was in the Bay Area, I had an important project to work on. I had been quietly scheming for a way to get back to this place on a permanent basis. I wanted the kids to grow up with a sense of belonging, a feeling of permanence and solidity, not having to change neighborhoods and schools all the time. I wanted them to mature in a coherent environment, a place where values felt a lot like mine, where culturally curious people could have access to a rich tapestry of possibilities, a place where by now I had achieved enough recognition to imagine that I could work steadily, without having to travel all the time to make a living.

But most of all, I wanted a way to realize my dream of helping bring the blues out into the mainstream, of presenting this music in a comfortable place where folks unused to venturing into Black communities would come and meet the artists as well as their fans on common ground. Even more, I wanted to have a place to present those audiences with what could well be the last performances of some of the founding fathers and mothers of the blues. I had witnessed the power of what they still had to give, and my vision was to present them in an atmosphere of respect and dignity, to move beyond the stereotyping assumptions that the blues was only booty-shakin' music.

I made a few inquiries about available locations, and when I heard that there was a shuttered club on Broadway, El Bordello, that was about to auction its lease and liquor license, I jumped at the chance to see it. The address was perfect: right across the street from the Jazz Workshop and down the block from El Matador, two of the best little jazz clubs in town. The size was perfect, just right for about 150 people, with a nice, long bar along one side, and already outfitted with a small stage and some booths around the opposite side. It wouldn't take a fortune to make it look just the way I wanted, and the timing was pretty good too. With my usual heedless optimism, I told the real estate person I would be back in time for the auction, which was only a couple of weeks away.

Something told me this was such a perfect idea that nothing could stop it now. I got to our next stop, Hollywood and home, and told Byron all about it. He, of course, thought I must have left my mind somewhere along the trail, but at the same time, he seemed to see it as an opportunity and an adventure, especially since we both had loved living in the Bay Area.

And then, at last, we arrived at the end of the Newhart tour in San Diego. At the end of the concert, a man came backstage and introduced himself as the escort of Norma Aston, a woman of means who lived in the nearby big-bucks beachside enclave of La Jolla. He had been sent by Ms. Aston to invite me to visit her home for a drink after the show, so, with the agreement of Kenny and Wellman, we followed him there.

In the lower part of this sumptuous spread, Aston had built a social room much like a small jazz club, with a jukebox on one wall and a piano that stood on a little platform with a sound system, lighting, and so forth. We sat at a stylish cocktail table, and one of her people came out of the shadows to quietly attend to our drink requests. After a lot of small talk about the show, Newhart's comedy, other performances she had enjoyed, and so on, Norma asked, "Well, what are you going to do now that the tour is over?" Without hesitation I began to describe my dream, the blues club I was going to open in San Francisco, filling in some details about which performers I was planning to book and so on. As I spoke, I watched something in her eyes begin to dance as she wet her lips and hesitantly asked, "Well . . . I don't suppose you could use a backer for all this?" And just so, the missing piece of my plan fell into my lap.

Next day in Hollywood, I called Ben Shapiro for advice. He was a close enough friend to trust with my plan, and of course Mr. Hollywood

Hipness Himself. I've never been one to do papers, so I knew I was going to need a lawyer to take care of all the business details, but I wanted someone who would impress Norma Aston, who was clearly in heat when it came to show business. Ben was quick to put me in touch with exactly the right guy, and I can describe how he looked and acted but I cannot recall his name, probably because he wound up near the top of my short shit list for life. But that day, I went up to his fancy Hollywood law office, where, after a brief handshake, he resumed his balancing act, a phone receiver in each hand into which he was conducting two separate phone meetings. As I sat describing what I needed from him, he continued holding conversations regarding big deals for big movies with big stars, tossing around the Marlon Brandos and the Liz Taylors, just as I hoped he would do within earshot of Norma Aston. How did I imagine this guy would come up to San Francisco and negotiate my little deal, and do it next week? But I laid the idea on him, and he quickly agreed. Maybe he liked excuses to visit the Bay Area. Maybe he just liked the notion of being part of a fresh new plan like mine. He was so cool he didn't even ask for a retainer to do this.

I met him at the airport, secretly amused at the way he walked in his clog-like shoes meant to make him look five feet nine instead of five feet six and the comb-over that was meant to disguise his balding dome. But what energy! Aston had also arrived in town, had seen the club and checked out what the auction was going to require of her. We headed for her hotel room, where I outlined my terms. Number one: I would only accept a silent partner. No meddling with my business policy, and nothing to do with my booking policy or whom I hired to work in the club. I would pay a determined percentage of the monthly income to Aston, who would have no say over any of this unless I defaulted for six months. She agreed, and we all shook hands. With my rush of elation held inward, I hoped to have seemed super cool, and more than that, hoped I looked like I knew what I was doing. But here's the thing: she was the one paying the lawyer. Now I realize that this meant she owned him, that I was not really represented here; and this proved to be the undoing of one of my best ideas ever. Here's a free lesson in life: no papers, no standing, no dream scene, *punto*.

Aston wasn't without an agenda of her own, and it wasn't long before she sprung it. It was she who had gone to the auction and put up the money when our bid was accepted, and whose name went onto the liquor license and the lease. Norma laid out the money to redecorate the premises using my simple design: dark-red banquettes around the walls, the walls covered with burlap for texture and then whitewashed, any new pine carpentry stained with dark walnut Minwax, small round tables, and some very good oil paintings of jazz inspiration by local artists. We bought a grand piano from the former owner at a decent price, and it turned out to be an excellent one. We upgraded to a decent sound system with good mics and added some stage lighting.

The room held about 150 people, and my policy was to give a fair drink for a fair price, in contrast to the many tourist-trap strip bars in the area using false-bottom glasses. We also dispensed with the traditional street barker normally stationed outside Broadway's club doors to drag in customers, and there would be no cover charge or minimum drink requirement. I wanted people to feel free to wander in and check out the music, and to feel equally free to leave if it didn't grab them. I only wanted people to stay if they were actually enjoying the music. I also hired only male waiters and asked them to dress in simple black shirt and pants, as a contrast to the scantily clad counterfeit Playboy Bunny waitresses found in all the other clubs on the San Francisco rialto.

In May 1961, I opened the first blues club in the nation that was not back-o-town but on Broadway, the main entertainment street of the city seen all over the world at that time as one of the most exciting places to be. San Francisco was the perfect place for this new idea, and I wanted the perfect name. At first I had planned to call it Mother's, as in the old joke about the businessman who calls his wife and says he can't come home right now because he first has to visit Mother's. Norma wouldn't hear of it. The term *motherfucker* had just begun to make its impact on the culture, and she felt that Mother's would make the place sound like a low joint. After a great deal of thought, I came up with the idea of Sugar Hill because the phrase has a resonance in both Black and white culture. It is the name of a ritzy part of Manhattan, north to south roughly 145th to 155th Streets, and east to west from Edgecombe to Amsterdam Avenues, where jazz musicians lived and played during the Harlem Renaissance, and at the same time it serves as the principal refrain of a bluegrass tune with the repeated line "goin' to Sugar Hill."

Sugar Hill, Home of the Blues. 430 Broadway, North Beach, San Francisco, 1961

>Get your banjo off the wall, grab your fiddle, Bill
>Hitch the horses to the sleigh, we're going to Sugar Hill

We finally settled on the full name: Sugar Hill, Home of the Blues.

Byron and I had put out the word to friends that we were in urgent need of a reasonably priced place to live, hopefully in Berkeley, and soon got word that Ted and Mimi Odza, a couple we'd known for some years, were splitting up and willing to rent us their house up in the hills. Mimi was a gifted modern dancer, and Ted was an artist and landscape designer, so we knew their aesthetics would be in tune with ours, not ostentatious and making economical use of simple, natural materials. The place was just large enough to accommodate the five of us, with unpainted redwood lining the inside walls and a large deck, also of redwood, off the kitchen. There was a sort of fantasy boat down the slope below, something Ted had built for his own kids out of redwood leftovers, and downhill from that a sea of tall grass. From up there, we could see nothing but trees and a bit of the bay, as if the house stood alone in the gently rippling oceans of green fields that surrounded us.

Kenny and Wellman were delighted at the idea of long-term guaranteed steady work, especially in this town so open to new ideas and cultural experiments. They took rooms in a simple workingman's hotel that stood down at the end of Broadway, otherwise occupied by pensioned longshoremen and ex-sailors, well within their means and just a short walk to work every night. I knew it was important to find a manager who would open the club in the afternoon for deliveries, someone who could be trusted with transactions involving tradesmen, and someone who was on our side, willing to keep an eye on our interests. Kenny and his Armenian friend Frank came up with someone who filled the bill perfectly. As for a bartender, everyone had been advising me about the need to find one who would not steal too much, since it was understood that anyone in that trade considered a bit of skimming a part of their perks. Norma found Don Currie, a redheaded man she trusted from the gay world, someone whose reputation around town seemed to be positive, so we put him in charge of that end of things.

From the first day the doors were opened, people began to discover us. We never had a night when we didn't make our nut, even at the beginning. It gave Byron a steady job, one that he enjoyed, acting as the host and greeter who welcomed people to the club and kept an eye on everything while I was busy on the stage, singing my heart out to an audience full of well-wishers and friends. He was inherently gregarious and perfectly cast for the job. He could make people feel they had come to a special place, and, as a matter of fact, they had. It quickly began to feel like a large public living room; in a way, that's what it really was. People knew he was my husband, so it felt as though they were being welcomed into my home.

Our door was directly across the street from the Jazz Workshop, and many of the nationally known musicians who played there stopped in on their breaks. Kenny and Wellman also proved to be a magnet for many of the local trad jazz players, who began to fall by, bringing their horns, augmenting our sound with musical surprises. Sometimes we let Sonny Terry's cousin J. C. Burris take a few minutes to demonstrate his way of playing the blues harp with one hand while keeping time with the "bones" he held in the other, or let us check out his limberjack, the traditional clog-dancing wooden doll he claimed to have made for himself, or show off his agility with the body-percussion moves called hand jive. Those were the nights when he wasn't staggering dead drunk down the street somewhere.

On several amazing occasions, Willie Mae "Big Mama" Thornton came by with her posse of girls, intent on doing a set with my musicians, who really did give her exactly the kind of support she loved. On those nights, she did some of the best singing I've ever heard. And it wasn't only blues. I wish you could have heard her sing ballads, something that would have surprised the kind of listeners who like to keep their favorite artists in boxes. I looked forward to featuring her at the club, and, as she was local, I thought she'd be the best possible person to hold our audience any time I might have to go out of town for a gig.

One of the regulars at Sugar Hill fixed me up with a radio show, on the promise that I would never have to come to a studio, but would be able to record it from my dressing room between sets. *Barbara's Blues* ran on KIBE radio in Palo Alto, KDFC-FM in Santa Rosa, and KJAZ-FM in San Francisco. Putting a show together with my comments and ramblings was fun and relaxing. I didn't have to go out of my way to do anything except make up a set list of some of my favorite cuts from my LP collection to be dubbed into place by the radio stations. I didn't get paid a dime, but it was worth it for the exposure, a way to let more folks know about Sugar Hill too.

Most nights at the club it was just me, with Kenny and Wellman, free from restraints and swinging anything that came to mind. I seldom made a set list for these live shows, and we never rehearsed. Often I would make up a whole new blues by asking the folks to throw me a few words or phrases and then weaving together a few unlikely images to make some kind of sense, usually humorous, sometimes salty, sometimes slick. I loved the challenge! But even more, I loved bringing in guest artists and providing the setting in which they could strut their stuff.

At first we presented the best local bluesmen as guests, including T-Bone Walker, Jesse Fuller, Brownie McGhee, Sonny Terry, and K. C. Douglas. Soon we reached out for more distant legendary figures. One of the most memorable of these was the great Jimmy Rushing, who was in town to appear at the Monterey Jazz Festival. His nickname, Mr. Five by Five, was an accurate description of this froggish-looking man. Promoter George Wein, who had brought him to Monterey, came along the first night and even played very decent blues piano behind Jimmy. Neither of them could have realized how validating it felt for me to have Rushing there, or how much a part of my life's soundtrack he had been since I was in high school. In fact, I hadn't realized it myself until I looked back at his repertoire and saw how much of that material was reflected in my own choice of songs.

My impression of Lonnie Johnson was mixed. On the one hand, he was the pioneering musician who had moved the guitar forward from its place as an accompanying chordal folk instrument to a single-string jazz soloing instrument, and was revered among other musicians for what he had accomplished. He'd recorded with Louis Armstrong, Duke Ellington, and James P. Johnson, and had even toured with Bessie Smith, placing him in the front ranks of jazz history. His influence on other guitarists, like T-Bone and Brownie, and on singers including Elvis Presley and even Bob Dylan, can't be overstated. After all these years, he still played with uncommon dexterity and skill, although to my ears now he was "mailing it in" more often than not. It seemed so easy for him that you could imagine him playing great riffs and runs in his sleep.

At one time, Lonnie had had a brush with becoming a crooner, having a major hit in 1948 ("Tomorrow Night"), which topped the so-called race records charts for several weeks, and he was reported to be quietly offended if the press referred to him as a bluesman. Those were the days when he probably was actually able to make a living in music, and it was this pop-like singing style he continued to use. Increasingly, his repertoire was loaded with sentimental, syrupy, brokenhearted tunes with lyrics about love gone wrong. Maybe songs like that were really metaphors for all the miserable ways society had done him wrong, but I was waiting for his real feelings about life to come out in song, waiting for that fierce survival undertone so basic to the blues, and I wasn't the only one.

Flash forward a few years to a small group of musicians gathered at my apartment in New York City one night, including Lonnie and Brownie McGhee. Brownie, who had had a few drinks, began to rag on Lonnie, first practically kissing his hands as he lavished praise, calling him the man he considered his greatest model, and then, without warning, launching a fusillade of invective that would wither a redwood tree, all about how Lonnie had quit putting himself into his music, had quit believing in himself. Lonnie had beamed at first, but in moments was reduced to tears and had to leave the room. I felt sad and embarrassed for him, but Brownie explained to the rest of us that he was only trying to get Lonnie angry, to make him stand up for himself, to show what he was really made of. To be a true blues man.

There were special moments in each of the bookings that followed. Tampa Red, so prolific a songwriter and so widely loved a few decades before, was a bit vague and shaky offstage. Some of the Chicago folks had gently warned me that he hadn't been himself since he'd lost both his wife and his best friend and musical partner, pianist Big Maceo Merriweather. But once back in the saddle, he fully satisfied the expectations of his collectors and fans, who respectfully and readily made allowances for his age. When I wrote him a letter inviting him to play the club, he replied kindly, signing himself "Hudson Whitaker, better known as Tampa Red." His many double-entendre tunes like "Let Me Play with Your Poodle" and "She Wants to Sell My Monkey" were his old-time moneymakers, but the one I sing myself, "It Hurts Me Too," is straightforward and touching. On his closing night, he held the entire room in thrall with his last song, as he quietly mourned his beloved friend Big Maceo, tears streaming down his face as he sang:

> Nights are long since you went away,
> I think about you all through the day,
> my buddy, my buddy,
> nobody quite so true.
>
> I miss your voice, the touch of your hand.
> I long to know that you understand.
> My buddy, my buddy,
> Your buddy misses you.

In the fall of 1961, Estella "Mama" Yancey finally made it west to sing for a couple of weeks at Sugar Hill. From the beginning, Mama had been one of the reasons I wanted to open this kind of club. Ever since she had been so kind to me in Chicago, connecting me up with people like Tampa and Lonnie, coming to my closing-night jams at the Gate of Horn, and singing for the folks, I had been trying to think of a way to let some of her glory shine on her. Finally that day had come, and we were ready!

We got in touch with a few of the traditional jazz musicians who we were sure would want to be part of a big musical welcome, and they quickly pulled together a marching band to meet her at the airport. We called those members of the press we knew to be aware of her history, and the best ones showed up. Byron and the children waited in the VIP lounge with the rest, bearing a gigantic bouquet of long-stemmed red roses and a banner that said "Welcome Mama Yancey to San Francisco." Bill Carter, clarinetist and brilliant photographer, waited at the ready, to play as well as to document this whole array.

I made my way down the covered gangplank that connected the plane with the airport building so that I could help Mama and tip her off about what was going to happen next. Completely unaccustomed to flying, she was drowsy and a bit dazed as the plane landed. I bent down to whisper in the ear of this tiny woman with the rumpled gray hair, explaining that there was a whole crowd of people waiting to greet her, including a jazz band and some reporters, and asking if she was all right with that. In a flash, she pulled herself up to her scant five feet and lifted her chin. Her dim eyes almost seemed to sparkle behind her thick glasses as she gripped my arm and said, "Let's go!"

As we stepped into the VIP lounge, the band struck up one of her signature songs, "How Long Blues." Bob Mielke on the trombone led the way, as Mama stepped in front of them and began half-singing, half-shouting those ringing words!

> I been down to the delta,
> Baby, and I've stood my trials,
> And I can stand more trouble
> Than any little woman my size.
>
> How long, how long,
> How long will it be
> Before you will learn
> To quit mistreatin' me?

She was handed the bouquet of roses almost her size, and we held our banner aloft as a half-block-long contingent of well-wishers paraded behind her down the long hall to the lobby. I'm sure most of the travelers

Mama Yancey and Barbara Dane. San Francisco, 1961

milling about the airport were wondering, "Who the heck is this Mama Yancey?" But we knew, and we would never forget the joy we all felt seeing her blossom with all the attention, so richly deserved but so seldom offered her for a lifetime of music. Mama was thrilled when she saw the scene depicted in *Jet* magazine the following week.

Her first night singing at Sugar Hill was a strange wonder. Jet-lagged; aching from too many hours of trying to fit in an airline seat; her limbs, already twisted with rheumatoid arthritis; then suddenly surrounded by strangers demanding that she be "somebody." But still, from the minute she heard Kenny and Wellman playing her intro, there she was, throwing all the emotion and energy she could muster into song after song. Next day, jazz critic Ralph Gleason wrote some snarky comment about that night, intimating that this poor old lady was being exploited even though she had little music left in her. But, to his own loss, he didn't bother to check in later in the week to see how things were going. Here's how they were going!

That first night, a middle-aged Black woman Mama had helped out with something important many years ago in Chicago came in with her daughter, insisting that Estella Yancey was *not* going to stay in any old hotel but that they were going to put her up at their home for the next two weeks and feed her lots of good home-cooked meals. Luckily, I had thought to give Mama an advance, knowing she was probably tapped out, and next day she and her old friend went shopping for something new to wear on the stage. That night, Estella showed up in a simple sweater and pleated skirt, like a college girl on her way to having her class picture taken; her hair was neatly coiffed, and she was tastefully made up and wearing a string of pearls around her neck. The daughter, a hairdresser, had done a complete makeover on Mama's tangled mane. Not exactly a blues singer's getup, but it was the way she wanted to present herself, with dignity and lookin' good!

Kenny and Wellman, of course, were the perfect accompaniment for the spontaneous, emotion-driven singer that Mama was. Owing to his longtime admiration for Jimmy Yancey's playing, Kenny seemed to know her whole repertoire, and she was completely comfortable with them behind her, lifting her and encouraging her all through the evening. Each night, she became more and more confident, and because of the good home cooking at her friend's house, she even began to put a little cushion on that skinny old rack of bones.

One of Estella Yancey's biggest fans was S. I. Hayakawa, future Republican senator from California but then a professor at SF State University, who came frequently to Sugar Hill and who even held an afternoon seminar for one of his classes there, during which Brownie McGhee and Sonny Terry performed. Hayakawa himself had been a student in Chicago in the 1940s and early '50s, during which time he became an ardent blues fan, spending many an evening enjoying the Yanceys' musical hospitality. Now that Mama was right here on his home turf, he made a point of showing up on a number of occasions. When it was finally time to wind up her engagement, we prepared a good-bye party at a private home in San Francisco, and Hayakawa offered to come early to slice the ham. I'll never forget the thin, orderly slices he produced with the special Japanese knife he brought in for the job, arranging the platter with the exactitude of a professional sushi chef. Our good friend Bill Carter took some great photographs that night too, and while we all felt sorry to say good-bye, there was a sense of satisfaction among this whole impromptu team in seeing the bloom in her cheeks and the smiles lighting up her face, knowing that our love and care had helped to put them there.

On one of our nights off, Wellman invited me to go with him to hear the Ellington band, then playing downtown at a fancy jazz club called Basin Street West. We sat listening appreciatively to the almost overwhelming power and beauty of the music this band brought to every number. As they were ending their set, Duke, to my amazement, made a little speech about his old friend and longtime bass man, Wellman Braud, and then added some appreciative remarks about me. When he finished, he asked the whole band to stand in salute, and there they were, these true giants of jazz, standing and bowing to us! Well, at least to Braud. Me? I felt like Zelig sitting next to him. An extra miracle that week was seeing one of them, the man whose tenor sax magic had been one of the strong pulls toward jazz for my teenage heart, sitting in the back room of Sugar Hill trading old stories with Braud a few nights later. Yes, Ben Webster in the flesh!

21

BUZZ, BIZ, BOOM, BLAM!

In the early fall of 1961, I went down to LA with Kenny and Wellman to record *On My Way* for Capitol Records. After so much work performing together under all manner of smooth or stressful conditions, our music was as tight as a group's can be, and we had a pretty endless supply of material we loved to play. Kermit "Curly" Walter, the super-savvy producer Capitol assigned to us, brought in guitarist Billy Strange, allowing me to focus on singing and virtually silencing my utilitarian rhythm guitar in favor of his studio-pro handling of the job. We were thrilled to have two alternating world-class trap drummers in Earl Palmer and Jesse Sailes, with Rocco Wilson on conga drums, an instrument I had never thought of needing but that added enormously to the swing of the spirituals.

A few weeks before the sessions, while taking part in a civil rights movement fundraiser in Berkeley where I shared the bill with Cannonball Adderley, Wes Montgomery, and Mary Stallings, I met a group of gospel-singing teenage girls called the Andrews Sisters. I spontaneously invited them to come to Hollywood to sing backup on "This Little Light of Mine" and "I'm on My Way."

Although they were very young and this was their first studio experience, they performed with solid professionalism, and with such an exciting sound, Capitol later asked them to do an album of their own

Rehearsal with the Andrews Gospel Singers. Berkeley, California, 1961

(using the name the Andrews Gospel Singers to avoid confusion with the pop-singing Andrews Sisters). I was very proud of them.

Kenny was mind-blowing on the cornet every time he picked it up, inspiring Curly to bring in another pianist, Ray Johnson (something of a Ray Charles clone) to spell him on piano for one tune, allowing Kenny to focus on his horn for "Good Old Wagon." And to top off all this excitement, Curly commissioned a few Gerald Wilson big-band arrangements to be recorded at the end of the week. In four full working days, we actually cut usable versions of forty-two numbers, largely because once we got going we just kept right on rolling, hardly ever stopping for playbacks. I am convinced that you will almost always get the best take on the first take, if you are prepared and confident and focused, which we were.

The engineer described my voice to me as the one that had "the widest dynamics" he had ever worked with. I think he wanted me to rein in some of that, but I didn't know how. It only registered with me a few days after the sessions that I had been standing there in the same space,

Capitol Studios. Los Angeles, 1961

with the same engineer, maybe even using the same microphones, as Nat King Cole, Frank Sinatra, Judy Garland, Kay Starr, the Kingston Trio, and so many others. Am I a real professional now, or just impersonating one?

And now for some true confessions. Please keep this close to your vest. Or under your hat. Or somewhere else dark and quiet.

Something I had wished for since at least 1947 appeared as a reality just a week before those 1961 Capitol sessions began. An Ash Grove regular by the name of Dave Hubert called me to say that after years of looking for the finances to get Horizon Records started, he was finally ready to record one of his favorite folk music projects, which happened to be me. And for reasons never clear, Dave's project would have to be recorded during the very same week that I was to be closeted in the Capitol studios making my first record for them as an exclusive artist. Impossible? Well, as you must have noticed by now, I love a challenge.

So of course it was impossible to say no, but how were we going to jump these particular hurdles?

Dave said that he could wheel his big Ampex console into my friend Noël's house, where I was staying, and we could record without attracting any of the notice that working in a studio might have done. Then he suggested that I tell Capitol that I needed a day off to "rest my voice." I happened to know that Tom Paley from the New Lost City Ramblers, one of my favorite folk instrumentalists, was in town, and asked Dave to find out whether he was available to play some guitar and banjo with me. It turned out that he was free and eager to do it. So with everything in place, smack in the middle of my first chance at recording jazz, blues, and spirituals for a world-class label, I finally recorded my first and only purely folk album. The music seemed to flow freely and full of life, like a stream does when the ice has finally melted and spring has arrived, and by the end of that one afternoon, Paley and I had completed an album we were both proud of.

I decided on the spot to call it *When I Was a Young Girl*, after the first line of the opening song, an ancient ancestor of the familiar "Streets of Laredo" about a girl who is dying of syphilis, rather than "a young cowboy all wrapped in white linen." I asked Dave to use a portrait taken of me a few years earlier by Zoe Lowenthal, a dear friend and student of the great Dorothea Lange, as the cover photo. I'm seen sitting in front of a rock wall covered with English ivy, which actually was just outside my front door, holding my guitar and looking quite young indeed, as I was, and the photographic quality was superb.

This record has been pirated and sold several times over the years, the cover mangled by a yellow tint overlaying Zoe's splendid silvery black-and-white photo, and the name opportunistically changed to *Anthology of American Folk Songs* without my permission. But still I'm glad I made it because otherwise that part of my work would be completely unknown. At least nobody added drums and fake stereo.

Clearly, I hadn't hesitated to break a few eggs in order to make this particular omelet. I was pretty well aware of some of the manipulations record companies were known to use for controlling artists and their material, and knew that some of the biggest companies were notorious for treating their artists unfairly. I'm sure this knowledge was in the back of my mind, helping dispose of any need for "fairness" toward

Berkeley, 1958. © Zoe Lowenthal Brown

Capitol on my part. But truthfully, the joy and energy let loose in me by making all this music had completely overtaken my senses, and everything else just faded far off to the edges. Other artists reading these memories will understand that thing which overtakes us in the process of doing our work.

One of Capitol's biggest-selling artists at the time was blue-eyed blonde singer Peggy Lee, with her hit song "Fever." Rumor had it that Capitol planned to use me as a threat to her supremacy in case her demands were too high when contract renewal time arrived. While Lee's pot was boiling, they could conveniently keep me simmering on the back of the stove in case they needed to put pressure on her. Another ploy that is commonly used in the business is to place a five-year exclusive hold on all the material the artist records. (Dot had tried to insist on seven!) It didn't dawn on me until sometime later that in our eagerness to record as much as possible of the music we loved, we had also given up our right to record these songs for any other label for the next five years. And as if that weren't enough, the company had now acquired a whole new list of material that in effect could be used as demos that might well be suitable for their name-brand artist to record. Their A&R (Artist and Repertoire) guys were always scrambling to find the good stuff. So they gotcha, coming and going.

Capitol also insisted on buying any unissued recordings I may have been planning to use otherwise or in some other form. In my case, I had just fronted the money to record our work live at Sugar Hill, with the intention of forming a house label. I was now in possession of a full week of recordings, dozens of songs recorded in ideal live conditions. But now I had to sell the master tapes to Capitol, basically at cost, thus giving them tight control over most of my immediate professional future.

Curly Walter made his own selection of cuts for the *On My Way* album Capitol issued, and I was fine with that. He did a great job of selecting and programming what went into it, although I have no basis for comparison since the company never let me have access to listening copies of any of the other tracks.

Capitol did send me out on a promo tour soon after the release of the record, taking me to Chicago, Detroit, and some other cities I can't recall. Because there was a school break, I decided to take my two younger children, Nina (six years old) and Paul (nine), along with me for a chance to show them what I did when I was away from home. They were great company for me too, and I was delighted with their ability to fit into things, watching them absorb new scenes, meet new people, and deal with new situations with such ease. They never caused the slightest problem or held me back from any of my commitments, either. If only I could have involved them more closely during those years, I wouldn't have felt so lonely for them. But although I managed to pay all their expenses this time, I couldn't have done that without coming home empty handed most of the time. The only sour note was when someone in the PR department at Capitol suggested later that perhaps it was because I had taken the children with me on the promo tour that the company had cooled on me. My own opinion is that they stopped answering my phone calls because the State Department or the FBI had been poking around and casting shadows on my character upstairs in the famous round tower on Vine Street.

A few years after Curly Walter had moved to another company, I tracked him down to ask what he remembered of the sessions. He insisted that all of it was worthy of issuing, and said that they might have refused to give me listening copies of the unissued material for fear that I would find a way to put it out without them, as indeed I probably would have done. As it stands today, more than fifty years later, close to thirty songs are still trapped in those dark metal cans, in some dank storage room, two-inch audiotape slowly deteriorating over the years, all that music busting to make people laugh and dance and love and feel happy. And contractually, the company is not obligated to issue anything an artist has ever recorded. Repeat, not obligated to issue anything.

After the sessions in LA, and before heading back to San Francisco, I was booked at the Hollywood Bowl, capacity close to twenty thousand, by an office called Concerts, Inc. But I wasn't impressed because the Bowl had been just over the hill in back of my home on Rockledge, a place where my kids went to explore on days when nothing was going on, so it felt almost like doing a gig in my backyard. Kenny and Wellman would be backing me, and the rest of the bill fit right in with the title of the show: *Dixie at the Bowl*. There would be Kid Ory with his band, Pete Fountain with his quintet, the Dukes of Dixieland, and the three of us. As I recall, everything went according to plan, easily and professionally, but it's all a blur now. My mind was on Sugar Hill.

The club quickly became well known as a great place to hang out for the local progressive politicians, and I'm told that the politically powerful Burtons and their friends were often in attendance. I was usually on the stage singing or in the back room catching a breather, so I was never sure who might be included in this crowd, but I could see faces I recognized and people I loved, like Tillie and Jack Olsen, Malvina and Bud Reynolds, some of the artists I had met when I lived upstairs from Margaret De Patta and Gene Bielawski in the house on Laidley, the North Beach regulars, poets and musicians and comics and actors and the whole gamut of contemporary SF bohemia. And there in the center of it all was Norma Aston, now spending more time in San Francisco surrounded by some of the most interesting people in town and even finding her name in the papers.

Some months before the Sugar Hill idea had come into Norma's life, she had booked a cruise that was to last for several weeks and take her far away. Maybe she had already been craving an escape from La Jolla and the life of a banker's wife, sick of driving her four children to soccer practice or whatever. Well, now it was time for her to leave on this voyage to wherever. I wondered what would happen with her out of reach for so long, since we didn't have any backup funds in case something unforeseen came up.

Things went quite smoothly during the club's first several months in business. We watched the clientele build as the musicians more than rewarded the regulars with great and heartfelt blues night after night, just the way I had dreamed the club would be. I was able to sing for a warm and receptive audience most every night, stretching myself sometimes in unexpected ways, and there was much joy in watching a real community building around Sugar Hill. Kenny and Wellman, too, were finding the work, the club, and the city ideal, and were accumulating their own circles of friends. I felt at home with all these people, the new friends as well as the many people I had learned to love ever since my first arrival in San Francisco back in 1949, who kept turning up. I was able to come to work every night with my husband and to be with my children every day, never doubting that I could go on like this for many happy and productive years.

And now it was time for a coup I had been cooking up for a long while: the first appearance on the West Coast of the great Mississippi piano blues and jazz man Mose Allison, in December 1961. I had first heard him on his early records that we often played during the breaks at Cosmo Alley, back in Hollywood.

Mose came from the white side of a little town called Tippo, Mississippi, not far from Tupelo, where Elvis Presley was born, yet he seemed to carry an enlightened racial attitude and modern thinking about many things. What he had that truly set him apart were his incredible jazz piano chops. He could seamlessly travel the keyboard from deep, dark blues to red hot and cool bop, including plenty of stride too, and as the years moved on, his talents had only grown deeper. He began writing songs, always rich with meaning, and some writer even dubbed him the William Faulkner of the blues. He continued touring until near the end of his life in 2016.

As soon as the word got out that Mose was in town, we had lines running in both directions on the sidewalk outside the club. The hunger to catch him live was enormous, and the ambience we had already laid down made Sugar Hill the perfect place for him to connect with this throng of admirers. Another little dream of mine come true.

And then, right in the middle of all this elation, Norma Aston returned from her cruise. Blam! That's when the shit hit the fan. She saw all these wallets lined up outside and decided that right now we were going to impose an entrance fee. I said, "Oh no, we're not," and it began to escalate from there, so I walked away, beckoning Byron to follow me out the door, past the crowds and down the street to the Matador, the better to reconvene in a quiet neutral place.

When Mose finished the set he was playing, I asked Byron to corner him and bring him to where I waited, saying we needed to talk about something important. Once we were out of earshot and away from the hysteria back at the club, I explained to Mose what Aston was demanding, and why it was important for us to resist any change of policy. I assured him that, whatever happened, none of this would affect his personal financial takeaway. Then I asked whether he would be willing to withhold his services—in other words, go on strike until we had Aston's commitment not to interfere with our standing policy. Apart from singing them, Mose is a man of few words and basically indicated that he didn't want to get involved, that he would have to go ahead and perform as planned, would have to fulfill his contract.

I'm not at all sure what more Byron and I did that night, probably just cut for home and some sleep. I have a sometimes frustrating habit of shutting the doors in my brain so that the bad stuff can't get in, and now, as I'm trying to take you through this mess, I find myself unable to re-create it. All I know is that we were suddenly on the outside. Norma got across to us that she was no longer going to tolerate my policies, that as of now, Byron was replaced by Warren, the doorman from the Jazz Workshop across the street and now her lover, and that from here on she would do the booking, which did not include my services. My beloved musicians Kenny and Wellman would have to deal with her directly now and decide whether they wanted to stick around. She also informed us that we could not expect any more paychecks, starting now. Oh yeah, the woman had a heart of gold.

Well, luckily, we had set things up so that we were employees, with the club paying each of us a regular weekly paycheck from the beginning. This meant we were now able to apply for unemployment insurance, and I began to make the rounds of various law offices, anywhere I had reason to believe someone would have been sympathetic and maybe even a fan of the club. I was trying to find a lawyer who would help me sue for my rights, and although all of them were kind, the best they could do was point out to me that because I had no written contract, I, in fact, had no rights, that there was really nothing that could be accomplished in the courts. Many weeks went by in this fruitless search, and finally Norma sent word that her banker husband was going to arrive in San Francisco with the intention of terminating any further business between us.

I made a date to meet with Aston and Aston in the office of one of the lawyers who had defended Harry Bridges, the world-famous organizer of the longshoreman's union whose many tangles with the law over the past forty years had required at least half a dozen on his legal team to keep him from being deported. All of them, Richard Gladstein, Aubrey Grossman, Vincent Hallinan, and the others, were among America's most noble and brilliant civil rights attorneys, overkill indeed for my little situation, but I was pretty sure that most of them had been to the club at some time and would understand the potential cultural losses at stake in addition to my modest livelihood. Their generosity in allowing us to play out this drama in their offices provided me with an atmosphere of security, the feeling that, while it might not be possible for justice to be done, at least I was not going to be disrespected or misused. It became crystal clear at this meeting that there was nothing further we could do through legal means, that the Astons had all the cards, and that we could do nothing but gracefully leave. As we walked out the door, I resolved not to enter Sugar Hill ever again, even to collect my clothes, LPs and tapes, papers, or anything else I could have claimed as my property. I thought of calling a press conference, but even that gesture felt undignified and useless. So good-bye to all that. A new door would open up ahead. Of this I was sure, and of course it is always true. Just don't trip over yourself by looking down as you make your way toward it.

Falling from the sky and right into our desperate income gap following the Sugar Hill disaster was an offer from Gerd Stern, one of the original Beat poets and one of the founders of KPFA. I didn't know him, but he had apparently enjoyed many visits to Sugar Hill, and just as the news reached him of the collapse of my dreams, he was about to leave for an extended vacation. In a fit of generosity, he decided to offer the use of his home on a big barge in Sausalito as a temporary folk music club while he was gone. I immediately saw what an appealing idea this was, and Byron readily agreed. We quickly printed up a fistful of invitations summoning the masses to the inauguration of the Barge, sponsored by the Muddy Bottom Folk and Blues Society. Back in business, if only for a few minutes.

 Sitting comfortably in the mud next to the legendary—or, more accurately, notorious—Juanita's Galley, the Barge would be easy for our followers to find. Checking out the premises, I saw that there was a big enclosed deck area, but very little furniture of any kind. Another denizen of Sugar Hill came up with exactly the right inspiration: he said that since he was a carpet salesman, he could bring me several big stacks of outdated samples from his store for folks to sit on. And how would we collect the admissions that would support this venture? As the visitors handed over their two dollars, they would be handed back a piece of carpet like a receipt, to be turned in at the end of the evening but that meanwhile would enable the listeners to avoid getting splinters in the butt from sitting on the old barge deck itself. People seemed to love this arrangement, and we were an immediate hit! Problem was, no piano and no room for a bass either. So there I was, alone again with my basic guitar and a little stool to sit on, the only rhythm provided by my foot stomping and the handclaps and finger snaps of the listeners, plus some tambourines I sometimes passed around.

I think Byron must have contrived some things to sell—glasses of wine or beer, coffee, and so on. But, with no liquor license, this time we had to depend on a two-dollar door charge, and nobody seemed to think that was out of place. We opened only two or three nights a week for a few months, but this brought in enough to help us out by augmenting our unemployment insurance while also serving to keep us in the lives of the fans we had come to love. The houseboat community there in Sausalito was constantly in danger of being shut down, accused of dumping raw sewage into the bay and other offenses, and was generally seen as a huge ugly wart on the high-end waterfront property the real estate machine was always working to expand. We knew this great little no-rent scene of ours couldn't last, but we enjoyed it to the max while it was happening, and I know that many folks who were around then still remember it fondly.

22

ON THE *EMES*, THIS IS TRUE

About this time, Albert Grossman was outgrowing the confines of one small folk club in Chicago and sold his half of the Gate of Horn to his partner, Alan Ribback. So now there was a brand-new Chicago scene featuring the opening of the reborn Gate of Horn, in a building specially designed and built to be a jazz club. Ribback had decided to "do it right," and he did, spending a large chunk of his trust fund, or wherever he got all that cash. OK, but the problem was that a club like the Gate would always feel more "right" in a grungy repurposed warehouse or other architectural dump. Here, we had a professional dressing room, with its own large mirrors and bathroom, matching chairs in the showroom, a super grand piano, well designed lighting, and so on. Still, none of this could make it "right." Money couldn't buy that.

For this grand opening engagement in early 1962, I was cobilled for a three-week run with Lenny Bruce, who was at the top of his form in those days. I had not been able to book either of my usual Chicago pianists, Memphis Slim or Little Brother Montgomery, so I took a chance on another legendary piano man well known by the name of the Honeydripper (or as his mama called him, Roosevelt Sykes), with Ransom Knowling on bass. Knowling was the same bassist who played on one of those old 78s with Big Bill Broonzy's guitar that had hooked me on the blues when I was a kid in high school, and he still knocked me

Barbara Dane with Roosevelt Sykes (left) and Ransom Knowling (center). Chicago, 1962

out. I found out that his day gig was as playground director at a South Side school. Even musicians as good as he was needed to have a reliable source of income. Sykes was accustomed to being the main focus, with his own "act," but he suppressed that in the interest of doing a great job for me, and probably hoped to be booked again on his own at a later date.

I had come in early that first night to make myself comfortable in this new set of circumstances, and someone else had come in early too, just to greet me and give me his best wishes for the opening. It was Big Joe Williams, looking like I had never seen him before: freshly shaven and with a new haircut, dressed in a nicely pressed suit over a white shirt, with a handkerchief in the pocket and a pin in his lapel signifying his membership in ASCAP! I was touched almost to tears at the effort he had made to come in looking like a proper gentleman, and even when I think of it today I'm touched and humbled. I knew he had wanted me to see that he could show up as a man of dignity, but I wonder whether he ever realized the high regard I had for him as a deep man, an authentic man. I even saw his struggle for dignity when he was dressed in the same clothes he had probably slept in for days, stinking of cheap booze and bad food, with his great heart that had clearly survived a thousand lonely nights without ever allowing him to be less than a gentleman as far as I could see. I miss you, Joe.

One night early that first week, Lenny invited a few friends into our small dressing room—the entire Harlem Globetrotters team, filling the room literally from wall to wall as well as from floor to ceiling! Beautiful buffed Black bodies, as graceful in life as in art, topped by the smiling faces of gods, beaming down on me from high above. A sight one doesn't soon forget. I might have experienced a slight frisson, but my job was to keep on doing my makeup and getting dressed, since I was the opening act and it was almost showtime. Lenny, for his part, entertained them effortlessly with improvised basketball jokes.

At this juncture of his life, Lenny seemed super clean, sharp, and eager to connect with all the show people in town, the loose-knit society of performers who floated around the country doing cabaret, stage shows, circus, theater, clubs, burlesque, and, yes, basketball ballet—almost any kind of way a living person could communicate with a live audience. He loved them all on principle. Growing up with a mother who worked in burlesque, he considered this amorphous society his "family" and his "hometown," albeit without real estate. So what did he do? He sent out telegrams to all of the showfolk currently working in live shows in Chicago at that moment, from clubs and stages all over town, inviting them to the Gate for a special late-night performance that would be open only to those who presented their telegrams or were on his list.

What unfolded onstage was one of the most masterful live performances I have ever seen. Once in a while, a figure from a familiar bit would appear, like Father Flotsky or Bela Lugosi or the Djinni in the Candy Store, but for the most part Lenny was off into even deeper territory than usual, improvising more rapidly and effectively, flashing bits of impersonation and mimicry more vividly and incisively than seemed humanly possible and, like never before, ripping to shreds the hypocrisy and chicanery then, as now, rampant in high places. There is no recording of this phenomenal evening, but you can get a glimpse of Lenny's genius on some of the collections still available. Please don't go on much further with your life until you connect with some of it, because, while you will be amazed at his humor and entertained by his hipness, your understanding of the human condition will be altered forever.

One night, Lenny and I both received telegrams from none other than Hugh Hefner: "I would like the pleasure of your company at a party in my home, tonight at 1 am until ? in honor of Dick Gregory." With an accomplice like Lenny, I was sure to have an interesting night. He'd obviously been there before and took it on himself to show me the highlights. We settled in for a drink in a room downstairs with a big glass wall where one could see whatever people were doing underwater in the pool upstairs.

We never did spot Dick that night, but I had met him a few years before when he was an unknown, out-of-work comedian. One night at the Gate, I was in the bar relaxing while the opening act did their thing, when a Black guy in a nice-looking suit said hello. I think he might have seen some of the recent press about me, or maybe he was just feeling lucky, so he struck up a conversation with me. He began by telling me that

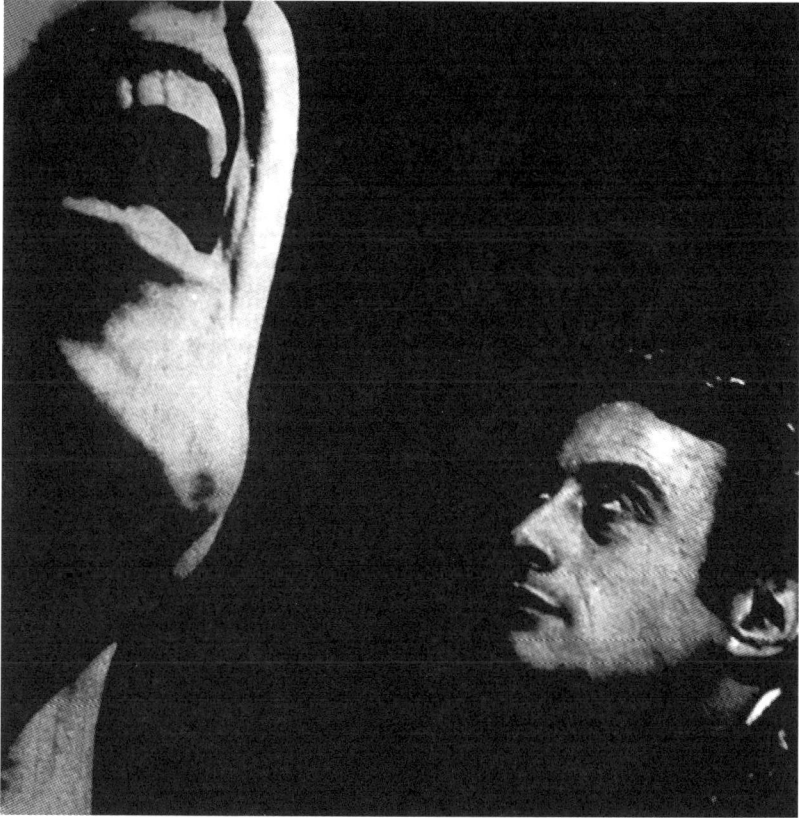

Lenny Bruce. Chicago, 1962

he was a comedian and talking about how hard it was for Black comedy to find an opening in any mainstream clubs. He even began reeling off a couple of his bits, and when I saw that he was actually funny as hell, with a decided political slant to his humor, I said, "Hey, one of these days I'm going to have a blues club in San Francisco, and I'll be sure to book you when I do." Who would have guessed that by the time I had finally opened my blues club, a year or so later, Dick Gregory would already be all over *Time* magazine and famous!

I have a photo of Lenny standing in the dark outside the Gate of Horn with snow falling all around, as he looks up at a giant blowup of my face and the big marquee with my name on it. He staged the photo, of course, as a little gift to another struggling artist. That was my last experience there, because the brand-new shiny club didn't last long.

By the early 1960s, they had begun busting Lenny just about every time he appeared on a stage. He had alienated too many Catholic cops with his cheeky Pope routines, while infuriating the secular others by contrasting the ugliness of racism and war with the simple act of making love to the object of one's affection, a practice known colloquially as "fucking." He had the nerve to go on shredding the sacred national delusion that we generous Americans only bring good to a suffering world, and he wouldn't stop exposing how routinely we punish our own for mere possession of a different kind of hair or degree of pigmentation, or for discovering a different way of expressing love, or giving our love to persons of the wrong gender. No, he'd never surrender to hypocrisy, which meant they just couldn't leave him alone. And anyone could see that there was no way he would back off from his mission.

A couple of months after our run at the Gate of Horn in Chicago, Lenny was arrested on obscenity charges after his opening set at the Jazz Workshop in San Francisco, right across the street from the Sugar Hill. During the trial, he asked the handful of friends who were hanging with him in his hotel room to lend moral support what we thought of his idea for avoiding the unflattering news photos that kept cropping up in the *Chronicle* and other publications making sport of him more often than not. He would take a lipstick and write the letters F-U-C-K across his forehead so that it would show up in the photo, thus rendering it unusable in those uptight family venues. Go for it, we said, and go for it, he did. It worked for a day or two.

He knew I was having financial troubles at that time, so, as he walked me to my car after that day in the courtroom, he pressed a twenty and a ten in my hand. That was the last time I saw him alive, leaving me with an incurable case of unresolved Lenny.

In 1966, after enduring years of constant harassment, arrests, and trials, Lenny was murdered by that notorious instrument of self-destruction that seeks out creative artists whose world has failed them—a drug overdose. The stark scene of Lenny's lonely and desperate death on the floor of a squalid bathroom haunts me to this day. Oh grieve, good hearts, for this brilliant soul, crushed by the empty, relentless offensive of law and order, destroyed for loving the world too much, eaten alive by that vengeful monster whose name is American hypocrisy. He was only forty.

23

WAKE UP AND SING!

Ten years had passed since I had my foray into the early days of TV with my show, *Folksville USA*. Now it seems that the suits upstairs had gotten wind of the fact that folk music was beginning to boom, and they wanted more, hoping to draw in younger audiences.

Wake Up and Sing was a weekly half-hour children's show I was drafted for in 1962 on KPIX-TV, one of San Francisco's major television pioneers. I used Woody Guthrie's trusty "Wake Up, Wake Up" as the theme song. I also introduced Malvina Reynolds's "Little Boxes" on that show, and drew on a considerable amount of our own favorite family songs to share as generously as possible with all these young potential folk music fans.

One week I lacked a babysitter and so had to bring two of my little ones, Nina, four, and Paul, seven, along with me. On the way over the bridge, I heard the sound of a harmonica in the backseat. Busy with all the other daily struggles, I hadn't been aware that my budding little musician was making all this progress on his own, so to encourage him I asked that he play along with me on some song I was thinking of using when we got to the taping session. He fell right in with the idea of fearlessly improvising either harmony or call-and-response parts, maybe picked up from having watched trad jazz bands or Sonny Terry rehearse for half his life, and I decided on the spot to have him play on the show.

We continued this game until we arrived on the set, where I instructed Paul to stand in a corner far at the rear, and explained that when I nodded toward him, he should start slowly walking across the back of the set while playing along with whatever I was singing, and then "disappear" on the other side. We may have run through it once, maybe not. Studio time was always limited. But I know that the taping came out very well. And who could predict that during the early years of the twenty-first century, Paul would be the one to introduce the blues harp to Cuba?

Beginning in June, I sang frequently with trad jazz bands on a nationally syndicated variety show called *PM East/PM West,* based on the idea of switching between live audiences on the two coasts. I heard Barbra Streisand for the first time on the *PM East* part, just a kid doing her first TV work and stunning everyone with that voice.

Around the same time, I was asked to perform in an episode of *Checkmate*, a popular TV show inspired by that master of detective fiction, Eric Ambler, filmed mostly on the Universal backlot. My scene in the episode, called "Side by Side," is set in a recording studio, and I am irrelevant to the plot, just someone cutting a record, a "gospel singer from the Rockies" who stands in bare feet behind the glass separating the control room, strumming her guitar and singing . . . what else? "I'm on My Way"!

I also appeared on an episode of *Alfred Hitchcock Presents* in 1962 titled "Captive Audience," starring James Mason and Angie Dickinson. I was charmed by Mason, a delightful person to work with, provoking little improv humor bits with the other actors during breaks in the shooting. Understanding that I was a novice at this kind of filming, he made a point of coming into my dressing trailer just to chat and help me relax. "You can't make enough of a living just being James Mason," he said, "so I take a lot of cowboy sidekick roles. You wouldn't recognize me because I wear a big ten-gallon hat pulled over my eyes most of the time." I'm 95 percent sure he was joking, but you never know.

What I appreciated most was the way he handled the scenes where I was singing. At first I am shown standing against a brick wall with my guitar, singing "I'm on My Way" while he watches intently. Then his girlfriend (played by Angie) comes in with a friend, who is suddenly "called away" when Mason comes over to their table. This is a planned meeting in which the two are supposed not to have seen each other for some years. I finish my first song, and begin singing "Goodbye, Daddy, Goodbye" as the camera leaves me behind.

But Mason continues to glance over to where I am singing, and it seemed clear to me, watching this later, that with his glances he was purposely helping maintain the viewer's interest in me even as he was scheming with Angie's character. A nice gesture toward a young cast member just breaking into theatrical TV. A few weeks later I received a congratulatory postcard from James Mason, and not long after that, a kind note from Angie Dickinson. Good folks.

My dad, watching the show in Detroit, was excited and proud, and he called to tell me so. But soon after that, I got the news that he had had a severe stroke and would be mostly confined to life in a wheelchair. His second wife, Dotty, was having her own troubles, her world beginning to fall apart after she too fell ill, diagnosed with lupus. They hired part-time help, a woman named Ruby who reported to my sister that Dotty had begun to hide money all over the house, accusing everyone around her of wrongdoing in her fits of paranoia. It wasn't long before Dotty left altogether, and Dad decided it would be best for everyone if he got a divorce. I was pretty overwhelmed with my own life just then, so there was no way I could head for Detroit. The job of helping Dad find an accessible and affordable duplex, settling him in it, and hiring a full-time caregiver was left to my sister. Julia shouldered the responsibility with no complaints, even though her own situation was precarious and difficult. I shut my eyes and turned back into my own swamp of circumstance.

In the summer of 1962, we moved into a big old house on Josephine Street in Berkeley. It was, in its way, the perfect home for us at that time because of its size and its location in the heart of Berkeley only a couple of blocks from Garfield Junior High (now Martin Luther King Jr. High) and a few more blocks to Berkeley High. Nicky was fifteen and had his own room at the back of the upstairs, giving him the privacy I thought was needed by someone his age. Paul and Nina each had a room too, next to mine, and the main floor had plenty of space, with a living room and dining room separated only by sliding doors, a typical feature in Berkeley houses of a certain age. The kitchen was small, but it had a separate pantry where the sink was. I remember once, having just returned from Chicago and all the attention and press, I was on my knees scrubbing that pantry floor and thinking that it was good for my character and even good for my work, that, besides being useful, these everyday tasks gave me an important balance between the stage spotlights and real life in a neighborhood, something that helped me keep my feet on the ground.

One day my younger son, Paul, came home from visiting a friend across the street, with some big questions: "Mom, why don't we have those little lacy things on the back of the chairs like Joey does? And why can't you be here when I come home from school, to give me milk and cookies like his mom does?"

"Well, Son, I could do that if it's important to you. But it takes a lot of time to crochet those antimacassars and doilies, and I would have to stop going away to sing if I was to be here every day. We wouldn't have much money then," I explained, "so we might have to move to a cheaper place. So what would you like me to do? I'm going to ask the other kids if they want the same as you, and we'll figure it out." His face became very serious, but after a few moments of thought he said, "OK, I think we should keep it like it is. Thanks, Mom." I guess we both wanted to hang on to this place, this life, as long as possible.

In October 1962, our quiet neighborhood, along with the entire world, was on red alert because of the possibility that a confrontation between the US and the USSR over nuclear-tipped weapons positioned in Cuba could trigger a nuclear war. Here, we call it the Cuban Missile Crisis, but in Cuba they call it the October Crisis to distinguish this one from so many others the US has visited on them. The real reasons for this terrifying situation, not to mention the obfuscations and manipulations, are important to understand. It sends a chill up my spine even now to think how close we were to doomsday.

As the tension built day after day, everyone's eyes were on the TV news, hoping to understand what was happening. People began to check on the whereabouts of distant family members, and all over town, folks were drawing their children together. I began to call Rolf's house looking for Nicky, who had been staying there, but there was never an answer. I had to assume that my older boy was in good hands with his father, although inwardly I was gripped with fear. I found out later that Rolf had literally headed for the hills, leaving his son alone to fend for himself. Byron and I took the other two children and joined the neighbors from the block at a house across the street that had somehow become the gathering place. There we sang and talked and sang and talked, long into the evening, nobody wanting to sit alone at home stewing in their individual fears.

Nina, now almost seven, had begun teaching herself long and complicated songs when I was away singing out of town. She first developed this interest in song texts by sitting with me in a big old rocking chair where she helped me learn my newest repertoire as we rocked, mother and daughter in perfect synchrony. On this particular night, she stood up in the circle of neighbors and declared that she had a new song for us. In a firm and steady voice, she sang, "There's blood on the coal and the miners lie, in roads that never saw sun nor sky" and "There's no more water nor light nor bread, so we'll live on songs and hope instead!" By the time she was finished singing "Springhill Mine Disaster," the room was pretty much struck dumb. But then with an uncanny sense of programming, she broke the spell by following up with "A Jug o' Punch," a comical old drinking song that everyone could join in on, and of course everybody did.

To the relief of millions, the missile crisis was resolved through diplomacy and not through warfare of any kind, except for the ongoing propaganda war against Cuba and the decades-long economic warfare of the blockade that prevents any ship unloading goods there from continuing on to the US for further trade. This is only one of the thousands of rules and regulations meant to deprive the country of normal trade relations with the world, rules that persist to this day, long after the demise of the USSR and any excuse it may have provided for our government's ongoing attempt to starve the Cuban economy.

24

DO YOU, MISTER JONES?

In the midst of one of New York's coldest winters, I went back to the city for a solo spot opposite one of the well-known hot jazz bands still operating. The club was down a long flight of stairs on the south side of West 4th Street in Greenwich Village. The featured outfit was called the New New Orleans Jazz Band [sic], with Sidney De Paris on trumpet and brother Wilbur on trombone, but the musician I most admired was a tall brown good-looking man from Ohio called Garvin Bushell, who had played with everyone from Fats Waller, Ethel Waters, and Cab Calloway up to Miles Davis and Coltrane, but at this moment was replacing the late Omer Simeon on clarinet. He could have been playing his bassoon, oboe, or English horn, but he took that clarinet seriously on those oddly uncrowded nights in the Village and heated things up considerably. It happened to be a week marked by spectacular New York snowstorms, and almost nobody was out there willing to brave the weather, nobody but musicians and other workers who couldn't afford to take the income loss if they stayed home, and the cab drivers who struggled to get them to their work. Some nights we played mostly for empty chairs.

An old acquaintance, Irwin Silber, the editor of *Sing Out!* magazine, got in touch and asked whether he could interview me for a story while I was in town. After nearly twenty years of reading Irwin's articles and column notes, I felt secure that the outcome would be worth the trouble, so I was delighted to make the trip to the apartment on the Lower East Side where he and his family lived. I arrived at dinnertime and greeted his wife, Sylvia, as she left, on her way out to a meeting with community peace volunteers, leaving Irwin to handle the care and feeding of their three children. I watched him move competently through the various tasks while we warmed up the conversation, happy to find myself in a comfortable, homey scene instead of the usual office or bar where most interviews were conducted then, as now.

And now, one of the most coveted television appearances any working performer could imagine was suddenly on my calendar. The *Tonight Show with Johnny Carson,* nightly from the NBC studio at 30 Rockefeller Plaza in New York, was the springboard to success for dozens of artists, and I was booked for January 10, 1963. I was given the usual allotment of two songs, and earlier in the day I discussed and rehearsed them with the bandleader and his big band. First I would do the most intense and philosophically deep blues I know, "Trouble in Mind," and then something peppy and funny, another blues but totally different.

The other guests that night were Horst Buchholz, an actor sometimes called the German James Dean and well-known for his TV work on *The Magnificent Seven,* and Jane Withers, who had been a famous child actress playing the foil, the mean older girl, to the darling little Shirley Temple, but now known for her commercials, most notably for a kitchen cleanser (Comet) where she plays an allegedly amusing character known as Josephine the Plumber. Buchholz did his thing and split. He was a star. Now it was my turn.

I was well aware that in 1963, the couch 'taters white or Black from coast to coast were mostly innocent of blues history and culture, and because of this, I always set up the songs by offering some background on the song and certainly something about whoever originally wrote or popularized the piece. All this was said, and I was digging deep into the emotional space the delivery would require when suddenly the band strikes up the intro to the peppy tune meant for the second song!! What was I to do?

Instead of shouting out "STOP RIGHT THERE!" I did what a team player would do: adjust what I'm doing to make sense with what the rest are doing, and keep going. I ended up inventing new lyrics on the fly, which of course couldn't have conveyed my original intention, the complexity of which would certainly have been reflected on my face, which made matters worse. I had to do the same thing when the second song came around, only this time to a slow tune, the one I had originally introduced. It was a mess. I wanted to crawl under a rock and hide, but there wasn't any. All I could think of to make things a little better was to wait for the talk time, when I could try to explain my dilemma and basically ask whether the bandleader had been drunk or what. You will forgive me if I'm not sure whether it was Doc Severinsen or Skitch Henderson running the music that night; I would have killed either one, but it's illegal.

Remember, this was the most popular TV show at the time, and it was running live. The last minutes are ticking away. Carson invites me and Withers to sit on the couch, but with Withers near him in the hot spot and me down at the cold end. He engages Jane in a discussion of how she likes playing the part of a plumber, she guffaws a bit, the theme music comes up, and the show ends. Maybe someone says something to me after the lights are snuffed, but I don't remember. I took a taxi to my mom's place and went straight to bed. I got my check in the mail, but no further comment from anyone. Maybe that's the biggest break I got from the show.

In the spring of 1963, I went back to New York to record a two-part Westinghouse TV miniseries, one of the first nationally broadcast shows featuring folk music. The first was *They Call It Folk Music* and the second, *Folk Songs and More Folk Songs*.

The show was built around John Henry Faulk, folklorist, storyteller, and radio personality who had just won a large settlement in a lawsuit against Aware, one of the primary movers of media blacklisting, effectively breaking their back. The talent roster was lengthy and included the Staple Singers, Bob Dylan, Carolyn Hester, the New Lost City Ramblers, Brother John Sellers, the Brothers Four, and others.

The producer, Michael Santangelo, with whom I had worked on the *PM East/PM West* shows the year before, was doing his best to work with a seriously cheesy set made of simple cartoon drawings to simulate, well, a train ride to nowhere. Hard to know what Westinghouse thought it was doing. The show seems to have been conceived of as a series for

Program for *They Call It Folk Music*, KPIX-TV, 1963

teenagers, featuring some two-dimensional version of "America" with a lot of patriotic dialogue. Something that could reinstate Faulk as a genuwine American, a kind of Will Rogers–like figure, the better to turn him into a marketable product again. Somebody upstairs must have realized there was a hunger for folk music, real or surreal, growing out there in television land, without a clue about how to capture or portray it.

On that last episode, I sang the folk songs wearing a simple corduroy dress to avoid the usual clichéd look of the 1960s revival singers. It was a chilly early spring in New York, and I had come to work at the rehearsal wearing some clunky ankle-high boots, something nobody in those days would have worn on a show. I kept them on through the day because we got so busy I forgot to change to my "ladylike" shoes. But Santangelo thought they were terribly hip looking. Well, he was a New Yorker and a slick professional guy, and I felt like a hick from California, so I didn't argue, and wore them for the "folk look."

For the blues, I changed to a dress I had made myself from a three-yard-long remnant of some beautiful grayish-violet crepe fabric, and canned the boots for a pair of low-heeled pumps. I even changed my makeup. I had spent a bit of time that past week in New York hanging out with Francesca Raskin, a new friend who was the warm and generous female half of a folkish cabaret team called Gene and Francesca ("Those were the days, my friend, I thought they'd never end"). She introduced me to the miracle of false eyelashes, so, for the first and only time, I wore them to achieve a more appropriate look for the blues part of the story, which is what I saw the whole program to be—a story. Santangelo brought in a first-class New York jazz trio to accompany me, what you might call "very cool cats," super experienced at studio work, so with almost no rehearsal we did a surprisingly good job together.

As the opening credits rolled, the whole cast was instructed to walk single file in front of the camera and on across the set. Dylan was walking directly in front of me, and you can see in the clip his flash of "OK, whatever . . ." to the camera, barely suppressing a rolling of his eyes, in contrast to the rest of us all grinning in jolly feigned conviviality.

But I had a little problem. Bob, in the way of many a neo-folk guitarist, often including myself, had left the wires of his guitar strings uncut and flying loose right in my line of sight. Having years ago had an eyelid ripped open by a similar wire, flung at me by my baby son, Nicky, as I held him up to see some duckies in a cage, these wires really spooked me. Back in the dressing room before the actual filming, I noticed Bob fluffing up his hair in the mirror, the better to make it look super wild, but I took courage in hand, explained my problem, and asked

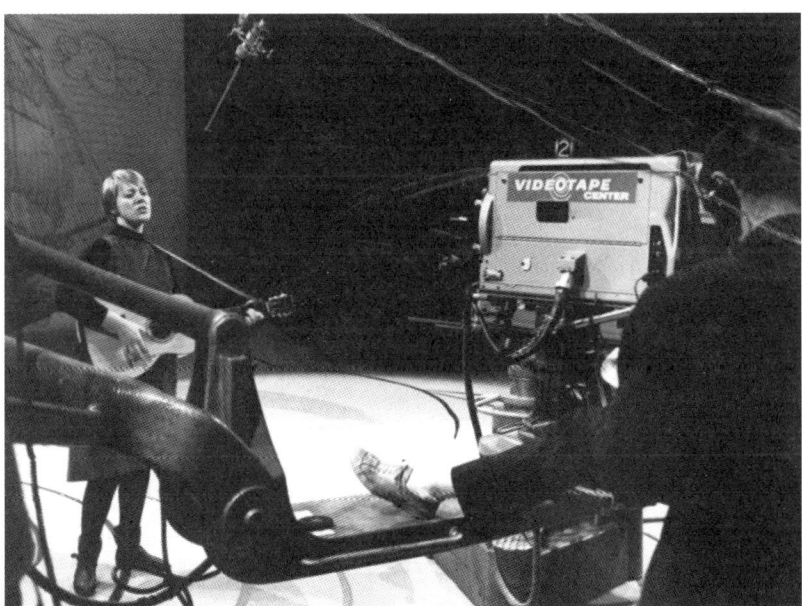

Westinghouse TV studios. New York City, 1963

whether he would mind clipping off the ends of those steel strings. To my amazement and relief, he apologized and immediately complied. In my heart I thanked his mother for teaching him to be a nice boy.

No, wait—I want to back off from making light of Bob's efforts to be accepted, to connect, to be seen, to give what he had to give. There were certain ways I too was still a youngster like that inside, a hick from the outskirts of Detroit, and a "chick" on top of that. I knew all too well what a fine line between being annoying and being helpful one had to walk in order to find your way into the place where the action is. Bob, of course, had that extra thing going for him: an enormous talent hidden inside an endearing young scalawag.

As we were leaving the TV studio, I mentioned that I was on my way to WNYC to do an interview on Oscar Brand's long-standing *World of Folk Music* radio show. Bob asked if he could come along, offering to play if I needed any backup. It was actually companionable and comforting to have him with me, and I believe he did play a little guitar or harp too.

On the Faulk show, Bob sang "Blowin' in the Wind," probably the first time America heard it, and then his version of "Man of Constant Sorrow" and "The Ballad of Hollis Brown," two chillingly etched stories of a farmer and his desperately hungry family, one from tradition and the other by the singer. In spite of the more seasoned performers on the show, myself included, it was obvious that he was the most effective, the most genuine. And then there were the Staple Singers featuring Mavis, her fresh young face and a voice that could move mountains. As for me, I was too busy playing roles that I thought were required for the story. Or maybe just thinking of ways to flaunt my versatility? Watching your own work on television can be a soberingly instructive way to learn what's wrong with what you do in performance. Mostly, I was not delivering the kind of performance I appreciate, not at all. I was perfect, but I was not good.

I first heard of Bobby the year before the Faulk show. I was strolling down Telegraph Avenue ("the Avenue") toward the Berkeley campus with the great Bessie Jones, founder of the Georgia Sea Island Singers and the person Alan Lomax valued as the single richest source of African roots music and lore he had come across in the US. She was there to perform at the Berkeley Folk Music Festival, but I'm sure most people there had no idea of the depth of her folk wisdom beyond music at this point. We were just getting acquainted, and I had invited her for a little lunch up on the Avenue, assuming that she didn't know a soul in town and might like some compatible companionship. As we passed the open door of a small record shop that habitually directed the sounds of some of its latest releases out to the street, the voice of a young man with guitar floated on the air, an oddly Woody Guthrie–ish nasal sound punctuated by some wheezy harmonica. Bessie halted in front and asked me to wait while she went inside. Soon she returned holding out an LP that she had signed with her thanks for the meal. "This here is Bobby Dylan," she said. "He came to visit us back home at St. Simon's Island, even stayed a while. You know, that Bobby is just a poor boy a long way from home."

Soon after the Faulk TV show, I found myself back in Los Angeles for another Ash Grove run. One morning, I received a phone call from Ben Shapiro. Without mentioning any names, Ben urged me to come by his house that afternoon to get acquainted with his latest discovery, a young songwriter-singer he was excited about. He suggested that I bring a recording machine so that I could capture some of his songs for my repertoire.

When I arrived at the Shapiros, Albert Grossman was there, as was Miles Davis, but the three of them soon vanished into the back room and left me with, guess who? Bob Dylan. Well, of course, we already knew each other from the John Henry Faulk special. Bob was eager to get on with his mission, so he unboxed his guitar as he offered to sing me a few of his latest compositions. I sat down on the carpet next to my faithful old Wollensak reel-to-reel machine, loaded a new tape into it, and we were off! I still have that tape, with a digitized copy for easier access, where between those incredible songs the only sounds you hear are my exclamations, mostly wordless gasps of amazement and delight. As he sang them one after another, each more surprising than the last, I realized I was hearing something that was going to change the landscape of American song. Bob was about to record a number of them for his second album. An unforgettable day, but we weren't done yet.

As I was packing up my recording equipment, I met Miles for a minute, said hello and good-bye to Albert, and wondered in passing whether he had been making a pitch to manage Miles as well. I thanked

Ben for inviting me over, and left to get a little rest at my motel before the performance that had brought me to LA. Dylan was sticking around town for a bit, getting ready to have his first gig at the Ash Grove, and asked whether he could tag along with me. I was busting with my usual curiosity, and he may have been too, a trait that seems to have led him down many a storied—or perhaps apocryphal—road in search of tall tales, songs, and experience. I'm fourteen years older than he is, and still questing.

So of course, what would I say? I said "Of course!" What better hope does a woman have of cutting straight through the protective walls into the inner courtyard of a man's personal emotional dwelling? Very little was revealed at the skin-to-skin level by this young genius except for the insight that he and I were very much alike in wanting to know everything about everything. But staying in character with his youth, Bob was not about to cop to the possibility that there was anything about these matters that he didn't already know.

Sadly for the Ash Grove audiences, Dylan had to cancel his performance. John Hammond had summoned him to the Columbia studios in New York, where he would finish recording *The Freewheelin' Bob Dylan* for the world at large, the world that was clearly waiting for this music. Still relevant, still fresh, still provocative, still comforting, still revolutionary, and, to this day, still spinning.

25

WHICH SIDE ARE YOU ON?

Talk began to circulate that a new show was about to be launched by ABC-TV featuring folk music. It was to be called *Hootenanny*, after that special participatory kind of performance flowing from the life's work of people like Pete Seeger, Woody Guthrie, and many inspired by them, and the aesthetic of People's Songs, People's Artists, and *Sing Out!* as shaped by producers like Irwin Silber, Harold Leventhal, Moses Asch (Moe), and others. Soon I received a phone call offering me a spot on one of the first shows, to be taped at Penn State, a campus I had visited before in relation to the peace movement. This was exciting news, because very few live music shows of any kind were ever seen on TV and also because this seemed like the day we had all been waiting for: a chance to reach the millions of viewers out there with genuine people's music, a way of helping create village-like music communities for folks who were choking on the false commercial culture normally being shoved in their faces, a place to remind Americans about the vast musical riches of our past and open their eyes to the new songs being written about our realities in the present as well as our hopes for the future. Huge possibilities!

But I had already heard rumors that Pete Seeger was to be barred from the show, and if that was true, there was no way I could participate. I decided to "accept" the job offer, with the idea that once I had verified the rumors I would cancel, but only at the very last minute just to fuck them up. I knew how much difficulty one normally encountered in getting to the Penn State campus, and the producers would have a hard way to go in bringing on a substitute very close to showtime. Or maybe ABC could get one of its army buddies to helicopter someone in?

Just about then, Pete himself was coming to Berkeley for a performance and planning to stay at our house. I remember now taking him to the Co-op to buy a few groceries on the way from the airport, and finding that the subject of *Hootenanny* was on both our minds at once. Pete began to make a little speech about how I should go ahead and do the show, partly for the sake of my contribution to it, and partly because he knew I needed the money and the inevitable career advancement that would follow this kind of exposure. I cut him off mid-argument to say that I would never agree to perform on the show if he was to be blacklisted, or if anyone else was to be kept off the show for political reasons. I explained that all the rationale in the world would not be enough to quiet the pangs I would have in my stomach if I were to cooperate with this kind of censorship in any way. A day or two later, I had a call from Joan Baez, who asked me how I planned to relate to the issue. She was pleased to know of my decision, and suggested that we begin spreading the word that a boycott was on.

The show took to the air without us in April 1963 and didn't take long to become a big hit . . . at least for a couple of seasons. It couldn't sustain itself much longer than that because the producers had to keep repeating the same old slick commercial pseudo-folk performers instead of providing the endlessly varied and engaging genuine article.

Bob Dylan published a poem/letter in *Broadside* not long after, where he refers to this incident:

> I dont understand the blacklist
> I dont understand how people aginst it go along
> with it
> I'm talkin about the full thing
> not just a few of us refusin t be on the show
> I'm talkin about the poeple that stand up
> against it violently an then in some way have something
> t do with it . . .
> not just the singers mind you

but the managers an agents an buyers an sellers . . .
they are the dishonest ones
for they are never seen
they play both sides against each other
an expect t be repected by everybody

the heroes of this battle are not me an Joan
an the Kingston Trio nor Peter Paul an Mary
for none of us need t go on that show
none of us really need that kind of dumbness
but there's some that could use it
for they could use the money
I mean people like Tom Paxton, Barbara Dane,
an Johnny Herald . . . they are the heroes if
such a word has t be used here
they are the ones that lose materialistically
ah yes but in their own minds they dont
an that is much more important
it means much more
we need more kind a people like that
poeple that cant go against their conscience
no matter what they might gain
an I've come to think that that might be the most
important thing in the whole wide world . . .
not going against your conscience
nor your own natural senses
for I think that that is all the truth there
is . . . an no more

Despite the mainstream media's attempts to co-opt folk music, this was a time in our nation's history when songs were particularly instrumental to social change. In May 1963, just a month after the *Hootenanny* caper, I attended an inspiring event. A multiracial crowd of over twenty thousand San Franciscans led by a coalition of religious, political, and labor leaders rallied at Civic Center to voice their solidarity with the intense civil rights protests taking place in Birmingham, Alabama. With the headline "We Shall Overcome," the *San Francisco*

Chronicle detailed the events with patent exuberance. "'They say that Negros are not ready for their freedom . . .,'" said Rev. Bernard Lee of Martin Luther King's Southern Leadership Conference. "'But we are saying this to the Nation: "Ready or not, here we come!"'" The article concluded its coverage noting that "Barbara Dane, a blond folk artist of national reputation," led the crowd of thousands—Blacks and whites together—as they sang the "marching song of the Southern Negroes." Deep in my heart, I do believe. Later that summer, Martin Luther King Jr. led over 250,000 people in the March on Washington for Jobs and Freedom and inspired millions with his speech "I Have a Dream."

Soon after, I participated in what resulted in one of my most satisfying recordings, not for my performance especially, but because of the circumstances and the outcome. Lucius (Lu) Watters, another trumpet master and a true mensch, was the recognized father of the traditional jazz revival that began in the San Francisco Bay Area just after World War II. Lu had founded the Yerba Buena Jazz Band in the late thirties with trombonist Turk Murphy, trumpeter Bob Scobey, pianist Wally Rose, and others. After a break during the war, the band reconvened at the Dawn Club on Annie Street in San Francisco, engendering a worldwide revival of traditional American jazz. In 1950, Lu opened the legendary Hambone Kelly's in El Cerrito. His horn was blazing hot, original and compelling, but by 1957 he was so burned out and disgusted with the commercialized musical world that he retired and began to work as a cook in a Cotati mental hospital. He also became an amateur geologist of some note.

When Pacific Gas & Electric, in all its corporate wisdom, decided to build an atomic energy plant at Bodega Head, on one of the most beautiful stretches of the coast and directly on the San Andreas earthquake fault, Lu saw his two biggest interests in life come together: music and geology. This drew him out of retirement long enough to reorganize the band for one more recording session, titled *Blues over Bodega*, for which he wrote a song he asked me to sing, by the same title. I am proud and happy to say that the nuclear plant was never built, but the song goes ringing onward, reminding us of a very significant victory for the movement toward antinuclear sanity represented by the many thousands of people who rose to the defense of the Pacific Coast and the planet. This unusual protest song—an early manifestation of the environmental movement—

played on a lot of local jukeboxes and on Bay Area radio. In 2018, I recorded it again on an album called *Throw It Away* to remind us all that great victories can be won by ordinary people working together with the same purpose: the preservation of life!

That summer, founder Jimmy Lyons had rounded up a sensational range of artists for his first-annual Monterey Folk Festival, starting with Peter, Paul and Mary, the Weavers, and the New Lost City Ramblers, and, thankfully, adding some of the vernacular musicians I loved most, Bessie Jones and the Georgia Sea Island Singers, Lightnin' Hopkins, Mance Lipscomb, and Doc Watson. He contacted me to ask whether I would like to act as MC on one of the three days in addition to performing, and I gave him the thumbs-up just because these folks would be there. I could drive down with Byron and the kids, and we would have a great weekend in the sun. The big buzz, of course, was Bob Dylan, billed as "the newest young folk star," but the real news was that Dylan and Baez were making a big hit with each other behind the scenes.

Popping up at some of the informal jams throughout the weekend

Byron Menendez, Mable Hillery, Barbara Dane, Nina Menendez, Michael Cooney, Paul Menendez. Monterey Folk Festival, 1963. © Jerry Stoll

was an unknown singer called Janis Joplin. I'm told by people who knew her that she often showed up at places where I was singing, and I am sorry that we never got acquainted, because to me she was a true blues heart. Sadly, she left us before she understood that the blues were invented as a tool for survival, not just for casting your heartbreak into the wind or for burning yourself up onstage.

Bessie Jones was on Sunday's gospel program, and I made sure to be there to witness that juxtaposition of song forms from different branches with shared roots. I thought I must be mistaken when I saw, standing not far from where I was perched, none other than the queen of gospel herself, Mahalia Jackson, apparently added to the festival lineup at the last minute and therefore unannounced. I greeted her warmly, and she sat down by me in the grass. We had met briefly a few months before in a TV network's dressing room where I had been busy fixing my makeup before some forgettable interview. I had noticed someone getting a massage in an adjacent alcove, so I made some kind of comment and we started to chat. When I gave her my name, she lifted her head under the towel, and said, "Aren't you that white girl who sings the blues? I heard some of your new record, and you got it going on!" That voice sounded so familiar, but it wasn't until she sat up that I saw who she was, and was naturally struck dumb! There in the festival sunshine, I was even more shocked, but I hid it. When I inquired about her health, Mahalia said that she was about to cancel a tour because her heart was acting up. Then she casually added, "Maybe you could do it for me?" Yes, this queen was about the most generous and down-to-earth person you could find, ready and even eager to lend encouragement to a younger artist.

I had fantasized for a while about a collaboration with Doc Watson, for me the greatest acoustic guitarist anywhere, and here he was in Monterey. A few days after the festival, due to some serious serendipity, we were offered a bit of studio time together. We recorded a few songs just to have a chance to see how things might work. We had a great time playing and singing together and came up with a some wonderful tracks, but both of us realized that there was no way our careers could dovetail. Each of us already had too many musical commitments in addition to living on distant sides of the country, and we each would have had to woodshed a while to grasp the fine points of the other's style. I had to let that little dream go.

A few months later, I headed south once again to play the Ash Grove as I did whenever Ed Pearl called me, and things always went well there. This fall, Ed was immersed in big plans, bringing Joan Baez, the number-one draw for the folk crowd at that time, to the Hollywood Bowl on October 9. It was an expensive gamble and a dauntingly large venue to be sure, but one he was confident he could fill, especially since it had leaked that Baez was bringing her new friend, Bob Dylan. I think Ed had almost forgotten to book the Ash Grove in his intense focus on the Bowl venture, but he called me and I came. He told me later that he was astonished that even on that night, with all eyes on the Baez-Dylan show, I had sold seven hundred admissions to the Ash Grove, something of a record. Ah, sweet mystery of life.

26

THE TIMES, THEY ARE A-CHANGIN'

The next few months were to bring a sea change to my life, and a turning point for my children too. The fall of 1963 was one of both national and personal devastation.

In the wake of May's intense civil rights protests in Alabama, resulting in key anti-segregation concessions, the Ku Klux Klan retaliated, bombing Birmingham's Sixteenth Street Baptist Church on September 15, killing four young girls. The nation was rudely awakened by this vile act of racial hatred.

On November 22, the young president who had introduced so much hope and promise into American life was "cut down in his prime," as the old songs say, just as he and his wife, Jackie, drove past an adoring crowd in Dallas. It was a fusillade attributed to an ambiguous young figure named Lee Harvey Oswald, himself cut down before he could become an embarrassment to anyone on the witness stand of American television. Millions of people in my country still doubt the Warren Report that was intended to act as a comforting conclusion to the mystery of who actually pulled off this cruel and traumatizing assassination, so much easier to bear if it was just this one crazy guy. This lack of trust in what we all had grown up believing to be a neutral and benevolent government was destabilizing then, and remains a source of unease and cynicism even today, well over half a century later.

Less than a week after JFK was murdered and LBJ installed as the leader of the "free world," Thanksgiving Day arrived, and I, like most good moms, was spending the day roasting a large turkey for my family and eagerly anticipating our dinner guest. Also, like every other mom in the nation, I was hoping the warm togetherness that Thanksgiving implied would ease the pain, or at least temporarily distract our families from the tragedy.

I had met Ben Legere at the home of the Berkeley Puppeteers, where he was renting a room, and had invited him to dinner. I especially wanted my children to meet and establish a relationship with this dear old man who carried so much history in his veins. Born in 1887, Ben was in his late seventies when we met. He had been a lifetime socialist and an active Wobbly (member of the IWW, or International Workers of the World), who had known and worked with Big Bill Haywood and Elizabeth Gurley Flynn, two of the greatest figures of American labor, even before 1912 when he went to Lawrence, Massachusetts, to lend himself to one of the first and most important events of labor history, the great Bread and Roses strike. I wanted to make sure that Legere, a person who lived alone now in spite of having so willingly dedicated himself to others for his whole lifetime, had a family to be with on Thanksgiving, a place where he could feel welcomed and even needed.

At the same time, things were getting shakier at our house. Byron had spent the first part of Thanksgiving day drinking Old Crow, and by dinnertime was at a staggering stage of drunkenness. For the past few months, he had been more and more occupied with his private affairs, which included a girlfriend or two. I had been doing what I could to turn a blind eye to all this for the sake of the children and my own mental balance, ignoring the humiliation I was completely entitled to feel and probably should have addressed. I knew that our family was about to unravel, but I wasn't ready to make a move until I could figure out how to arrange life for the least possible impact a break-up would have on the kids. However, I was nearly reaching the end of my tolerance and whatever ability I had to keep steering a steady course.

When Ben arrived for dinner, the children and I greeted him as brightly as possible, and we all quickly sat down at the table, where the brown and fragrant turkey I had set out now glistened in the center awaiting the traditional ceremonial carving. When Byron lurched in from the kitchen brandishing my great-granddad's long, sharp machete-like carving knife in the manner of a samurai warrior, something inside me snapped, yeah, snapped again . . . you could almost hear it! A decision had been made. I danced the knife out of his hands as smoothly as I could and turned him toward the door, shut it behind me, marched him out to the curb, and sat him down. "That's it," I said as firmly as I could. Adios.

And of course it was never good-bye, because I really loved this man, in a physical way reflected in the two wonderful children we shared; loved him with a deep regret for all the potential twisted up in him, stolen by the effects of a war that would never leave him; loved his sturdy masculine beauty, his innate dancer's grace; loved his deep intelligence that was of so little use to him because of forces I could never know, things that happened which he himself has never come to understand; loved his profound appreciation of nature and respect for all its creatures; loved his ingrained musicality and the way he allowed music to come into his life from every conceivable angle; loved his inborn sense of design and the ability to make motion and beauty out of a flat sheet of silver. And there was all the love I had wanted from him but could never be sure was mine. Oh no, this wouldn't go away. My love would remain an undertone, a vibration inside me that I would allow to slumber but would never be able to release. No final good-bye.

Together, neither Byron nor I had any substantial assets, so there was nothing to divide. About custody of the children, my heart told me that we could better work those things out between us based on current realities rather than on some legal decisions made by strangers. I asked simply that Byron make the payments of fifty dollars a month on the a sporty but inexpensive little blue Triumph I had just purchased with a loan from the credit union. That seemed just to me, since I would not have needed a car if we were still together. This would help me through the period of readjustment, and also it was finite. He held up his end of this arrangement, and thus the marriage was dissolved.

PART THREE

MY AMERICAN DREAM

27

IRWIN CALLS, LIGHTNIN' STRIKES, MISSISSIPPI BECKONS

One day in the spring of 1964, a phone call came from an old acquaintance, none other than Irwin Silber from *Sing Out!* magazine. He was in town representing Oak Publications and Folkways Records at the American Library Association convention.

Would I like to have dinner with him the next evening? You bet I would. I had nothing but respect and admiration for Irwin, going back to 1947, when I had met him on the way through New York heading for the World Youth Festival, and later that year had seen how smoothly he ran the People's Songs convention and concert in Chicago. For nearly twenty years I had avidly followed his writing in *Sing Out!* and had been educated by it. Most persuasively, it had been a considerable time since I had had dinner with someone who brought a brilliant mind to the table and was willing to share it.

Irwin asked me to choose the restaurant, and the first thing I thought of was a rather elegant new place in San Francisco offering Japanese cuisine, then quite a novelty in the US, even in the Bay Area. Between the sushi and the sukiyaki, the tempura and the teriyaki, I had some idea of what to order, and that impressed him, since he had never tried Japanese food before. I could tell we both were feeling very lucky to be doing this together.

After dinner we went to a new club called the Committee, which featured an inventive new type of theater called improv, known for its humor and political edge. At the ticket window ahead of us we ran into Mark Lane, investigative reporter and writer, former NY state assemblyman, and an old friend of Irwin's. We invited him to join us, which quickly raised the intensity of discussion as well as the hilarity.

As our eyes and ears focused on the stage, I became aware of Irwin's hand resting quietly on my knee. I felt a warm wave of something like gratitude, an unexpected feeling that mixed with the sense of surprise sweeping through my body. I glanced at him and smiled, and softly moved my hand to cover his.

As we left the club, Mark jumped in a cab and waved goodnight. Now it was time for me to drop Irwin off at his hotel, the entrance of which was exactly on my route to the Bay Bridge and home to Berkeley. I confess to some trepidation about writing this next part of what happened, because it may sound like a dime novel, but it was just this simple. As the attendant opened the car door at the hotel's porte cochere, Irwin leaned to kiss me quickly good-bye and started to get out. With no time to think, I whispered into his nearest ear, "Would you rather come home with me?," and without a word or hesitation, Irwin tipped the doorman and signaled to close the car door again, and we headed for the East Bay.

I had always slept with my bedroom door closed because of the noise the children usually made in the morning as they got themselves up for school. Twelve-year-old Paul was the first to knock on my door, insisting, "Mom, I have to get in there to iron my pants!" I told him to go and brush his teeth first, while Irwin dressed quickly and tiptoed downstairs.

I was usually working late at night, so I had seen to it that my children were well prepared from an early age to get themselves together in the morning. Routines are great things, and soon they were off to the day's academic adventures, leaving Irwin and me with a little time to talk.

There was so much to be said, and so little need to say anything. We both understood without a word that this was not a casual moment but the beginning of something profound and enduring, although neither of us could have predicted that it would become a partnership of forty-six years, lasting until his death in 2010.

Irwin, not yet thirty-nine, was clearly feeling the burden of the many responsibilities he had taken on over time to make ends meet, running the magazine as well as writing a good bit of it, and working for Moe Asch's Folkways Records, which involved a great deal of travel. He was also running Oak Publications, a publishing house he had formed with Moe's backing. (Most of the folk music material one could find in those days bore his Oak imprint.) Irwin was being drawn further and further into business details without finding the time for his own writing and research, especially the opportunity to write about events beyond the folk scene. He also craved time for his own political activity. I could see that he genuinely loved his three children, but that in spite of his respect and affection for his wife, Sylvia, he had outgrown that relationship and was feeling trapped in the quicksand of the business world. Big changes were about to take place, regardless of the catalyst.

After my own difficult marriage that had stretched over about fourteen years, I was sure I had no interest in jumping back into a relationship. Yet here I was, in spite of myself, looking deep into the eyes of someone I had only known as a colleague and acquaintance, now seeing him for the first time as a warm, sensitive, and democratic man, feeling that perhaps at last, in this man, I had found my true partner.

The night before Irwin was returning to New York, I was to sing again at the Cabale, a wonderful little music venue started by a group that included my first husband, Rolf Cahn. From its opening in 1963, the club had quickly become one of the most important venues for traditional music on the West Coast. I was excited to be singing there that particular evening, knowing Irwin would be in the audience. Also, I was trying out a little Gibson guitar whose cutaway and built-in electric pickup interfered not at all with its great acoustic sound. It was an exceptional night for me in every way, as I sang with my heart beating almost visibly through my clothes, and the Gibson feeling as though it had been mine since the day it was built. Heedlessly, I left it locked up at the Cabale dressing room overnight. Someone broke in and stole it, and I never saw it again. That morning, I had to say good-bye to Irwin too. As he was leaving, I felt a tug in the gut, felt my heart swell along with the lump in my throat. As the plane lifted him up and off to the east, I began to repeat this mantra: "Oh please let him be safe; don't let any harm come to this dear person. We will be together again soon."

Barbara Dane with Nina and Paul Menendez. Protest against the Vietnam War. San Francisco, 1964. © Erik Weber

Only a few days later, I too was lifted up by the chance to join several hundred people in one of the first demonstrations calling for an end to the rapidly increasing US military involvement in Vietnam, a country most Americans had never heard of. We sang and marched right up to the gates of the San Francisco Presidio, in one of the earliest civilian confrontations at a US installation. Of course, I brought my kids along.

In June 1964, James Earl Chaney, Andy Goodman, and Michael Schwerner, three young civil rights workers, were kidnapped in Mississippi, and disappeared. Because folk music was currently attractive to the press, someone came up with the idea of forming a caravan of singers to go to Mississippi in support of the Freedom Schools, a system of volunteer community schools that had been set up earlier that summer in some of the poorest, most isolated areas of the state to teach literacy and help more folks register to vote. The idea was that this might bring national press attention, which would call on the authorities to move faster with their search and investigation. I instantly volunteered and set about raising the money to get there from California.

Irwin and I exchanged several phone calls (ridiculously expensive at the time) and many handwritten letters. I was seriously considering moving to New York, and in that dizzy and impulsive mental state that often accompanies new love, without a real plan for what was going to happen if I did move, how all this would affect the futures of my children and anyone or anything else, I set things in motion to make it happen. I went about organizing my belongings and selling off furniture, outgrown children's clothes, books and surplus LPs, anything that would clear the decks and simplify the move if indeed I decided to go through with it. This also brought in some of the funds that I needed for the trip to Mississippi.

My "Sublet, Short Term" sign on the Co-op market bulletin board soon brought me a renter who seemed just right for the situation and even saw himself as helping out my mission by renting the house. When I went to buy a suitcase, the owner of the store wouldn't take my money, saying that he wanted to make his contribution this way. People were stopping by almost daily to buy from my in-home thrift shop in the same spirit. It seemed that everyone wanted somehow to be part of the enormous sea change that was flowing across the nation, propelled by the courage and determination of the sit-in students and freedom riders, bus boycotters and marchers, schoolchildren and grandmas, plowmen, cotton pickers, cooks and cleaners, teachers, preachers, and even lawyers who were undertaking to overcome the sickness of racism in America.

I explained to my children that, by behaving like the responsible and considerate young people they were while I was gone, they would be part of the movement too. My dear friends Myrna and Andy Conn were happy to have Paul and Nina visit them and their kids for a few weeks down in Venice Beach. Nicky would be staying with his dad, Rolf, who currently lived several blocks from our home with folksinger Debbie Greene.

Flash forward: Right in the middle of my most intense moments in Mississippi, I phoned the man who was subletting my house just to check on things. He was relieved that I had called, because, just a few days before, Nicky and his belongings had been dumped on the porch by Rolf, who simply left him there and drove away with no explanation. The renter was kind enough to let him stay in his old room, since he wasn't using it anyway, and I think he was also giving Nicky some food out of sheer decency. I had asked him to deduct anything like that from the rent, but he had been mainly concerned for the boy's welfare. Not much I could do from where I was, except assure him that Nicky, then fifteen, would be all right until I got home. I wasn't sure that was true, but what else was I to do?

Chris Strachwitz, the spirit of Arhoolie Records, asked me to record some favorites from my folk song life before saying good-bye to California. We decided to do this inside the Cabale in Berkeley, on an afternoon when we would have the place to ourselves and where Chris could easily roll in his big old Ampex recording machine. The acoustics were great there even when it was empty, but I knew I would always sing my best with some folks on the receiving end, so I asked my old friend Carroll Peery to round up a few people to create a small afternoon audience. It happened to be a time when Lightnin' Sam Hopkins was in town, and since he usually stayed with Carroll, he showed up along with the others. Sam had dropped by the house a few days before, but we only had had a minute to talk as I was busy cooking and dealing with the kids, so I was glad to see him walk in.

    I had already recorded a good-sized handful of my songs when they arrived, and I think to Sam it looked as if the whole thing was a jam rather than a recording session. Oh well, what the hell, whatever happens can't be bad. He spared no time in unpacking his guitar, and we easily launched into a blues give-and-take, making up verses as we went, most of which incorporated inside jokes that Carroll and some of the others would understand, not thinking for a moment that any of this was being preserved.

    Chris, not surprisingly, kept the tape reels spinning and even found time to take a few really good photos of Hopkins and me together. A couple of years later, some of that session turned up on the B side of an Arhoolie LP called *Lightning Hopkins with His Brothers Joel and John Henry / with Barbara Dane*. My folk tracks had disappeared into a dark hole at the Arhoolie headquarters in El Cerrito. Thirty-two years later, Strachwitz stumbled across those nice photos of Lightnin' and me, inspiring him to release a CD opening with that very unorthodox spontaneous blues session and wrapping things up with those tracks—some of the few recordings available anywhere of my folk singing days. He took the title from something Sam said in one of his improvised blues verses, "Sometimes I believe she loves me." Lightnin' was right.

Before heading down to Mississippi, I had a very important stop to make in New York City. It was urgent that Irwin and I take a good look into each other's eyes again, the better to search each other's hearts. There were questions that needed to be asked in person and facts to

Barbara Dane with Lightnin' Hopkins. Berkeley, 1964. © Chris Strachwitz

be examined. We both needed to find a way to make sense out of what we were feeling. Most of all, we needed to wrap our arms around each other for reassurance, to know that whatever was to come next would be based on the kind of trust and understanding that would enable us to get through some of the hardest decisions either of us would ever make in our personal lives. Would we determine that, for the good of our children and many other considerations, we would need to invent some kind of long-distance collaboration, sacrificing the happiness and fulfillment that could have embodied a life together? Or would we come to the conclusion that if we could pull it all together, if we could find a way to be live-in partners for life, this would provide the foundation for the greatest happiness of all concerned, for our children, our work, our goals, and our dreams?

Irwin's wife, Sylvia, didn't fly, so she had booked a week-long ocean crossing to Europe. Their plan was for Irwin to fly over later, renting a car for a trip through the UK and France during the period their children were away at summer camp. When he began to beg me to come to New York for the week following Sylvia's departure so that we could have some uninterrupted private time together, my everyday self might have found the idea duplicitous and even dishonorable. But I was in the grip of a jones so compelling I couldn't see beyond it, driving me to hurriedly work out an itinerary that enabled me to pass through New York on my way to Mississippi.

Everyone who could leave New York for that Fourth of July weekend was gone. In the streets of a sweltering and humid Greenwich Village, Irwin and I held hands heedlessly or walked with arms intertwined, hardly able to believe we were right there together. Almost delirious with joy and the sensation that our lives were about to take an entirely new direction, we felt that anything seemed possible. We would find a way to make these huge changes work out positively for all concerned, certain that our love would spill over to all those whose lives would also be most deeply affected.

I had a fantasy that if I could talk all this over with Sylvia when she returned, if I could explain things as I saw them, I could help her see that Irwin was in no way rejecting her personally or undervaluing their lifetime of child raising and activism together, but was simply going through a reevaluation of his own life and finding it desperately in need of refocusing. I could explain that it is possible for people to love many others, for many different reasons, that this doesn't ever have to stop, so that he would continue to love her for the reasons he always had. I could point out that people sometimes may need to have different partners at different times, depending on where life is taking them. I wanted her to know that I could see that she was a strong woman with a creative spirit who could chart her own course and perhaps find an even more rewarding life ahead.

Yes, there I go again, thinking I am the only one in the room who understands what's going on. There I go again expecting that the right words will fix everything, blinded by my own needs and expecting others to simply understand, pushing ahead at my own speed. Of course, reality—events outside ourselves, undeniably more significant than the lives of any individual—soon took over, and our precious few days together in a dream came to an end.

28

GO TELL IT ON THE MOUNTAIN

Over that summer, more than twenty artists took part in the Mississippi Caravan of Music, including Len Chandler, Judy Collins, Peter La Farge, Gil Turner, Pete Seeger, Phil Ochs, Alix Dobkin, and Bob Cohen of the New World Singers. We were not all in the state at the same time, and we moved around to the towns and villages in small groups, which meant that many of us never had the chance to meet one another, but we all were considered a part of the cultural wing of the Mississippi Freedom Project.

That first day, a number of us were brought directly from the Jackson airport to the Student Nonviolent Coordinating Committee (SNCC) office, where we were introduced to the legendary civil rights activist Bob Moses. He was there to lay out some ground rules: never discuss our itineraries on the telephone; don't call attention to ourselves in public places; try to avoid having Blacks and whites together in the same cars. He explained that we would be traveling to a lot of small-town and backcountry places, and our hosts would be risking considerable danger just by allowing us outsiders to stay and mingle with them.

If any of us had thought we were immune to the dangers in feudal Mississippi because we were white, we needed to realize that the powerful whites and their minions saw us as race traitors, outsiders, agitators, commies, or worse. They hated us because of our sense of entitlement, unlike the Blacks who, through centuries of enforced custom, mostly knew how to "stay in their place." We were performers, people whose usual work required being intentionally conspicuous, but now we would be more useful—and less of a danger to all—if we could learn to function discreetly and discipline ourselves to quietly blend in with the circumstances.

In the Freedom Schools, they were teaching literacy, political organization, voter education, and Black history. The daily routine included talking and singing with students ranging in age from grannies to grandkids, helping them see how much of their own culture, which for generations they had been taught to think of as unworthy, was not only known but sought after, studied, imitated, and especially enjoyed and loved in the outside world. We would find that everyone wanted to sing at every opportunity, because the movement itself, like the churches historically, had revealed the power of song. Songs helped build and consolidate unity. Songs could intimidate the enemy, stop a riot, provide a shield, or hold back a sword. They provided the singer with a self-image that was strong and courageous, raising everyone's spirits, chasing away fear, and delivering large doses of love to those with righteous hearts.

Just as I had been packing up to leave Berkeley for New York and on to Mississippi, my old guitar-playing comrade Jimmy Wood happened to drop by the house to say good-bye, and showed me a song that Malvina Reynolds, beloved singer-songwriter, friend, and Berkeley neighbor, had just written. "It Isn't Nice" was full of details reflecting tactics used at the recent sit-ins at the Palace Hotel in San Francisco, where people occupied the floors of its elegant lobbies for days. This purposefully nonviolent but certainly aggressive demonstration set forth the message of the Ad Hoc Committee Against Discrimination, demanding that the hotel open its employment rolls to Blacks for the first time. Although many protesters were jailed during the struggle, in the end, that demand was won, and the victory reverberated throughout the Bay Area, setting a precedent against discriminatory hiring practices.

The song was just what I needed to show that the movement was growing even way out west! I added a beat to make it danceable and more appealing to young people, and a chorus attempting a Sam Cooke–like cadence designed to allow the listeners a chance to sing along. Judy Collins, seeing the impact it was having during our days in Mississippi, asked whether I would mind if she recorded it with my alterations, and of course I urged her to go ahead, knowing that her high visibility would help folks find it all the sooner. (I later recorded it myself with the Chambers Brothers on Folkways Records.) It also might bring Malvina royalties, and she agreed to the arrangement.

Meeting the great singing organizer Fannie Lou Hamer was for me like meeting one of the legendary women of the past, women like Harriet Tubman or Sojourner Truth. She was so determined that her people would have a voice in how not only Mississippi but the country itself should be run, so clear in her mind on both tactics and strategy, so courageous in pursuit of her objectives that she forged ahead despite the almost total lack of financial resources available to her, the constant threat of physical danger, and the lifetime disabilities resulting from the brutal beating inflicted by police while she was in custody for trying to register people to vote. Fannie Lou just kept on moving forward, relentless and unbowed.

I had the privilege of singing with Mrs. Hamer one night in a packed church basement in Ruleville, her hometown. As usual, the local police were circling outside, jotting down the license plate numbers of all the cars and generally creating a menacing atmosphere. The people gathered inside the church were absolutely undaunted, singing lustily and loudly along with us and nearly lifting the building off its foundation with their fervent demands for freedom, implicit in every song. After standing in the midst of those sounds, anyone could understand why the jailers tried to ban singing when they locked up the demonstrators all over the South.

We singers traveled from town to town in dusty older cars, with a volunteer driving us to the next destination. Right out of the box, I had been sent off into the backseat of one vehicle, with Phil Ochs huddled in the leg space under the front passenger seat. He was ashen and shaky from the start, and I began to wonder how he was going to manage through these next days. When we got to the humble home of the local supporters who were allowing their back rooms to be used as a sort of HQ, Phil asked right away if he could make a call, and without waiting for an answer he was in the back shouting into the telephone. He was giving out all the details of our next moves, in a voice loud enough to be heard across the fields outside. As soon as I realized what was going on, I rushed in and insisted that he stop, but his frantic reply was, "Be quiet!

I'm talking to *Newsweek*!" The SNCC folks must have had to reorganize our whole itinerary. They knew, of course, that the lines were tapped, and we had already been sternly warned not to give our itinerary to anyone. I tried not to travel with Phil anymore.

And yet, and yet . . . In spite of whatever overwhelming mental distress eventually ended in his suicide twelve years later, Phil proved to be one of the bravest artists of the period. "I Ain't Marchin' Anymore" validated the resistance of thousands of young potential recruits during the Vietnam War, "We're the Cops of the World" ripped the masks off American military intervention, and "Draft Dodger Rag" celebrated the draftees clever enough to stay out of the mess. Phil's interests ranged broadly, his scalpel cut deeply, and in spite of a burning ambition to be recognized, to be mainstream famous, he never held back or took an opportunist's stand that only looked like protest. No, his legend doesn't approach Dylan's as the poet of the era, but his songs will not be forgotten, and his courage lives whenever they are given voice.

It was June 21, 1964, when Andrew Goodman, Michael Schwerner, and James Chaney were abducted and lynched by the Klan in Neshoba County, Mississippi. Their bodies were not found until August 4, forty-four days later, buried under an earthen dam near the murder site. Millions of people across the country, and across the globe, had been holding their breath until then. Even so, it took years before the killers were identified and any sort of justice was meted out, even though everyone in town, Black and white, probably knew who they were. But the nation reacted to these horrific crimes and so many others committed in the name of White Power and homegrown terrorism by passing the Civil Rights Act of 1964 and the Voting Rights Act of 1965. Almost sixty years later, many of those gains are threatened, some have even been reversed, and the Ku Klux Klan is far from eradicated. We can never stop fighting the deadly poison of white supremacy that has its knee on the neck of our democracy.

I had my own close encounter with the KKK, though I didn't know it until I read about it in Izzy Young's *Sing Out!* column. Among several performances that Phil Ochs and I did together, one was at a community center in the small Mississippi town of Milestone. Later that same night, after we had left, the center was bombed.

The Mississippi Caravan of Music brought my notions about the power of song into concrete reality and demonstrated that, beyond lightening the heart and pointing the way, music could actually affect the future. Lives could be saved. A writer for a small movement paper wrote,

> Perspiration poured off our bodies as we sat crowded into a small church and singing, with Miss Dane leading, "It Isn't Nice," "You're Gonna Reap Just What You Sow," "You Just Can't Make It by Yourself." Perhaps I was not the only one who thought as we sang of the girl who had been shot a few weeks before as she stood by an open window during a mass meeting in a church in Hattiesburg or of the tear gas thrown into so many mass meetings over the Deep South. I realized then, as so many others before me had, that it didn't matter: the police outside didn't matter; tear gas didn't matter; shots didn't matter; fire bombs didn't matter. We were safe because we were right, we were together, we were singing and the songs made us strong. There were more of us on this stage and all over the country who sang them than there were of the racist gangs, and we would win. We were not afraid.

One night near the end of my stay, at a gathering in a place called Pilgrim's Rest, so far up in the Mississippi hills that it wasn't on the map and so remote that escaped slaves had managed to hide there until manumission arrived, a man named Link Williams stood up at a meeting and said, "If this lady can leave her three children and come all the way from California to sing for us, then the least that we can do is all go down tomorrow and try to register."

29

NAVIGATING OBSTACLES BLANKETED IN BLISS

I went back to New York to meet Irwin, who had returned from Europe a week ahead of Sylvia. He was covering the 1964 Newport Folk Festival for *Sing Out!*, so we immediately headed up to Rhode Island. So now, here I was with Irwin for three precious days. We couldn't help but show our newly minted attachment, and I know some of his old associates and friends were curious, some even shocked. This only became clear to me later, when I was told that the Seegers, Pete and Toshi, were upset when they realized they were witnessing the end of the Irwin-Sylvia couple they had known since the early 1950s, not to mention the Barbara-Byron couple they had known, although not as well, for nearly as long. Some folks don't take too well to rearrangements of families.

But for these precious days I was wrapped in a blanket of bliss. Partly because of the enormous audiences loving and supporting this music that over many years I had been loving and supporting when it sometimes seemed a lonely obsession. But mainly because with every moment, I was more sure of my connection with Irwin, more in love with his brilliant way of looking at things, his self-confident manner of moving through the world, his honest appreciation for my own best qualities and willingness to ignore my worst, his sophisticated humor as well as his endless store of old Jewish jokes, his athleticism in contrast to my physical sloth, his respect for my opinions while never compromising his own. Shall I go on?

During the festival, Irwin and I had a few odd moments with the young singer-songwriter who seemed to be the object of everyone's attention. Bob Dylan was sitting with Joan Baez and chatting with a couple of us older "insiders" when we spied some youngsters making a move to join us. Up went a towel he had been holding, over his head and covering his face, a Do Not Disturb sign if ever there was one. He sat that way as I continued to rattle on about my Mississippi journey until we went inside to a hotel room, where some musicians had gathered to share their new material. As a jug of red wine was passed around, a guitar was thrust at Bob, and he seemed eager to display some of his brand-new stuff, most memorable of which was "It ain't me, babe. No, no, no, it ain't me babe. It ain't me you're lookin' for, babe." Joan was not amused.

The drive back to New York found Irwin and me in a sort of reverie as we spoke of the kind of life we could fashion together. The past few days had demonstrated our mutual ability to tolerate endless musical exploration, often seasoned with analysis and conversation about it. The worldview we held in common was evident in all our dialogue, and a lifetime of

Irwin Silber and Barbara Dane. Newport, 1964. © David Gahr

following a peace and justice agenda was only going to blossom with the support we could offer each other. On the lighter side, our shared gusto for great food and lively people and good Scotch or wine—that is to say, laughter amid an atmosphere of clashing ideas and passionate devotion to their exploration—offered both of us the sensation that happiness, not just fun and good times but real joy and fulfillment, was almost within our grasp.

But first we had a mountain of obstacles to be cleared, and each of us would have to find their own way to work things out. We both had many obligations as people active in our communities, with many expectations held by the people close to us—family members, old friends, and colleagues. If we could find a way together to unleash our most creative and joyful spirits, we told ourselves, everyone around us would benefit, especially our children, our families, and those same friends and colleagues who shared our vision. So where do you start?

Irwin was deeply enmeshed in his many commitments as editor of Oak Publications, to the authors and musicians already embarked on projects and to the enormous network he had built through that work and through his lifelong stewardship of *Sing Out!* magazine. His boys, Fred and Josh, were twelve and thirteen years old, and his little girl, Nina, same name as my daughter, was about five. Irwin still hadn't explained to me any conversation he may have had with Sylvia in Europe, but expressed his intention of talking to her in the next few days about his future plans. Presumably, this meant as soon as he could figure out what they were.

My situation was almost the opposite. I had definitively ended my marriage with Byron, although we stayed in contact and worked out the ending amicably. I had consistently raised my children to stand on their own feet, acknowledging the fact that, given my work, I would be away often, but also as the best insurance that they would be able to survive as adults in an uncertain world. Byron, I was sure, would continue to be there for the younger kids in his own way, and Nicky had already declared his independence from me by trying to move to his father's place. My kids had plenty of experience fending for themselves in a number of unfamiliar environments. Irwin's kids had always lived in their same eighteenth-floor apartment on the Lower East Side. Their grandparents lived only a few steps away, and their mom was nearly always home after school. My kids had only vaguely known their grandparents, who lived in faraway places, and I was the kind of mom who could be counted on to leave as surely as she could be counted on to return home.

As we massaged these difficult questions over the next few days, it began to look as if it would be nearly impossible to uproot Irwin from his New York City locus, while my situation seemed to have more flexibility. It occurred to me that I could probably work as well with New York as home base as I could with the West Coast as my anchor, maybe even better. It didn't become apparent to me until I had left it how much my own network mattered to me. My relatively high profile in the folk music and jazz circles of the West Coast was what made it possible for me to easily present my music, make a living with it, and continue to work with whatever organizations or campaigns I wanted to support.

But I knew with every cell in my mind, heart, and body that my future lay with Irwin, and I realized that if I didn't make this move to New York now, my future would never stand a chance of unfolding as it should. How in hell was I going to manage it? Would it create more havoc in my life and those of my children than I could ever repair? Or would it open unimagined doors for all of us? Just how I would manage a cross-country move was unclear, but I knew I would have my mother's help in a pinch. Surely she would be delighted to have me near, and would have more opportunities to see her grandchildren if I lived in New York. In turn, they would finally get to know Grandma Dorothy.

As things hadn't worked out living with Rolf, Nicky asked me if I would allow him to move to a room near the campus that was only fifteen dollars a month and, if I didn't mind, would I buy him some white paint to make it nicer. He took me to check out his proposed digs, a shabby little room in a run-down student rooming house a few blocks away, and I reluctantly agreed to his plan. Rolf lived in the same Berkeley neighborhood, and though he could barely manage his own life, I figured he would at least be some sort of backup for Nicky in case of trouble. A move across the country for my boy would have meant leaving his own plans, his friends, and all his musical connections too, which he took very seriously.

Over time, I had developed a lot of trust in Carroll Peery, my old friend from the Ash Grove days, and he became invaluable as I was getting ready to move to the East Coast and trying to figure out what might be best for Nicky. By this time, Carroll had moved to Berkeley, and, besides running the Cabale folk club with Rolf, he found himself in the role of a sort of psychologist without portfolio to many young people roaming Telegraph Avenue in search of themselves. With all the grace and generosity of spirit he was known for, he stepped up to the plate when trouble arose, and became Nicky's legal guardian.

My plan for Paul was that he stay in Berkeley with Byron for the near future, a decision that was heartbreaking for me. But it seemed wrong to move a boy so far from his father at that particular age. At twelve, he also had a strong network of friends, and everything I read about this stage of a kid's life seemed to advise that this was when they were forming their own agenda, their own personhood apart from their family's demands, and that this needed to be respected.

Nina was only eight and a half, and I hoped that as soon as I could get things together she would come to live with me and Irwin in New York. But for now, I had to leave her in Byron's care, in her home place with her dad, who had always given her tender and loving attention. There she could continue to freely move around Berkeley's streets, parks, and open fields with her best friend, Zibby, and her faithful companion, Seamus, a beautiful red Irish setter, as sweet and unforgettable as a dog could be. Those were the days when we still left the keys in the car, the doors unlocked, our dogs unleashed, and our children unshackled.

By the end of the summer, I had become desperate to see my little Nina, and sent for her to join me. She traveled by herself on a plane, wearing a big tag with her name and destination on it. I already knew that she was going to miss her dad, her brothers, her dog, and so many other big and little things children cherish. New York would not be easy for either of us. While I was struggling to get my life in order, Nina and I stayed with my mother, and I started looking for an appropriate apartment where we could begin our new life.

Thanks to rent control—and very good luck—I found an incredible four-bedroom, three-bathroom apartment for a paltry $350 in a Stanford White–designed Beaux-Arts architectural treasure on the Upper West Side. We wound up living there from October 1964 to September 1966. But there were still things that I needed to wrap up before making this monumental move, so I took a quick trip back west.

One day, as I was wading through piles of tough decisions related to moving, I got a frantic phone call from Peter Franck, everybody's trusted young "movement" lawyer, informing me that there was a major student protest going on at that very moment on the UC Berkeley campus and that I might be needed. A former grad student named Jack Weinberg had been sitting at a CORE (Congress on Racial Equality) literature table on Sproul Plaza passing out flyers when the campus police tried to arrest him. Just now he was trapped inside a police car, with two to three thousand other students surrounding it in an attempt to prevent his arrest. Peter said that a charismatic young student named Mario Savio had been speaking from the roof of the police car and moderating the flow of other speakers who had begun showing up, but that Savio was on the verge of collapse from exhaustion after a couple of days like this without sleep.

Peter was urging me to come down there and hold the crowd together with songs while acting as a sort of MC for a few hours while Mario got some rest. I dropped everything and headed right over. I could see that this protest was a turning point. The Free Speech Movement proved to be one of the most significant and far-reaching events of the era, a flagship for the many campus movements that were to follow in its wake.

As Alameda County sheriffs and campus police began to surround us, and rumors of mass arrests rippled through the crowd, I sang three or four songs from the top of the police car, stomping my bare feet as I led them in singing Malvina Reynolds's inflammatory "It Isn't Nice" and other songs I had just been singing in Mississippi, such as "Go Tell It on the Mountain" and "I'm on My Way." Our beloved listener-sponsored KPFA radio broadcast the whole thing.

Next day, after summoning the moving guys to pick up my rocking chair, refrigerator, and countless boxes, I really was on my way.

30

YOU DON'T KNOW ME

While I was furnishing the new apartment with wonderful vintage furniture from what New Yorkers referred to as junk stores, Irwin had that dreaded talk with his wife, and then with his children, which was, of course, terribly painful for all of them. He made it clear that he would continue his financial support, and it was decided that Sylvia and the kids would remain in their apartment on the Lower East Side, near their grandparents and where Irwin could easily continue frequent parental contact. Soon he began moving his own belongings to 71st Street.

Apart from my relationship with Irwin, I had my own relationship to *Sing Out!* to think about. I had been in those same circles since the earliest incarnation, when Pete started the *People's Songs Bulletin* in 1946, and considered my relation to these folks as if we were all part of the same moving village. Now that I was living in New York, I started writing articles for *Sing Out!* and began to enjoy the process, because it gave me an outlet for letting the world know more about performers I admired, such as Jesse Fuller and the Chambers Brothers.

In celebration of Lead Belly's seventy-fifth birthday, Irwin produced a program at the Town Hall and I was honored to be on the show. Although I had never met Huddy Ledbetter, he inspired and influenced me deeply, and I did my best to reflect that.

Around this time, I was singing occasionally at Gerdes Folk City in the Village. Mike Porco, the sweet Italian guy who ran the place, got started booking folk music early on, taking cues from the Folklore Center's Izzy Young about whom to book. Izzy's credentials as the founder and proprietor of the Folklore Center meant that he knew nearly every singer, player, and songwriter in the Village and beyond, and his *Sing Out!* columns meant that everyone knew his opinions and ideas.

Mike's innocence had the effect of giving the proceedings on the stage all the freedom in the world, and if he liked you, he'd bring you back whenever you were ready. A couple of music critics, most notably Robert Shelton at the *New York Times*, took a shine to the scene there, and pretty soon everyone was wanting to do their thing in this accidental folkie haven and showcase. I liked it for the informality and because Mike just seemed so pleased when someone went over well with the crowd and he saw people having a good time.

Most of my nights were solo gigs, with occasional guests dropping in. One night when I was singing my heart out on some basic twelve-bar blues, with only my usual rudimentary guitar for support, I heard somebody starting to plunk away with me on the upright piano at the back of the stage. I looked around to see that it was that kid in the corduroy cap who liked to hang around Mike's place and was taking the liberty of joining me. When I moved to another song, maybe a Woody ballad, there he was again, standing in back of me and singing harmony like it was meant to be. I had known Bob Dylan since we did the TV show the year before and had gotten to know him even better when we met up in LA, and here he was, showing up again. He added a nice touch of solidarity, and since he didn't try to take over or make more of it than it was, I appreciated the fact that he trusted me and the music and the audience enough to just do what came naturally. And so, a belated thanks, Bob.

Another wonderful Gerdes night was when the legendary Victoria Spivey floated in like a queen, her vassal Len Kunstadt near at hand. She had cut her first record in 1926, but by 1965 had outlived most of the other women of the classic blues period and still had plenty of glamour and vocal power after forty years of rockin' the house with her "Black Snake Moan." She was having a bit of a comeback at the time, appearing throughout the US and at one of Horst Lippman's American Blues Festivals in Europe with a cohort of other old-timers. And she had

Barbara Dane and Bob Dylan. New York City, 1965

recently launched her own blues label—Spivey Records—with Kunstadt. I was deeply gratified that she bothered to come to hear me. She seemed to enjoy herself all evening, with the occasional admirer dropping by her table to pay their respects.

Soon after I arrived in New York, I had a call from Chris Albertson, author of the first biography of Bessie Smith and an ardent devotee of the classic blues. At the time, he was also the program director at WBAI-FM, the New York part of the Pacifica group that had begun in Berkeley as KPFA, the first independent listener-sponsored station in history. He was asking whether I would be interested in hosting a radio show. I'm sure what Chris anticipated was a show focusing on the blues, although he didn't specify. But they had no folk music show on the roster—in fact, almost no station anywhere had one—and here I was living with the editor of the country's leading folk music magazine. I told Chris that the show would be called *Sing Out!* and that my cohost would be Irwin Silber. We would feature live guests playing music that ranged from blues to bluegrass and beyond, drafting whoever was available. We started right off with old friends Brownie McGhee and Sonny Terry, and after them came a steady stream of brilliant musicians, anyone we could grab who was passing through town. We discovered, as I had suspected, that almost any musician would be happy to play live on the air and talk about their performance and recording plans, along with their ideas and personal history. You can bet we had nothing but the best! The show ran for about a year.

Most of the organizers and writers and editors and producers around the folk music scene in general didn't seem to have a lot of actual music in their daily lives unless they were going out to a club or a concert to review it. Well, that would change for Irwin, since any home of mine would never be long without musicians hanging out, rehearsing, or just enjoying the making of their own music as they jammed or practiced. It rarely would be anything planned, but more often was a case of musicians simply being in a space where it was OK to play. More than once, I have heard musicians say that there are only four things a musician needs: a bite to eat, a drop to drink, a place to sleep, and a place to make music.

When Christmas of 1964 came, Irwin, Nina, and I had a wonderful reason to leave New York, with its chilly winds and holiday madness. I was invited by Guy Carawan and local activist Esau Jenkins to sing at a local festival at John's Island, South Carolina. This was the home of the Moving Star Hall singers, the group that had moved me more than most anything at the Newport Folk Festival that summer, so the opportunity to meet and hear Janie Hunter, Mrs. Mary Pinckney, Benjamin and Ruth Bligen, and others in their home place, to stand in their aging and unadorned wooden hall and hear their voices blending, their feet stamping, and their hands voicing the various clapping tones as they have done since their parents and grandparents before them was a dream come true.

This was a festival without pretensions, without commercial trappings, but with voices and hearts giving everything they had to be together in concert with one another, barely a distinction between the so-called professionals and the people who came to listen. This was more like the way I imagined people had gathered and shared their music since before there were microphones or stages, contracts or managers, or recording companies circling like vultures. The music was flowing from our lives and woven into our everyday experiences. I could see that Nina was drinking deeply of all this, and what she was taking from it could never have been found in a classroom.

There was a sparkling-white clapboard church on a little hill in the village, where the faithful spent their Sunday mornings in whatever finery was accessible to them. But it was at the praise house down on River Road called Moving Star Hall where the traditional and more personal spiritual life was expressed in the evenings. For as long as anyone could remember, the souls who tarried at Moving Star Hall had spent the hours of New Year's Eve singing, praying, shouting, and stomping out their intricate rhythms until dawn. I was yearning to spend those hours with them, to allow myself to open up to the spirit they were celebrating, although interpreting its meaning according to my own heart's secular ways.

This was not part of their festival, but a very private meeting of neighbors, many linked by family ties, but all known to one another most of their lives. The other out-of-town visitors who had come for the festival had left, and it was humbling to realize how rare it was for outsiders like us to be trusted enough to be invited to share that night.

The voices of the worshipers were sometimes soft, sometimes strident, but always saturated with emotion. The improvisational lead voice blended homemade biblical poetry and prayer, intensifying the mood in concert with the polyrhythms created by the high- and low-toned hand clapping and the simple but precise foot stomping. During the "shout" part that came later, we were cautioned not to take our feet off the ground or cross them. As the voices rose, the handclaps became louder and more intricate, and every sentient being in the room began to move rhythmically across the floor. Maybe that's the meaning of the building's name? Nothing like that night has ever moved me more deeply, and I believe it left an equally deep message in my daughter, a gift of a lifetime.

For these men and women, Moving Star Hall was a sanctuary where one could unburden the heart and draw strength and courage from one another. In this special place, the masks of the day could fall away, fears or doubts could be confessed, private joys could be expressed, and each singer seemed to feel a direct connection to their personal deity. These people were not going to crumble, regardless of the hardships life handed them. The suffering and humiliation of the generations before had shaped these tools, and the ancestors had taught them well how to use them.

One of the things that makes the preservation of pockets of African American cultural survival like this so important is the way it connects the people all across the African diaspora, from New Orleans to Cuba to Haiti to Brazil to Peru to the Dominican Republic and anywhere else in the hemisphere where much of the human capital required to build the so-called New World was brought, through kidnapping, human trafficking, and enslavement. Through the cultural connections, the immensity of these crimes is revealed, the superhuman effort involved in resistance may be celebrated, the sustaining belief may be reinforced that an ultimate overcoming is possible, and the envisioning of oneself as part of a proud and noble majority rather than a despised minority can be achieved. Through recognition of one another as part of an enormous web of humanity with a common culture, people can see themselves not as victims, not as people without agency in modern life, but as possessors of a powerful set of tools that have enabled their people to survive through the flames of hell on earth. This is no small achievement.

31

HARD RAINS ARE A-FALLIN'

Back in New York, I took to getting up uncharacteristically early just to make Irwin an elegant and sustaining breakfast—fresh-squeezed orange juice, crisp bacon, eggs sunny-side up, hot coffee, the works. After all, I didn't want him to be hungry before I went down to Times Square, where the *Sing Out!* office was, to meet him for lunch at that wonderful old-fashioned American comfort food emporium on 46th Street called Gus and Andy's. Irwin was struggling to lay off the most fattening foods, without much success. I myself had thrown all caution to the wind. We would then each go about our afternoon's affairs until time to meet again, now for dinner at La Strada on 45th Street, probably a steak with asparagus on top, à la Pepe, a specialty of the house, preceded by my favorite appetizer, *prosciutto e melón*, and probably a martini. I know it sounds unbelievable that we ate that much day after day, but our juices were flowing, and we both always seemed to be starving. Yes, we both took on some of that old avoirdupois to be sure, and later we had to pay.

All went literally like a dream for a few weeks, until one day without fanfare Irwin announced that he just couldn't handle all these changes, that he was feeling too much guilt about leaving his children—even though he knew he would be able to see them as often as he wished—and now found it necessary to move back to Grand Street and Sylvia's household. He professed his enduring love for me but kissed me good-bye and left. I remember that when the door closed behind him that afternoon I lay down on a nearby daybed and thought I was literally going to die. I felt that all the blood had drained out of me and my brain had gone to sleep. I went numb all over and had to lie there for an hour or two before I could function at all. And I remained in some sort of mental blackout, which seems to be preventing me, even now, from completely untangling what happened next.

Irwin moved all his books, records, and clothes back downtown, a huge logistical task involving a moving truck and a team of workers. But here is the oddest turn of events: it was only a matter of days before he asked whether he could move everything back again and declared that this time, he was with me for good. What could have happened to help him work out his thoughts and get through these days remains a mystery, but of course I came back to life, opened my arms and my heart to him again, and that was the last time we spoke of it. The next two years there were some of the happiest of my life, and certainly some of the most productive. That is, if you can be happy in the midst of being depressed.

I was, as usual, up to my eyeballs in projects and problems resulting from my move to New York. I only realized much later that for psychological reasons I was covering up an unrecognized but inescapable case of depression by disguising my disorientation with a Lady Bountiful costume and an "I can cope with just about anything" mask. Anyone who has uprooted themselves from a place where time has awarded them some social currency and familiarity, only to find themselves looking up from the bottom of a basket of crabs, will recognize how I was feeling. I had left a West Coast world where I could easily pick up the phone and get a booking or press coverage, where people came to me for advice and counsel. Now here I was, in Noo Yawk City, the Big Apple, the Center of the Universe, with my new life concentrated in the highly charged, overly romanticized, and competitive little world of "the folk scene" just as that community was evolving from what had started out, in the Cold War atmosphere, as a kind of substitute for a politicized youth movement into what I would mordantly describe as "the folk biz" in this era of relative openness and prosperity.

In my imagination, there would be a warm welcome waiting for a stranger in a new land, especially one bearing good credentials and an open heart. Instead, I felt that I was seen as a carpetbagger cutting straight from nowhere to the front of the line—at least in the minds of not a few strivers—and, of all the nerve, bundling with the boss, the guy with the power of the pen. That attitude may have been largely in my imagination, but still I was feeling the sting of being seen as the outsider where in another setting I had been kind of a queen bee.

That pain was not eased by having to deal with Irwin's frequent family contacts, the ones where I was habitually assigned to waiting in the car outside their Grand Street apartment while he made an after-dinner visit to the kids. I sincerely respected his efforts to keep them as secure about his connections to them as possible, but wouldn't it have been more natural for them to see me coming and going with him as well? And I had no experience with being seen as a nonperson, a pariah, a leper, or maybe the "wicked stepmother." Oh yes, there was a price to be paid for all this redesigning of lives, and always the nagging possibility that this was all wrong.

By 1965, a great sense of pain and disillusionment was spreading over the country. Alice Herz, a survivor of the Nazi horrors during World War II in Germany, was a kindly, dignified woman in hat and gloves who was always a gentle presence in Detroit at antiwar activities and protests against atomic weapons. As a teenager I had known her as we took part in the same demonstrations, and she had encouraged my youthful unrest by assuring me that everything would be all right some day. But on March 16, 1965, she publicly immolated herself in Detroit at the age of eighty-two, the strongest statement she could make against war. She lived ten more days due to a misdirected rescue attempt, making her purpose clear through a letter she left for her daughter Helga. Her intention was to follow the example of a Vietnamese Buddhist monk who had recently taken this desperate way of demonstrating his own opposition to the war, in solidarity with him. I was, of course, devastated by the news, but somehow I saw it as a terribly lonely act, a failure of our movement to have provided to Alice, and perhaps others, the sense of strength in numbers, the kind of united opposition that might have helped her find the joy flowing from confronting the war makers with a power that could actually stop wars. Or perhaps she had just become exhausted from her eighty years, a lifetime, of confronting mankind's inhumanity to man that seemed to know no final defeat.

A few days later, President Lyndon Johnson described our objective in Vietnam as "the independence of South Vietnam, and its freedom from attack," after which he ordered the escalation of a fierce and deadly air war, bombing that small country of peasants indiscriminately, with cruel and previously unimagined weapons of destruction.

In response, on April 17 the SDS (Students for a Democratic Society) mobilized the largest Washington demonstration against the Vietnam War to date, illustrating the ability of increasing numbers of Americans to cut through the curtain of official lies in order to express themselves in opposition to what was, by now, clearly not a war, a contest with two opposing sides, but an American invasion. It was a lifetime thrill for me to sing for the assembly of twenty-five thousand people who had made their way to DC from all around the country, united as they were in pursuit of immediate withdrawal and peace. It would be the first of many times I sang there with the growing throngs of dedicated demonstrators.

UC Berkeley, 1965. © Mike Alexander/*The San Francisco Chronicle*

On May 5, several hundred people carrying black coffins set off for the Berkeley Draft Board. At least forty of them burned their draft cards on the spot. My son Paul was then living in Berkeley with his dad, and friends spotted him in the march, not old enough yet to have a draft card but upset enough about the war to be there. Yes, even junior high school youngsters were beginning to march to the antiwar drums now echoing all across the country. Over the weekend of May 21–22, approximately thirty-five thousand people in the Bay Area took part in Vietnam Day, organized by Jerry Rubin, Abbie Hoffman, and a cohort of other UC Berkeley students. Jerry asked whether I would fly out to participate, and sent me a ticket. Nothing could have stopped me.

That trip back to Berkeley also allowed me to spend some time with Paul. I knew he was on his own most of the time and suspected that he was beginning to hang out on the Avenue, where the fragrance of cannabis drifted through the streets. I also found out that Paul had been leading the trombone section in the school band at Garfield Junior High School until the teacher noticed that his sheet music was upside down! He had been learning all the parts by ear on first hearing and leading them confidently without benefit of any sight-reading skills. Time for him to start taking some serious music lessons!

32

THREE-MILE WALK OF HOPE

In 1965, the Newport Folk Festival ran July 22–25, and as Irwin and I drove up to Rhode Island, all we could talk about was the fearsome expansion of the military intervention in Vietnam and what it could mean for the people of the US. Both of us had a sense of wanting to do something to expose the dangers more broadly, to find something we could do to help people express their growing and increasingly justified fears, and even to encourage popular resistance to the escalation. Reflecting on the interest being shown in the teach-ins that students were holding on many campuses, Irwin came up with the idea of a giant *sing-in*, and since we were on our way to a large gathering of the very people who might be enlisted in making this happen, why not start talking it up this weekend and see what response we would get from the movers and shakers?

For most of the "folk" world, Newport 1965 is remembered as the year of Dylan's famous defection from the ranks of acoustic guitar twangers, as some would see it, or his deviation from the path of righteous politically themed poetic endeavor, as others insisted. But apart from Dylan, Newport 1965 was full of important new developments. For example, the New Folk and Contemporary Song workshop presentations by Len Chandler, the Kweskin Jug Band, Mark Spolestra, Dick and Mimi Fariña, and others brought compelling examples of the rising youthful energy and creativity that would provide relevance to the whole idea of folk song as the future unfolded. In the traditional realm, there was even a workshop that focused on the dulcimer and featured Dick Fariña right alongside Jean Ritchie, the woman who had introduced the instrument to the wider world beyond Appalachia.

Before I moved east, a young gospel quartet from Mississippi showed up at the Ash Grove, and when I invited them to sit in with me, everyone could see that, together, the Chambers Brothers and I could bring new life to the freedom songs that were helping change history. We worked together so seamlessly, I took to inviting them to share the bill with me several times over the next couple of years, mostly in their gospel quartet mode, although they would often open the show with their wonderful bottle band, which they had invented as kids in the Mississippi cotton fields using a washtub bass, a jug, and various bottles filled with water at different levels to provide for different pitches. We raised money for voter registration projects in Mississippi at quite a few of our shows together, but when I asked whether they would consider going there with me to sing at the Freedom Schools, their answer was understandable: any young Black man who had made it out of there alive was never going back just to visit.

By the time I moved to New York, I couldn't stop thinking about recording those songs with them. The Brothers agreed wholeheartedly. Moe Asch at Folkways quickly recognized the value of offering the public an example of Black and white people singing so easily in harmony, especially since the material would feature songs from the contemporary civil rights movement.

I called Pete Seeger and asked whether he could get them onto the roster of the upcoming 1965 Newport Festival, which would pay for their flights east and make it possible for Asch to move ahead with the project. I reached Pete just in the nick of time, and he phoned back within minutes to say that everything was a go.

Once in New York, the Brothers went into a whirlwind of activity, but the day before they were to depart for Newport, I managed to get them into Moe's studio, where he customarily served as engineer. No time was left for rehearsal, but after a quick agreement on key and tempo, we recorded each song with one take only, voices and hearts in deep, if temporary, harmony. I am still very proud of the results, and all these years later, I get messages thanking me for that recording.

At Newport, the Brothers invited me to sing a couple of songs with them on their Sunday morning gospel set, where someone took that wonderful photo that appears on the Folkways record jacket. This is one of the first album covers on any label showing a white woman and Black men singing together, and that will go down in history, as it is something that—as I had been told at Capitol Records just three years before—couldn't be done.

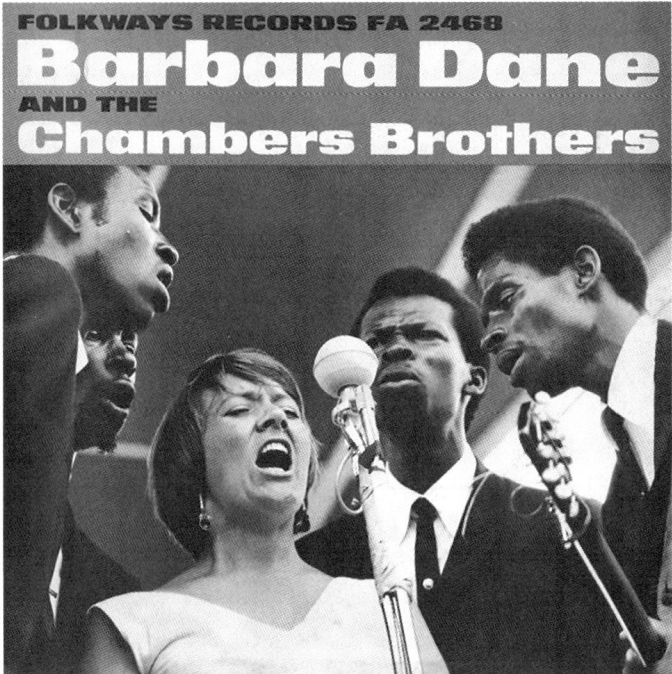

Barbara Dane with the Chambers Brothers at Newport Folk Festival, 1965. (Smithsonian Folkways)

A few days later, I invited the Chambers Brothers to join me for a show at Cafe Au Go Go in NYC, sharing the bill with the Paul Butterfield Blues Band, who had just backed Dylan at Newport. That night my son Paul, who was visiting from California, played with us, and remembers that a young unknown guitarist named Jimi Hendrix came to jam that night and blew his mind. Although Paul was technically too young to be in there, he was already six feet tall, helping him look older than his fourteen years, so I had no worries about that.

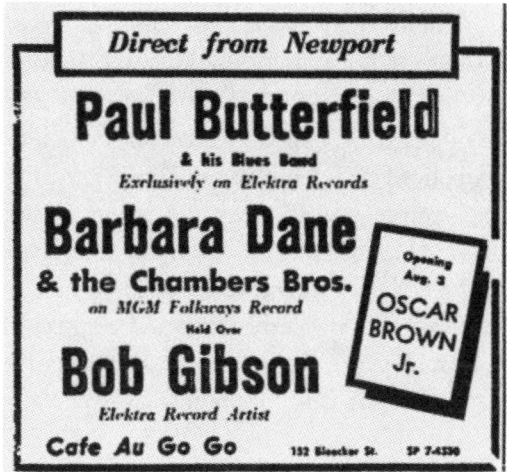

Village Voice ad for the performance at Cafe Au Go Go

As for the infamous Dylan performance at Newport, I was thunderstruck by the honesty and bravery of it, both the electric part with its monumental songs and his tearful acoustic denouement. Something was indeed happening here, not exactly clear, but set out there plainly and painfully for us all to examine. This was a time to open ourselves up to new directions, not only in music.

> The vagabond who's rapping at your door
> Is standing in the clothes that you once wore
> Strike another match, go start anew
> And it's all over now, Baby Blue

Almost a year before the Newport performance, Irwin had written an open letter to Bob in *Sing Out!*, often quoted but generally misunderstood, expressing his concern that Bob was, in effect, throwing away his base of support—turning from his groundbreaking lyrical expositions of the peace and justice issues boiling all around us, those great songs that were providing singers with tools of unprecedented poetic eloquence with which to express these things—and instead beginning to focus on the more mundane personal issues of youth. Disappointment, yes, but far from disdain or disillusionment.

In truth, though, apart from the Dylan brouhaha that year at Newport, perhaps the clearest signal of the disintegration of the cherished "folk ethic" pipe dream came at the very end of the festival. The previous couple of years had ended with gestures of a kind of organized spontaneity, symbolic of the democratic and inclusive mission envisioned by many in the crowd as well as on the platform, with performers returning to the stage to lead one final song together with the audience. This year, someone had the brilliant idea of asking the legendary Fannie Lou Hamer, one of the most dearly loved and respected leaders of the Mississippi freedom movement and also a great singer, to lead the closing song. Here is part of Irwin's description of what took place:

> [H]ordes of singers, musicians, self-appointed participants and temporary freaks take over the stage in a tasteless exhibition of frenzied incest that seemed to have been taken from a Hollywood set. One singer called it a "nightmare of pop art," one of the more apt and gentle of the comments heard in the audience. The stage invasion took place during the singing of Mrs. Fannie Lou Hamer, one of that incredible sisterhood of Mississippi heroines who are in the process of reshaping America for us all. It seemed as though everyone wanted to make sure they were in on the great "civil rights act" and a moment that might have become the high point of the entire weekend was suddenly turned into a scene of opportunistic chaos . . . reducing the meaning of Newport to the sense of a carnival gone mad.

We walked slowly away along with the crowd sorting its way through a general sense of disorientation, our own eyes wet with tears and our hearts determined to create a more focused musical event.

We called it a Sing-In for Peace in Vietnam and set it to take place on September 24, 1965, at Carnegie Hall. Almost all of the folk *machers* Irwin approached agreed to be on a committee to make this happen, with one glaring exception, Al Grossman. I had been appointed coordinator, and I sent invitations to every last singer whose address I could get hold of—from the hills of Kentucky to the Georgia Sea Islands—to Pete Seeger, Joan Baez, Phil Ochs, Alan Lomax, and of course the people in the Grossman grouping, asking for their personal participation or a brief recorded statement or at least a contribution to help make it happen. No response from the Grossman gang. People in his stable reliably showed up for the most newsworthy events of the civil rights movement, and if there would be TV cameras and national press, Albert made sure of that. But in an effort to stay firmly on the fence regarding the war, he vetoed the participation of his artists in our sing-in, so the event took place without Bob Dylan, Peter, Paul and Mary, and Odetta. Grossman, with his own peculiar logic, had decided that "it would harm their civil rights work" to appear at a peace concert. It must have been hard for the artists to sort it out: Do we choose peace advocacy, or do we choose Albert? I guess they decided to let their work stand for itself. Anyway, even without these so-called superstars, we sold out every seat in Carnegie Hall twice that night, a total of approximately seven thousand admissions.

Harold Leventhal (who managed Pete Seeger, Judy Collins, and others), Jac Holzman (whose Elektra Records featured several key folk artists), Moe Asch of Folkways Records, and Art D'Lugoff (who ran the Village Gate, where many top performers appeared) all got on board with enthusiasm. An overwhelming sixty performers responded, each paying their own way to come to New York for the opportunity to sing only one song. Leventhal was able to convince Carnegie Hall to let us run two shows that night to accommodate them all. We were profoundly honored by the presence of Fannie Lou Hamer, as well as of Bernice Reagon and the Freedom Singers, who brought their inspiring songs to the evening. Bob Moses, the legendary leader of SNCC, was in the audience. It didn't seem to hurt anyone's civil rights work at all to take up the call for an end to this dreadful war.

People calling about tickets kept asking which show Joan Baez would be singing on, so we asked her to appear on both shows, but everyone else had their single moment, the only way we could make room for about thirty different performances on each program. To save time, Irwin came up with a genius device: no MC would introduce the performers. Each person would simply step out and say something like "My name is . . ., and I am here because . . ." The effect was stunning. One after another,

Sing-In for Peace in Vietnam. Carnegie Hall, New York City, 1965. © Dan Kramer

a direct and heartfelt statement uninterrupted by any kind of puffery. Performers and audience alike were there in that magnificent space with but a single purpose: to confirm and validate the enormous wave of antiwar sentiment that was building in the nation. And, of course, to bear witness to one of the historic occasions when the folk community came together as one, in the pursuit of peace.

At the end of the music, at nearly 3 a.m., everyone was invited to take part in a candlelight march down to Greenwich Village, where coffee would be waiting at the Village Gate courtesy of owner Art D'Lugoff. This was one of the first times something like this had ever taken place in this city that has "seen everything," and there was an uncharacteristic hush as we silently passed down through the still-darkened street and the early dawn traffic of 7th Avenue in the slow lane, a blocks-long double file of faces lit only by flickering candles. A three-mile-long walk of hope.

The world outside our apartment was beginning to break out everywhere with signs of awareness that there was something terrible happening in Vietnam, and an awakening to the realization that Americans of conscience could no longer look the other way. By January 1966, 170,000 young American boys had been drafted and another 180,000 had enlisted in the armed forces, while another two million had qualified for college deferments. There had already been nearly nine thousand US casualties. The nation was divided on that level alone, and the ramifications of this began to reverberate through every other level of civil society.

Over the course of the next several years, I managed to sing at literally every single peace rally in Washington, partly because I saw this work as at the center of my own commitment, but also because of the way it always fills up my soul to feel that same commitment being expressed by thousands and thousands of people acting together. It was endlessly inspiring to watch the numbers of protesters constantly growing and the level of sophistication about the issues growing too.

33

GOOD MORNING BLUES

Something I had been hoping and working for most of my life finally happened in the mid-sixties when the Newport Folk Festival recognized the centrality of the blues to American music. Just as their lives were on the shaky edge of viability, Fred MacDowell, Bukka White, Son House, Skip James, Robert Pete Williams, Howlin' Wolf, and a few others of these survivors were gathered together in what became a celebratory event. These were the giants who had created the bedrock of the blues out of their need to "make a way out of no way" in an American culture steeped in racism. This turned out to be one of the key starting points for a worldwide blues revival that would be unprecedented and unstoppable.

The roots of African American culture have produced branches and flowers of enormous variety, and the blues sprang forth as one powerful way of expressing the deeply personal, which of course is often the path to the heart of the collective experience. The blues were born out of the worst conditions one people can force on another—out of slavery and exploitation—and were given to the world in the spirit of turning madness into sanity, pain into joy, bondage into freedom, and enmity into unity. This is music for survivors, and this spirit is something to be learned from, shared, and spread as far as it will go!

Musicians like these had appeared on the festival as individuals in the past, something like a dash of pepper in the stew, and most of

Newport Folk Festival, 1966. © David Gahr

them were already playing clubs and coffeehouses, and some even had electric bands to back them. This time, however, they were an assembly representing the long history of the many others on whose shoulders they stood. This day, without reservation, they gave of themselves and their music for most of an afternoon from a stage in a large field, before a sea of nearly all white faces that numbered in the thousands and felt like worshipers. The great revival of country blues was on!

Yes, I was there, and yes, I sang a blues or two. At some point, one of the elders had passed a guitar to me and motioned me to join the group onstage. What could be more validating, more unexpected, and what would feel more natural than to accept the invitation? So there I was, flowing into the moment and feeling so free and happy. I was photographed as I sang, and this added to the mistaken idea that I had been officially invited to sing at the festival, but I am grateful for the picture that brings the moment alive again for me.

The blues revival was mostly a male scene, but still there were several women who had a lot to say, although they were most often underacknowledged. Estella "Mama" Yancey had certainly served to show me the way for a while now, and one of my dreams was to see to it that she could make a well-recorded collection of her signature songs while she was still packing plenty of vocal power. I was overjoyed when Verve/Folkways Records agreed to front the money for me to fly to Chicago for the purpose of producing the project, and I proposed that her accompaniment would be that great blues piano man Art Hodes. I had worked with Art myself at the Cafe Continental years before, and I knew the spirit of Mama's late husband, Jimmy Yancey, was alive under his fingers in a way that would make Mama feel right at home and very happy. That was, in fact, the way the whole recording session unfolded. She was in pretty good health and not drinking too much, and, with Art's ability to lay in the unique features of that special Yancey style to perfection, she blossomed. I still think *Mama Yancey Sings, Art Hodes Plays Blues* turned out to be one of the best recordings she ever made.

In the spring of 1966, Dr. Bernice Reagon and Anne Romaine, both folklorists, singers, and civil rights activists, teamed up to form the Southern Folk Cultural Revival. Theirs was a groundbreaking idea: to illustrate southern history in song and demonstrate that even through the long years of segregation, Black and white musical cultures have cross-fertilized and intermingled. With the support of the SSOC (Southern Students Organizing Committee) and SNCC, they pulled together a contingent made up of eight young and old, male and female, Black and white musicians. Hedy West; Mable Hillery; Gil Turner; Len Chandler; Rev. Pearly Brown; Eleanor Walden; Bernice and her small baby, Toshi Reagon; and me, with my ten-year-old daughter, Nina, made up the passenger list in the two secondhand cars that would carry us across the South.

We presented our music for folk clubs, campus groups, church groups, and human relations councils, traveling in three weeks' time through eighteen cities from Florida and Virginia to Arkansas and Texas. In Atlanta, we were privileged to perform at Ebenezer Baptist Church, the spiritual home of Martin Luther King Jr. Every night was different from the last, with other guests sometimes joining us. Even Pete Seeger joined us in Austin. Everywhere we went, we were met with a warm welcome, and audiences—sometimes forty or fifty, sometimes a thousand—were ready to sing with us. Although we knew the world outside was engaged in a historic struggle for civil rights, we did not face any racist encounters directly related to our performances, surely due to the social skills of our leader, Bernice, and others experienced in southern customs. Somehow we held it together in spite of traveling crowded into two elderly cars that burned a lot of gas. This I remember from a close call in Tennessee, where the station attendant eyed us with a hard face and suggested he was going to "call for help" if we didn't move on. Well, move on we did, just barely making it to the next available source of gas.

This tour had been organized primarily by Bernice Reagon, and it ended with a sense of gratitude, satisfaction, and joy. I'm sure that there were moments during the sweaty days and unpredictable nights when we each said silently, "What the hell am I doing here?" But I don't think any of us would pass up the chance to do it again. You couldn't find a better way to draw closer to your fellow musicians, to use music for a better purpose, to see the real South, and, most important, to reach audiences more clearly open and eager to learn, to feel, and to grow.

Barbara Dane with Bernice Reagon. Philadelphia Folk Festival, 1966.
© Diane Davies (Smithsonian Folkways)

34

CUBA SÍ, YANQUI NO!

My life took another major and unexpected turn later that summer. Estela Bravo, now a brilliant documentary filmmaker with thirty award-winning films behind her, was then working as a programmer for Radio Havana. She had come to New York to gather some recordings for her folk music show and visit her family. She had also been asked to look for an American folksinger willing to perform a series of concerts in Cuba in spite of the State Department's formidable travel restrictions, hoping to clarify that the revolutionary slogan "Cuba Sí, Yanqui No!" meant Cuba yes, Yankee *policies* no! and was in no way calling for any rupture with the historically warm ties between the people of the US and the people of Cuba.

A Brooklyn girl who had grown up with radical ideas, listening to Pete Seeger's music and the Almanac Singers, Estela had cast her lot with the Cuban revolution after her husband, Ernesto, had to flee his Argentine homeland rather than risk being jailed or worse. She first approached Pete about making the tour, but he had reservations about how defiance of the State Department might be seen by his Beacon, New York, neighbors, who served as his barometer of Middle America. He said that he would gladly come to Cuba later in the context of a full Latin American tour, which would have a logic that balanced out the picture for those neighbors. He then suggested that she ask me whether I would be interested in the proposition.

I guess Pete saw me as an artist who was habitually incautious about this fragile thing known as a career. That was true, of course, because it never would have occurred to me to weigh an idea in that light. On the world stage, nothing was happening anywhere that was more exciting than the Cuban revolution. The Cuban people, especially the young ones, were creating a whole new way of organizing society, and only ninety miles from our shores. Nothing could have kept me from saying yes to the invitation. Even less when I saw the official invitation with President Dorticós's signature right there on it! People often ask me in interviews whether I have regrets about any of what may have seemed, to some, to be rash decisions in my life. My answer is a resounding NO, and in the case of my Cuban adventures, I consider it one of the very best decisions of my life.

Irwin was excited about the opportunity to investigate and write about developments in the first country with an avowed socialist agenda in the Western Hemisphere. Like me, he didn't know a lot about Cuban music or musicians, but was eager to learn. We were to be hosted by a cultural project of the Cuban government, and this would give him the avenue to write about a burgeoning socialist system within the parameters of *Sing Out!*, "the folksong magazine." He started by notifying the State Department that we were requesting travel licenses for two journalists to visit Cuba, the most likely way we would be able to obtain permission to make the trip. He would be going as editor of the magazine, and I would be writing some articles for it upon our return.

We made arrangements for all the kids to be taken care of while we were gone, and my old friend Noël—who had already been staying with us in Manhattan for some time—agreed to house-sit. After too much time passed with no response from the State Department, Irwin called to advise them that whether the licenses came or not, we were going to exercise our right to travel, and that we would be traveling as journalists. *Punto*, no further discussion.

Passing through Immigration in Mexico was a strange experience. Because we were traveling with only our birth certificates for papers, the Mexican officials stamped their backs with *Salida a Cuba* (Departure for Cuba) in big red letters, hoping this would cloak their impotence to do anything about it. Then a tall white American fellow in standard FBI or CIA drag took these and our passports and ran them through a cumbersome old-fashioned copying device the size of a microwave oven. He warned us that we could not return to the US through Mexico without the proper licenses from the State Department. Of course, we expected that anyway, so without saying anything that might be considered confrontational, we boarded our flight. Our mission was not to test our government's will at this moment but to get on with making whatever contribution we could toward the building of bridges between our two peoples. From my Freedom of Information Act (FOIA) papers accessed in 2015, it's clear that Irwin and I were accompanied by informers and maybe worse on that flight to Cuba. That was probably the case for most flights from Mexico City to Havana at the time. Your tax dollars at work again.

As we flew toward Havana, my thoughts were filled with anticipation and hope. Until these last few hours, I had not fully realized how much I yearned to see people in the process of building something good for themselves with the support and encouragement of their government—building solidarity among dozens of grassroots organizations spread all over the country, instead of having to feel the constant pressure of being part of the opposition. My spirits were in deep need of a concrete example that could confirm what I have believed in all my life: the power of selfless cooperation in pursuit of a shared dream. In a world filled with so much noxious air, I needed something like the purifying winds Silvio Rodríguez wrote of some years later in his song "Rabo de nube."

We couldn't have been more surprised by the reception when the plane landed at Martí airport. As we stumbled down the portable steps strapped with all our carry-on belongings, we were blinded by the spotlights of a crew filming us for one of renowned film director Santiago Álvarez's weekly newsreels. Next, we were warmly embraced by a welcoming band of officials and their assistants, eager reporters throwing questions at us in Spanish, and at last, the familiar face of Estela Bravo, who spoke not only English but *NewYorkese*. With all this official hospitality at work, we were soon in the VIP lounge sipping Havana Club Añejo (the new name for what was the recently departed Bacardí family's best rum) on the rocks, as requested. Oh bliss! Soon the moist green air, infused with the warm brown nectar, was working its charm.

Every single thing was new to me. The language, the customs, the fragrant air, the humidity, the heat, the faces, the attitudes, the food, the relationships, the bureaucracy, the transportation, and most of all, the expectations. Over the course of the following days, I came to understand that my role was to be a symbol of the friendship between the peoples of our two countries, a relationship that was enduring despite the political differences between our two governments. I was proud to stand for the millions in my country who saw in Cuba a ray of hope for a new kind of social contract, especially one that meant kicking out the gangsters, the banksters, and the kleptocrats and creating new systems that could put power in the hands of ordinary people, counting on their collective wisdom to make things work.

It was clear that Cubans had a long-standing enthusiasm for all things American, and they expressed great warmth toward our people. But they were also very aware of the long history of catastrophic events that continued to burst out all over the globe in pursuit of the Yankee obsession with power. Cuba would never again become a subservient victim of American foreign policy. To be Cuban would mean to be fully in charge of one's own destiny.

We checked into our room at the Hotel Habana Libre, formerly the Hilton, up on a high floor where we could look from our balcony over the lights of the city. An enticing and unfamiliar scent was filling the air, a sexy gardenia-like fragrance, but stronger, insistent, nearly overpowering; then there it was: a tall earthenware vase filled with an abundance of creamy white blossoms, with a card personally signed by Haydée Santamaría, cherished heroine of the revolutionary struggle and now founder and protector of the Casa de las Américas. Everything I came to know about her later could have been summed up in that bouquet of Mariposa, Cuba's national flower: down-to-earth but romantic; sensuous, but dead serious about elevating the human spirit; generously honoring and welcoming to friends of her beloved country.

The next day, Estella took us to meet with the Cultural Council (Consejo de Cultura) representatives to discuss our agenda. We were to tour the island, stopping in several cities where I would sing and we would have an exchange with important cultural figures. But first we'd spend some time in Havana. I was to be given an entire Saturday evening to present a concert at the Amadeo Roldán Theatre, Cuba's equivalent of Carnegie Hall. Not only that, the concert would be televised across the whole country, and I could invite any guest performers I would like to take part. I asked what length the segments should be, how much time to allow for the usual commercials, and the producer laughed! "No, no, nothing like that. No commercials. The TV is ours now!"

I turned to Estela Bravo for advice about the musical guests, and she astutely recommended that we invite some of the heroes of Cuban popular music and jazz to open the show. What resulted was a lineup beyond any music lover's dreams. An all-star jazz group—including Frank Emilio on piano, Orlando Lopez (Cachaíto) on bass, and Tata Güines on congas—came first, followed by José Antonio Méndez, the singer and composer who embodied the romantic genre called *filin*, or "feeling." The great Carlos Puebla was invited to kick off the more topical part of the program. And then came Joseíto Fernández, composer of "Guantanamera" and sublime improviser of décimas detailing current events.

Irwin came up with the brilliant idea of having Adolfo y Justo, two stars of Cuban country music who were also skillful improvisers, introduce me with a traditional *contraversia*, one of them singing about the strange phenomenon of an American woman who came to sing songs of friendship with Cuba, and the other insisting that this was a crazy idea, it must be a fantasy, such a thing was not possible. When I walked out from the wings on cue, it proved to be an effective way of setting up expectations of more humor that would come through the music.

Since my songs would be in English, and because I liked to frame them with little improvised stories intended to give a context, I would need a really good translator up there with me. I was relieved and honored to have the best! My straight man and interlocutor turned out to be Manolo Ortega, the one who did this same sort of thing for Fidel himself. No matter what crazy spontaneous idea I threw out there, he managed to translate it for the audiences and apparently make sense of it, because I got laughs where I was hoping for laughs, and seriousness when that was the right note, while all the time he maintained a dignified flow to everything.

What did I sing? A mixture of folk songs, blues songs, union songs, and plenty of social commentary. Probably nothing any Cuban had ever heard before, and very little that would even be musically familiar. The reaction was generous and immediate, with representatives of many groups calling and sending notes of appreciation, periodicals and photographers setting up interviews, and best of all, the general public offering Cuban-style hugs and kisses whenever we passed on the street. Oddly, a man from the Masons even got in touch, saying he found out that my father had been a Mason and welcoming me to Cuba on their behalf. *Granma*, the Communist Party's newspaper and official national newspaper of record, published a nice article in its international weekly magazine, available in several languages and distributed throughout the world.

I couldn't go anywhere without being recognized, and often gathering a crowd. An unaccustomed circumstance for me, and one I wouldn't like to live with full-time. What made it bearable, and even welcome, during those weeks was the understanding that I was representing something much larger than myself, something Cubans were hungry for, and it was easy to see what that was: a clearing away of the political and economic obstacles between our two countries, a normalization of relations, and an opportunity for the world to see and understand Cuba's desire to make something new of their own, to design a future now free of the old constraints of foreign domination. The revolution had given its people a voice, after centuries of being defined by outsiders, and they were ready and eager to use it.

Irwin, of course, was accustomed to the way the public reacts to performers, how they often barely notice the people who happen to be accompanying them, and of course he met this with his usual equilibrium, maybe even a little relief, considering how often he was usually the main event back home. But the Consejo de Cultura began scheduling opportunities for him to meet with some of the country's most significant writers and poets: Nicolás Guillén, Roberto Fernández Retamar, Lisandro Otero, Pedro Pérez Sarduy, Pablo Armando Fernández, and others. Miguel Barnet was just coming out with his most celebrated book, *Cimarrón: Autobiography of a Runaway Slave*, and he generously introduced us to the scope of it. Many of these writers spoke fluent English because they had spent some years working and studying in the US during the Batista years, returning to their homeland after the triumph of the revolution to take part in the building of the new society. The fact that they were comfortable speaking our language and also experienced in various aspects of US culture was a big help to Irwin, and to me, because of course I went along with him to those meetings as often as possible.

Before I left Havana for the trip across the country, Estela had taken me to the home of Carlos Puebla, asking him to help me learn "Cuba, que linda es Cuba," the song she knew I would need to sing as an encore everywhere. Puebla had been making and singing songs against the barbarities of the past all his life, and these days was in his glory, with so many positive themes he could write about. This did not happen to be one of his own songs, but he generously struggled with helping this at-the-time-English-only speaker to see that I got it right.

To my amazement, as I made my way, concert by concert, across the country, each time Fidel's name was mentioned in the song, the crowd interrupted with thunderous nonstop applause, without any prompting and without exception. Estela was right! Seven years after the triumph of the revolution, it would have been foolish to attempt to end a concert without giving the audience a chance to sing this song, simply and sincerely expressing love for their homeland, their appreciation for its beauty, their pride in the fact that it was now seen as a beacon of liberty instead of a pathetic victim of imperialism, all summed up in the name of the man whose vision and dedication had led them to this place. The key line was "Cuba, how beautiful is Cuba; those who defend her love her best."

Don't forget, this is a country whose revolutionary leaders were barely into their thirties when they kicked out the US-backed Batista thugs and Lansky mobsters. These faces before me were their younger siblings or their kids, who would not have to grow up in a world distorted by people like that. They were the ones who were engaged in transforming their country into a place guided by love and respect for those stevedores and cane cutters, cigar rollers and ranch hands, domestic workers and their families who had survived the starvation and isolation of the past, the ones who had put their lives on the line to bring their country to this new place of dignity. Of course they wanted to celebrate this, and at every opportunity.

Our tour across the country had two threads. The first was made up of my concerts, sometimes in big halls but often outdoors, where I eagerly and gratefully drank in the energy and enthusiasm of the hundreds, often thousands, of Cubans of every generation but mostly young, who came to see what this American visitor would have to sing about. The second thread was for Irwin and me to witness and engage with as many aspects of Cuban culture as possible within the time we had. We traveled with a car and driver, accompanied by Estela Bravo, who was not only translating for us day after day but also giving us the cultural guidance that helped us avoid embarrassing ourselves.

There was, even then, a fairly decent highway that made its way the length of the country from east to west, and it was wonderful to have someone else responsible for the driving. We stopped for performances in most of the major cities and some smaller towns too, although I have to confess that the newness of everything, and the pace, prevented me from keeping track. Estela Bravo was indispensable in making sure that we arrived when and where we were expected. The local Consejos de Cultura made sure the venues were always jam-packed when we arrived. In my opinion, the audiences' enthusiasm was mostly due to the novelty of it all, because the level of musical skills at my command was certainly no match for the legendary riches of Cuban music.

It was astonishing for me to realize that only seven years after the revolution triumphed, they had managed to put together some kind of Casa de Cultura (cultural center) in nearly every city and town. These were sometimes in former municipal buildings, church basements or schools, or converted private houses, and even with the enormous shortages of every kind, bits of sound equipment or theatrical lighting, paint, paper and canvas, costumes and greasepaint—whatever could be found of the thousand other things needed to make art had been pulled together and made available to anyone, along with free classes. Since my specialty is music, our brief visits to the Casas were usually filled with informal performances, and some of those were opportunities to meet and listen to singers and poets who are legendary in Cuban musical history.

At the start of one of these encounters, I understood from the atmosphere of veneration that I was about to meet someone of especially great value to the history of Cuban music. A very small brown man, barely five feet tall, with strong Indigenous features, was gently ushered in and seated. This was, in fact, Sindo Garay, the man often described as the greatest composer of Cuban traditional poetic song known as Trova.

Although he was now one hundred years old, he could manage a song or two, and one could easily see that there was real gold under the patina of age. The tender care with which the others handled his needs gave assurance that his legacy would long outlive the man, and I felt humbled by the effort he had made to be with us for an hour.

In the Escambray Mountains, because of the occasional eruptions of counterrevolutionary violence in that region, armed civil guards had been judiciously stationed outside our hotel room door. But when we traveled up into the Sierra Maestra, to Minas del Frío, Cuba's highest elevation, where the guerrilleros had historically been encamped and where Che Guevara had his most discreet and useful headquarters, no guardia was needed. Nothing like what you would call roads existed to get up there, but something more like streambeds and animal trails, meaning that it would take eight hours of bone-shaking road time to arrive at the top in the jeep we were now using.

Up there, a new generation of Cuban teachers, mostly youngsters in their mid-teens, was being trained to lead others, in a country where teachers and schools of any kind had historically been the lowest government priority for the disenfranchised. Their classrooms in this remote place were still nothing but sheds with dirt floors; crude planks served as seats and desks, with palm thatching for shelter.

Many of the kids had been recruited from humble shacks called *bohíos* scattered throughout the hills, where subsistence was all they knew, but others had come from towns and cities where choices were available. To make sure everyone had adequate clothing and shoes, each person was given a uniform that would indicate simply that you were a student, neatly eliminating these visible distinctions. In spite of any cultural differences they may have been carrying on the inside, the great sense of solidarity, enthusiasm, curiosity, and just plain joy pouring out of these young people was rare and beautiful. In the next years, I traveled back to Minas de Frio a couple more times, finding the rough trails gradually being transformed into passable surfaces, the time required to reach the school cut much shorter each time, and conditions generally improved. But this beautiful spirit was something that didn't seem to have dimmed or worn thin, and if anything, had deepened.

Soon after our return to Havana, Irwin telephoned Noël in New York to check on the home front. She reported that he had just received notice from the State Department to the effect that his license was finally granted, allowing him to return home via Mexico. Its verdict regarding my case was different. Because I was not a full-time journalist, I was not considered eligible for the license. My only way home, then, would be a flight to New York via Spain, but there was an extreme shortage of seats on flights from Havana to Madrid at that time. Irwin immediately booked his flight to Mexico and on to New York, since various things at his office had become pressing, and I was happy to have some extra time in Cuba until I figured out my itinerary.

One day, Estela called to say that the Consejo de Cultura had a request for me to sing for the workers at the Antillano de Acero steel mill there. The weather was extraordinarily hot, but there is no way I could turn down these men who were helping to keep the revolution moving forward with their labor under almost impossible conditions. When I arrived, there were just a few of them in the assembly area, doing whatever they could to find shade while they waited. What would serve for a stage was a simple, unpainted loading dock, and I would have to exert my vocal powers with all my might because there would be no sound system.

"Welcome Barbara Dane," Cuban Steel Plant. Havana Province, 1966

I climbed up onto the dock, and some sort of signal was given. Men began to pour out of the factory until several hundred stood on the ground in front of me. I greeted them as best I could, not knowing whether I was participating in a special occasion of theirs or whether I was the one who was supposed to provide it, and began to sing, with Estela gamely trying to translate my remarks and give an idea of what the songs were about. I worried that many men had no place to sit and were standing in the sun, and I could see the weariness in their faces, so I searched my head for something appropriate to sing, uplifting without requiring a lot of explanation, rhythmic without trying to extract a big physical response, soothing without putting everyone to sleep.

The heat that day was so intense and unaccustomed for me that I couldn't go on for long, but when I finished, as the applause was fading, I heard a voice rising from the crowd, beginning the familiar strains of "The Internationale." As I heard the voices joining in, listened to the sound of the words in Spanish mounting higher, I broke down in unexpected tears, suddenly overcome with the realization that this was the first time in my life I had ever heard this most beloved and emblematic revolutionary song being sung unselfconsciously and without fear, right out loud, by workers standing at the doors of their own factory, a place that now, at last, belonged to them. I recovered myself enough to begin singing, in turn, the English words I had never sung in my country under conditions remotely like this, had never led a big room full of people singing this song, of all songs, at full voice. We ended together, our fists in the air, with both languages blending and with full hearts, mine brimming over with love and hope.

> Arise ye prisoners of starvation
> Arise you wretched of the earth
> For justice thunders condemnation
> And a new world is in birth!
> No more tradition's chains shall bind us
> Arise, ye slaves, no more in thrall;
> The earth shall rise on new foundations!
> We have been naught, we shall be all!

[CHORUS, with my changes]
'Tis the final class conflict
Let us each take our place
The International working class
Shall be the human race.

Realizing that my time was almost up in Cuba, I made up my mind about one thing that I had been considering since before coming. I knew that the Provisional Revolutionary Government of Vietnam, the PRG, had representation here, and in view of the near impossibility for dialogue between simple citizens of the US and representatives of this entity with which we were supposed to be at war, I was particularly keen on a contact.

Estela Bravo easily arranged an appointment, and soon I was sipping some tea from a tiny cup, sitting across from a cordial man with a pleasant round face, dressed in a Cuban *guayabera* but clearly Vietnamese. This was Huỳnh Văn Ba, whose job before coming to Cuba had to do with caring for American POWs in the south of Vietnam, which probably explains his very understandable English, even occasionally punctuated with contemporary slang, which he heartily enjoyed. I learned that it wasn't called a war in Vietnam but rather a *giac my*, an invasion. He expressed deep gratitude for my testimony to the existence of an active and growing opposition to the war back in the US.

As a parting gift, Văn Ba gave me a few examples of something I found profoundly touching. These were small strips of cardboard folded over into little four-page booklets, each with simple artwork in color on the front, with musical notations and texts of songs inside. He explained that one of the first things the NLF (National Liberation Front) members did when they entered a village was to distribute these to the villagers. He underlined the importance of songs and other cultural expressions as they undertook to educate largely illiterate peasants about their efforts to reunite their country in peace and even enlist them into their ranks.

I was finally told I had a seat on a plane from Havana to Madrid on September 5. My country was still engaged in this ugly thing called a

"Cold War" with the USSR, so why not be bold and ask Estela if we could pay a visit to the Soviet embassy to explore the possibility of an invitation to sing in that country? She was able to easily set up an appointment, but we were just sitting down to the customary welcoming glass of tea when the phone rang with a caller asking for Estela. "Unfortunately," she announced, "we will have to postpone this meeting and return to Barbara's hotel immediately."

A car was waiting for us, and off we went toward the Capri Hotel where, to my amazement, we found Fidel himself standing on the front steps with right hand extended. He courteously asked how I was, and then glanced around for a suggestion of a place to sit down for a talk.

Well, what is a girl to do in a case like that? I invited him, his right-hand man Dr. René Vallejo, and Estela, of course, to come up to my room where we would have quiet and privacy. Up we went in the elevator, to the high floor where I was staying. As we rose, I began to recall that I had washed all my underwear in anticipation of packing my bags that night, and with no other convenient options, had draped them over every available lamp and bedpost. To make matters worse, due to my low-income way of life, they were somewhat the worse for wear, and in my habitual way of turning disappointment into opportunity, I had dyed them all purple! It was too late to turn back, so I opened the door.

Fidel had intended a twenty-minute courtesy call to thank me for the risk I had taken in coming and the work I had done on behalf of US-Cuba friendship, but he soon sent word to the head of the National Bank, waiting below in his car, that he would be detained for some time. Vallejo sent down for some coffee, and we launched into a three-hour discussion about the various social movements then stirring the people to action in the US. I talked about the traveling and singing I had been doing, especially as part of the antiwar movement, but even more, I tried to convey my impressions of the movements and organizations that were directing all this action, and the government's efforts to suppress them. He spoke of the OLAS (Organization of Latin American Solidarity) conference being planned by Cuba for the summer of 1967 as a response to the US-led expulsion of Cuba from the OAS (Organization of American States). He asked me which Black leader I would recommend they invite from the US, and I suggested Stokely Carmichael, who as a central leader of SNCC had been one of the first to emphasize the need for Black power and who saw the importance of linking the civil rights struggle to the movement opposing the war in Vietnam.

Midway through this discussion with Vallejo and Bravo translating, I realized that Fidel actually spoke and understood English fairly well, but since I was far from any fluency in Spanish, I was glad we were conducting things this way. One of the great advantages of this kind of communication is that you get to hear everything twice, and also get some time to think about your responses. My overall impression was of a man long accustomed to having identified his own life with that of his country, thinking constantly and broadly about how this new Cuba would fit into unfolding events in a world of incredible economic and military imbalances, a tiny nation now being run for the most part by inexperienced young people. He seemed intent on gathering all the understanding he could about things, in order to impart any useful information to others who would then analyze it and put it to use. A mind that habitually operated in a collective mode, but with the courage to lead with clear individual decisions when necessary.

All in all, it was a very comfortable exchange, and although inside myself I thought about how much richer it would have been for Fidel if he could have talked with Irwin as well, I never felt that he took what I

Barbara Dane with Fidel Castro. Havana, 1966

had to say lightly or as if I were limited by my profession or my gender. He was plainly accustomed to taking women seriously, and that gave me courage and ease with the whole encounter. For this, I owe thanks to the great women of the revolution: Celia Sánchez, Wilma Espín, Haydée Santamaría, Melba Hernández, and so many others.

As he rose to leave, Fidel paused to ask whether I wouldn't like to stick around a couple of weeks to rest and enjoy the beach at Varadero after all my traveling and singing. Nothing could have pleased me more, but I answered that it was important for me to get back home now to see about my children.

Suddenly the thought struck me that a far greater reward would be a year of school in Cuba for one of my kids, a chance for at least one of them to get a sense of what a real revolution could be like, and, I hoped, to study music. His face lit up as he replied that Cuba would welcome the idea and promised to arrange it.

My son Paul had done well at Garfield Junior High and was supposed to enter Berkeley High in the fall, but I knew he wasn't thrilled about the idea. He was always a very self-motivated and self-reliant boy, who already knew that he wanted to be a musician, picking up trombone and harmonica on his own while he was just a little kid. While Irwin and I were in Cuba, he was in New York working part-time in the garment district to earn his first good electric guitar. I had just visited the National School of Art (Escuela Nacional de Arte, or La ENA) and seen that while the students were being given the usual high school education, they were also receiving a serious education in their chosen art field. From my own disappointments with our education system, I knew that it would be a life-changing experience for a young person to be able to focus on their passion for music or art or theater in that way, at that age. Most of all, I had just been exposed to the enthusiasm and hope I saw on the faces of young people all across Cuba, so different from those back home, trapped in a circle of anxiety about the draft and the shrinking chances of ever making a living without contributing to an economy controlled by the military-industrial complex. At the first opportunity, I telephoned Paul in New York to find out what he thought of this new idea, and with almost no hesitation, he agreed to give it a try.

35

PAUL BECOMES PABLO

As soon as I hit town again I had to start looking for another place to live. Our two-year lease was up for renewal, but it had become pretty clear that "Needle Park" at 72nd and Broadway was not a great neighborhood for the long run, especially not for a child. I spotted an ad in the *Times* for a house in Brooklyn with a miraculous number of rooms and even a backyard for what seemed like a misprint: two hundred dollars per month. It was on a one-block street near the docks of Red Hook in a section that real estate people called Cobble Hill, home to a large population of Italian immigrants, mostly working class, just as depicted in Arthur Miller's great play *A View from the Bridge* and in the film *On the Waterfront*. After meeting the salt-of-the-earth family occupying the basement flat, we took the plunge and signed a lease. When I think of the decade spent there at Strong Place, and realize what a parade of fantastic people and interesting discussions and succulent meals and satisfying political work took place there, I'm almost overcome with the urge to relive it as much as possible by describing it for you in all the redolent detail it deserves. But so much was going on in the world around us, there was little time to savor, let alone document, the richness of life at home.

Paul Menendez. New York City, 1967

My plans for rearranging the space in the house had to be put on hold because I had to go back to Cuba to place Paul in school and on the path to his new life. Irwin's oldest son, Josh, would be going with us as well. Irwin was super busy with his work at *Sing Out!* and Oak Publications, but he happily agreed to take care of Nina's needs while I was away, just as she was creative about helping him out however she could. Paul packed up the few clothes he had brought from California, adding to it a new pair of Levi's and as many seven-inch reels of tapes as he could carry, loaded up with all the music that seemed to make up his world at the time, copied from my overflowing collection of LPs. With his new guitar and amplifier, plus a second-hand Wollensak recorder of his own, he seemed to feel well outfitted to face this new life he was about to enter.

Once in Cuba, we were taken to a house not far from the Escuela Nacional de Arte, where we stayed until the boys were settled in a school dormitory nearby. Soon we were summoned to the apartment in downtown Havana shared by Fidel and Celia Sánchez Manduley, his longtime companion and closest advisor. This was to be an opportunity for Paul and Josh to meet these two historic figures. Estela Bravo conducted us to the appointment, translating with her customary expertise. Josh, noticing a basketball court on the adjacent rooftop where Fidel took his daily exercise, couldn't resist shooting a few hoops, and, without warning, Fidel jumped up and joined him in a friendly competition. As we were leaving, Celia reassured me that she would keep an eye on the boys as they settled into Cuban life.

It wasn't any accident that all three of my children have carved out a meaningful life in the world of music. Raised in a household where music was central, they each began to forge their own musical identity early on. Growing up in Berkeley, Nicky had an unparalleled opportunity to personally know many of the great originals among North American blues and country players, learning from observation, from conversation, and sometimes from direct instruction. Still in her teens, Nina fell in with a small but dedicated community of flamenco aficionados in Northern California, becoming acquainted with genuine Spanish Gitano culture as she observed the dance, practiced the vocalizations, and internalized the poetry of the songs.

But it was Paul who drew the lucky number when it came to having access to formal music education, while all around him Cuban folk and popular culture was reawakening and evolving. Paul—who would soon become Pablo—was about to experience some of the most exciting developments occurring in this particular time and place.

By the time Pablo arrived in Cuba, new architecturally experimental buildings had been constructed to house La ENA in the part of Havana called Cubanacán, on that broad greenness where once Havana's elite white gentlemen had golfed and sipped their daiquiris. Now Pablo became one among dozens of scholarship students housed in the mansions in the surrounding area, left vacant by gangsters, foreign investors, and corporation managers fleeing for Miami to avoid those scary bearded men in olive drab. These mansions, now stripped of their gaudy objects of conspicuous consumption, had been outfitted with bunk beds and simple dormitory furniture. Everyone ate in the dining room of the former country club, simple food but in an atmosphere unlike anything most of the students had ever seen before. Pablo lived full-time in this way, as a scholarship student at La ENA, an experience he says has stayed with him for life. Talented youngsters were being recruited from small towns and villages all across the country, many coming from remote mountain villages where they had grown up in bohíos with thatched roofs and dirt floors. Not a few of them had never even seen a film or owned a book before coming to the school in Havana. Pablo was exposed to a full spectrum of Cuba's cultural legacies: some of his classmates were from families with deep Afro-Cuban roots, others carried campesino cultural traditions, others were descended from prominent popular artists or well-known musicians and intellectuals. The diversity of the students' backgrounds was matched only by the diversity of their fields of study. One could major in music—Pablo's chosen field—plastic arts, drama, modern dance, or ballet, and this diversity fostered many fruitful collaborations among the budding artists.

We spoke occasionally on the phone, but telephone calls to Cuba then had to be booked several days in advance, and it might take days just to reach the operator taking those bookings. After your call was finally placed, the dilapidated phone system made it impossible to conduct much of a conversation even if you reached the intended party. Postal communications of any kind were also difficult. Letters took at least a month to arrive in Cuba, probably due to US government detention for the purpose of inspection. Packages were no longer accepted by Cuba from the US after several bombs had been mailed from Miami. It became a continuous and daunting task to find folks traveling to Cuba who would be willing to carry a letter or small package, a sort of people's Pony Express. Sometimes, Pablo would make wonderful long audio letters on his Wollensak. Mostly, I depended on making the trip to Havana every few months, each time requiring some ingenious circumvention of the travel ban. And I always was hoping that Pablo was so busy acquiring a new culture, a new language, and a new life that he wouldn't have time to be lonely. He formed his first band, Los Gallos, and soon began composing. Not long after, he started dating another scholarship student, the young actress Adria Santana.

36

HE'S GOT THE WHOLE WORLD IN HIS HANDS

On April 4, 1967—a year to the day before he was killed—Martin Luther King Jr. gave his fateful speech at the Riverside Church in NYC, linking the struggle for racial and economic justice at home with the opposition to US involvement in Vietnam, calling for an immediate ceasefire and withdrawal of all US troops and saying, "I speak as a citizen of the world, for the world as it stands aghast at the path we have taken." It so clearly delineated the connection between the terrible injustices at home with those in Vietnam and elsewhere in the subjugated and impoverished world that it may very well have been this speech that resulted in King's assassination.

> I knew that I could never again raise my voice against the violence of the oppressed in the ghettos without having first spoken clearly to the greatest purveyor of violence in the world today—my own government. For the sake of those boys, for the sake of this government, for the sake of the hundreds of thousands trembling under our violence, I cannot be silent. . . . If America's soul becomes totally poisoned, part of the autopsy must read: Vietnam. It can never be saved so long as it destroys the deepest hopes of mankind the world over.

This was the one man who personified unqualified incorruptibility and who had paid his dues, had earned the nation's respect and love to the point that he might catch the ear of the most disappointed and spiritually defeated American. This was the man who could see through the sham and expose the true heart of the nation, calling on its self-image of generosity and courage, challenging it to oppose and defeat this system of murderous venality in the interest of saving its soul. In other words, he was the leader who had the potential to show us the way out of the capitalist system into some more humane and just way of organizing our society. A savior, if you will. And like that earlier savior, Jesus Christ, he would have to be destroyed by those whose system would remain all-powerful. A new man had come now to throw the money-changers out of the temple, and that, of course, was intolerable. But he left us with the tools to understand that a better world is possible, and to realize that the only way to defeat an evil system is to unite and organize toward that world.

A few days after this momentous speech, in the sparkling beauty of a sunny spring day, the peace movement invaded New York's Central Park, organized by the Mobilization Committee to End the War in Vietnam (fondly known as the Mobe). It was April 15, and together Irwin, Nina, and I set off to join the demonstrating throng, which numbered in the area of three hundred thousand before the day was through. The participation of several key leaders from the Black community and the demographics of the crowd signaled a historic turning point in the peace movement; a new wind was blowing. Dr. King himself addressed the crowd, building on his passionate call at Riverside Church days earlier and underlining the urgency of unity among all progressive people.

"I would like to see the fervor of the civil-rights movement imbued into the peace movement to instill it with greater strength," he said. "And I believe everyone has a duty to be in both the civil-rights and peace movements. But for those who presently choose but one, I would hope they will finally come to see the moral roots common to both."

After the rally, the marchers were to proceed from Central Park to the United Nations Plaza. But by mid-afternoon, things had become chaotic, and in the surge of people we lost track of Nina, who often had her own idea of what to do in a demonstration, being an old hand at them by this time in her young life of just over eleven years. Irwin and

I decided to separate in order to look for her in different directions, and soon lost track of each other too. We always had the understanding that we would meet back at home in Brooklyn once the demonstration began to ebb, so I wasn't overly concerned. I knew that Nina was accustomed to getting around in New York on her own and could find her way back to Brooklyn. Repeatedly casting my eyes over the crowd checking for any disturbances, wherever I noticed some sort of trouble spot I tried to see what it was, but I found no trace of Nina.

It was several hours later when I finally heard her voice on the phone saying that she was on her way home. She had been walking toward the UN Plaza against the traffic down 6th Avenue with the other marchers when some plainclothes police suddenly jumped out of an unmarked garbage truck and began striking out at the demonstrators, one of them a young man in a wheelchair. Nina had been carrying a picket sign stapled to a hollow cardboard tube, and began crying out, "Leave him alone!" as she angrily banged on one of the assailants with it, not realizing he was a cop. One of the others grabbed the child by her long hair and slammed her down against the curb, leaving her unconscious as they rushed on to bash their way through the rest of the crowd. Some older students who had witnessed this took her to a safe place and iced her head until she recovered enough to remember her phone number and call me. Even as I write about it now, I feel anger rising from deep down in my mother place, and I'm trembling.

Barbara with daughter Nina Menendez at antiwar rally. New York City, 1965.
© "Eli Lucky" Finer

37

SINGERS OF THE WORLD, UNITE!

In late July 1967, Cuba's Casa de las Américas hosted a groundbreaking event: the Encuentro de la Canción Protesta. Founded under the leadership of revolutionary heroine Haydée Santamaría, Casa's mission was the building of links with like-minded artists, writers, and other cultural figures throughout Latin America and the Caribbean and the development of a new and international awareness of their value, placing Cuba squarely at the center of a Latin American cultural renaissance. The Encuentro was inspired by the explosion of new musical forms emerging in Cuba in the first decade of the revolution, particularly the budding Nueva Trova movement, and the Nueva Canción movement that was flourishing in Latin America, reflective of the struggles taking place throughout the continent.

We would be performing for the Cuban public, hearing one another's work firsthand, experiencing the work of new young Cuban artists, exchanging ideas and experiences, and piecing together networks that would enable our songs to spread beyond the borders of our own movements and travel throughout the world.

Irwin and I were enlisted to help contact potential US attendees, so we assembled a list of the best-known, most engaged and outspoken folksingers and songwriters, as well as some of the more obscure but militant artists. Irwin drafted a carefully worded letter indicating that we were not the hosts but were merely acting as messengers, and that the event would last for two weeks with all expenses covered. We sat back and awaited what we assumed would be a flurry of excited and enthusiastic replies accepting the invitation.

One by one the replies drifted in. "Oh, I have such a full schedule I can't possibly . . ." "Sorry, but I can't risk having any trouble with my passport . . ." "If only I had more advance notice." In other words, "The dog ate my homework." What I felt then, and feel now as I write, was a certain sickening sensation of disappointment, a great sadness for my fellow "folksingers" because of what seemed to me a general surrender to self-absorption and self-delusion.

The importance of this event cannot be overstated. It was an audacious concept in the first place, coming from this small island nation, half the size of California, then with a population of less than 8.5 million, mostly young people, struggling hard to overcome the daily shortages and difficulties caused by living under a tight economic blockade. Part of the founding mission of the Casa de las Américas was to build solidarity with writers and artists unable to function in their homelands because of their opposition to military dictatorships and their pursuit of social and economic justice.

We may have been the only ones there from the US, but more than fifty musicians from four continents arrived, ready to spend two weeks together, weaving bonds of solidarity that would prove to be unbreakable. Our Cuban hosts were well aware of the difficult conditions that most of us worked under in our home countries, where we rejected the idea of music as a commodity rather than as a means of intercourse between people, so they had arranged for our networking sessions to take place at Varadero, that world-famous beach where only the white elite had frolicked before the revolution.

Our discussions touched on a broad range of topics: we thought about whether didactic or socialist-realist songs were effective, what relation artists should have to parties and political organizations, the relation of form to content, and obstacles and victories we had experienced. One overriding understanding was that a new kind of united front was badly needed, and that our songs could play a role in helping people come together in that way.

It was such a relief to be at a gathering where we could speak freely about this kind of work, with all its hazards as well as its joys. I was personally rewarded with a sense of fraternity seldom available to me back home, whether in the competitive commercial music world or in the broader political arena where I was usually the one in the back of the room, upsetting everyone by insisting that the emperor had no clothes. In our final statement of unity, we agreed that as artists, we would continue to oppose imperialism and colonialism in all their pernicious forms, use our songs to help break down barriers between people, work *with* people as opposed to being sold *to* them as consumer products, and always strive for high standards in our work, remembering Che Guevara's famous guideline, "Quality is respect for the people."

On one of our free evenings, the father of political song in Cuba, Carlos Puebla himself, joined us with his Tradicionales, bringing with them their vocal harmonies, their maracas, marimbula, and bongos. He was eager to teach us a song he had just written, one that has since become the most loved and widely sung of any in the genre, "Hasta siempre, Comandante," in celebration of the Cuban people's love and respect for Che, who had just slipped out of Cuba for Bolivia, where he intended to participate in the liberation of its people. This was an extraordinarily emotional moment for all of us, and the perfect way to embed the song forever in our hearts.

We traveled all around the island singing for students, campesinos, and factory workers, from Santiago de Cuba to the mountains of the Sierra Maestra. Toward the end of our tour, we were taken to a part of Cuba usually missed by casual visitors, one with a separate special history of its own. The Isle of Pines, off the south coast of the mainland, had been immortalized long ago as Robert Louis Stevenson's Treasure Island. Before that, its many caves served as hideouts for pirates, and even before that, it was a penal colony. In 1898, at the end of what the US called the Spanish-American War but that was in fact Cuba's War of Independence from Spain, speculators instituted US currency; settled the place with English-speaking schools, churches, and citrus groves; and began shipping fruit to New Orleans. Once Cuba took possession again in 1925, the Machado regime turned the place into a giant prison complex where, in 1953, Fidel and his brother, Raúl Castro, along with thirty other members of the 26th of July Movement, were locked up following their attack on the Moncada Barracks that signaled the opening of the revolutionary period. It was from there, in a prison cell, that Fidel wrote his legendary declaration, "History Will Absolve Me."

Within a decade, this place would be renamed Isla de la Juventud, or the Isle of Youth, and transformed into a haven for young people from around the world, wherever conditions were unlivable and possibilities for education were nonexistent. As long as its own fragile economy could provide, Cuba would do its best to share what it could, out of a sense of revolutionary solidarity and also with the hope that seeds of fraternity and mutuality would grow on fertile ground once these young people could return home with a better understanding of the world's problems, but also of its interconnectedness. Eventually as many as thirty-five thousand international students, mainly Africans, were studying there at any given time in around sixty-five different schools.

On this occasion, we were to sing at the ceremony to inaugurate the island's first reservoir, "Vietnam Heroíco," presided over by Fidel himself. As I sang my songs, I felt as if I was being lifted in a sort of grace, forgetting myself in a sense of oneness that causes the distance between audience and singer to disappear.

Later that night, we gathered under a palm-thatched roof to jam a little by the light of a couple of kerosene lamps. There were rumors that Fidel might join us, and suddenly a jeep pulled up in the dark, scattering the gravel, and the man himself vaulted out. Someone remembered it was his birthday, so we welcomed him by singing "Felicidades, Fidel, en tu día." Most of the singers from Latin America had special songs they wanted him to hear, songs with stories of conditions in their respective countries, and they began a round of those while others quietly passed around some rum to share, and the party was on! It was deep into the early hours when Fidel finally headed off. It seemed as though the man rarely slept, judging by the distances he traveled, both geographically and socially. We mere mortals collapsed into the hammocks of the student barracks where we were billeted, and fell to dreaming of things to come.

Before leaving the Isle of Youth, I went to visit the students from La ENA, budding ballerinas, actors, musicians, and painters, who were spending their summer vacation planting grapefruit trees, rows and rows and rows of them, which would eventually contribute to the Cuban economy by providing the grapefruit juice to be canned and exported to its trading partners all over the world. My two special reasons for being here were, of course, Pablo and his sweetheart, Adria, who were among those volunteers.

They invited me to join with the other students in their supper of beans and rice, after which most of these exhausted part-time campesinos headed for their hammocks. The darkness was unbroken by any artificial lights, but we could make out one another's faces because one or the other of them would be smoking a strong Cuban black tobacco cigarette—Populares—more like the French Gitanes than any chemically altered American brand.

Pablo and Adria had just decided they wanted to marry, and were in the process of considering the complications that might result from joining two lives with such different backgrounds. They wanted to know how I would feel about such a momentous decision. I wondered how Adria's father and mother would view the idea of marriage to a foreigner, not to mention that this one was only fifteen years old. How would travel restrictions between our two countries affect their future together? In which country would they live? What were the political implications? A series of other important questions were also on the table, most of which could hardly be answered that night. But I expressed my confidence in the extraordinary maturity and sense of responsibility I saw in both of them in spite of their ages and their lack of worldly experience. And I told them that if they truly had respect as well as love for each other, and the willingness to face any difficulties in the future together, this would be enough to build a wonderful life. In other words, I gave them my blessing. The rest would be up to Adria's parents, Rogerio and Cuca. It was time for me to go home.

Some of the other singers went to jail on arriving back in their countries, just for the crime of having gone to Cuba. Some, such as the Vietnamese, were going back home to practice their healing musical arts under the bombs of US planes. Some had traveled clandestinely to Cuba because they lived under brutal dictators at home. Some, like Irwin and me, had the luxury of living in a country where the fiction of "free speech" was still maintained, so we weren't too concerned with blowback.

But one day, two men in FBI drag knocked on my door in Brooklyn demanding that I surrender my passport. Yes, they actually had a warrant, so I had no choice but to hand it over. All those trips I had already made to Cuba, circumventing the rules each time by traveling home through a third country, had not been enough of a bother to them to incite this response. Ah, but a song conference, now there's a conspiratorial event that might prove threatening to our national defense, or defensive to our national threat, or denationalizing our natural fence, or something worse.

So I beat it on down to the law office of one of my heroes, the renowned civil rights attorney Leonard Boudin, longtime scourge of poor old J. Edgar Hoover. Boudin famously always stood ready to defend everybody from Paul Robeson, Daniel Ellsberg, Philip Berrigan, Julian Bond, and Dr. Benjamin Spock to many of the humbler people harassed by the House Un-American Activities Committee.

Leonard told me to hang on for a few weeks, because the Supreme Court was on the point of rendering a decision regarding the use of passports in the case of Staughton Lynd, Herbert Aptheker, and Tom Hayden, who had gone on a fact-finding trip to North Vietnam, another country on the US "no-go list." He thought that I could probably reapply for a passport and get it with no problem after their ruling, which is exactly what happened, just in time for my next foray outside US borders.

All through the years, since age eighteen, I had been surveilled and documented by the FBI, but out of curiosity I asked Boudin why he thought that, even with all my comings and goings, I had not been harassed as some others had, had not been subpoenaed by HUAC or stripped of my rights in some way until this passport confiscation. He said it was probably because I had always been so open about all my activities and had never tried to hide anything, that I was clearly not easy to intimidate, that there was no easy way to put the screws on me. Well howdy, J. Edgar, how they hangin' these days?

The reason the FBI and CIA have been, and remain, so afraid of a few nonconformist singers willing to express their own ideas and that of people's movements without restraint is that they understand, much better perhaps than we realize, that singers, actors, painters, and dancers can motivate, educate, unite, and inspire people to rise up and defend their own, can cut through the brain invasion meant to make people feel powerless and to perceive their own culture as worthless.

38

LEVITATE THE PENTAGON!

In 1967, the next big DC action was scheduled for the weekend of October 21–23 by the Mobilization Committee to End the War in Vietnam. Lifetime pacifist Dave Dellinger was chief coordinator this time, and he and a large number of other peace movement activists had created an umbrella broad enough to include several Communist Party veterans; members of the various Trotskyist, socialist, and other left groups; many different pacifist and faith-based organizations like Clergy and Laity Concerned; and all the way over to counterculture figures like Jerry Rubin and Abbie Hoffman, whose advocacy of so-called free love and the use of recreational drugs offended Dr. King, along with their fanciful promise to "levitate the Pentagon," causing him to refuse participation.

Early in the day, nearly one hundred thousand people assembled for a concert and rally, with speeches by Dellinger and Dr. Benjamin Spock and music by Phil Ochs and Peter, Paul and Mary over at the Lincoln Memorial. As more and more buses full of demonstrators arrived, the march over the bridge to Arlington and the Pentagon began. The predicted size of the whole event—which by the end of the day had grown substantially—apparently terrified McNamara and his team, causing them to call out about twenty-five hundred soldiers to separate the throng into sectors so that people in one part could not reach people in the other parts. Their battle plan was clear. The soldiers were outfitted in combat attire, with helmets and rifles pointed at the mothers, dads, students, and elders attempting to approach their building. The troopers were young, and probably many were uncomfortable with what they had been asked to do. Some people began talking to them, looking for a crack in their military composure where their humanity might spill out. As photographers famously captured for posterity, some young women playfully and courageously poked flowers into their gun barrels.

Irwin and I were among those who managed to get almost all the way to the Pentagon. Military helicopters began circling over our heads, and we were so close that McNamara himself could be seen peeking out from a curtained window. Some of the protesters went so far as to attempt breaking through the line of soldiers, and tear gas began to permeate the air. As if by plan, we all sat down on the concrete and began to prepare ourselves for whatever was to come, including being dragged away as we had seen in so many other demonstrations.

And now the power of song once again took charge, weaving a bond of comradeship and mutual protection among many hundreds of people, some trembling from the tension and some from the chilly evening air. A voice in the crowd began to intone, "Oh beautiful for spacious skies, for amber waves of grain," quickly joined by every other voice in the crowd, not loudly but firmly and fully, as if in prayer, or as if in mourning for a lost dream of a country so dear and once so full of promise. It was the sound of mass heartbreak mixed with ancient hope. We repeated the song over many times, until at last somehow we were able to disperse, quietly dragging our bones back across the bridge again into DC and wherever we were to sleep that night.

But, as we prepared to leave, we couldn't find Nina anywhere among the thousand or so in our sector. Nina, it turned out, rightfully viewed the demonstration as a festive occasion and had decided not to hang in with the "straight" old-school peace demonstrators but to follow the fun, dancing, and chanting around the bonfires with the young ones set on levitating the Pentagon. Toward the end of the day, she made her way to our designated meeting spot, but soon realized that we were probably in an area walled off by guardsmen and wouldn't be able to meet her. So, with night falling, she followed some of the others to one of the many homes and shelters prearranged to accommodate out-of-town student demonstrators.

Wondering whether we'd been arrested or injured, and eager to reconnect for the long ride home to Brooklyn, Nina began calling police stations and hospitals all over the city. It wasn't until the following day when we finally found each other. The police, now standing at a respectful distance, had arranged for one of her new friends to bring her to a meeting point in a park. As she rushed into my arms for a motherly hug she whispered, "Pretend you know Jimmy!" Of course I played along with "Well, hello, Jimmy, how's your mom?" at which point the police felt they had done their job, so they left. Nina had been quick to realize that this kind young man who had brought her to us would quite possibly have been in deep jeopardy if the cops got it into their heads that this eleven-year-old white girl had "spent the night with a Black stranger."

In December, a phone call came from my father's home aid helper saying that I had better come to Detroit now if I wanted to see him alive one last time. I met the woman only for the three or four minutes it took her to greet me at the door of his small ground-floor apartment. As I stood by my dad's wheelchair pressing his shoulders in a fumbling attempt to hug him, I heard a vehicle pull up outside, and through the little glass window in the front door I caught a glimpse of his helper and her suitcase. She had run out the back and jumped into the taxi, which quickly sped away. When I saw how translucent his skin had become, how dimmed and dull his eyes looked, how little he could make his limbs move, I realized that she had not exaggerated. This man needed help immediately! The woman had pressed a paper into my hand with a few phone numbers on it, including the one for his doctor. When I finally made my way through the phone tree and was able to speak to him, I began to plead, half crying, that we needed an ambulance, that my dad needed to go to the ER right away.

"It's too late," the doctor said. "I'm sorry, but we've done all we could, and now it is time for Mr. Spillman to pass on." With an anguished sense of defeat, I hung up and began to sort things out.

"Are you hungry, Dad?" I asked.

He nodded. And what would you eat? He spoke hoarsely between parched lips. Some tomato soup, maybe, and a cracker. Nothing in the cupboards. I phoned my sister, Julia, who said she'd rush right over with a can of soup. Now I would have a few peaceful moments with this man who was all wound up in my psyche but whose face I had seldom seen since leaving home in 1948. I glanced down and noticed his robe had fallen open, exposing his naked maleness, so I reached to close it for him.

"It doesn't matter anymore," he said in resignation.

I found a brush in his room nearby, and began gently stroking his hair, which was soft and gray and tangled. It occurred to me that it might be comforting if I sang to him, so I quietly began one of those old sentimental tunes he loved, "When it's springtime in the Rockies, in the Rockies far away, once again I'll say I love you, while the birds sing all the day . . ." He began to make a low sound, almost like purring, as I sang.

Dad slipped away in his sleep on December 9 and was laid out at the funeral home of his Lion's Club friend Mr. McCabe, a ritual for which he had provided years ago. His deer-hunting buddies came to the viewing of his body, as did a good number of the folks of the Brightmoor neighborhood near where his store had been, people who had known him all through the Depression years. I was surprised and touched to see how many showed up the day he was buried at Acacia Park, in the grassy hillside plot he had bought and paid for back during World War II, when the money had finally begun to come in at the drugstore.

39

UNITED WE ARE STRONG

The Cultural Congress of Havana in January 1968 would bring together intellectuals from every field, representing close to seventy (mostly Third World) countries. A place for these voices to be heard and given credence was being created, and a united front was being forged. It would also have the function of helping Cuba reach out for meaningful interaction with the intellectuals of the world who understood its intention of taking its rightful place among nations, and its leadership in the emerging movement of non-aligned countries. The opportunity to attend this historic gathering was impossible to turn down, especially since it would coincide with the planned wedding of Pablo and Adria.

We arrived at the Havana Libre, where Irwin took charge of checking us in. Right there next to the counter, our guide from the Cultural Council was politely introducing me to a small group of gentlemen also waiting to check in. The first was Roberto Matta, one of Chile's best-known painters and a seminal figure in twentieth-century abstract expressionist art. Standing opposite him was David Alfaro Siqueiros, one of that holy trinity of Mexican muralists who, along with Diego Rivera and José Clemente Orozco, had literally transformed the world's view of art. Matta was introduced to Siqueiros, but he drew back and pointedly refused to shake his hand, saying in a firm and unquiet voice that he could not possibly give a warm greeting to a man who may have been complicit in the murder of Trotsky. What a way to get this week off to a comradely start!

Approximately five hundred intellectuals made the trip to Havana to participate in this momentous gathering: writers, poets, artists, philosophers, musicians, athletes, sociologists, economists, scientists, professors, journalists, publicists, and more, drawn from seventy extremely diverse countries.

Irwin made sure to keep the printed translations of all the papers presented at the congress, and once he was back home in NYC, each night after a long day at *Sing Out!*, he would climb to his small third-floor home office, where he worked on the tall stacks of mimeographed texts, shaping these passionate demands for cultural dignity and independence into an accessible and coherent collection called *Voices of Liberation*. Reading through the resulting book after more than forty years, I'm deeply moved by the testimony echoing centuries of struggle against rampant cultural genocide faced by the peoples in all parts of the globe historically relegated to what was at the time called "underdevelopment"—countries that have been ruthlessly plundered by imperialism in its many guises.

Circulating these voices of reason and truth was exactly the kind of work that Irwin's own passions were demanding of him, and this was part of why he began to arrange meetings to design the best way for transferring his folk music connections to a working collective, in the case of *Sing Out!*, and to a larger company, in the case of Oak Publications, allowing him to move on to political research and writing as the focus for his energies.

January 20, a few days after the close of the congress, was the scheduled wedding day that would unite my fifteen-year-old son, Pablo, with Adria Santana, the budding actress who had easily won his heart with her modesty and intelligence, her beauty and her passionate commitment to life as well as art.

Adria had moved to the capital city with her family from the provincial town of Victoria de las Tunas, where sugarcane, bananas, and cattle have historically kept the people of the region alive. She was chosen for the drama school at La ENA, and after graduating she became one of the enduring principals at the renowned Hubert de Blanck

Theater, developing a long string of leading roles that defied any kind of typecasting, each an indelible and original characterization. She starred in a number of long-running TV series, including *La Delegada*; made several films; and created the unforgettable protagonist of the monologue called "Las penas saben nadar," written for her by the country's leading playwright, Abelardo Estorino, a solo vehicle now known throughout the Spanish-speaking world.

When doctors advised her to take a hiatus from the stage because of her struggle with cancer, Adria decided to finally take time for college, graduating from the ISA (Instituto Superior de Arte) with honors at age fifty-eight. When she finally lost her fierce battle with breast cancer a few years later in 2011, the nation mourned one of the most brilliant actresses of her generation. To us, she will always be the intense and beautiful young girl who risked it all to marry a fifteen-year-old foreigner named Pablo, and whose wonderful family took him in like a son, as he remains after more than fifty years.

Now it was time to become better acquainted with her family. We arranged to visit their home in the run-down working-class district of Havana known as Lawton, and with the help of a young interpreter who had been working with us as a guide throughout the congress, we did our best to communicate. The family's modest home in Las Tunas had doubled as the local Communist Party office during the Batista era. Facing repression for their support of the revolution, they fled to Havana in the late 1950s. Now, Adria's father, Rogerio, worked in the industrial sector, and her mother, Cuca, worked at the Cultural Council. Adria's brother, Jimmy, was heading for a career in the foreign service, eventually to become Cuba's ambassador to Syria in the early years of its horrific civil war, after dedicated years of consular service in Norway, Uganda, Canada, Denmark, and elsewhere. I believe her sister, Ivis, was then studying to be a teacher.

The day we visited, Cuca was busy contriving a short modern wedding dress for Adria from the scarce selection of fabrics available, adding a quite stylish little fur collar. Rogerio generously offered us añejo rum on the rocks, which he had been saving for this special occasion. Pablo was lit up with smiles from deep inside, and if he was nervous, he didn't let on. Adria was serious, determined to carry off her last few days of single girlhood with dignity.

Adria Santana, Pablo Menendez, Cuca Rodríguez, Irwin Silber, Rogerio Santana. Havana, 1968

The ceremony was a simple signing of papers, followed by a luxurious dinner at the famous restaurant 1830, generously hosted by the Cultural Council. I felt a strong sense of rightness, a feeling that these two budding artists would form a lasting marriage of love and cooperation, a marriage that would be admired by many and a credit to both families. My son's experience in Cuba was no longer to be a yearlong study-abroad parenthesis. I knew I would somehow find ways of visiting frequently, in spite of the idiotic travel barriers my government was enforcing, and this I did, sometimes two or three times in a year. Many have asked me why I didn't just move there, where my son has made his life now for all this time. But I have always felt that the problems back in my own country demanded my energies, that a country without watchdogs and gadflies like me could not remain much of a democracy, so here I stay, for better or worse.

40

UNIDENTIFIED FLYING OBJECT

During the first months of 1968, the world witnessed a rapid series of game-changing events, and without my going into the details of each, it would be helpful to keep them in view in order to understand the context we were living in. January 30 brought the beginning of the Vietnamese Tet Offensive, a major turning point of the war and one that sent a strong message that this whole military misadventure was not going to end well for the US. Then there was the horrifying My Lai massacre, when US ground troops killed more than five hundred Vietnamese civilians. Increasingly unpopular due to his escalation of the war, President Johnson announced on March 31 that he would not be running for a second term. As the world was digesting that, Martin Luther King Jr., the most spiritually powerful leader alive, was assassinated on April 4 in Memphis, where he had gone to support striking garbage workers. The candidate set to replace the dethroned LBJ was Robert Kennedy, and on June 5, he too was gunned down, shot by the by now standard "demented lone assassin" minutes after winning the California presidential primary. These events sparked an intensification of the peace movement and ongoing resistance from Black communities across the country. The government crackdown was brutal, a signal that all constitutional rights were closed now for serious repairs.

Fred Gardner, a young Harvard graduate who had completed a

tour in Vietnam as a member of the Army Reserve, wanted to figure out how he could best help to end the US devastation of Southeast Asia. Brainstorming with his young friends Devora Rossman and Donna Mickleson, they all agreed that a key element in stopping the war might be support for the young soldiers who were beginning to resist it. Peace activists were stopping troop trains and raiding draft boards, even counseling those who were considering a conscientious objector (CO) status, but few were actually working with the young people most directly affected. Why not reach out to them where they were enduring the mind-bending experience of basic training, where they were facing immediate life-and-death decisions about their future? Why not provide a safe haven where they could meet like-minded comrades, a place for thinking things through without constant military pressure, for finding help with CO counseling if needed, and, of course, a place for some badly needed relaxation and cultural enrichment?

During the 1950s, counterculture coffeehouses had been springing up all over the US, started by people looking for a way to break out of conformity and explore new ideas together while sipping a coffee or a glass of wine, checking out alternative music and poetry, reading and discussing cutting-edge literature, or simply hanging out with other free spirits. I did sing my share of folk songs and blues in these places and was identified as helping lend these gathering spots a certain air of hipness and cultural audacity, along with letting my red flag fly. Unlike sports bars or churches or lodge halls, coffeehouses were understood to be places where new ideas could be freely explored and where resistance to the norm was acceptable, if not expected. So why not open one for GIs, near a military base where there would certainly be plenty of confused and lonely young men looking for shelter from the storm of basic training and a space to express themselves without pressure? It was an idea whose time had come.

Fred decided to focus on Fort Jackson near Columbia, South Carolina, the army's largest and most active training base from which soldiers were being shipped overseas. A group of GIs was already active there in support of Captain Howard Levy, who had been court-martialed, convicted, and sent to prison for "willfully disobeying orders" and "promoting disaffection among enlisted men." He described the Special Forces as "killers of peasants, women and children," and ironically, the colonel who presided at the trial said: "The truth of these statements is not an issue in this case." As a lesson to any others tempted to openly express such ideas, Levy was made to serve twenty-six months of a three-year sentence at hard labor, and was given a dishonorable discharge and stripped of all benefits, after which he immediately made himself available to the protests cropping up everywhere in opposition to the war.

Devora recalls that Fred was eager for their participation because "he needed some long-haired chicks." But in spite of some irritation at this, she and Donna went along, with the hope of contributing to the antiwar movement in a more concrete way. They were expecting no more compensation than free housing and five dollars in pocket money per week, but of course, it would also be an adventure for these two young northern-bred women in their mid-twenties.

Fred moved ahead by renting a storefront on the main street of Columbia, using ten thousand dollars of his own money, and shortly afterward, he, Devora, and Donna opened the first GI coffeehouse, naming it the UFO, or Unidentified Flying Object. It looked and felt nothing like the official USOs (United Service Organizations) sponsored by the Defense Department, dispensing coffee and doughnuts with a chance to meet and dance with girls. Opened on a shoestring, this new kind of meeting place felt decidedly unofficial, with psychedelic posters on the walls, various alternative papers and magazines on the tables, the hippest music playing, live performances and jams with local musicians, and even a chance to volunteer by helping staff the place. Jeff Zinn, son of beloved historian Howard Zinn and barely out of high school, joined the staff as a sort of in-house musical director, and within a short time you could find hundreds of GIs spending their time there, away from the pressure-cooker atmosphere of the base.

Local civilians began gathering there too. I sang there a number of times, as did other singers such as Bernice Reagon, a founder of the Freedom Singers, and Drink Small, also known as the legendary "Blues Doctor." The UFO was also one of the only venues in town where Black and white young people were able to gather without a problem. Of course, all these "strange goings-on" also attracted the attention of the law-and-order boys. The military police, the local cops, and the FBI began careful surveillance, and most probably also began looking for the kind of opportunists willing to infiltrate and spy on these activities. The UFO organizers quickly realized they would have to strictly enforce a "no drugs" policy to avoid trouble.

Often after singing for the GIs gathered at the coffeehouse, I would stay on and talk to some of the guys one-on-one. Many of them were feeling trapped by the basic training mantra, "I am a killer!" and were grappling with tremendous anxiety about the role they were being forced to play, but worried they'd be labeled a coward or traitor by friends and family back home if they didn't stick with the army. My counsel was always the same: "Be true to yourself. If you don't follow your heart, you may not be able to live with yourself in years to come. But if you stay true to yourself, in the future you may find that people will see you as a hero for choosing what is right."

Barbara talks to GIs after concert. Oleo Strut, GI Coffeehouse, Killeen, Texas.
© Carolyn Mugar

Fred Gardner was able to secure ongoing support from an organization called Resist, an antiwar collaboration formed in 1967, made up of activist intellectuals—Noam Chomsky, Norman Mailer, Benjamin Spock, Allen Ginsberg, and others. This group had begun its life by issuing *Call to Resist Illegitimate Authority* to support draft resistance in opposition to the war in Vietnam, a document that was quickly signed by over twenty thousand people. In the following years, Resist supplied a large part of the funds needed to continue and expand the GI coffeehouse network. Today, almost fifty years later, the organization has grown to become one of the most critical funders of grassroots activism in the US.

Right on time for the February 1968 Tet Offensive, almost as if it had been coordinated, a handful of GIs from Fort Jackson donned their uniforms and went to the chapel on the base, where they would pray together for an end to the war. Nobody could fault them for that, could they? Thirty GIs showed up, but the MPs were ready. They announced that the meeting was over, arrested two of the soldiers who had dropped to their knees to pray, and sent the rest back to their barracks to ponder the future of free speech and assembly in America. I recall talking afterward with some of the GIs there about that pray-in. The deep disappointment and disillusionment in their faces was matched by the pain in my own heart. It was only going to get worse.

Encouraged by the impact the UFO had made in South Carolina, Rennie Davis and Tom Hayden, two seasoned peace organizers "up north," set to resourcing the funding and staffing for other locations, forming an aptly named organization called Support Our Soldiers (SOS). Over the next couple of years, with the coffeehouses helping create new platforms for resistance as the GI movement spread, a revolving list of speakers grew, which included Howard Levy, lawyer and investigative writer Mark Lane, Black feminist lawyer Florynce Kennedy, actress-activist Jane Fonda, comedian Dick Gregory, former Green Beret Donald Duncan, and a few others, including me. There was, of course, a far larger pool of speakers who appeared at the many peace rallies and marches, but when it came to the GI coffeehouses and the many events they generated, we were the "rogues' gallery" who could be relied on to show up.

The most viable of the coffeehouses, and the one I remember best, was in the town of Killeen, Texas, home of the largest tank base in America. Josh Gould, a longtime civil rights activist, and a former Radcliffe student named Jay Lockard, opened the Oleo Strut (named after the shock absorber on a helicopter) a couple of miles outside Fort Hood—a base that contained about 35,000 men plus about 65,000 auxiliary family—and got things rolling by the early summer of 1968.

The Strut had only been open two weeks, and the town fathers already saw the place as a decided threat. They didn't know *what* it was, but they knew it was *different*. The local cops busted two GIs one afternoon because they were sitting on the sidewalk in front of the Strut, smoking Bugler Tobacco in a hookah.

I was invited there the first time to help create the Fourth of July "festivities" with a "Love-In for Peace." The event was a huge success, attended by more than eight hundred local young people, including a large number of GIs who became hard to single out because many showed up wearing wigs, love beads, and "JC boots" (sandals). Looking out at the faces of these young people, I could feel the weight on their shoulders as they joined me in singing, "We want to end this war right now, bring 'em home, bring 'em home."

Oleo Strut, GI coffeehouse, Killeen, Texas. © Carolyn Mugar

When it was nearly dark, the organizers prudently decided to call it a day. Word had it that goat ropers—local vigilantes—were reportedly ready to make a charge off the hill. As we all dispersed, they came down in mass, moved to the center of the crowd, and seemed to wait for instructions. I noticed a plainclothesman conferring by walkie-talkie. There were a few minor scuffles, a camera was smashed, and a drummer attacked, but the determined nonviolence of these soldiers, even though trained every day to reflexive violence, won the day. The troublemakers moved off in a body, and we started melting off toward home. The Fourth of July 1968 may have been officially over, but independence had been firmly declared by these courageous young soldiers who had attended the love-in peacefully, in spite of every attempt to intimidate or provoke them.

There is a direct line between the resisters active around the country and the projects Support Our Soldiers was helping get off the ground, beginning to resist the military in greater numbers. These activists arrived at the summer of 1968 seasoned by events like the Columbia University student takeover in NYC, the teach-ins on campuses everywhere, sit-ins and freedom rides in Texas and Alabama, the Free Speech Movement and HUAC protests in California, massive peace marches in DC or in their own hometowns, and so much more. Unwilling to tolerate a rotten status quo and unafraid to challenge it, these resisters must be understood as America's most authentic patriots. Theirs is the spirit that would bring so many to the Grant Park demonstration at the Democratic Convention in Chicago, meant to send a clear message to the world that racism, repression, economic insecurity, and especially the war agenda were not what the American people would any longer endure without protest.

And this awakening was not limited to the US. By 1968, anger and frustration found students, young workers, and others in the streets of Mexico, Argentina, Japan, France, Germany, Italy, and Czechoslovakia demonstrating their opposition to the escalating war in Vietnam, and to the poverty and exploitation, lack of democracy, mounting police violence, and other forms of repression in their own countries.

41

PLAY YOUR GUITARS, AMERICAN FRIENDS

In 1969, I was invited to the Newport Folk Festival to participate in an afternoon workshop to be called Songs of Liberation. This would be the only festival event focusing on the war, effectively sidelining the main topic on most minds worldwide. The US invasion of Vietnam was on its full rampage of genocidal destruction, and that should have been a central theme of this festival that purported to express our American hearts and minds. I was, of course, grateful to have been invited, given the ongoing blacklisting I had been experiencing since the aborted tour with Louis Armstrong, but I determined that it was not possible for me to participate. I wrote a lengthy article explaining my position, published in the *Village Voice* on July 10. Mine was a small gesture, but it proved to be momentous in "career" terms. The commercial folk-world hierarchy, headed by George Wein, must have read it and determined that I was never again to be invited to perform at a major American festival. But in a way, this was liberating. I was now able to give my full attention to some of the many worthwhile projects in my dream book.

This was the height of the antiwar movement, and there was a veritable explosion of songs of opposition and resistance all across the world. I was deeply moved by the power and diversity of these songs, and, realizing what an important tool it would be for activists, Irwin and I began to collect materials for a joint project we would call *The Vietnam*

Songbook. Irwin's experience as an editor of many songbooks gave him the necessary research skills and the ability to write or select meaningful headnotes for the songs. He also came up with the logical scheme of arranging the songs to begin with a simple pacifist song and move through the increasing anger, confusion, and horror of war all the way to involvement and clarity of purpose and the fighting song of the NLF (the Vietnamese National Liberation Front). Irwin also had a keen eye for how to illustrate each song, and we had access to some good journalistic photo files. If you begin at the beginning, reading the notes and the song lyrics, and inspecting the photos as you go, you can get as vivid a picture of the war and its meaning and effect on a generation as you might from a documentary film.

We had to publish the book ourselves, without a budget, and faced the prospect of distributing the book in guerrilla fashion, but despite these handicaps, we sold out the entire printing and had to go back for more. I believe it still is the only such collection ever published.

We managed to get some boxes of *The Vietnam Songbook* into the hands of the Vietnamese representatives in Paris, who then sent most of them on to Hanoi. The response was more than gratifying, because the next thing we heard was that a gala event was held in their largest concert hall to celebrate the arrival of the book, with the country's leading singers and songwriters taking part. One of the greatest, Phạm Tuyên, wrote a song called "Play Your Guitars in Washington, American Friends" partly in tribute to our book.

By 1969, opposition to the war within the military itself was intensifying every day. GI coffeehouses were springing up all over the country, and the United States Servicemen's Fund—a handful of dedicated peace movement folks in New York—wanted to sponsor my continuing work singing outside military bases around the country. We organized a coast-to-coast tour of the coffeehouses that summer. I knew I would need support, musically and logistically, as well as personally. Fortunately, Pablo was able to take a break in his own busy life to accompany me, generously becoming my ideal partner. We bought a cheap old Mercury convertible with plenty of room in the trunk for all our instruments and other necessities and headed west.

In addition to our musical program for the GIs at the coffeehouses, I was using my Cuba slide show to give talks, augmented by Pablo's description of his experiences living and studying there. We made an appealing presentation together: the mom who brought her songs to support the war resisters, her son who went to live in revolutionary Cuba rather than be drafted into the "Green Machine." I think it helped the listeners to see that we were walking the walk, not just singing about peace.

We were ultimately headed for Seattle-Tacoma where a healthy GI movement group called the Shelter Half was running a coffeehouse to help organize other resisters at Fort Lewis. But first, we made a pit stop at our old California stomping grounds.

Arriving back in Berkeley in July 1969 felt like a kind of homecoming. Pablo managed to carry himself like a cool, normal Oakland kid, but he confessed that inside he felt like a total foreigner. He had lived in Cuba now from ages fourteen to seventeen and had no idea how to do a lot of things most people took for granted, such as open a checking account or avoid a parking ticket. He was even afraid he was losing some of his English, and was glad to have a few weeks of using it.

Pablo ran into Pat Brown, a friend from junior high who was now active in the Black Panther Party, and he spontaneously invited her to join us on our trip up to Washington State. Nina, now thirteen, had been living in Berkeley with her father, Byron, for about a year, and I had been missing her terribly. I arranged for her to go north with us, and I was really looking forward to spending time with her and giving all of us the opportunity for some bonding and fun time together, the way a road trip should be. Pat seemed like a good leavening agent in the mix, and I knew that both Pablo and Nina would enjoy spending some time with her and learning about her experiences as a young member of the Panthers.

We began rolling along quite nicely up Highway 5 toward the Oregon border, but by the time we reached Medford, the old Mercury was showing signs of serious problems with its suspension system, so we stopped to have new shock absorbers installed. While we waited, we decided to take a stretch and eat some lunch in a pretty little park across the way. I began to lay the picnic things out on the table and sent the kids across the street to a small butcher shop to buy some milk, ham, cheese, and such. To their astonishment, the butcher came out from behind his counter, advancing toward them waving his cleaver, screaming, "Get out, get out, we don't serve your kind in this place or anywhere else in town!" I guess our racially mixed and decidedly non-conservative-looking group was straight out of his paranoid fantasies and, apparently, more than he could handle!

Meanwhile, I was eagerly measuring my Peet's coffee grounds into a small portable coffeemaker in anticipation of a steamy cup when a very large police officer slinging two large pistols stomped over toward me and declared that this park was "off-limits to strangers. Pack up and get out! Now!" The kids were coming back on the run, and we quickly piled into the Mercury and eased it out to the highway. Pablo remembers the cop shouting after us that we had better hope we had fillings in our teeth so we could be identified in case something happened to us on the way out of town. "Human kindness overflowing . . ."

Even after growing up in Detroit, one of the country's most racially divided northern cities, and even after my Mississippi experiences, I really wasn't prepared for this kind of open, angry racism and prejudice against the "other" in Oregon, a place I had always thought of as enlightened, mellowed by the beauty of its bucolic surroundings, easygoing, and friendly. No question that racist attitudes are still an undercurrent even in forward-thinking places like the San Francisco Bay Area and Cuba, but they are generally dressed in restrained language and polite behavior. Now we couldn't wait to get out of Oregon, so off we went on our new shock absorbers, heading north to Washington State on trusty old Highway 5.

When at last we rolled into Tacoma and found the Shelter Half, Barbara Garson was there to meet us. This talented playwright had recently caused quite a New York sensation with her 1967 play *MacBird*, which adroitly tweaked Shakespeare's *Macbeth* into an excoriation of LBJ. She had been active in Berkeley as a founder of the Free Speech Movement, so we felt comfortable with her. The place was buzzing with GIs and students from U of W, a large number of whom had just participated in a Seattle march for returning troops, some with signs reading "Welcome home! We will stay in the streets until every GI is home!" One night Nina surprised us all by singing "Masters of War," leaving the soldiers and their student friends' eyes bright with tears, and mine too. I'll never forget it.

Heading back south on I-5, you pass through one of the most spectacular and biodiverse parts of this country, with mountain ranges and river valleys the rival of the Alps or the Himalayas. Eureka is the first town you reach in California, and the next town south is Weed, with Mount Shasta, the second highest volcano in the Cascades, on one side and the vast Klamath National Forest on the other. Wouldn't you know, that was the very spot the old Mercury decided to die? And it was fast becoming hotter than Hades that day.

What else could possibly go wrong? Well, it seemed that Nina had come down with the measles, so I had to get her back to a doctor in Berkeley as quickly as possible. The only solution was to jump on a bus headed south, but we didn't have the fare for the four of us. The car couldn't be moved at all, so Pat and Nina walked several blocks to the bus station, where they would wait for Pablo and me to arrive with the luggage, which was formidable. Then Pat and Pablo bravely agreed to hitchhike back home, a risky proposition especially after the Oregon reception, but what else could we do?

Pablo and I loaded our bodies with guitars and suitcases, way too much to carry all at once, so we had to move things in relays. By now the temperature was unbelievably hot, over a hundred degrees. We looked at each other with that *This is impossible, but we're gonna have to do it* expression you hope you never have to see again. Then out of the depths of our musical raison d'être somehow we both began to whistle the same melody: "We Will Liberate the South," the fighting song of the NLF. No way we could have made it without that invincible tune, the same one that helped the peasants of Vietnam defeat the American invaders. At the station, we exchanged anxious hugs all around and loaded our stuff onto the Greyhound for the eight-hour ride home. Pablo and Pat showed up safely in Berkeley just before we began to panic, and we all hugged and hugged again, before we crashed for a healing night's sleep.

Pablo arrived back in Havana in October, just in time for the birth of his son, Osamu Menendez Santana. This little fellow would turn out to be my only grandchild, and the father of my three great-grandchildren.

42

LA VOCE DELL'ALTRA AMERICA

The Communist Party of Italy (PCI) had been driven underground by Mussolini during World War II. Nevertheless, its partisans consistently supplied the most trusted and courageous clandestine leadership in the struggle against fascism during the war. By the early 1970s, though, they were about as militant and leftist as today's centrist Democrats. Still, it sponsored the Festa dell'Unità (Festival of Unity), the annual cultural extravaganza of the Italian left. This festival specialized in drawing performers from all around the globe, mostly high-profile artists giving musical expression to whatever political issues were then gripping the Italian public. I was proud to be invited to perform there for the first two editions.

The festival's poster called me "la voce dell'altra America" (the voice of the other America). Only a few months before, in November 1969, I had been one of the artists, along with Pete Seeger, Rev. Frederick Douglas Kirkpatrick, and Phil Ochs, who led the singing of literally half a million Americans marching on Washington in what the United Press called "the greatest protest Washington had ever seen." I was determined to bring songs to this festival that suggested the breadth of the US antiwar movement.

The Festa dell'Unità 1970 was held in Firenze (Florence) and was dedicated to exposing and opposing the fascist military junta that was

Pablo Menendez, Martha Galli, Barbara Dane, Mable Hillery. Festa dell'Unità, Turin, Italy, 1971

holding Greece in its jaws. In 1967, a handful of junior officers, led by Colonel George Papadopoulos and backed by the US, had overthrown the Greek government and declared martial law, outlawing "strikes, labor unions, long hair on men, mini-skirts, the peace symbol, the Beatles, Sophocles, Tolstoy, Aeschylus, Socrates, Eugene Ionesco, Sartre, Chekhov, Mark Twain, Samuel Beckett, free press, new math, and the sound of the letter Z [which means "he lives!" in Greek]."

It was there that I experienced one of the most thrilling events of my performing life. Mikis Theodorakis is the greatest Greek composer in its history, and arguably the greatest living European composer of our era. He belongs on Mount Olympus alongside Zeus for his extraordinary musical talent and his lifelong commitment to peace and justice. The only way most Americans will recognize his name is if you mention the soundtracks for *Zorba the Greek* starring Anthony Quinn, *State of Siege* and *Z* directed by Costa-Gavras, or *Serpico*, directed by Sidney Lumet. Many saw him as a major symbol of resistance to fascist rule, and a widespread international campaign forced the junta to free him from imprisonment shortly before the festival, although his music was still strictly banned in Greece. And there he was, just in front of me that afternoon, up on the stage taking his group through their sound check. His energy and commitment to the music were palpable, and I was spellbound just watching.

I noticed a striking woman sitting beside me, and when I turned to look at her, I was astonished to see the face of Maria Farantouri, who sat quietly waiting for Mikis to call for her turn. Whenever an interviewer has asked me, "Who is your favorite female singer?" I answer that there is not one but a small handful that includes Nina Simone, Violeta Parra, Mavis Staples, Mahalia Jackson, and . . . Maria Farantouri. I had listened to Maria's recordings time and time again, as she made the passion in the music of Theodorakis come to life vividly enough to break your heart, strongly enough to evoke the unshakeable resolve of her people to be masters of their destiny. Now she was right here in Florence, right next to me, and about to run through her preparations for tonight's performance. I was nearly tongue-tied with excitement, eager to introduce myself and thank her for all she had given me through her interpretations of Theodorakis's work over the years and hoping to tell her about the English lyrics I had written for the first three songs of *Romiosini* in case they would be useful for her.

My greatest personal ambition was to use the medium of song, bits of poetry and music made from the artistry and heart of so many, to carry a piece of each movement across every border, to build a bridge between struggling peoples everywhere. This meant stretching my modest musical and language skills nearly to the breaking point. Inspired by the evocative and ferocious poetry of Yiannis Ritsos, which Theodorakis had brilliantly set to music, I had worked hard for weeks, poring through poetic translations of *Romiosini* I found in various collections, checking the meaning of the poetry through the sensibilities of intellectual Greek friends as well as the eyes of a short-order cook in the local greasy spoon in Brooklyn and a neighboring Greek housewife, drilling down below the surface of meaning to the heart of this eloquent cry for justice, there to find the timeless Greek yearning for self-determination, that indestructible and untranslatable *kaimo*. The first song in the trilogy insists on the unbending historic resistance to tyranny of the Greek people. The second evokes the long years of suffering they have endured, and the third song beckons us to join the advancing liberators as they appear wave after wave. Here is my singable translation of one of the most illustrative verses:

> These trees, these trees will never bend their heads,
> Nor submit to restricted skies.
> These stones, these stones won't easy take the tread
> Of a footstep with a foreign stride.
> This face, these faces we have known so well
> Answer only one master: the sun.
> This heart, these hearts that we have loved so well
> Answer only that justice will be done!

Maria immediately insisted that I tell Mikis about my work, and when the musicians took a break, she literally pulled me up onto the stage. When I actually shook the hand of this man whose music and heroic activism I had revered for most of my life, he seemed like an old friend. He greeted me warmly, and spontaneously invited me to sing the three songs for him, accompanying me himself on piano. I'm no expert in the complex rhythms of Greek music, and I'm sure I made horrid missteps as I sang, but of course he nimbly adapted, and when I finished he rose and wrapped his arms around me, asking, "Will you sing this with us tonight?"

After finishing my own set—a combination of fresh antiwar songs and timeless American freedom songs—I returned to the stage later that evening to sing my English lyrics for these three magnificent Greek songs with the composer himself, before a huge enthusiastic international audience. Later, Mikis asked whether I would join him on tour in Australia the following year, and asked me to stop by his home in Paris before returning to New York to pick up more of his material and prepare more singable versions in English. I could never have imagined any of this, even in my most hubristic dreams!

I was devastated when, just before that tour was to take place, I had to cancel due to a serious bout of pneumonia that was initially diagnosed as tuberculosis. However, I was able to perform with Theodorakis again a few years later, after the US-backed junta was finally sent packing

Barbara Dane onstage with Mikis Theodorakis. Florence, Italy, 1970

in the summer of 1974, when he came to New York to celebrate the reestablishment of democracy in Greece. Welcomed with great warmth and enthusiasm to Astoria, Queens, the heartland of the largest Greek American community outside of Athens, he presented an evening of song, and I was proud to be asked to perform my three *Romiosini* songs in English with him there.

The truth is, I have always seen the invitations to tour with Louis Armstrong, indisputably the most treasured American jazz musician, singing the classic blues with him, and then from Theodorakis, the most beloved composer of his country, to tour with him singing classic Greek poetry to his music, as the most precious highlights of my musical life. Although unwelcome circumstances prevented me from realizing either of these tours, the invitations alone made me feel that on some basic level I was succeeding in my goal of demonstrating through music that borders are illusory, that culture flows unrestrained no matter how high the walls, that music has the power to flood through the driest and hardest of arteries and bring hearts back into the rhythm of life itself.

The fall of 1970 found me preparing for what was to be a clandestine tour of Spain. Franco was still living, and his draconian rules required that translations of the songs I planned to sing be submitted to the censor's office before I could be given a visa. "Ramon Padilla," a friend working as a translator under that pseudonym at the UN in New York, had advised me to submit nursery songs and similarly "innocent" texts for the censor, but for performances use translations of the songs I would really be singing. He and his entire family were lifetime anti-Franco, so he insisted on translating it all for me. My visa was already in my pocket.

The idea for this tour had come from Raimon, a singer I had met at the 1967 Encuentro in Cuba, banned in Spain since he would not sing in Spanish but only in his own language, the outlawed Catalán. He and another Catalán singer, Pi de la Serra, contacted the Worker's Commission, the group that had built the most effective oppositional network in the country, and they all agreed that someone from the US would stand a good chance of delivering the kind of moral support and information they would have liked to have done themselves. It was known that Franco would do anything he could to stay in favor with the US government and so might be blinded to my efforts to do what otherwise would have found the local singers behind bars.

I stayed at Raimon's flat, where I met Julia León, now a gifted singer of Renaissance Sephardic music, who was to be my guide and translator. My first performance was at the University of Madrid, on a completely dark and seemingly deserted campus with no visible announcement, where we slipped silently downstairs to a door that opened on a huge hall jammed with students waiting for us. Julia had warned me they would not be able to applaud but would snap their fingers in approval. That was the way we conducted all subsequent performances, and I quickly got used to the small thunder of clicking thumbs. When all was done that night, someone checked outside for the all-clear signal: so many blinks from the cigarettes of two simpatico Guardia Civil, normally the most feared law enforcement guys, stationed on the nearby hilltop to make sure nothing strange happened there. Students had tactically made friends of these two, and this is how the others knew it was safe to leave campus.

I was pretty exhausted, still jet-lagged, and was put to bed in a tiny student apartment where I heard the muffled sounds of books being moved. There was to be a large demonstration in downtown Madrid the next day, and it was known that the police would come to search this place in advance, making it necessary to hide anything that would look "red" to them. I insisted on going to the demo, hoping to learn what tactics the Spanish opposition had developed to evade arrest. I was coached on the proper behavior: never walk with more than two other people, and make it look like window-shopping; if stopped, show my US passport and speak English respectfully; meet back at the place where I'm staying. What an education! I saw thousands of trios of "window-shoppers" on what appeared to be a normally quiet day, strolling the main avenues. But suddenly, on a soft signal, a large group converged and, from the obscured center, a few hundred leaflets flew with the message of the demonstrators. At that, the shoppers quickly resumed their stroll. A very effective tactic, but still a few hundred were arrested that day. Fortunately, most of my student hosts managed to make it home.

In Barcelona, I was surprised to discover that our concert would be public. More than a thousand students gathered at the university, and the concert was described by the press as "aposteosic." What was truly impressive was the courage of the audience, there at great risk to take a stand against the fascist regime.

Of all the places we visited on the tour, the País Vasco, Basque country, gave me the most detailed memories. First lesson: never use the name of the country, or any other Euzkadi word I may pick up, in public. In only one place, the Basque Cultural Center, was the language permitted by law. We had two translators on the stage, one to read the Spanish translations of songs like "Skip to My Lou" and the other to read the words of the real ones, such as "Kent State Massacre" or "Study War No More" in Euzkadi.

When it was time to leave Spain, I said good-bye to Julia and her crew, assuring her we would meet again, as we did years later when she invited me to attend a peace conference she organized between Israeli and Palestinian women held in Zarautz, País Vasco, where she lives today.

I sang again in Spain in 1978, three years after Franco's death. It was a profoundly changed country. My trip culminated with a huge concert at the Casa del Campo park in Madrid, where I was accompanied by my son Pablo. Suddenly, in middle of our set, as a dense fog rolled in, something from deep inside moved me to begin singing the Spanish Civil War song, "Jarama Valley."

> There's a valley in Spain called Jarama
> It's a place that we all know so well
> It is there that we gave of our manhood
> And so many of our brave comrades fell

Covered in a thick mist, the assembled audience of over ten thousand people were transformed into the ghosts of the thousands of Republican soldiers who were killed on that very spot by Franco's forces forty years before and the hundreds of international troops who died there with them, including the one-hundred-plus Lincoln Brigade volunteers from the US who sacrificed their lives to fight fascism. When I looked over at Pablo, he was in tears, and I realized that had he been born years earlier, he might very well have been among them.

43

BUILDING A BIG WALL OF MUSIC

Ever since returning from the Encuentro de la Canción Protesta in Havana, I had been looking for ways to connect the songs and artists I had heard there with audiences and activists here in the US. Why not create a record label that could collect this outpouring of music and poetry flowing from movements all over the world and put it where it belongs: into the hands of those struggling every day to change it? Making the music available to American audiences as performed by the originators would be far more in keeping with my mission than trying to sing everything myself. It would be more credible, more personal, and certainly more culturally grounded that way.

    We secured a modest donation of start-up funds and were able to issue and market the first group of four LPs. From that point, any money that came in from sales was plowed back in to pay for future productions. In those days, an enormous amount of voluntary expertise and energy was given to projects like these, never intended as commercial ventures but developed in order to encourage connection between the resistance and revolutionary movements breaking out everywhere. I believed we could count on many committed people to do writing, researching, translating, original art, and the like in order to create the kind of booklet I planned to include with every record. We approached organizations like NACLA (North American Committee on

Latin America) and the PSP (Puerto Rican Socialist Party), US-based supporters of the IRA in Ireland, opponents of the Greek junta, Chilean refugees from the Pinochet regime—whatever groups were doing good work in relation to the issues represented on the recordings—and unfailingly, they offered their support. Most of these groups would sell the records to raise funds for their work and use them as educational tools in recruiting and informing their supporters and for spreading their message outward on the airwaves, in classrooms, at events—wherever music could flow.

Well, what to name it? I had to come up with something quickly, and somehow a word I had heard in Spanish popped into my head: *Paredon*. It was easy to pronounce in English, and if you knew it meant "big wall" in Spanish, you might be hip enough to think of the Fugs' semi-satirical song taunting the bourgeoisie, "Up against the Wall, Motherfucker!" To me, with the US blockade against Cuba in mind, it meant a big wall of culture opposing imperialism. But it never occurred to me that the term *paredón* had disturbing connotations as well, indicating a firing-squad wall, against which either your friends or your enemies may have been executed. I wish I had not been as ignorant of the language or the history as I was then. Of all the words I could have chosen, that one was a mistake that I hope has not cost the label too many friends.

Irwin was the perfect partner in this endeavor. Although the whole thing had originally been my idea, and I ended up doing almost all the selection, acquisition, and production of the recorded material, plus the editing of the extensive booklets, it was Irwin who knew the nitty-gritty of the manufacturing side and who had plenty of experience with distribution and marketing. He had worked with Moe Asch and Folkways Records over several years, and so understood exactly the kind of things I needed to learn. Plus, when it came to the contents of the booklets, I could always count on Irwin for a superb political introduction to any of the subjects, or he could point me to someone else who was expert in that particular area.

For me, the most thrilling part of all this work was the discovery of music or poetry or oration that flowed from the political struggles, offering undeniable evidence that each movement existed, was viable, and was moving forward, and, by this, demonstrating that victories were possible, that victories had been achieved. The very writing of a poem or

Paredon cover art

a speech or the raising of a song was a kind of victory in itself, a triumph over censorship or marginalization, disparagement or even death.

My work with Paredon throughout the 1970s had always been woven into the strands of peace movement urgencies, family obligations, and even, with a little luck, the occasional bread-and-butter activities, but I never saw it as a burden. Rather, it seemed so logically something that needed to be done—like eating or breathing—that I simply accommodated it into whatever else was going on. Whatever singing I was doing during the Paredon years, no matter where, one part of me would be keeping an eye out for material that could become a record in order to communicate that same spirit as far as possible. The voices of movements that cried out to be heard were calling from every part of the globe during the seventies, and I was a part of the chorus.

44

FREE THE ARMY!

In 1970, I attended an ambitious gathering of left and progressive individuals and organizations that was convened in Chicago, largely through the initiative of Arthur Kinoy. The most revered and trusted leaders of the day—including Ella Baker, fierce civil rights defender and beloved founder and mentor of SNCC—had brought together as many sectors of the peace and justice movement as possible: folks like Dave Dellinger, the Bellecourt brothers from AIM, Dolores Huerta from the United Farm Workers, and more. The idea was to consider the feasibility of building an electoral national third party. It would take the power of a united left to mount any serious challenges to our national problems, but was this the moment when it might be possible to build that unity?

Apart from the plenary sessions and panels, people were milling about and exchanging ideas in the halls and hotel rooms. A somewhat agitated man we had never met before asked me to join him along with Jane Fonda in a room where he could tell us about "something very important." He introduced himself as Lou Wolf, saying that he had been living in the Philippines for some time doing peace movement work and was in contact with GIs who were struggling to build a movement. He had recently launched a GI rag called the *Whig*, funded by the Lawyer's Guild and the Pacific Counseling Service (PCS) with encouragement from the United States Servicemen's Fund (USSF). He told us that he had attended the conference specifically to ask whether we would be willing to travel to the Philippines with some cultural support of the sort we had been providing in the US, perhaps bringing other musicians and actors. His hope was that we could help inspire a strong antiwar GI movement there.

Both Jane and I took his request very seriously. I declared on the spot that I was prepared to drop everything I was doing in order to give the organizers whatever they felt was most urgently required, predicting that if we let anything delay us, we would likely show up to find the organizers busted or shipped elsewhere and the nascent project dead. We had already seen how quickly the military was prepared to move when they saw a need to extinguish any type of organized opposition.

On the other hand, Jane had recently come up with the idea of creating a real USO-style presentation, an antiwar alternative to the Bob Hope–style tradition, which could also be filmed and used as an organizing tool for future work, something more high profile than underground. She had already been seriously thinking about this, encouraged by Howard Levy since the previous autumn. And with her resources and access to the Hollywood community, she would be the ideal person to pull it off.

Jane and I were proposing two different strategies, and only time would tell which would be more effective. I wasn't privy to the discussion within our funding group (the USSF), but I think there were voicings of both points of view.

Jane soon set out to recruit the cooperation of like-minded actors, musicians, writers, directors, and funders, whatever it would take to develop a script and mount a live show as a pilot project for what was now being called *The FTA! Show*. With scriptwriters like Jules Feiffer, Carl Gottlieb, Herb Gardner, and Barbara Garson, and direction by Alan Myerson, how could you go wrong?

Meanwhile, as 1971 was dawning, an organization called the Citizens Committee of Inquiry had already set in motion a momentous event called the Winter Soldier Investigation, and Jane, along with the Vietnam Veterans Against the War (VVAW), Mark Lane, Don Duncan, and others, took part in its planning. A collection of US officers and enlisted men were to gather in Detroit to testify publicly regarding the many shocking war crimes in which they had personally participated. The My Lai massacre was already all over the front pages, as was the CIA's record of human rights violations in the Phoenix Program, but these vets were concerned that the media was painting incidents like these as if they were isolated events, when they knew from bitter experience that they reflected existing Pentagon policy.

As a way of raising funds for the Winter Soldier Investigation, an event called Acting in Concert for Peace was devised, held on January 29, with the participation of Dick Gregory, Donald Sutherland, Jane Fonda, and myself. Two other concerts by David Crosby and Graham Nash, as well as Phil Ochs, helped pay the cost of transporting and housing the veterans who would be testifying.

I will never forget the experience of the Winter Soldier Investigation. We sat for three days both horrified at what the vets were describing and proud of these men for their courage in confessing their participation in what were undeniably a considerable number of cold-blooded and merciless acts of cruelty. Shamefully, rather than treating this historic event as a tremendous scoop, the media gave it very little attention, the way they treated "routine" antiwar activity in general in those days. Only KPFA and the other Pacifica stations gave this important investigation the extensive coverage it merited.

In March we launched *The FTA! Show*. Yes, in the army propaganda, FTA! meant "Fun, Travel and Adventure," but the GIs had long ago transformed it into "Fuck The Army!" or, in polite company, "Free The Army." More or less the same idea, right? Get the military out of your life before they fuck you!

Fred Gardner had stepped in to work with Jane, along with Donald Sutherland. Gary Goodrow from the San Francisco Mime Troupe, actor Peter Boyle, Jerry Williams and his Swamp Dogg band, and even Dick Gregory joined us in Fayetteville, North Carolina, where so many thousands of young Americans were being hammered into becoming soldiers at Fort Bragg. Hosted by the organizers of Haymarket Square, the local GI coffeehouse, we put the show on to three full houses. They came in droves, in spite of a phony bomb scare, surveillance photos, and other intimidation attempts, hungrily applauding the show with over-the-top enthusiasm for its message, which was, unequivocally, stop this war now!

The FTA! Show: Gary Goodrow, Jane Fonda, Peter Boyle, Dick Gregory, Barbara Dane, and Donald Sutherland (front center). Fayetteville, North Carolina, 1971.

With this concrete evidence of a need for such a presentation, a Hollywood producer named Francine Parker was drafted to take over direction, and singers Rita Martinson, Holly Near, and Len Chandler were added to the troupe. Through the autumn, the show was presented near several army bases in the US, ending its tour at Philharmonic Hall in New York. It was determined that the show would then be taken to the troops in the Pacific region who were on their way to Vietnam, and a documentary film would be made.

I found myself quietly sidelined, possibly because I continued to insist on the urgency of sending support to the projects in the Philippines. In a compromise, the USSF leadership agreed to send me to the Far East, along with Pablo for accompaniment. We would be sponsored in Japan by the peace organization Beheiren, and in the Philippines by the Kabataang Makabayan, founded in 1964 as "the patriotic and progressive vanguard of the Filipino youth." We would go to Hawaii first and then to Japan, Okinawa, and, at last, the Philippines. That would mean a lot of traveling, but it was only part of the picture for Pablo and me.

In the summer of 1971, it was time for two-year-old Osamu's first visit to his father's home country, and his mother Adria's first look at this vast and complex place. Skirting travel restrictions, they began their adventure with a sea journey from Havana to Montréal, two weeks of eating strange Russian food and counting the flying fish from the back of the boat. They were more than glad to make land. The Melamed family, progressive expats from the US, generously opened their home, offering a safe place to rest while they waited for me to drive up from New York to fetch them.

Adria had no papers for entering the US, but we concocted a story that Osamu was my kid and Adria was his Puerto Rican nursemaid in case the border guy asked, and he did. Near the border, we bought the baby and Pablo those corny tourist T-shirts declaring that they had just had a great visit to Canada, and put more tourist trash on the dashboard for show. Slick as a whistle, we were in New York!

Back in Brooklyn, Lucy Ranghelli, our downstairs tenant, turned into instant granny with the prospect of having a darling little toddler in residence for a few weeks. Her husband, Luigi, even put together a little tricycle for Osamu from discarded parts he scrounged in the neighborhood. Their daughter Teresa, then a young teenager, took Osamu on as her personal treasure, and you couldn't have asked for more love and attention. She giggled with pleasure whenever he pointed proudly at his tiny new red sandals and said, in baby Spanish, "pato roro!" meaning *zapatos rojos* (red shoes).

After a quick trip to Italy to sing at the second annual Festa dell'Unità, Pablo and I were about to begin our second cross-country GI organizing tour, bringing Adria and baby Osamu with us. The plan was to buy a relatively new VW ragtop for the drive west—since it offered somewhat more space than the old model and was said to be equally economical on gas—and then sell it at the end of the tour. By this time, there were GI coffeehouses or similar projects springing up in more places, and we played at several: Fort Bragg in North Carolina; Fort Campbell in Kentucky; then west to Fort Chaffee in Arkansas; Fort Hood in Killeen, Texas; Fort Sill in Lawton, Oklahoma; and Fort Bliss in El Paso, Texas. Heading out from San Antonio, we hit New Mexico and Arizona, finally arriving in California, where we actually had a paying engagement at the Ash Grove.

It was quite a feat to find space in that little car for the four of us,

Pablo, Adria, Osamu. Southwest United States, 1971

with two guitars, enough clothing for each person, a couple of toys for two-year-old Osamu's entertainment as we traveled, and maybe even a place to stash some snacks for the road. Miraculously, a Puerto Rican woman who looked vaguely like Adria actually loaned her an expired passport so that she wouldn't be without resources in case she was challenged.

One of the most impressive and touching things about the entire trip was the welcome that greeted us in every town where we stopped, with activists and supporters freely opening their homes and giving us bed and board, great conversation, even extras like a little sightseeing, medical assistance if needed, accommodations for the toddler, maybe laundry or help with car problems, most anything we needed. These folks didn't know us in advance and were taking it on faith that we were going to be good houseguests and honest people, worth the risk, since we had come in support of the wave of resistance to war and in celebration of our mutual longing for peace. Without fail, we would leave with teary eyes all around, big hugs, and promises to stay in touch forever, which of course was not possible.

The only hostile moments I recall took place in Arkansas, after we had left Jonesboro, where we paid a quick visit to my Grandma Totsie so she could meet her great-grandson Pablo and embrace her little great-great-grandson Osamu for that one time in her life. We were sad not to be able to linger, but it was urgent that we get an early start. We headed up and over the Ozarks on the road to Oklahoma and oh, America the Beautiful, we saw you at your best that summer, passing through those forested mountain roads where wildflowers twinkled everywhere in the shade.

A little after noon, a small clearing revealed a gas station and cafe, and we stopped there for lunch. We found several beefy middle-aged white men sitting around a table near the rear. Taking our seats near the front window, we couldn't help but notice the stiffening of those men when they saw us, the hushing of their conversation and the hard stares. A sense of dread began to fill the air, as they shifted slightly, and slowly moved their hands near their holsters, mumbling something about damned long-haired hippies. We began calculating whether it would be a good idea to simply retreat or whether that would get us in worse trouble, when without warning our little two-year-old slid down from his seat, walked over to their table and extended his hand in the universal gesture of peace. The men were so surprised, they actually returned his handshake, and the air suddenly seemed to clear. Now that we know Osamu as a grown man, we understand that nobody had to teach him how to handle situations like that. He's just made that way.

At last we arrived in California for our Ash Grove performance, but I was focused on getting to Berkeley, where we could spend some family time. Nina was eager to introduce us to her new boyfriend who she had recently moved in with, and Nicky was helping Tina, his old crush now his partner, make a home and raise her two little boys. To my relief and joy, life with these folks seemed to be moving along on a reasonably even path, even with its somewhat "original" arrangements, but then my own arrangements were hardly like those of most people.

Before leaving California, Pablo and I had one more important job to carry out: to sing at a rally at the Alameda Naval Station in support of the sailors from the USS *Coral Sea* who were refusing to participate in its next mission, the mining of Vietnam's Haiphong Harbor and Tonkin Bay. Deep unrest was already spreading throughout the navy, but this apparent escalation kicked off protests that had begun weeks before, when the ship was still in the San Diego harbor. After an initial confiscation of petitions circulated on the ship, the sailors kept up the pressure until one fourth of the crew had signed. Even in that historically military town, civilians supporting them collected hundreds of signatures on street corners.

In an innovative move, San Francisco Bay Area peace activists welcomed the *Coral Sea* to its staging visit in Alameda with a giant peace rally, purposefully without the usual lengthy speeches. The program would primarily feature music, with speeches only two or three sentences long, exclusively by men from the ship. As the sailors stepped up to the mic, it was amazing to hear each one with his own variation on the theme: "I don't believe in this war," "I don't think we should take part in any escalation," "I'm personally not going to participate!" and even "I ain't gonna go." One remark stood out for me: "I'm going to stay on the ship where I might be able to do some good." When it was my turn to sing, I shared a song I had just written, explaining the campaign.

Here is the first verse and the verse that I added later at the end of the song to explain what that last man's comment had actually meant:

THE CORAL SEA SHOUT (SOS, Stop Our Ship!)

I know you've heard of the Vietnam War
And you know what we were fighting for:
Standard Oil, and Republic Steel,
And I'll tell you how all the people feel:
Seventy percent say it just ain't right,
And a whole lot of soldiers just won't fight.

Air Force pilots setting airplanes down,
And a whole lot of sailors coming back to town,
And a thousand men of the Coral Sea,
Expressing the conscience of you and me
SOS! Stop our ship! SOS! Stop our ship!
. . .
Well, the orders came for the sailing day,
To mine Haiphong Harbor and Tonkin Bay,
So they mined that harbor, but there ain't no doubt,
The sailors took all the fuses out! Yes, they mined that

harbor
And there ain't no doubt,
The sailors took all the fuses out!
SOS! Stop our ship! SOS! Stop our ship!

The next day, we took off on our antiwar GI organizing tour in Japan, Okinawa, and the Philippines. In Japan we were met at Narita airport by Tsurumi Toshiyuki, a national leader of Beheiren, the organization representing Japan's peace movement, and taken to a large room jammed to the walls with journalists. The only observable female in the room apart from me was dressed in traditional kimono and consigned to the back corner of the room. Reporters began addressing questions, but only to Pablo, a nineteen-year-old boy at the time. But this boy spoke to them directly and clearly. "I think you need to address your questions to my mother. She will be glad to answer anything you need to know." With that, they actually shifted their attention.

Later, by coincidence, on a train we ran into the woman journalist who had stood in the back of that room, now dressed in Western clothes. In perfect English, she filled us in on the kind of discrimination she has endured for her entire career, and thanked us for taking her questions, which most Japanese ignored.

Our concerts were held near US military bases all over the country, but access to the bases themselves was always impossible. As for the GI movement, its most visible expression was a small underground newspaper called *The Owl*, sponsored by the Pacific Counseling Service based in the US. Nevertheless, we were able to interact with some GIs in a limited way.

It was at the Iwakuni Marine Base that we met with some very disturbing information. A young marine insisted on talking with us in private, where he breathlessly described discoveries he had made that he felt should be urgently brought to the attention of the US legislature, asking our help to contact New York's Bella Abzug, then the most visible peace advocate in Congress. He knew it was illegal to bring nuclear weapons materials into Japan, and he was sure that there were large quantities being kept in the secret underground areas where he worked. His military training had given him the ability to identify the classified materials to which he was assigned. He asked if there was any way we could help him get the information out. We promised to try, but then were swept off to our next stop, at the mercies of an agenda planned by others.

When we circled back to Iwakuni a few days later and inquired after this man, we were informed, shockingly, that he had been run over by a jeep and killed on the base. In her autobiography, Jane Fonda talks of others there who were urging her to demand a search of the base, but in her words, she too "got nowhere."

We went to Okinawa, where there are thirty-two US military bases, occupying almost 25 percent of its territory. Since 1945 and the end of World War II, these islands had been under US administration, viewed as an occupation by most of its people. In 1971 when we arrived in the capital city, Naha, it was obvious that there was a generalized and strong objection to this foreign military culture, its impact on the local ecology, and the corruption it engendered in local life. There was an almost palpable insistence on native culture everywhere, and we were delighted to find that distinctively Okinawan music, with its unmistakable lilt and instrumentation, was played even in the taxis and restaurants.

A local Quaker activist from the US was living in Okinawa, trying to build a movement there among the disaffected GIs. He organized a concert for us at a local high school. The students didn't understand enough English to get a lot out of our lyrics, but we discovered that they had prepared a song we could all sing together—"Michael, Row Your Boat Ashore"—creating a sense of unity and solidarity. Several GIs had been invited to attend, and we spoke to them after the concert, bringing news of the movement in the US. Pablo hung out with them later, getting an insider's view of GI life off base and lending moral support.

Before leaving Japan, we went to Hiroshima to visit the Peace Museum. When the US launched the nuclear era by bombing Japan in 1945, more than 100,000 died here and another estimated 80,000 people in nearby Nagasaki. As we approached the museum entrance, our guide pointed out some small camps along the nearby river bank. These were the shelters of survivors of the nuclear attack, the deformed people not absorbed into the general population even twenty-five years after the bombing. Of all the things I saw in the museum, the form of a little schoolboy melted into a rock and clearly identifiable touched me most. Of all the things I heard, it was the sound of silence that upset me with the absence of any mention of the US as the perpetrator of such deliberate devastation. An inexcusable silence.

On November 18, we landed in Manila to find that Marcos had the whole country on alert with his threat of imminent martial law. It was shocking to see the tension in the faces of our hosts. We met Melinda Parras, the eighteen-year-old Filipino American girl assigned by the underground socialist youth organization Kabataang Makabayan (KM) and its cultural wing Student Cultural Association of the Philippines to handle our visit. Melinda had arrived from California only a few weeks previously, in search of her roots, and was determined to do her best at this test of her abilities. Thankfully, her sense of humor was reasonably intact, and her taste for adventure was evident too. She did well by us.

When we arrived at our lodging, we were presented with a letter from the immigration office mockingly called an "invitation," demanding that we show up for an appointment. We were quickly advised that this was in fact a summons—a sort of subpoena—and it meant sudden and possibly dangerous expulsion from the country. "A one-way helicopter trip over the China Sea" is how one comrade described it. A consultation was arranged with lawyer friends of the KM to decide what to do. After

Melinda Parras, Pablo Menendez, Filipino activist. Manila, 1971

some discussion, I informed the KM representatives that Pablo and I would not accept the "invitation," that we had come for a specific purpose: to lend cultural support to the GIs opposing the war and any allies who cared to work with them, and so, with their consent, we intended to carry out our mission. They agreed, and promised to make sure that there would be a lawyer at all our performances ready to act on our behalf if police or other officials tried to intervene.

Our first test was a crowded concert at the Angelus University, a large Catholic college in Manila. As we prepared to go onstage, we were told that police were waiting outside, apparently to arrest us as we exited the theater. So we made a plan: we would present our musical messages during the first half of the event, and, when the packed house roared out its request for more, we would issue the false promise that we were coming back with our best stuff after the intermission. Reassured when we spotted Melinda and the lawyer in the front row, we exited offstage, where a priest grabbed my elbow, advised us to put our jackets over our heads, and quickly hustled us down a long dark hall, up some kind of fire escape and over the roof, down to a waiting car with license plates unknown to the police.

We were driven to the home of sympathizers already in bed asleep, since they were schoolteachers who had to be up early. Our driver let us in and left hurriedly, but we saw that there was only an empty living room with no evidence of beds or even couches or cushions. We found some newspapers to cover the cold tiles and did our best to catch a few winks of sleep on the floor. I could only surmise that the salaries of teachers in the Philippines were not enough to cover the price of sheets or pillows, or much else for that matter.

Join the movement and see the world! We traveled on the worn-out local buses, along with farmers, schoolchildren, and housewives with live chickens or ducks in baskets—all the local commerce made possible by these rickety conveyances. We presented our music near the US bases that are peppered all over the country: Clark Air Force Base on Luzon, the naval base at Olongapo, Camp John Hayes in Bagio. Not surprisingly, the audiences were made up mostly of young Filipinos, although the KM comrades had made every effort to contact any GIs looking for a way to express their feelings against the war.

But there were many forces competing for the hearts and minds of these young men, many away from home and on their own for the first time, some filled with the understandable fear of what was to come in the 'Nam, and for others the crushing confusion and regret that wouldn't stop gnawing at their guts after they'd done their time there. Military towns survive on the money spent by soldiers, sailors, and airmen looking to cut loose from all that. As one observer said of the town near his base, "If there is one place on earth where a person can act like an uncivilized animal, it is this place." Sleazy nightclubs selling watered booze and prowled by underage prostitutes, careless food stands, overpriced jewelry shops peddling shiny junk, sex shops where you could get anything you wanted, nonstop and no questions asked.

Near the end of our stay, Melinda had taken a room for us in the cheapest place in town, since her fund allotment was running low. Every surface was covered with dust or was sticky and grimy, with a moldy smell that was nearly unbearable. All three of us had to find a way of sleeping there, but because I was the oldest, they insisted on giving me the only soft spot, a musty old couch complete with broken springs. They were teenagers, but they didn't complain. They realized that, after all, they had volunteered for this gig, so what could they do?

When we got the word that Jane Fonda and the official *FTA! Show* had just arrived in town and they were staying at a big modern hotel, we rushed over, our first objective a hot shower in those clean white bathrooms, with actual towels! After some greetings and hugs, we asked whether they would lend their room keys, and left them to their press conference and the palpable VIP air that surrounded them. The Filipinos saw them as visiting Hollywood royalty, and this was a huge advantage. They drew large crowds of GIs, who did see them as stars of a USO Bob Hope–type celebrity show, although with a critical twist that was just what they were ready to hear. Alas, the organizing cadre that would be needed to shape this enthusiastic but amorphous mass into anything like an ongoing movement was essentially nonexistent.

Leaving the Philippines, we felt disappointed that the GI movement we had hoped to encourage in this part of the world was still just a hopeful dream. According to my FOIA files, I was brought to the Philippines to help attract and recruit dissident servicemen. I guess that's what is meant by the word *subversive*. People like us were, and are, depicted as the bringers of discontent, when as any fool can see, the discontent is the social motion that causes us to show up.

What we hadn't realized was the depth of dissent surging all through the armed services, the range of forms it was taking, or the kind of numbers it was reaching. Actions were already being taken that no coffeehouse could have contained. This GI movement had spread to bases all over the world by 1971, even in Vietnam. More than a hundred underground newspapers were being produced, over half a million troops had become deserters, officers were being killed by fragmentation grenades placed under their beds by their own rebellious troops, entire units were refusing to fight. It was reaching the point that the war could not be prosecuted because, in effect, the troops had all gone home. We hadn't seen the forest for the enormous number of trees.

45

SOLIDARITY FOREVER CROSSING BORDERS

Arriving back in the States, Pablo and I still had to drive the VW convertible back to New York from California, and winter was already setting in. But I was eager for Pablo to meet two of my dearest friends, so we headed north for a visit with Carolyn Mugar and Mark Lane at the Covered Wagon project near the air force base at Mountain Home, Idaho, where they had lived for over a year now, helping organize the air force resisters and eventually spending more than two years keeping the project afloat. Carolyn and Mark, of course, met us with their familiar warmth and good humor, although harassment and attacks of every imaginable kind had been taking place on a regular basis at the project. We were shocked to hear that their headquarters had been burned to the ground by arsonists just days before we arrived.

Several days later, back in Brooklyn, I sold the VW for a little more than I had paid, and I wonder whether the new owner could ever have imagined the adventures that little car had already been through. Then I made a quick survey of the possibilities of buying yet another VW ragtop, one of an earlier vintage that I could afford to give Pablo for all the adventures he anticipated once he returned to Cuba. I stumbled across a dealer who had at just that moment taken in trade the exact car we were looking for, in reasonable shape, and because he hadn't invested anything in it yet and would not have to guarantee its condition, he was willing to sell it to me for only a few hundred dollars. We checked it out and snapped it up, and Pablo hurriedly loaded it with the many household items on his list, along with several important things for his musical work in Cuba. He would now be heading up to St. John, Newfoundland, in the dead of winter, where he could load the car onto a Cuban freighter and head back to Havana. I must have been crazy to send my precious boy, not yet twenty years old, off on his own for such a potentially perilous journey in midwinter, in an unproven vehicle. But in the end, he made it home all right, and was able to transport his band, his family, and his friends all over Cuba for several years in that same little rusty red ragtop VW.

Now I was headed for Paris, where I was to sing at a Vietnamese Tet celebration at the historic Mutualité Theatre as part of the Paris Peace Conference. The event was impressive, replete with high-level Vietnamese officials, refugees, and expats as well as their French supporters and antiwar activists. In this legendary hall where many French presidents had spoken, Edith Piaf had sung, and Charlie Chaplin had recorded his film music long ago, we gathered on that night to demonstrate growing worldwide condemnation of the US intervention in Vietnam and our solidarity with the liberating forces of the Viet Minh and the National Liberation Front (NLF) who were struggling to end it.

 There I encountered my friend Joe Bangert, a very special vet, a man who had been assigned to one of the most deadly and cruel jobs the military could offer. As a Marine helicopter door gunner, he had routinely flown close enough to his helpless victims to see their faces as he riddled them with firepower. Deeply marked by the experience, he was determined to give absolutely everything he had to help stop the war. He had learned Ewan McColl's "Ballad of Ho Chi Minh" some time before, and as he belted out the chorus during a dinner we attended at the Vietnamese embassy, the ambassador and his staff broke out in smiles. Next, I sang the English lyric I had written for "We Will Liberate the South," the anthem of the National Liberation Front. Then Joe, by now proficient in Vietnamese, ended by singing it for them in the original! I know these experienced ambassadors had seen it all by now, but this was a musical finale they could not have expected.

I was staying at the perfect refuge for an itinerant activist-artist, the thoroughly unpretentious but elegant home at Place des Vosges of Delphine Seyrig, one of the most generous and politically committed actresses in French film. This wonderful woman was also a full-on activist in the French pro-choice movement, literally a life-and-death issue in this overwhelmingly Catholic country. Marguerite Duras called her "the greatest actress in France and possibly in the entire world."

Right there in Delphine's very comfortable and private guest room, wrapped in her stylish bedding, I awoke in the middle of the night with a combination of hideous problems. I suddenly began throwing up at the same moment that uncontrollable diarrhea attacked, and in the middle of all that, the first intense hemorrhaging as a result of the surprise onset of perimenopause. I had a fever and felt awful, not to mention a little irrational, but I had come a long way to take part in some serious stuff, and there was still a long way to go.

Irwin would be meeting me that same week in Paris, where he was to attend the World Assembly for Peace and Independence of the Peoples of Indochina, at the Palace of Versailles. I did my best to downplay my sorry state, but of course he knew me too well to be fooled. Even today I am humbled at the thought of how graciously and carefully he absorbed this dramatic alteration of his own plans for a badly needed working vacation in Europe, with all its politically challenging as well as potentially romantic possibilities. I attended the event with Irwin, but I was too out of it to follow the proceedings. Fortunately, the French movement had set up a medical tent, and when I asked them for help, their medical volunteer examined me and provided me with an antibiotic, which I continued to take for the next couple of weeks.

As planned, after the conference was over, Irwin came with me to the East Berlin Political Song Festival. I had played the festival a couple of times before and saw it grow over time to become one of the largest of its kind anywhere, ultimately bringing several dozen of the world's most well-known political singers each year. In this way, young East Germans were exposed to the music of movements in many other parts of the world, helping ease some of the sense of isolation that had set in with the building of the wall. This was an important Vietnam solidarity event and was attended by the German Democratic Republic's head of state, Erich Honecker himself, along with several Vietnamese dignitaries. The event was held at the country's largest theater, hosted by the Oktoberclub. This was to be another celebration of Tet, the most important holiday in Vietnamese culture, and now also a time to commemorate their successful military offensive of 1968 that had proven to be a turning point in the war.

Feverish and delirious, I made it to the stage with Irwin's help, and managed somehow to perform my songs alongside the Vietnamese artist who had come all the way from home to deliver their own musical symbols of solidarity. It was all I could do to stay upright as I was taken by wheelchair back to my room, by this time almost unable to breathe.

Festival organizers arranged for me to see "the most famous chest doctor in the country" for consultation the next day. He took a series of x-rays, observed my general condition, and reached a verdict. In his firm opinion, I had tuberculosis, which meant that I must cancel all impending work and go home for treatment, which would be long term. He gave me several different kinds of pills, which he said I must take to cover all possibilities until the particular strain of TB I was carrying could be identified.

With a heavy heart, I sent word to Theodorakis that I would have to cancel my participation in his Australian tour. Irwin worked out all the details of getting me home in the best way possible, and soon I was in Dr. Marvin Belski's office in New York. To my surprise, I had begun feeling somewhat better by the time I arrived. To my profound relief, the diagnosis this time was pneumonia; Belski told me that it was probably the original antibiotic from the French medical volunteer that had saved the day. I threw all the German TB pills in the trash and was soon back in action.

A few months later, New York's Manhattan Center would be jammed with Greek patriots protesting the brutal CIA-backed military regime, an event brought together by the United Hellenic Front. Melina Mercouri, star of Jules Dassin's hit film *Never on Sunday* and later to become culture minister of Greece after the fall of the junta, spoke out forcefully against the fascists, as did the future president, Andres Papandreou. I was asked to sing my English versions of the first three songs of Theodorakis's masterwork *Romiosini*. I am always thrilled by that exhilarating music, its insistence on the Greek people's unbending historic resistance to tyranny, and the promise of eventual victory it holds.

In the greenroom after the program, Papandreou approached with a hearty embrace to thank me. As if that wasn't thrill enough, he followed by saying that he had often visited my San Francisco club Sugar Hill, Home of the Blues during his years as head of the Economics Department at UC Berkeley, becoming a lifelong fan of the blues in the process!

The following year, Theodorakis was able to bring his orchestra, along with Maria Farantouri, to New York's Avery Fisher Hall. It immediately sold out to Greeks eager to hear his music and express their opposition to the fascist junta back home. With difficulty, I was able to get one ticket to witness a stunning example of the reason why Mikis owns an unassailable place in the pantheon of modern Greece. When encore time arrived, the accompanying musicians left the stage, leaving Theodorakis alone at the piano. Without speaking, he began to play the themes of his old songs as the audience, unbidden, began to sing. For more than an hour, their voices rang through the hall, the man at the keyboard sometimes singing, sometimes humming with his beloved community, these songs that have become as deeply embedded in the culture as folk songs—music and poetry providing the matrix just as they have since the days of Homer.

I was profoundly grateful when Theodorakis agreed to record a project for Paredon while in town. You should have seen his face as we mounted the steps to Sweet Sixteen (named for its sixteen-track recording console) on Manhattan's 14th Street, the studio we almost always used. Over the door hung a faded sign from some bygone travel agency touting "Cosmos." "Yes! To the Cosmos! That's where this music will go now!" quipped this man who throughout his life had been imprisoned and tortured many times and had only a few years previous been held in a concentration camp by the fascists in his homeland. Then he sat down at the piano to play for an entire afternoon with barely a break, on and on into the evening, pouring out the poetry of three complete song cycles plus a composition in the special form he calls a *song river*, providing all the vocal lines himself. I have no words to describe the depths to which the music touches the listener, his guileless non-singer's voice expressing these powerful and tender melodies. How destitute of language I feel without the tools to grasp this poetry in its full Greek dimensions, so nostalgic yet so urgent, seeming to flow without interruption from the solace of the ancients to yesterday's entreaties to tomorrow's promise. It was plain to see why the fascists were so terrified of his moving music that they banned it and any reference to it as soon as they came into power.

46

WILD WOMEN DON'T GET THE BLUES

One day in the spring of 1972, I got word that my mother Dorothy's third husband, Ambrose Casner, was hit by a massive stroke, leaving him wheelchair bound and unable to speak. I wondered how my mom, at the age of sixty-five, would manage to cope with this devastating shift in their lives, but within a month or so another blow ended his days. I swear it was not more than a week after his death that Dorothy informed me all in one phone call that he was gone, he was already cremated, she had sold her Manhattan apartment with everything in it, and was moving back to her hometown in Arkansas! All she needed from me was that I come over to say good-bye. With dry eyes and a big hug, we bid each other farewell. But I was used to travel anyway, and had long wanted to know more about Jonesboro, so I would be seeing her as often as I could, given the commitments I continued to constantly accept, which often took me far from mid-America.

Life goes on, and change will always be the most constant feature of it. Consider what life was like in the US for women even into the 1970s. A small thing, but for example, I was always uncomfortable with the idea that a woman's marital status was required at nearly every interaction. I was still quietly insisting that people simply address me as Barbara, no Miss or Mrs., no titles please, until someone invented Ms. Far more important was the fact that women were rarely taken seriously in business situations. I could not own property or open a bank account without a husband or father to back me up. On any contracts a husband would be listed first, and whenever one was lacking, a father or brother might do. To take my own son or daughter with me out of the country, I would need a document of permission from their father. The oppressive system of coverture adopted from medieval English common law was still operative within US practices.

Women who tried to act independently were disrespected in a thousand ways. When you dropped your car off at a garage, the mechanic would not explain what work was needed, sure that a woman couldn't understand. And just try to get waited on in any place where substantial money might be expected, like a furniture store or an automobile showroom. You could wait all day in a shop that sold home hi-fi sound systems because it was a man's hobby, and surely the little woman wouldn't know what she wanted or have the power to make any decisions about spending. Even salesmen knocking on your door would ask whether they could please see the man of the house, assuming the husband controlled the purse strings.

In the professional music world, it was difficult to even speak with record company executives, managers, bookers, and so on unless you had already established a solid standing as a performer. Entry-level females were mostly invisible to them, with others speaking over their heads to determine their course. Granted, I had been labeled a "brassy blonde," a term meant to imply "ballbuster," but for me this only reinforced my grip on the reins of my own horse.

So I was pretty excited when in May 1974, I got a phone call from Kristin Lems, a student at the University of Illinois in Champaign-Urbana, wanting to book me for what would be the first National Women's Music Festival. Amazingly, she had gathered a cohort of other women who together were determined to launch this groundbreaking project, where the roster would be entirely female and the audience would be there specifically to enjoy the work of their sisters. What a concept!

I began to prepare a set of songs that would verify and advertise the strength and leadership of women in many spheres and claim our musical space, but more than that, our place in world history and struggle. I learned the original Spanish words of the Puerto Rican national anthem, written by Lola Rodriguez de Tió as a call to arms. Then it was "Bella Ciao," song of the partisan peasant women who confronted the fascist German armies in Italy, to which I composed an English lyric. Earlier, I had composed English lyrics to a Vietnamese song of women making uniforms for the soldiers on small sewing machines in leafy jungle workshops under the bombs. Then it was "Go Tell It on the Mountain," the anthem most identified with one of the greatest African American leaders, Fannie Lou Hamer. There was so much to say! The chance to present these songs and their anti-imperialist message to a massive gathering of American women was thrilling to me.

But as it turns out, the festival had another emphasis that I was unaware of. It quickly became clear that this was one of the first opportunities anywhere in the world for many women to exhibit their special affection for other women, for same-sex romances to bloom and flourish in a large public place. The obvious need for a space like this must have been overpowering, with artists frequently marginalized or closeted because of their sexual orientation now taking center stage and performing songs that verified and helped normalize this part of our lives.

Perhaps because of my broader agenda, I was never invited back to the festival. But what became known as women's music continued to expand, and the demand for it has gone beyond what anyone had dreamed. Other and larger women's music festivals have sprung up all over the nation, and there is no end to the creative energy unleashed by this demand, no limit to its penetration of the mass media and our national personality. And about time!

47

GIVE PEACE A CHANCE

In the fall of 1974, as the nation was reeling from the revelations of the Watergate scandal, an invitation that had been hinted at during our trip to Paris a couple of years before suddenly became a reality. Irwin and I were to travel to Hanoi, where I would present a concert at the Workers Auditorium celebrating the US release of the *Vietnam Songbook*, joined by the best local singer-songwriters. We came bringing the solidarity that was flowing from the hearts of millions in our own country and were received warmly by the Vietnamese public as we expressed our hopes for a speedy end to the US invasion.

Arriving in Hanoi was like those experimental films where the black-and-white picture suddenly changes to Technicolor. We could see everyday people going along the streets leading everyday lives, although we soon were told that the manhole covers appearing with regularity were actually what the name implies: covers for mini air-raid shelters into which people could duck as soon as an alert was sounded. Then there was the infamously bombed-out hospital standing among otherwise normal buildings. A doctor pled with us to let the world know about their many medical needs.

From there, we traveled south down Highway 1, the only way to reach the first liberated province of Quang Tri, just over the DMZ (demilitarized zone), stopping to meet and sing for folks in small villages

North Vietnam, 1974

along the way and even up the mountainside to a Hmong village. I noticed that the small group of Vietnamese artists who were with us would spend a great deal of care making up their faces and changing to special clothes before performing, in contrast to my way of applying a bit of lipstick and quickly brushing my hair. When I asked them why they bothered, they answered that it was out of respect for the public, who appreciated seeing something out of the ordinary, something bright and hopeful along with their songs and dances.

We reached Quang Tri after crossing several rivers on pontoons, necessary since the bridges had all been bombed, and were taken to the rudimentary hospital where we noted that the beds were little more than thin grass mats. A nurse guided me to the room where a young man of about twenty had just been brought in, his body burning up from the inside from a US phosphorus mine he had hit while sweeping the area for the safety of others. There is no cure for this condition. Smoke was pouring from his eyes, and he had the unmistakable look of one who knows he is doomed. We left for home soon after that, Irwin loaded with material for future articles and I with a heart so heavy from that sight that even now, fifty years later, I find it hard to describe.

On a glorious spring day a few months after our return, in the spring of 1975, the news broke: the Vietnam War had ended at last. A wave of relief and joy spread across the nation. I was booked that night at Gerdes Folk City, and I arrived to find a full house, packed with a crowd looking to share this historic moment. Looking out at the audience, I saw a sea of familiar faces from the many marches, rallies, and teach-ins over the years, among them the great Nuyorican poets Pedro Pietri and Sandra María Esteves. I tore up the set list, and the night turned into an enthusiastic sing-along lasting for hours. A week or so later, we reconvened at a massive rally in Central Park organized by Phil Ochs, and the celebration continued with a stream of activist singers including Pete Seeger, Joan Baez, Reverend Kirkpatrick, Phil, and myself.

These were the days when I was busy transforming our wonderful new house on State Street into a perfect place to live, work, and grow old. The house on Strong Place was comfortable, but had its space limitations, so I had found this one, a few blocks away but half again as wide as

Peter Yarrow, Pete Seeger, Barbara Dane, Phil Ochs, Joan Baez. Central Park, New York City, 1975

the first, where I could better accommodate the Paredon work. You can actually fall in love with an aged house like this one, built in 1832, and I guess that was what happened to me. I was in my glory, learning more about materials and methods dating all the way back to its beginnings than I had ever dreamed I could know, let alone manage. Luckily, Irwin knew or cared little about such things, although he deeply appreciated all my enthusiasms and successes, so we never had a dispute about anything I was doing.

One chilly day in early winter, I was dressed in my usual work outfit: jeans, lumberjack shirt, and construction boots, necessary since I would be up on the roof one minute and down five stories to the cellar the next, stepping on every kind of surface, checking and supervising various workmen. I had to chase down the phone when Irwin rang me saying I should hurry over to Brooklyn City Hall because we must get married today.

We had been living together for many years without bothering with papers, knowing in our bones that we would always be together. So what was the need? But Irwin explained that our accountant had just urged him to get married right away because it would save us a great deal of money on this year's taxes. OK, I'm all for that, and besides, I was vaguely aware that conforming to the legalities might make things far easier at the time either of us were to die. "They're very short on appointments now because of the holidays, but I was able to get a spot at 3:00 p.m.," says Irwin.

All right—making a quick decision that a change of clothes would be a waste of time, I wash my face and comb my hair, check on the workmen, grab my ID, and head out the door with my bike. City Hall was only blocks away, with only my thoughts to slow me down. The fact that for years I had been putting on a disparaging act toward my friends still tethered to marriage contracts meant I'd have to make a U-turn on the subject, but for a pragmatic person like me, this was a small price to pay. So here we go.

The "wedding chapel" was a joke: some dime-store "stained glass" Con-Tact paper stuck over the office window. The ceremony was really nothing, a few pro forma words read by a clerk. We all signed a few things. Then the clerk reached out for handshakes, announcing: "I'm running for alderman next election. Please vote for me!" and handed us literature. We shared hugs all around: Irwin; his dad, Ben Silber, and his daughter, Nina Silber (our witnesses); and me, a newly minted Silber. Then off went the four of us to the Hungarian restaurant on nearby Montague St. for some delicious pork goulash and a toast: *Egészségedre!* (To your health!)

Our dear friends Madeleine and Bob Bedell, who lived a few blocks away, were having their annual Christmas party a few days later, inviting us to make a sort of wedding out of it after we'd all eaten their traditional roast goose with fixins. I pulled an antique wedding dress from Goodwill out of my rag bag, where it had been stashed because it was way too small for me and also quite shabby. I washed it and did a little sewing magic so that I could get into it somehow. I forget what Irwin wore, but two party guests who had brought a cello and violin played "Here comes the bride" as we slowly came down the long steps from the second floor. We took as long as we could, and at the bottom we stood together with our hands clasped while Bob read a verse or two of his choice. I was handed a small bouquet of yard flowers, we said "I do!" and kissed. Then we all sang the whole ten verses of "Red Fly the Banners, Oh!" at the top of our lungs. Back upstairs to put on more comfortable clothes, and the party was on!

We had another occasion to celebrate in the neighborhood when

Irakere, then the hottest band in Cuba, arrived in 1977. The hip members of the New York jazz world had been waiting breathlessly for the band's arrival. Because of the tangled political and economic relations between our two countries, very few representatives of Cuba's flourishing jazz scene had been able to play in the US for a good many years. Now suddenly George Wein, with the Newport Jazz Festival, was to present them in a surprise midnight concert.

The band would be in town only a few days, but, realizing they knew few people in New York, I wanted to organize as much hospitality as possible to make them feel at home as the Cubans had always done when I visited there.

My daughter, Nina, was visiting me before moving to Cuba to embark on her undergraduate studies at the University of Havana. She was already friends with some of the musicians in the band from past trips to the island over the years, so with her friend Karen Lynch, she offered to help me pull together a party at my house, which had ample space for a good-sized gathering. Nina's friend Steve Peterson was drafted to make a giant batch of paella for everybody. I called my friend David Amram, one of those beloved and rare musicians who can play just about everything with just about anybody, and asked him to invite a few other New York musicians to meet and jam with the Cubans after dinner. The party was just about the most fun you can legally have in a Brooklyn brownstone! I don't think any of us will ever forget it.

The fact is, I will never forget the sense of wholeness I felt after hosting this rich gathering of artists in my own home, the place I had been working so hard to perfect as a residence that could accommodate my daily life, my musical projects, my record label and all its holdings, my husband's work and his hobbies too, and of course our political work. It would need constant upkeep and vigilance, but that 1832 brownstone on State Street now felt like the place where I could live out life to the fullest and then fade away in time. And by now the old rivalries and power struggles I had felt when I moved to New York had become meaningless. I had made my place. I was home at last!

PART FOUR

NOBODY GONNA TURN ME 'ROUND

48

PACK UP YOUR SORROWS

By 1980, Irwin had become deeply involved in what was then called "the party-building movement," requiring a great deal of travel, speaking, and writing on his part. Since 1972, he had been executive editor of the *Guardian* (subtitle: *Independent Radical Newsweekly*), and in its pages he had built a strong reputation for his writing and analysis, covering the wars in Southeast Asia, the struggles breaking out everywhere in the Third World, and developments in the socialist camp, while at the same time continuing to cover the antiwar movement and the various currents emerging on the American left. In what most people would call their "spare time," he also handled the promotion and distribution of Paredon Records.

With Irwin's encouragement, the *Guardian* organized several locally based clubs through which readers and supporters could begin to explore steps toward forming some kind of new revolutionary organization. He saw it as basing itself on a new Marxist theoretical construct, one without ties to either Maoism or Stalinism but firmly rooted in homegrown conditions, with particular emphasis on race. He soon found himself in ideological dispute with others of the paper's editorial staff, already ridden with sectarianism, and was eventually forced out. But a collection of activists on the West Coast was in the process of launching a new organization with ideas closer to his. An invitation to join them meant making a quick decision to pack up and move to California, and he decided to accept the challenge. Eventually, a theoretical journal was developed called *Line of March*, also the name chosen by the group; and their newspaper, called *Frontline*, allowed Irwin an outlet for continuing to publish his analyses as before.

Irwin's decision to move to California came just as I had completed a pretty complex renovation of our house on State Street, into which I had installed a place for the Paredon office, its files and master tapes, and my rudimentary audio equipment, all set to stabilize and move forward with the work of the label as effectively as possible. It was a disheartening and disorienting moment for me personally, and privately I felt undermined—any idea of how this would affect my own work was apparently left out of consideration. But I could see that, along with this political sea change, Irwin was in the grip of a midlife change, one at least as drastic as when he had completely altered his family situation to become my partner, and I knew it would be useless and even possibly devastating if I were to veto the idea.

All through this last period, when I had backed away from income-producing musical work and placed myself at the disposal of the GI movement and the national and international peace movements, Irwin had essentially been underwriting our daily needs. Now he would have no income, and it would be up to me to figure out a way to sustain us. The only way I could see was to divide our home on State Street into a duplex, which, in addition to the top-floor flat, would give us three rentals. I could see exactly how to do that without any huge new investment except my time, which turned out to be about a year because of the restoration of the 1832 facade, a required part of our initial mortgage agreement. Irwin hurriedly moved to Oakland, where he shared a place with some comrades in the new group. I stayed behind, contracting and overseeing the new construction work by day and reading a lot at night. It was a lonely time, full of confusion inside, and no Irwin around to help sort it out.

One day, out of curiosity, I stepped into a neighborhood health club, a type of establishment I had never been in before. I took a sauna and steam bath, for the very first time in my life. In fact, this was the first time in decades that I had done anything "just for myself." At age fifty-four, after three children, three husbands, all the singing and marching and meeting, and no telling how many thousands of miles of travel, it was about time, don't you think? And I signed up for another brand-new experience: some yoga classes. I stuck with the health routine for the rest of my time in Brooklyn, and it probably saved my sanity. Work on the house went well, and by early 1981, I was ready to leave for Oakland myself.

As for this new political direction, I was excited and animated by the thought of a party that would attempt to build on the best ideas of those earlier social experiments, that would make a serious effort to learn from their historical mistakes, and most important, that would be founded on a deep understanding of American history and built to respond to the needs of the American people, not some theoretical constructs conceived half a world away. As the great Ossie Davis told Irwin one day when these ideas were laid out to him, "I've been waiting all my life for this."

When I was kicked out of the Communist Party way back in the 1950s, I swallowed my broken heart and set out to make my own way on that limitless, perilous, and glorious path toward peace and justice, those two most noble and holiest of grails. But I'd never gotten rid of my craving for some sort of collective, for a group of collaborators with whom I could discuss and determine and who would have my back, just as I would have theirs. I had witnessed the power of a strong national organization fighting for social justice, and the changes effected by the international communist movement in its heyday, and I see some of its lingering benefits even today. Without it, you wouldn't know about the worldwide movement that rescued the nine Black Scottsboro Boys convicted on a phony rape charge in Alabama, foreshadowing the current Black Lives Matter movement; without it, you wouldn't know about the quiet heroism of Sacco and Vanzetti, two Italian anarchists framed and murdered by the state for onerous reasons; without it, you would never have heard about Tom Mooney, young San Francisco labor organizer who served twenty-two years in jail on a frame-up, only saved from execution by another worldwide campaign led by communists; without it, we probably wouldn't have the eight-hour day or any decent labor laws. We'd still be like serfs, who must live and die by command of the king.

When this new party-building idea began to emerge at the end of the 1970s, I had spent most of my adult life fiercely singing out and standing up for social justice without benefit of any solid organizational support, the way I imagined a strong party would have taken care of its activists. No one had ever followed up on my appeal for reinstatement in the CPUSA, and I was even further ostracized because of my relation to Irwin, who himself had been painted by its chairman, Gus Hall, as the very devil because of his critique of Stalinism and the pusillanimous US party. All right, I would do all I could to support and assist these new folks in their pursuit of a serious organization.

But as I went about getting settled in Oakland, I began struggling with a persistent depression. Given all the changes I was facing, much of what happened in that period is still a blur. I do recall several concerts in solidarity with Cuba—more than one with the great Cuban singer Sara González—and with the struggles in El Salvador. Pablo and I, along with Mississippi Freedom Singers Wazir Peacock and Hollis Watkins, played a festival in Nicaragua in support of the Sandinistas. We also participated in an Anti-Imperialist Song Festival at the enormous Auditorio Nacional in Mexico City, sharing the bill with Pete Seeger, Daniel Viglietti, Amparo Ochoa, Danny Valdez, and more. And we played dates in Sweden, Germany, the USSR, and Italy.

I traveled to Cuba once again, to play one of the first Havana Jazz Plaza Festivals. While there, I recorded *When We Make It Through* for Paredon at the EGREM studios, a culmination of the many years of working partnership forged with my son Pablo. He produced the album and arranged several of the tracks, bringing in great Cuban musicians like Lucia Huergo, Jorge Reyes, Jorge Aragón, Carlos and Ele Alfonso, and more. Pablo put his heart and soul into this project and once again helped lift my spirits at a time when I was struggling to rediscover the self-confidence that had always come so naturally to me. I am privileged beyond words to have had his support over the years both musically and personally.

Irwin and I had founded Paredon Records in 1970, and by 1980 the interest in and demand for more of what we were doing had shown us that the label had become a kind of institution on the left. The possibilities for building on this were endless. We had watched it expand and grow to

Pablo Menendez and Barbara Dane. Havana, c. 1982

nearly fifty titles, its reach held back only by the lack of a promotional budget and its scope restricted only by our other commitments, which required so much of our time. We realized that somehow we had to either capitalize the label and turn it into a regular business, or collectivize it by recruiting volunteers willing to shoulder a lot of the responsibility.

I liked the idea of turning the whole thing over to a political collective so that I could once again focus on my singing. Now in my fifties, with my voice and my energies still available for this, I felt it was probably now or never. My voice was still very much at my command, but it takes more than a voice to be a singer of the kind I aspired to be. I needed to continuously develop a contemporary repertoire and renew the way I would sing the old favorites, had to do the work it takes to remain current with political developments, had to reach out to my counterparts to continue our networking, and do all this before time robbed me of the energy and ability to give it my best. No sponsor, no manager, no booker, no agent, so, as usual, it was up to me.

The past several years had involved exhausting travel, a lot of self-motivation, and a lot of lonely confrontation of situations way bigger than I. I was badly shaken by the need to pull up stakes so quickly, just as I had finally gotten a grip on how I could best function based in New York. But when I got to the Bay Area, I discovered with relief that there were people waiting to gather around Paredon Records and continue with the work, even willing to work on issuing material already half complete. Good people, smart and dedicated people, several of whom I came to love.

We met many times as we talked about ways of passing on the work, and under the leadership of Hilton Obenzinger, a wise, funny, and talented comrade, I was able to lift the label off my shoulders and place it firmly in the hands of the collective he had formed. They went on to issue three precious albums following the style of the previous Paredon issues. I was very proud of all their efforts and especially their courage.

What we hadn't considered was that the main way materials had come to the label was through my travels and contacts. And then there was this group's innocence when it came to business matters. Some barely knew the difference between accounts payable and accounts receivable. Sadly, there came a time when they realized it just wasn't going to work.

In a moment of grace, the solution appeared during a conversation with dear friend and Smithsonian cultural expert James Early. He mentioned that Smithsonian Folkways might be open to acquiring other labels. Remembering Moe Asch's brilliant idea of a partnership between his life mission, Folkways Records, and the Smithsonian, our nation's pride and enduring legacy dedicated "to the increase and diffusion of knowledge," I nearly ran to the telephone to make contact with them, and with astonishing luck, Professor Anthony Seeger, then managing things, was on the line. He immediately warmed to the idea of a link with Paredon, saying he had already been following and using these recordings for a time, since his uncle Pete had called attention to them, and felt they would be an important addition to the Smithsonian Folkways' legendary catalog. With that, Irwin and I donated the label in its entirety with no strings attached other than that magic word *perpetuity*, thereby guaranteeing that these historic recordings—still so relevant in today's world—will continue inspiring future generations of artists and activists with their messages of peace, anti-imperialism, and social justice.

49

A MUSICAL ROAD TRIP TO NOWHERE

After a sumptuous and satisfying dinner in Oakland's Chinatown, early in January 1983, I broke open a slightly stale fortune cookie to find a slip of paper inscribed with a seductive phrase proposing to inform me of my future, insisting: "You will travel to many places." So how could that little cookie know I would probably travel that year to more cities and countries than my FBI shadow's budget would be prepared to cover? Like most years, it was full of joy and pain, good and bad days, miracles and disasters, but it would hold more astonishment, disappointment, discovery, delight, and despair than even the most clairvoyant freakin' cookie could have predicted.

The year started right off with the prospect of a trip across the country in a van with a Swedish film crew who would be coming to make a documentary about my work. This sounded like an amazing adventure, especially if Pablo could work with me. In fact, it would be impossible without him. Anders Lönnbro, the inventor of this whole idea, had pretty good credentials and seemed to be on my political wavelength. We spoke several times by long distance about his project, and as soon as the necessary funds from the Swedish Film Institute became available, he made a quick trip to California to plan an outline and an itinerary. Then he headed off to meet his crew in Chicago, which was where we were to begin this slightly mad endeavor to capture my work on film, as well as its far more interesting context: the rebellious spirit raging across the country at this moment in our history.

One of the first things I noticed about Anders was that he drank far too much beer, and this proved to be true of his crew as well. Maybe this partly accounts for the chaotic ending of the whole project. More likely, he had thought he'd be able to film Pablo and me doing a few performances in interesting places, grab some interview footage along the way, maybe some street life for atmosphere, and bingo! he would have his film. He had seen us work in Sweden a few times, and from there it looked easy, I guess. But once here in the US, he began to glimpse the intricacies of our political landscape, the immense size of the country itself, and the historic tensions gripping the nation in the early 1980s—endemic racism, conflicting ideas about war and peace, and a recession—all being played out in our streets. Not so easy after all, but all right then, let's have at it!

Whenever I came to Chicago, I contacted my special blues buddy and mentor, Estella "Mama" Yancey, as soon as I hit town. This time, I was hoping to create a good situation for her to be filmed doing what she did so well, even though I knew she was not in good health and age was beginning to take a heavy toll. But when she picked up the phone, she hollered, "Come right on over!" I suggested that we go out to Buddy Guy's club, where she could show me her latest stuff. She said she'd sprained her ankle "and can't hardly walk at all." I said, "Well, Mama, don't worry about that. I got four big Swedish guys with me who can pick you up and carry you wherever you want to go!" Without dropping a stitch she hollered right back, "Wait just a doggone minute! I said I couldn't walk . . . *but I can still hop!!*"

Well, that is the spirit of Estella Yancey and a glimpse at the kind of lessons in life that I learned from her. You had to keep your ears open around her at all times, because nothing ordinary was going to come out of her mouth, certainly nothing of surrender or defeat. Now in her later years, she was half blind, skinny as a stick, and all twisted up from rheumatoid arthritis. Stone broke and sleeping on a couch at her niece's apartment on South Loomis Street, she still mourned the death in 1951 of her beloved partner Jimmy Yancey, the man whose legendary piano inventions had been the magnet for every blues musician in town. Hear this line from her signature "How Long Blues":

> I been down to the Delta,
> And I have stood my trials,
> And I can stand more trouble
> Than any little woman my size.

Well, in the end, we did take her down to Buddy Guy's Checkerboard Lounge, where she bravely sang a couple of her classics with the aid of Magic Slim and his band. She was delighted to be singing, and we were proud to have made it happen, but sadly, the skimpy audience in the house that night didn't seem to remember or recognize what this frail little old woman and her husband had meant to the blues. The effort she had made to bring them her love had been met with indifference, even here in a place dedicated to the music she had given much of a lifetime to keep alive.

The Swedes had inadvertently poisoned the waters by going there earlier without us, thinking to pave the way by spreading a little money around, and who knows how that little drama had played out. Part of their plan was that I would sing a bit there for the camera, but there was clearly no welcome for anything of that sort. Buddy Guy had only nodded slightly as we walked in, and moved further to the far end of the room, staying at the bar with his friends, as they glared at us with a hostility that said plainly, "Why did you come all the way down here to film that white woman instead of us?" It felt chilly and awkward, and we left as soon as we could without seeming too rude.

Thankfully, the next day, we managed to organize a small gathering of Mama's friends at the home of Erwin Helfer, a wonderful pianist devoted to Jimmy Yancey's style and frequent accompanist when Mama got any work. Estella was in unexpectedly fine form. Enjoying her role at the center of attention, she sang strongly and beautifully in spite of her infirmities, the best I had heard her in years, giving me the great satisfaction of seeing her being filmed in a warm ambience of respect, the mirrors on the walls reflecting her every unforgettable nuance. Helfer remembers eliciting one of Estella's spunky remarks like this:

"Mama, are you afraid to die?"
"I don't know. I haven't did it yet!"

Next stop, Detroit. When we pulled into town, we went directly to my sister Julia's house, out in a working-class suburb of town, which in those days, when the unions were strong, still meant a pretty decent neighborhood. Anders and company went off to look for the downtown part of Motor City. We tried to explain that there literally was no downtown there anymore. They must have imagined a Motown scene alive and jumpin' in Detroit, but in fact Motown Records had left for Tinseltown by the early 1970s. Anders and his buddies were baffled. A writer once described the events of 1967 as "one of the most violent urban revolts of the 20th century," and even sixteen years later when we and the Swedes arrived, it was, as it still is, remembered as the Great Rebellion. Set off by a mishandled raid on a Black after-hours club by what were probably all-white police, five days of rage had ended with more than two thousand buildings destroyed by fire, seven thousand arrests, and more than forty dead. Then there was the fear-driven "white flight" that followed, when hundreds of thousands of white homeowners abandoned the city and any further civic responsibility along with it. The decimation of the tax base that followed with their departure, along with the adoption of a defensive climate of fear instead of one of reconciliation and bridge building, began the long, slow decline that ended in 2014 with this once-great metropolis, my beloved hometown, in bankruptcy.

Julia, who now went by the name Julianne, was living alone, choosing to stay in Detroit even after her two daughters had both moved to California. She had started life dreaming of becoming a regular June Cleaver, the perfect wife and mother whose main concern would be the comfort of her man. Three serious attempts at marriage had killed that dream, and by the early 1980s, the need to support her two small daughters as well as herself became urgent. She was just about out of hope when a friend tipped her off that, because of pressure from the women's movement, Henry Ford was going to hire some females for production work for the first time since the end of World War II. Her hourly pay would be whatever the union had won after years of bitter struggle, more than she could have imagined.

As it happened, she was the first woman hired, and she was assigned to a job almost guaranteed for failure. The work involved picking up heavy steel bars, measuring them with a micrometer, and cutting them on a giant band saw, daunting for anyone unused to handling machinery.

Seven days a week in the gray light before dawn, she was forced to clock in for a twelve-hour day, Ford finding overtime more profitable than hiring more workers. No days for rest, no time for personal matters, no life outside the factory. That outrageous situation went on far too long.

Anders and company had insisted that I be filmed performing in my hometown, but there had been no lead time to set up a concert. As luck would have it, my song-sisters Holly Near and Ronnie Gilbert (that powerful alto always soaring over the male voices of the Weavers) were presenting a large event in town during that same week we were there. I had contacted Holly in advance to ask whether it might be possible to film me singing a couple of songs on their concert, and she had graciously accepted the idea. And so it was that I was captured on film singing in my own hometown after a thirty-three-year absence from its stages.

Then on to the Detroit City Hall, where I was to receive a scroll along with the keys to the city. Remember that decades-earlier encounter at the Barlum Hotel Coffee Shop when they threw us down the stairs? It was my dear old friend Erma Henderson who led me and my American Youth for Democracy comrades in that protest challenging racial segregation. It was Erma who innocently sparked the fire under my departure from my family home. Erma, whose mother took me in when I showed up with my belongings in cardboard boxes back in 1946. And now I was receiving that scroll and those keys from none other than Erma Henderson, now president of the city council.

We were not yet finished with our visit to my home state. One of my most important goals was to visit the home of Sarah Ogan Gunning, the Appalachian woman who wrote so many powerful songs about the life of the coal miners and their families in Harlan County, Kentucky. I had already issued an LP on Paredon titled *I Hate the Capitalist System* after a song of hers that paints a vivid picture of the pain she felt at the loss of her child from starvation and of her miner husband from tuberculosis or black lung or both.

> I hate the capitalist system,
> I'll tell you the reason why.
> It has caused me so much suffering,
> And my dearest friends to die.
> . . .

> Well they call this the land of plenty,
> And for them I guess it's true,
> For the rich and mighty capitalist,
> Not for workers like me and you.
>
> Well what can we do about it,
> To these men of power and might?
> Well I tell you Mr. Capitalist,
> We are going to fight, fight, fight.

Since Sarah was now living near Detroit, this was my best chance to thank her in person for having created this powerful song and to let her know that I would always sing it as far and wide as possible, to carry her story forward as best I could. More important, I thought it would make an indelible statement in this film, one that was seldom delivered outside its home turf. Sarah's songs and those written by her older half-sister Aunt Molly Jackson and her brother Jim Garland about the struggles for survival and dignity of the mining families of Harlan County had become a permanent and ever-present part of my repertoire. I sang them especially when I traveled abroad, as a way of remaking the prevailing impression that all white people in America are rich, all live like the folks in the movies, and everyone has at least one car.

I had recently discovered that I had a personal connection to the life of the people who live in that hard-hit place. The day my dad died, I finally worked up my courage to ask him about the mother he had lost when he was only three years old. All he said was that her name was Hattie Turley and that she had come from Harlan County, Kentucky. I was stunned to hear him say that my own grandmother was from those very same ravaged and pillaged hills. Oh, ghost of Grandma Hattie, which side were you on?

Born in 1910, Sarah Ogan Gunning would have been in her twenties during the Great Depression, and the times that she was singing about, even now in the early 1980s, were still painful for her to talk about. I will always admire how she used her songs to inform the world of the misery and injustice her people had endured—and continued to endure—in this so-called land of plenty. Her courage in doing so was nothing short of astonishing. For me, this day was another indelible episode on an unforgettable emotional journey, and for Sarah Ogan Gunning possibly the last time she would be captured on film. She died the following year at the age of seventy-three.

Heading to the East Coast, I called Pete Seeger, friend and mentor since my teenage steps on the path of music and activism, to tell him about the film project, and my feeling that any story that failed to highlight his influence would be hollow and incomplete. I asked whether we might come up to Beacon, New York, where he and Toshi still lived in the log cabin they had built on a hill overlooking the Hudson River.

He was bedridden at the time due to a minor injury, but he generously agreed to let us come ahead, and so it was that Pablo and I, sitting on a corner of his bed or a chair nearby, listened to him tell the camera about the energetic and dedicated young girl he had met in Detroit who struck him as a good bet for organizing a People's Songs chapter. Then Pablo played our arrangement of Pete's wonderful and somewhat under-used song "As the Sun" while I sang.

Keeping the visit short out of respect for his state of health, we took our leave and drove down to New York City, along the wide, sparkling Hudson, the river Pete has worked so tirelessly to make habitable again for fish as well as humans.

That little visit with Pete will always stay with me, but whatever happened next has vanished down the rabbit hole of memory with most of the horrid experiences of my life. We might have played and filmed a gig somewhere in New York City, and then again we may have only rehearsed. But Pablo and I both recall that out of the blue, Anders's wife, Bodil, arrived from Sweden. We heard a lot of arguing between them, in Swedish. From what we could tell, she was the one in charge of the finances, and they were running out of money. It wasn't long before Anders, Bodil, and the whole crew decamped and left for Sweden, leaving us to make our way back to California. No thanks, no fond farewells, no footage.

A few months later, I got word that the film was finished, and eventually a copy arrived on a videotape. The title? *Barbara Dane's Amerika*. I watched it once, or maybe twice, in a stunned sort of fog. What Anders had extracted from the three months' time we had dedicated to the project was a montage of the street scenes and demonstrating crowds and background material meant to give the Swedish public a sense of American activism in the early 1980s. No Mama Yancey, no Sarah Ogan Gunning, and I don't even think there was much of the interview with Pete Seeger. In short, all these great people who had generously contributed their time and talent to the project on the basis of their goodwill toward us were royally ripped off. I still feel a great sadness looking back at the experience, almost as if these cherished people had been made to disappear.

Pablo and I appear in the film for one or two quick glimpses, one while riding the Chicago El and something similar in another moment, never while performing or even talking to the camera. No further communication from Anders has ever followed. He claimed to have no idea what happened to the footage. Who knows what the true story is. Maybe Anders and crew had neglected to secure releases from the artists or didn't realize they would need to license the music. The last friend who contacted Anders on my behalf was told to ask me to stop bothering him, stop inquiring, there was no more to be said.

Maybe I'm a fool for failing to recognize that most artists want a contract with proper signings before they rush in, but so many songs would never be sung or films made or books published or paintings painted if the papers had to come first and the art was only a second thought.

50

YOU JUST CAN'T MAKE IT BY YOURSELF

In the summer of 1984, I was off to take part in the Vancouver Folk Festival, where I would be able to meet a large Canadian audience for the first time. In spite of having been occupied far off the folk stage for some years now, I intended to make this performance special. Pablo, who had recently founded his own group, Mezcla, in Havana, was able to take a break and willing to spend precious time with me, so of course I drafted him as musical director. Our young Berkeley friends Barbara Higbie and Laurie Lewis were already superstars in the acoustic folk and jazz worlds, but were happy to come along and back us up on piano and bass for the companionship and the fun of it, having already been featured performers in previous festivals there and loving the Vancouver scene. Percussionist Al Guzman of the San Francisco Mime Troupe joined us too. Pablo and I rented a rooftop carrier for my trusty little brown VW Rabbit, loaded our gear into it, and took off. The others would meet us in Vancouver.

It was so inspiring to be on that stage in glorious weather singing to the large and happy audience of almost twenty thousand faces, looking out at the unbelievable beauty of the Vancouver landscape spread before us. I would gladly do this for free every day if the music goddesses would permit me!

Remember that I had been left out of the US folk festival circuit all through my peak performance years almost without exception, probably because of my problem with producer-promoter George Wein, who had come to own or manage most of them and most of those in Europe too. Back in the days when I had dreamed of actually creating and running a festival myself, I was always striving to observe them, not only from the producer's point of view but from the perspectives of both the audience and the musicians. Here was a festival that took no money from Big Tobacco or the oil monopolies and didn't emphasize the easy-sell "big-name acts" the way that Wein's festivals did. This one blossomed out of a different kind of soil, creating a celebratory, creative coming together in a noncompetitive atmosphere that, in a perfect world, would define the word *festival*.

If I had been in my thirties like Pablo instead of fifty-five, I would have made an effort to become acquainted with the organizers, but by now I had no need to seek or offer more cooperation with my own projects, scramble for work, look for more recognition, none of that. By now I was content to sing my songs and go home. But honestly, here I already felt at home.

It wasn't until years later that I came across something that indicated how ideologically close to home I was—a statement by the director Gary Cristall that explained his reasons for devoting his life to the festival: "I was a committed socialist activist throughout the period I ran the festival and I was determined to put socialist ideas into practise in both the production of the festival and in its programming. The latter meant using the festival stages as platforms for ideas that suggested the transformation of society into something beyond capitalism." It seems that he and cofounder Mitch Podolak had started with the shared perspective of two socialists, people who wanted to create a festival that would mean a lot more than a weekend getaway for its participants. A younger me would have considered moving to Canada just to be part of it.

Making a detour on our way home, we turned off to Orcas Island, a place I'd always wanted to see and where we'd heard there was a jazz festival going on. As we sat enjoying the show, the bandleader asked for requests and someone shouted "St. James Infirmary"!

"No, not possible. That is, unless one of *you* wants to sing it."

I stood up and walked toward the stage. He looked a bit dubious but he waved me up, and the band struck up the intro. Still energized from Vancouver, I let loose and, modesty aside, I knocked it out of the ball park. Afterward the bandleader turned to me excitedly and asked, "Hey, has anyone ever told you that you sound just like Barbara Dane?"

Back home, I found myself pulled into the trad jazz world again. Bands began to book me for special dates, among them Earl Scheelar's New Orleans Syncopators and George Noblauch's Black Diamond Band, both of which featured Bill Barden on trombone. Encouraged by this, I brought together my favorite local players, drawing from the survivors of the Bay Area's legendary jazz revival of the 1950s, and named us the Good News Bonanza Band because that's what we would deliver. Bob Mielke agreed to be the trombonist, and he doubled as musical director. He had encouraged and supported me since the days when I first stuck my toe in trad jazz waters some thirty years ago, even playing on my first album, *Trouble in Mind*. With George Fleming on trumpet and Richard Hadlock on reeds, we had a dream front line. Add to this Pete Allen on bass, Bill McGinnis on drums, and the inimitable Ray Skjelbred on piano, and we were unstoppable.

In 1986, a photo of then president Ronald Reagan appeared on the front page of the *San Francisco Chronicle* as he was performing the strange annual Thanksgiving ritual of pardoning a huge white turkey, sparing it from becoming his holiday dinner. On the same page, but not as prominently featured, ran articles about several especially deadly American military adventures, including what had instantly become known as the Iran-Contra scandal, recent mayhem caused by the backroom boys in our State Department that had the nation in an uproar. The contrast was more than I could take, and my mind began making rhymes unmasking some of the villains, a song without a punch line. Suddenly, "I haven't done anything wrong, and I'll never do it again!" seemed to tell it all, and "Gipper Gate Blues" was born. ("The Gipper" was the nickname of a character Reagan played in an old football movie, and, demonstrating his difficulty with separating truth from fiction, he adopted it in real life.)

I had to get that song on the radio ASAP! Calling around to find out who could be drafted to record it, I found all my first-choice musicians enthusiastically agreeing, everyone as outraged as I was about the state of the union. Same went for Mike Cogan, engineer-owner of Bay Sound. We set a date to meet at Bay right away. But who could manufacture and distribute one crazy song fast enough to make a difference? Remembering how effectively he had handled Country Joe McDonald's "Feel Like I'm Fixin' to Die Rag," I called Chris Strachwitz at Arhoolie. "We can put it out quickest if we make it like those twelve-inch 'dance singles' that play at 45 rpm," he said. Before I could sneeze, we had a thrillingly played and superbly recorded piece of work, and there it was, playing on KPFA as the theme song of the nightly news program covering the scandal. It ran for weeks! Nobody had asked for money, nobody had stalled or even asked questions. We had a real community, and it worked when it was time to move.

It wasn't long before producer George Buck asked me to record for his GHB label in New Orleans. Bob Mielke, Richard Hadlock, and Pete Allen were eager and ready to go. Then Pete made a disastrous decision. He wouldn't bring his own bass, but would rent one there, hoping to snag an old one with that mellow NOLA sound. Only when we arrived for the after-hours session—after the shop was closed—did he discover that his prized rental bass was missing its bridge! What saved us was the chance to have Butch Thompson—then a radio star on *A Prairie Home Companion*—with us on piano, and a couple of Buck's local hot players too.

We cut the record in 1988, but due to the need to re-record the bass and add Marc Caparone on trumpet and Clint Baker on guitar, not to mention some unrelated distractions, it wasn't released until 2002, just in time for my seventy-fifth birthday and the three sold-out concerts that the Good News Bonanza Band and I played together at the old Freight & Salvage.

You might think that after a life with such a rich diet of travel and cultural diversity, I was ready to stay home and count my blessings. I guess my brain was dancing around this possibility. But that's somebody else, not me. Long ago I had formed the habit of saying yes and "We'll figure it out later" whenever the chance came along to learn more about the world and the many cultures that have helped us survive as a species. When the invitations came, I was still saying yes without worrying much about the consequences.

So I was headed for East Berlin, where I was to link up with Pablo and his band, Mezcla, making their first European run in 1988. The German media fastened on "the blues-singing mother from the USA meets her son who lives in Cuba." No, not what we were after. For him, this was a tour meant to launch Mezcla in Europe! I learned to lay low as they played Dresden, Halle, and Leipzig, then back to Berlin for two final concerts. Then we piled into a minibus with all the instruments and what seemed like a thousand drums, arriving in Copenhagen within minutes of Mezcla's most important date: the famed Montmartre Club. The bus had broken down at least once, the musicians had not eaten or rested, but the house was jammed with an audience eager to hear this new Cuban band. Yes, the band played like there was no tomorrow and left the audience screaming for more.

Barbara Dane with Mezcla. Varadero, Cuba, 1982

From there, I had a series of dates lined up in Sweden, organized by Roger Hinchliffe, an American expat folkie who had met Pablo while on a visit to Havana. He loved Pablo's new band, and when he heard about Pablo's blues-singin' mother he decided to invite us both for a double bill. These events were all jam-packed, and nobody seemed confused by these evenings featuring both a Cuban band and an American blues singer.

Next we traveled to Helsinki with the whole gang. We had been invited by the Finnish Peace Council to take part in a cruise to several cities in the USSR on the good ship *Konstantin Siminov*. Our job was to ensure that this boatload of elderly Finnish peace warriors had as much relaxation and joy as possible as we traveled to Tallinn, Riga, and Leningrad. What we had to offer was just what they craved: the chance to sing and laugh and dance together in the beautiful harmony that we represented—Cuban, US, Finnish, and Soviet musicians making music together with respect and fellowship in that time of terrible Cold War tension. It was less than two years before the collapse of the "Socialist Camp."

Back home in Oakland, I pondered my musical future. Pablo's work with Mezcla meant that he was less available to work with me, and I was beginning to wonder whether it made sense for me to continue performing at all. I was in sort of a swampy depression again and struggling with questions about the relevance of my work in general, when I met Barrett Nelson, a super-skilled acoustic guitarist who often played with the SF Mime Troupe. Throughout this stretch in the late eighties, he was one of my most important collaborators. He would come all the way to Oakland from south of San Francisco to work out arrangements of new material and plan for performances, riding buses and trains to travel since his poor eyesight prevented driving. A man of unusual kindness and enormous gifts, he taught me a lot about music and an unforgettable phrase that has helped me immensely over the years, one that was current in the gay community as it was suffering the worst devastation of AIDS: "Get over yourself!"

51

WILL THE CIRCLE BE UNBROKEN?

On my last visits to Jonesboro in the early 1990s, during my mother's final illness, it was still uncommon to see people of color in the main gathering places of Jonesboro. The thrill of the week for white folks would be a trip to the Walmart with maybe lunch at the Catfish Cafe over on Main Street or, if you were among the town's elite, luncheon at the Elks Club featuring iceberg lettuce wedges with Russian dressing, chicken à la king, and the heavily sugared drink they call "sweet tea." But even after the gains of the civil rights movements of the recent past and the outlawing of segregation, no noticeable Black, red, yellow, or brown people even worked in the public rooms of these places, let alone ate in them. Maybe they were in the back rooms washing dishes or carrying out the garbage?

My mother's lady friends played bridge at one another's homes once a week, the sort that genteel ladies play, not the serious professional contract bridge Mother had played in Detroit or New York. But her lack of respect for their card-playing abilities did not keep her from loving them for their kindness. These dear aging ladies did steadfastly visit the sick, bringing companionship and home-cooked goodies, offering their fashion commentary, making sure that their world kept on turning in the most predictable way. And then Rachel Troutt, whose family had always owned the town's most reliable source of local information, appropriately called the *Jonesboro Sun*, would fill everyone in on the latest scandalous gossip. I noticed that their welcoming drink would not infrequently be a highball or bloody mary or a "coke-cola" with some kind of hooch in it, in honor of the fact that Craighead County is still dry and proud of it. You wouldn't want to act like a hick or insult your hostess by turning down a backhanded salute to that long-standing law, now would you?

Those Methodist and Baptist churches of Jonesboro have stood like mammoth immutable monuments for generations, looming over their respective street corners where they compete for the souls and dollars of the town's more prosperous citizens, who by right of their mutually understood economics, "quite naturally" were white. Once when I took a taxi from Jonesboro to Memphis to catch my plane home to New York, I mentioned that, as an adult, I'd never visited the nearby town of Paragould, where my dad had been born. Although he himself was white, the young taxi driver from Memphis commented, "You know, that place is kind of scary; Klan country to this day."

On July 25, 1992, my mother lost her years-long battle with emphysema. My sister, Julianne, and I were together at her bedside in the skilled nursing facility for her final few days, trying our best to find ways to comfort her and let her know how deeply we loved her. The intense pain in her legs caused by lack of circulation and, of course, the constant need to struggle for breath seemed impossible to assuage. There was no way to know how long this could go on. Painful for me was the fact that I had to leave her in that condition because I was contracted to teach at Jazz Camp West in California, but with Julianne remaining, we would maintain contact. I was only a day or two at Jazz Camp when a message arrived saying the end had come. Soon dozens of campers I scarcely knew were embracing me and giving what comfort they could. I learned a lot about the powerful effect of kindness in unexpected places.

Those days at my mother's bedside with Julianne taught me so much about my sister and our relationship. It wasn't anything we said or did, but the very act of taking care of our mother together gave me the sense of the deep ties that existed between the three of us that I had never quite grasped before. Over the years, I had come to see Julianne as this distant but familiar woman in Detroit taking care of her own life, her daughters, and our aging dad's needs, and of myself as a sort of admired outsider. Standing together on the brink of the sad moment when we would both lose our mother made me painfully aware of how many times Julianne may have needed me to stand with her when I hadn't been present. More than that, it made me aware of the strong steel my sister was made of that undergirded the deep love for everyone she had demonstrated so many times over the years.

When Mother died, Julianne went back to her factory job in Detroit, and I took up the task of wrapping up her affairs. I sold her car and sent the money to Nicky as she had directed. I prepared her duplex for sale and packed up her exquisitely ordered closets full of nice clothes, most of which I managed to send to our family in Cuba.

In a few weeks, we held a memorial at the First Methodist Church where she had been in attendance for some years, and as I had done at my grandmother Totsie's funeral, I sang "Just a Closer Walk with Thee." With mother's siblings also deceased, there were now no more living members of this family line in Jonesboro, so Julianne and I were the only family in attendance. Now Dorothy was at rest, leaving vivid and warm memories with everyone in her Jonesboro circle and far beyond, to the satellite circles of her three husbands, Gilbert Spillman, Louis Samuels, and Ambrose Casner, and her many contract bridge friends on both coasts. And of course, her five grandchildren: Julianne's daughters, Jean and Jill (now Julie Lazar), and my three kids. She was eighty-five years old.

In our shared grief, Julianne began to confide in me about how hard things were for her at the Ford factory back home in Detroit. She had very few chances to talk things over with anyone she trusted. It seems that, bristling at having a woman in their work space, some of the men would spit on her work as they passed or post obscene pictures torn from men's magazines with her name scrawled across them. Her foreman even took to stopping by her home at night demanding sexual favors. Where was she to turn in the face of such unbearable conditions and humiliations?

Once we had both returned to our respective homes, I began to spend long hours on the phone with her, trying to shore up her self-respect and encouraging her to look for ways of reminding herself of her true value. In a sudden burst of self-confidence, she recalled fantasies of becoming an actress, and, once normal working hours were finally reinstated at Ford, she joined the Red Door Players, a well-established amateur theater group housed at the big Unitarian church downtown. It wasn't long before she was playing leading roles and even directing plays.

In 1999, Julianne decided to move to California where her daughters were living. I went to Detroit to give a concert at the church in salute to her. The house was packed, and one of the actors read a touching farewell from her theater group that glowed with appreciation for her talents, her commitment to the group, and their love for her.

All on her own, Julianne courageously managed the cross-country move to Glendale, California. But by this time she could barely get around without her scooter because of her painful arthritic knees. Determined to find a way to voice her political views, she established a local chapter of the Raging Grannies, older women who write parodies to well-known tunes, dress in vintage clothes, and sing together at demonstrations to help explain the issues. Then 9/11 happened and the invasion of Iraq began. Julianne made a big sign demanding an end to war and began a vigil, one lonely disabled woman making her way from the nursing home to a nearby busy corner on her scooter to take a stand. The local newspaper ran large photos of Julianne and her vigil, and began to print carefully crafted op-ed pieces she submitted from time to time. The vigil grew to a large contingent of regulars who have occupied a main corner of downtown Glendale every Friday evening at 5:00 p.m. without fail, through all these years of wars and even until today. Julianne's example teaches us that it is possible to find ways to contribute your opinion and your energy to a just cause no matter how great the obstacles.

52

TAKE IT SLOW AND EASY

When I think of the last couple of decades I shared with Irwin, the overriding theme seems to have become doctor trips, with the attendant unwelcome dietary changes, awkward loss of mobility, and diminishing capacity for creative work. In short, creeping old age. I was still in relatively good shape, but Irwin's troubles proceeded from one knee replacement, to another, to a new hip, cancer of the bladder, degenerative spine surgery, detached retina, two ministrokes, and at last dementia.

But do you think Irwin gave up tennis? Instead, he became a poster boy for keeping up his game after all those surgeries, and I was more than glad. It kept us in the loop for those jolly parties the tennis guys liked to host, and most of all, it kept us in touch with Mike and Joan Healy. Mike had retired from his role as spokesman for BART, the Bay Area transportation system, leaving him with time to finish his book about its history. He remained one of Irwin's truest friends through it all, visiting him often, helping him continue to feel part of their tennis gang.

Given all of Irwin's maladies, I slipped into the caregiver role with ease at first. Physically this wasn't yet too taxing for me, despite my having been hospitalized for ten days with a life-threatening bout of sarcoidosis in the late 1980s, but emotionally it took its toll. I soon realized I should stop making many elaborate plans of my own.

To keep my balance, I began to accept some local gigs. In 1998, I was booked on a double bill at the Freight & Salvage with Odetta, and, although it had been almost ten years since my last major performance, jazz critic j. poet was enthusiastic, exclaiming that my stage presence was "pure fun, a celebration of the human spirit, accented by a bawdy feminist humor and a healthy sense of the absurd" and that my set of "foot-stomping" blues and classic American standards "left the sold-out crowd slack-jawed." Wow—I hadn't expected that!

In 2001 my oldest son, Nicky Cahn, who had by now changed his first name to Jesse and had relocated to Oklahoma City a few years before, arranged for me to play the Dusk 'Til Dawn Blues Festival in nearby Rentiesville. He'd done the festival previously, backing the unforgettable Miss Blues. This time he recruited a local band, the Zen Oakies, to back me, and I played the main stage with Jesse on guitar.

From there we drove down to Krum, Texas, together to visit Harvey Gerst, who had been the sound engineer for the Ash Grove in Los Angeles years ago. I was thrilled to find that he had preserved an excellent recording of my 1961–62 New Year's Eve show with Kenny Whitson and Wellman Braud. He graciously gave me the masters, and as soon as I was able, I issued a small run of CDs of this historic live performance.

Later that year, just after the shocking events of September 11, Jesse and I went to Europe for a string of performances in the Netherlands, Germany, and Italy. I remember one night in Venice when the power went out during our show. Jesse switched to the acoustic guitar, and we finished by candlelight. Impressed, the club owner tempted Jesse with the idea of staying on permanently, saying he could do well for himself playing the blues there in Venice. A couple of years later, Jesse and I went back to Europe, this time to the Canary Islands, invited by Juan Salán, a local promoter, who had organized a concert tour for me a few years before. Salán also booked Jesse a few of his own gigs, where he charmed the locals with his originals and his steel resonator guitar.

Back in the Bay Area, I formed some remarkable new musical alliances around that time. Ellen Hoffman, much more than a piano accompanist, is a general music maven, well known in the Bay Area. For two years (2003–04), we collaborated on shows for International Women's Day at Berkeley's Freight & Salvage, assembling a stellar cast that included Mimi Fox, Jackie Rago, India Cooke, Ronnie Gilbert, and Anna de Leon.

Johnny Harper, an electric guitar player and producer with great taste and imagination, worked with me off and on for over a decade. His ability to make the old songs sound new without violating their integrity, and to learn complex unfamiliar tunes in a heartbeat, forced me to stay awake to my own possibilities just as I was in danger of losing faith in them. Each of these musicians played an important part in helping me stay motivated and showing me ways to grow even as I aged.

I decided to do a big concert for my seventy-fifth birthday. This would be the time to display the many genres of music I had drawn from over the years, to show myself and the audience that I could still bring forth these songs and ways of singing that had sustained my creative life for so many decades. I asked Ola Andrews whether she and the other Andrews sisters would help me open the show with gospel-style songs, and they agreed. From the Greek Festival held each year at the temple nearby, I knew I could find extraordinary bouzouki player George Milordos. He could accompany me as I sang my English lyrics for Theodorakis's *Romiosini*. The jazz band was easy to assemble, since most of the players, including the amazing hot pianist Ray Skjelbred, were still active in the Bay Area. Ellen Hoffman could cover anything with a more country feel and beyond, and was eager to play. I drafted acoustic guitarist Jody Stecker to back me on the folk songs. What made it all hang together was Johnny Harper's willingness to handle much of the production, and his guitar work would give freshness to my old favorites and the confidence to offer new material. Oh yes, this time I would prove that I could do any music I liked. This would be my swan song.

I plunged into organizing set lists for each section, picking my favorites and holding back little, without any of the careful timing I usually employed. Would the audience stay for it all? To my amazement, most of them did. The Andrews sisters left early, but most of the other artists came onstage to help me make a rousing finale, with the audience standing and singing with us "Oh Freedom" and "I'm on My Way." The concert ran over four hours, and honestly I was on the verge of collapsing, but we had done it. I was impressed that so many of the white-haired folks in the crowd stayed up so long after their bedtime! This was not my swan song after all, and I would begin a tradition of celebrating every milestone with another birthday concert, sometimes more than one.

In March 2003, Irwin and I went to New York to take part in a project too exciting to turn down. A young musician by the name of Don Fleming had taken up the challenging and unquestionably invaluable work of handling the archives of Alan Lomax, the great folklorist who laid much of the groundwork for the American folk music revival. One day, Fleming and an associate by the name of Kim Rancourt had stumbled across an artifact in the Lomax collection called *The Vietnam Songbook*. Yes, the book Irwin and I had assembled and produced on the kitchen table over thirty years prior. They saw immediately that this was a collection of material that was particularly relevant in the hysterical run-up to Bush's "shock and awe" war in Iraq, and envisioned it as a vehicle for encouraging a new wave of antiwar songs. They developed the idea of a presentation they would call Songs of Protest: *The Vietnam Songbook*, and booked Joe's Pub in lower Manhattan for the occasion. Besides Irwin and me, they would invite a cohort of artists—ranging from Thurston Moore and Jim O'Rourke of Sonic Youth, to Pete Seeger himself—to bring the songs in the book to life.

Joe's Pub was packed, with even the standing-room audience uncomfortably squeezed together. *Variety* wrote a review, declaring *The Vietnam Songbook* to be "the definitive protest music sourcebook." And *Billboard* writer Michelle Mercer did such a fine job of describing what transpired that I quote it here at length.

> Jenni Muldaur . . . kicked off the concert with "Universal Soldier." She was followed by Dan Zanes, the popular children's musician whose hair is permanently shocked into a mad professor-muppet style. His selection, "Boonaroo," told the story of some Australian merchant sailors whose ship, the Boonaroo, was seized by the U.S.

Pete Seeger. Joe's Pub, New York City, 2003

Navy in 1967 when they refused to deliver weapons to Vietnam.

An unannounced special guest was eighty-four-year-old folk legend Pete Seeger, whose frail frame was habitually energized with the spirit of dissent. He led the audience in an inspiring sing-a-long ending with his emotional personal take on "Over the Rainbow."

A more modern presence was felt with Stephan Smith's radio-friendly protest ballad, "The Bell." The cut addresses U.S. policy towards Iraq through allegory. . . .

Sonic Youth's Thurston Moore emerged onstage carrying a 1964 poster hand printed by Allen Ginsberg with the words "Down with Death, War is Black Magic," and then offered up a sonically dense version of "Fourth Day of July." Matt Jones [formerly of the Freedom Singers] came out in a dashiki and skullcap to deliver his soulful classic "Hell No, I Ain't Gonna Go." The most abrasive music of the night came from Patti Smith's guitarist, Lenny Kaye, who returned to his folk roots with Bob Dylan's "Masters of War."

When Vietnam veteran Joe Bangert took the stage, he announced he'd been waiting to perform the "Ballad of Ho Chi Minh" in the U.S. for 30 years. He gave an a cappella reading of Ewan MacColl's ode to the president of North Vietnam, and everyone joined in on the familiar refrain. As they marched down the Ho Chi Minh trail, soldiers sang a tune less familiar to western audiences, "Giai Phong Mien Nam." Bangert, who lived in Vietnam for several years in the '90s, sang the song in its original Vietnamese. Another veteran on the bill was Watermelon Slim, the only vet to have recorded a full album of protest music. The singer covered "Draft Board Blues" and "Vigilante Man." . . .

One of the show's favorites was Tuli Kupferberg, who has the distinction of being the artist with the most songs in *The Vietnam Songbook*. Tuli brought a New

Yorker's dark humor to protest music with selections like "Day in the Death," which he sung to the tune of the Beatles' "A Day in the Life."

But the amazingly vibrant 75-year-old Barbara Dane was clearly the star of "Songs of Protest." She sang with gravitas and bluesy bounce on both of her selections: "Brother Can You Spare a Dime," a tune from between the two World Wars, and the "Ballad of Richard Campos." The latter song received the biggest response from the audience with its querulous refrain: "Should a man have to kill [in order] to live like a human being in this country?"

Dane also led the show's . . . finale, "Insubordination," for which all the performers crowded onto the Pub's small stage and led an audience clap-a-long, with Watermelon Slim waving his hands gospel style.

To my mind, the *Billboard* writer missed two of the genuine highlights of the whole evening: Beverly Grant's searing rendition of the Phil Ochs song "We're the Cops of the World," and African American vet Noble I'm Manu-El:Bey throwing his immense energy into "Insubordination" at the end. But I was struck by the enthusiasm of the normally jaded "show biz" chronicler who clearly stuck it out to the end and took the trouble to write such a thorough article. Producer Don Fleming capped off his comments with this: "It's a way to show how great songs can make a movement, from some living examples of people who created and performed them." I think he and Kim Rancourt understood that they had pulled off something worthwhile and that it was right on time.

For Irwin and me, this trip also turned out to be a time for retracing footsteps and reconnecting with people who meant a great deal in our lives, reexamining events and decisions, extracting lessons to be learned; a kind of harvest time, a gathering in of the fruits of many years filled with vibrant friends and dynamic events, commitment and struggle, creativity and risk-taking, poverty and ease, disappointments and success. In short, experience. A last lingering look at life itself.

Two of our dearest old friends, both of whom had come from distant cities to attend the concert, stayed over for a day of reunion and reminiscing with Irwin and me. Carolyn Mugar and Mark Lane had worked together in many of the country's most important movements, but hadn't seen each other for several years. These are two of the most tireless and effective activists on behalf of justice, peace, and truth that this country will ever see, and possibly the least recognized. Mark is the author of *Rush to Judgment* (1966), the first book to challenge the Warren Report's conclusions regarding the assassination of JFK, bringing him considerable notice in the press as well as serious harassment from government agencies. Carolyn has been a lifelong activist for many social issues, including labor, environment, literacy, and community empowerment, serving as executive director of Farm Aid and founding a reforestation project in Armenia, among other endeavors. There was so much to talk about, after so many years of separation, but mostly we just quietly internalized the deep affection and love we've had for one another through so many twists and turns of American life. We stirred up some old jokes and memories of the times when they had stayed at our house, great meals we had shared, and people we admired or disdained or disagreed about, and rehashed some old ideas and theories that have sustained our friendships over decades.

Before heading back to California, we took the train up the Hudson to Beacon to visit Pete and Toshi Seeger. When we arrived at the train station, Pete was there to meet us right on time. But you couldn't just get in the car and drive up to the house. First there was the ritual gathering and disposal of any litter that had accumulated on the ground around the station since Pete's last visit. Then up the winding drive to the cabin, now grown into more or less a proper house. As we settled down in front of a welcoming fire, the conversation quickly moved into high gear. So much to tell, so much to recall, and then so many plans to unfold. Our ages ranged from seventy-six to eighty-four, but most of the talk was about what we were going to do next.

In the years before his dementia set in, Irwin had continued to write. In *Press Box Red* (2003), he took on the job of telling the story of the battle to integrate baseball, led in large measure by his dear friend Lester

Rodney, retired sports writer for the *Daily Worker*. Another of his last books was *A Patient's Guide to Hip & Knee Replacements*, published by Simon & Schuster and made available in hospital gift shops all over the country. And, with his final efforts, he completed his most serious analytical work—still relevant today—titled *Socialism: What Went Wrong?*, incorporating much of the research he did on our unofficial 1989 journey to the USSR.

With his customary concern for others, as soon as he realized what was going on, Irwin took to advising friends of his dementia diagnosis in order for them to sidestep any embarrassment. I located a peer group guided by Dr. Adam Rochmes at the Alzheimer's Association in Berkeley, which was a great help to Irwin, and the sister group for caregivers held across the hall was both informative and comforting for me. It became our weekly outing, like a date, with a nice lunch afterwards at Pedro's, an outdoor Brazilian café we both loved.

My daughter, Nina, had been directing an overseas study program for American students at the University of Havana, the same place where she herself had done her undergraduate studies back in the late 1970s.

Byron Menendez, Irwin Silber, Pete Seeger, Barbara Dane

Now, in 2004, she was moving back to Oakland to find herself in an unexpected situation. I myself had just recovered from major surgery to remove a cancer, had developed atrial fibrillation, and was in the early stages of chronic heart failure. Her father, Byron, was planning his move back to the Bay Area from Yelapa—the remote Mexican village where he had lived for over thirty years—realizing that at his age, he was putting himself at risk by living over two hours and a bumpy boat ride away from critical medical care. And then there was all that Irwin was going through. Before long, Nina found herself lending her loving support to three octogenarians all at once! As our elder powers slowed, she moved gracefully into supporting position, scheduling doctor's appointments and ensuring that we could get to them, making sure we understood doctors' orders, making sure that we ate well and drank enough water—endless things. All three of us came to lean on her, a heavy weight for a young woman with her own plans.

After completing a PhD at Stanford and teaching at the University of Florida for a few years in the 1990s, Nina had determined that life as an academic was not the one she wanted. While never thinking of it as her profession, she had continued to develop as a flamenco singer, often performing in support of the local dance scene. Over the years, inspired by her love for the art form and for the many musicians, singers, and dancers she came to know and admire, she began presenting local flamenco artists in performances around the Bay Area. As her audience base grew, she was able to start bringing artists from the Gitano clans of southern Spain to perform and teach in the US, creating a bridge for cultural exchange. These extended families have kept flamenco culture alive for many generations, even through the horrific years of Nazi attempts to exterminate the Roma people altogether and oppression by the Franco regime. The vitality and passion of their art had captured the imagination of audiences everywhere, and now, with the help of Bay Area aficionados ready and willing to celebrate and support Nina in these projects, her annual Festival Flamenco Gitano soon grew to be a major cultural affair.

I have managed to attend nearly every flamenco event Nina has presented over the years, getting to know many of the artists in town from Spain. Some have stayed at my house, even though I strictly banned their constant cigarette smoking! Some occasionally cooked us a delicious

Spanish meal, and there was always music ringing through the house. Some were deeply private, and others were curious about my history and even wanted to learn something about the blues. All of them were splendid guests, and although my head has refused to learn any of the technical side of their music, my heart has been universally swept away by their dedication to their craft, their deep respect and even reverence for their roots, and their willingness to dedicate their lives in keeping with all that their history has handed them. A culture of resistance as uniquely bound together by its arts cannot fail to survive. Or, in the words of a Spanish Republican–era song: *Pueblo que canta no morirá!*

I only wish the same sort of cohesive, community-supported atmosphere could have found a way to continue its existence here in our Bay Area traditional jazz scene. During the mid-1950s, an event without a "Dixieland band" was almost irrelevant, and there was an entire postwar generation producing excellent musicians who could deliver it to you. After my exposure to the swing and inventiveness of trombonist Bob Mielke and his Bearcats, I learned to know and admire quite a few of these "youngsters," but it was the older generation—George Lewis, Kid Ory, and others—who made the tuning fork inside me vibrate. They, of course, came from long established communities in New Orleans, and their history was a big part of their charm. Much like the Gitanos with flamenco, their music said to me: we have dignity; we have agency; we have community; we shall not be moved! The men who played it may have worn frayed trousers and struggled to play battered horns through unattended teeth, but they were brothers.

As I write this in 2021, Irwin has been gone for more than ten years, and add to that the five or six years he was not in full possession of his old self—or, better said, the vibrant younger man that lived inside him. For my own mental health, in this narrative, it probably would be best to let him stay as he was in his healthy years.

Pete Steffens, son of the notorious muckraking journalist Lincoln Steffens, was one of those people often described as unforgettable, a journalist and professor at UC Berkeley from 1961 to 1969, mentoring Mario Savio and the other Free Speech Movement students during those fateful days. Pete loved Irwin's book *Socialism: What Went Wrong?*

with a passion, and sent a very congratulatory note in the spring of 2010. Irwin was a man whose morning desk during his decades as writer, editor, and publisher had been engulfed in mail. This note from Steffens happened to be the last bit of personal correspondence addressed to him before he died.

By then, Irwin's brain had become so muddled with Alzheimer's that I had moved his desk, computer and all, out of the house so that the sight of them would not be too dispiriting. But now he demanded to have a desk and computer access again in order to craft a reply. My heart had already been in pieces after taking away his old desk, but seeing his poignant desperation to resume his familiar posture as a writer, I scrambled to provide and assemble a small desk in his room. For a couple of long days he labored to make sense of his reply, but soon it became clear even to him that this was impossible. I dropped Pete a tender thank-you and took the desk away again. A double heartbreak memory. Irwin passed away later that year, and Pete followed soon after.

53

THROW IT AWAY

Once they have reached their late eighties, most folks have slowly surrendered many skills and delights, and life goes quietly from one day to the next with repeated patterns of habit and the sense that if you just continue to do this, and then the next thing, putting one foot in front of the other, you might slip unnoticed and undisturbed along a pleasant and familiar path until at last you just fade away into the sunset.

I was no different. But I hadn't counted on Pablo and Nina and their conspiracy aimed at keeping me alive and active for as long as they could see down the road. This is a story of how it feels when, as you are on the verge of turning ninety, the lights suddenly go up and the music begins to play, someone announces your arrival and the crowds part before you, everyone offers you their arm, and the familiar old path has turned into a red carpet. No fading away, not just now.

When in the summer of 2014 Nina and Pablo approached me with the idea of making a new recording, I thought maybe they were hoping for a final statement from an old lady with little hope of singing like the old days, but Mom all the same. But actually, Nina was genuinely excited about my fresh musical alliance with pianist Tammy Hall. And Pablo had already been talking to me about a different recording project I was vaguely considering, some Noel Coward–style songs with two guitars. So, always ready for a challenge, I agreed when our Cuban friend,

Grammy award–winning engineer Oscar Autie, offered some time at his well-appointed El Cerrito Studio.

I did want to try my best, and began to jot down titles of songs that suited my mood. In a bold moment, I called Tammy Hall to ask whether she would make the date. She immediately agreed, and my heart jumped up! She suggested Ruth Davies for the bass, and I recruited old pal Bill MacGinnis to add the drums, not knowing he was fighting lung cancer and that this would prove to be his last date. "All Too Soon," the Ellington song for which I had written new lyrics a while back, was meant to feature an alto sax solo by Richard Hadlock, another old trad jazz friend, and he agreed to try it, although he had nearly given up playing. In the end, his rendition made me weep with joy. To top it off, Pablo had arranged once

Barbara Dane with Tammy Hall. Home of Mike Healy, Oakland, 2015

again to bring his harmonica, his guitar, and all his positive energy and musicality to the project.

As each new song appeared on my list, I sent it as an mp3 to Tammy; we might have a few words about it, but circumstances really didn't permit much rehearsal. When we arrived at El Cerrito Studio, Tammy might have had a brief word with the others, but mostly we just stretched a little and began to record. Miraculously, song after song rolled out, leaving us satisfied and too excited about trying the next one to stop and listen back. In a total of six or seven hours over two sessions, we had enough music on tape.

Tammy had provided such a solid and inspiring platform for all of us that we worked like a group, and now, at age eighty-eight, I had a new recording that made me feel I'd reached that point on jazz mountain I had aspired to achieve: not the peak, but a spot high enough to look back on my past with satisfaction. I sent the results to Melanie Berzon, dear friend and director of music at KCSM, the Bay Area's treasured jazz

Nina Menendez and Barbara Dane, c. 2016. © Tom Ehrlich

Judy Schonebaum and Barbara Dane at Yoshi's, Oakland, California, 2016. © Tom Ehrlich

station, asking for her thoughts about how to program the CD. She fired right back that she liked it all a lot, generously offering her idea of how to sequence it, allowing me to avoid the days of anguish this process usually involves. Then Oscar mixed and mastered the whole thing, providing the final gloss of professionalism, and soon we had a finished product in our hands. We named it *Throw It Away* for Abbey Lincoln's classic song. Now it would have to be launched, a daunting job that would be handled by Nina, and what she produced was far beyond all expectation.

When Nina told me she had booked a concert at Yoshi's, Oakland's world-famous jazz venue, to celebrate the 2016 release of *Throw It Away*, I secretly thought all concerned were a little bit crazy. But I agreed, mostly to see what would happen. Would anybody come? We hit the trail, doing interviews on all the Bay Area public radio stations, and we got some great press as well. In January, the audience filled the house, and Yoshi's even invited me back in August. We filled it again. All right!

Outraged by the uptick of news about police killings of Black men and women around the country, I added the haunting song "Another Man Done Gone," a searing condemnation of post–Civil War–era lynchings, to the set list. And, with the elections on the horizon, everybody got it when I sang Allen Toussaint's great song "On Your Way Down," with my new verses talking about "shiny towers" and "bling" that caution, "The same folks you abuse on your way up, you gonna meet 'em on your way down."

Before I could catch my breath came an irresistible but challenging invitation from Cuba. My last visit to Havana had been in 2008, a joyful journey to attend Pablo and Adria's fortieth wedding anniversary. After that, I concluded that my traveling days were over. It had seemed so difficult getting around in airports, with the intensified security and the confused and stressed crowds. All this had convinced me that it was time to give up pursuits that had afforded me incomparable joy and enlightenment over decades of international travel.

Pablo was proposing that I come back to Havana one more time, meet his new wife, and even consider inviting a couple of my favorite musicians to do some performances with me. Pablo's first wife, Adria, had passed away in 2011 after a years-long battle with breast cancer, and when the painful period of grieving began to subside, he once again found an exceptional partner in Dr. Barbara Leyva, a leading Cuban gerontologist. However, after several frustrating attempts, they had been unable to pry loose a visa from the US authorities. It seemed the only way I would get to meet my new daughter-in-law was to go to Havana. She mentioned to one of her patients, the famed author and poet Miguel Barnet, that there was a chance I would be coming to Cuba.

My first trip fifty years before, in 1966, had caused quite a stir, and during that visit, I had met Barnet, then a young writer who had also just caused a stir, with his groundbreaking book *Biografía de un Cimarrón* (*Cimarrón: Autobiography of a Runaway Slave*). "Well, if she comes," Barnet declared, "we will want to induct her into UNEAC (Cuban Union of Writers and Artists) as an honorary member." With that, Pablo began looking for a place to produce a musical event. When he mentioned the idea to María Elena Vinuesa at the Casa de las Américas, she proposed that a concert commemorating my 1966 visit would be an appropriate way to kick off celebrations marking fifty years of the Nueva Trova movement, begun a year later with the Encuentro de la Canción Protesta. Nina called Tammy and Ruth, and both were thrilled with the idea of playing in Cuba and visiting the island for the first time. Meanwhile, I began planning visits to my doctors and making lists of all the nitpicky details it would take to successfully travel again for an old sedan like me.

In our family's headquarters in Miramar, Pablo and Dr. Barbarita had made several special arrangements to handle my needs. A brand-new hospital bed had been borrowed and set up in the back bedroom, and a very special person had been invited to help me start my days and to supervise my shower and other matters requiring personal attention. Her name is Zoraida, and her beautiful smile was often the first thing I saw on those precious days in Havana. Only after she had spent several mornings with me did I discover that she had been one of the nurses who volunteered for duty in Angola in the mid-seventies, spending two years there taking care of the wounded during the Cuban engagement that helped to definitively end the South African apartheid regime. Now, in her own old age, she was volunteering to care for this creaky old American woman come to bring some songs and visit family. Her gentle touch said more than words about her reverence for life and respect for others.

Soon I noticed that Pablo had created a sort of "Mom museum" on the wall surfaces facing me as I awoke in the mornings, decorating them with old posters and flyers from our travels, reminding me of past adventures and collaborations. That was the past, but the future was upstairs above my head. The flying footsteps of Oliver, my newest great-grandchild, chased by the cautionary words and laughter of Miriam and Daniel, his mother Yory's parents who had come from Camaguey for the holidays, became the soundtrack of a perfect world.

I had been one of those self-educated kids who rejected college, calling it a time-consuming exercise in brainwashing. But now I was about to be initiated into UNEAC, one of the most highly respected intellectual bodies of Cuba. Did they have the wrong Barbara? As I made my way down the long walkway to their impressive building, I could see that many friends from over the years had come to take part in the proceedings, and I would need to make stops all along the path to greet

UNEAC. Havana, Cuba, 2016

them. Many were actually old friends of my daughter, who had lived and worked among Cuban intellectuals for a good many years. I was glad to relinquish Nina's supporting arm so that she could return their warm and welcoming embraces.

As we reached the large assembly room, I was surprised to see one of my dearest friends, James Early, recently retired from years of leadership at the Smithsonian in DC, sitting in the front row next to actor-activist Danny Glover. And right there alongside them sat Abel Prieto, Cuba's minister of culture and former head of UNEAC. After his brief induction speech, Barnet presented me with a three-dimensional handmade wooden shadow box with a proclamation and the face of Cuba's nineteenth-century independence leader, poet José Martí, looking down on us all.

A representative from the Cuban Institute for Friendship with the Peoples (ICAP) then presented me with a certificate acknowledging my efforts over the years toward building ties of friendship between Cuba and my country. Then, surprising even myself, I burst out singing "Ain't Gonna Let Nobody Turn Me 'Round," and to my immense delight, this room full of Cubans joined right in with the emblematic American freedom song, loud and clear and, of course, with plenty of swing!

Film director Maureen Gosling and cinematographer Jed Riffe had come from California to film this and other events of my trip for a forthcoming documentary, and there they were, on the job. Working beside them were the legendary Cuban documentary maker and photographer Roberto Chile and his son, covering the event from the Cuban side.

In the garden after the event, James Early was asked to do an interview with me, and is filmed giving a candid explanation of how he came to know and respect my husband Irwin Silber when they met during an early 1970s trip to Puerto Rico in support of the independence movement, a friendship cemented by long evenings discussing Marxist ideas in our Brooklyn living room accompanied by smooth Scotch on the rocks. James went on to work at the Smithsonian Institution, where he was able to rise to a position of high responsibility in the inner circle even though he has openly been a communist at heart, and a Black activist at that. Talk about courage, and diplomatic skills! He is a model for any young person who hopes for a career inside the establishment with the least possible sacrifice of personal ethics.

I was already pretty high up on the buzz scale already. But now I was actually meeting Fernando González, one of the five Cuban heroes who spent years jailed in the US for espionage, specifically for unmasking Miami Cuban terrorists plotting to sabotage the revolution. He gave me roses and embraced and kissed me Cuban-style, and even reminded me that I had written him a postcard while he was in solitary.

That evening, Abel Prieto and his wife, Lilian Álvarez, came to Pablo and Barbarita's place along with Miguel Barnet and his companion

Raúl, where we relaxed over some nice wine and a delicious home-cooked arroz con pollo. Prieto may be the minister of culture, but he is also the long-haired jeans-wearing writer who oversaw the placing of a life-size bronze statue of John Lennon in Havana's most popular park in 2000, the twentieth anniversary of his death. In 2011, he supported the opening of a popular nightclub called Submarino Amarillo, or Yellow Submarine, where my grandson Osamu's band often plays, performing Beatles covers for a packed house.

Only a few weeks before my arrival, Fidel Castro—one of the most defining world leaders of our era—had died at the age of ninety. With the whole country in mourning, our conversations that evening were filled with memories and acknowledgment of his audacious and principled leadership, his obvious and undying belief in the possibilities of the Cuban imagination, and his reliance on the courage of those millions who demonstrate their patriotism as well as their internationalism with each day's simple acts of survival. Talk turned to the recent US elections and speculation about what the policies toward Cuba might be when the xenophonic narcissist sits in the Oval Office. The economic blockade then, as now, was still unequivocally in place, and the people were still suffering from it on a daily basis. Obama's diplomatic opening the previous year had generated enormous hope and brought some improvements to people's standard of living, but much more would have to be done to release Cuba from the weight of more than six decades of US sanctions. And now it was clear that, with the impending shift to the right in US politics, the country would need to gear up for a devastating decline in the economy, affecting the availability of food, medicine, gasoline, and much more, causing untold suffering to the Cuban people.

I had heard that Casa de las Américas was facing a couple of serious crises in preparing for my concert. Their treasured grand piano had been finally destroyed by a termite invasion, and the elevator to the third-floor Che Guevara Auditorium, their largest venue, was broken. When I arrived that evening, I was amazed to be taken upstairs by elevator without comment and relieved to see a grand piano on the stage being tuned. More than fifty years of living with the frequent unobtainability of repair parts has taught Cubans something money can't buy: the magic word *Resolver!* meaning "Got a problem? Well, solve it!"

I was excited to see that the audience assembling was both young and old, and when Pablo greeted me with a hug and I saw the band setting up, I felt a rush of anticipation. Tammy and Ruth were already in place, as usual prepared for anything, and Maureen and her film crew were circling around getting their bearings. Then Nina took her place, ready to introduce each song with a bit of context, something for which she was ideally suited since she had worked at the Casa for a spell when she was a senior at the University of Havana in the early 1980s.

Energized by the packed house, we started to swing with Osamu's arrangement of my old opener, "Good Morning Blues," led by his superb guitar playing, and followed it with several songs from the *Throw It Away* CD featuring Tammy and Ruth. Later, with Pablo on guitar I sang my English version of "Su nombre es Pueblo," the indelible song by Sara González and Eduardo Ramos written years earlier in tribute to all fallen guerrilla fighters, but this time dedicated to the life and intention of the recently fallen leader, Fidel Castro.

When I looked around the stage during our final song, I saw that even Osamu's wife, actress-singer Yory Gomez, had added her voice

Barbara Dane onstage with Pablo Menendez at Casa de las Américas, Havana, 2016

along with Mezcla's backup singers Lien and Yuki. What a rich mixture of humanity stood up there with me through that improbable evening, giving their all to this night of music and love. And as the audience stood in appreciation, my two-year-old great-grandson Oliver jumped up unbidden from the audience to join us in the chorus!

With the stage lighting in my eyes, I could barely make out the faces in the front row. Sitting next to Roberto Fernández Retamar, president of the Casa, was a small elderly man who seemed familiar. As the lights lifted at the end of the concert, I stepped down from the stage and found myself embracing Ricardo Alarcón, now approaching eighty years of age and recently retired from the presidency of the National Assembly, a position like our Speaker of the House. When Ricardo was barely in his thirties and just dispatched to New York as Cuba's representative to the United Nations, Irwin and I had met him and his wife, Margarita Perea. We shared several stimulating evenings with them, even attending baby daughter Maggie's first birthday in their New York apartment. Now Margarita is gone, and Maggie is half a century old. I was deeply touched to hear Ricardo insist that he had enjoyed the concert a great deal and would phone me next day for a chat. And yes, he called.

Before we knew it, it was time to go home, and although parting was as hard as ever, I think we all felt a glow of pride for what we had achieved. For now, I needed the downtime to recover. Also, my ninetieth birthday was coming up, and I knew there were plans afoot to make sure it would be royally celebrated!

The Bay Area is fortunate to have one of the best venues for jazz ever built, the Miner Auditorium at SFJAZZ Center. I had heard great performances there, but didn't dream of singing on that stage myself until Nina told me I was booked to present a concert there commemorating my milestone birthday. Tammy and Ruth were ready; our new drummer, the effervescent Daria Johnson, was available; and Pablo arranged to fly in for the date.

Then, to add a historical note and another musical dimension, Nina arranged for the Chambers Brothers to join us. Their 1968 hit "Time Has Come Today" had made them a psychedelic sensation, but their roots in Mississippi remained strong. We had always harmonized

Joe and Willie Chambers, Barbara Dane, Ruth Davies, Pablo Menendez. SFJAZZ Miner Auditorium, San Francisco, 2017. © Tom Ehrlich

effortlessly, and I was eager to bring that to the SFJAZZ audience. When Willie and Joe Chambers agreed to join us, I knew we could deliver a program to remember. The album of freedom songs we had recorded together was being rereleased by Folkways as a collector's vinyl LP at Nina's suggestion, and fans were thrilled to get their hands on the first pressing. When I saw the audience that packed the place, many familiar faces among them, I knew we would all go home steppin' high. And we did! "Ain't gonna let nobody turn me 'round," we sang, and the house sang along lustily, like a familiar congregation.

You might think this was the grand finale, the end of these ninetieth-year endurance challenges, but no. There were two more big ones ahead, one in LA and one in New York. My niece Julie Lazar—former director of experimental programs at the Museum of Contemporary Art in Los Angeles—had opened the door to the storied Royce Hall at UCLA, and Nina took up the task of producing a concert for me there in the fall of 2017. Executive director Kristy Edmunds and her crew could not have been more kind and generous in their support, and things went seamlessly. The UCLA library staff set up a retrospective exhibit in the lobby highlighting my social justice work, and there was a lovely reception after the show with proclamations from the Los Angeles mayor's office and the County Board of Supervisors. I was delighted when George, the oldest of the Chambers Brothers, who had decided he was too infirm to sing at SFJAZZ in July, now found himself fit enough to join his brothers for the concert in October at Royce Hall. The audience loved him!

Tammy and crew were on fire that night. Pablo too, as he sang one of my favorite Silvio Rodríguez songs, "Sueño con serpientes." Osamu sang "Ajedrez," one of his originals, playing a scorching guitar solo, with Yory joining in on the choruses. The whole audience was on their feet as we ended the concert singing Beverly Grant's inspiring anthem, "Together We Can Move Mountains." As the song says, "Alone, we can't move at all." Fans and friends I hadn't seen in decades had turned out for the show, including Roselva Rushton, the old Detroit comrade who had driven my car out to Los Angeles when we both moved there seventy years earlier in 1949!

The following summer, Joe's Pub in NYC's East Village beckoned. Smithsonian Folkways had just published a two-CD compilation of my musical history, *Hot Jazz, Cool Blues and Hard-Hitting Songs*, and this would be the celebration of that release and the finale of the string of concerts commemorating my ninetieth year. Taking advantage of the rare cross-country trip, Nina organized a string of interviews with New Yorkers who have been influential in my life for Maureen's film crew to capture. And, most important, she scheduled an on-air performance and interview with Amy Goodman on her highly regarded nationally syndicated TV show *Democracy Now!* For me, Amy is one of the greatest journalistic figures of our times, a woman with a vision that almost everyone said was impossible, a woman with the spirit and persistence to build it anyway. *Democracy Now!* is now available everywhere, perhaps the only uncensored and unbought news broadcast in this truth-starved nation.

We arrived at Joe's Pub to find a packed house full of New York friends and fans. My band hit the stage running . . . and I followed behind on my walker. What a great feeling to have my dream trio—Tammy Hall, Ruth Davies, and Daria Johnson—with me that night, and add to that the

Barbara Dane with Amy Goodman. *Democracy Now!* studios, New York City, 2018

irreplaceable support of Pablo and Osamu. I had invited Beverly Grant as guest artist, and, accompanied by my band, she sang her compelling ballad, "I Am a Sewing Machine." Toward the end of the night, I taught the standing-room-only audience to sing UK singer-songwriter Robb Johnson's chorus: "Be reasonable and demand the impossible now!" With so many issues currently demanding answers these days, they began to shout it with feeling. Reassuringly, I reminded them that we can make change despite seemingly insurmountable odds. According to Muhammad Ali, "Impossible is not a fact, it's an opinion."

I look back with deep satisfaction at the string of events around my ninetieth year. When Nina and Pablo first proposed all of this, I examined my ebbing stamina, heart failure, and general shaky health, and secretly thought it a slim possibility that I could pull it off. But I made up my mind to give whatever I had to the project, as long as I felt I could provide the audiences with something musically and spiritually rewarding. Now I see that they were right to challenge me. To tell the truth, it may have added years to my life. And there is still more to go.

So what lies ahead for me? If I can manage it, I'd like to be around to see the completion of the documentary film in which Maureen Gosling, Jed Riffe, Ashley James, and my daughter have invested so much energy and creativity. I know it will unleash a flood tide of memories when I finally see beloved family and friends and precious moments on the big screen, larger than life and reassuring, promising a certain fragile immortality.

But without you, dear reader, listener, audience, friend, all this would have been pointless and, in fact, not even possible. We are all part of a giant and endless game of catch. So I am tossing you a jumbo-sized ball of love, appreciation, and . . . here they come . . .

SOME RULES FOR THE ROAD AHEAD

Looking back over ninety years of raising my voice, raising my children, raising some eyebrows, and raising hell wherever possible, I've learned a few things that I'd like to share with you.

- The best way to survive any challenge is to jump right in. You can't run, you can't hide, so you may as well be a player.

- Few resources? Reach out—they are there. You are not the only one to see the needs.

- Do not attempt to go it alone. Remember, the kindest, dearest people you will ever meet are in this together with you, people who always hope to do their best. Get out and experience the joy and fulfillment that come when people work together, sing and dance, dream and struggle together. Those feelings will help see you through the difficult times that we often face, and offer you opportunities to join in the chorus of voices sounding the future.

- Mistakes are not anybody's fault; they just happen when circumstances collide.

- Resentments are too bitter to hold long in the mouth. Spit them out quickly in favor of lifting your eyes to the promise of each new day.

- Throw away guilt, fear, shame, and blame. Fear alone may keep you from some of the best experiences you could ever have in life.

- With no one to suggest that you need to do this or do that, you also have no critic to tell you to leave well enough alone.

- Keep your eyes on the prize. It's all about having your own agenda. If one doesn't work, make a new one. Keep going.

- My understanding of the world is actually pretty simplistic. I see life breathe in and then breathe out. I see people come together and then disagree, only to find common ground again when conditions are right. Nothing is ever perfect, but it is in the imperfections that creativity dwells, that discovery and enlightenment await. Just don't get your mind to believing there is a permanent, complete, and perfect world anywhere.

- We are the ones who deliver the goods. The real joy is born from the work we do, and the journey always rewards us far more than the destination.

- A big part of our job as artists is to help people see through the fog of our miseducation, our corrupt media, the insistent commercial persuasions, the false promises of self-serving politicians, the white supremacy brainwashing, and even our own fantasies of either dystopia or utopia. Truth and reality are what we are after. Don't be satisfied with less!

- Follow what your gut tells you is the right thing to be doing. Then when you get to your nineties, you can be like me, an old person with a peaceful heart.

Because I have chosen to live my life against the grain, loving our still imperfect Constitution too much to believe in the tropes of professional patriots; because I reject the idea that any nation is "number one"; because I admit to either all gods or none; because my idea of being a woman does not include big hair and plastic tits, tight dresses and dangerous shoes; because I can't bend low enough to kiss asses; because of all this and more, I've arrived at my old age with a clean conscience.

Yes, from time to time I felt as though I was out there alone on a long limb in danger of being cut off at any moment. No manager, no bankroller, no political organization, no church. But I knew it was a waste of time to predict my own disaster. I came to enjoy the thrill of risk! Life taught me to take a chance, to improvise, to reinvent myself.

With time one learns what it means to be alive—to value life above anything and rage like a tiger to keep it, to spend it with care instead of trading it for a new car or a fur coat, to treasure the moments that are real between human beings without counting the cost or trying to bargain.

There's no price on that beauty. The only thing we have, really, is our time alive, and I don't think they've printed enough money to buy mine. How about yours?

As I write the final lines of this book in the fall of 2021, we're experiencing one of the most dramatic moments in American history. We've had four years with a sociopathic, authoritarian mobster running the country, the emergence of an invasive white supremacist cult blind to truth and science, over a half a million lives lost in the pandemic, severe economic devastation, and above all, the urgency of the climate crisis.

But things do get better, sometimes even better than you can imagine. People all over the planet are rising up to demand justice—not just for themselves but for all people. Our new president has begun cleaning up the mess and even forging new directions that may help save the planet, but we must keep the pressure on, hold leadership accountable, and keep them on track.

Times like these have changed the heads of many, and even some of the hardest heads can learn the wisdom of following the heart. And for those who have chosen the work of the changer, I would offer Che Guevara's caution: "The true revolutionary is guided by great feelings of love. Large amounts of passion and audacity will be required."

It will take time, and it surely will take plenty of struggle, but I promise you, the human race is moving in an upward spiral, not running around in circles or caught in a maze. Look up and keep pushing toward the sun of science and the stars of justice. You have only one life, so make it count! And remember to sing!

GRATITUDE

Each of us is our own special sum of the millions living in our times and the billions who have lived since humans first drew breath. It is to all these that I first offer my respect and gratitude. There is nothing I know that I didn't learn from you. So whose idea was this book anyway?

Carolyn Mugar, my best friend, and the best friend of so many, started pushing me to think about it in the 1960s. She never stopped, and in the end, it has been her enthusiasm and support that has seen this project over the top.

Nina Menendez brought her intellectual powers to this book from its inception and has poured heart and soul into its pages in a way that only a beloved daughter could. She knows my mind and my heart almost as well as I do, and this book could not have found its shape and finally come to fruition without her guidance. Yes, I wrote every word, but she has been the one to make sense of it all.

Pablo Menendez has been my musical partner and inspiration, traveling buddy, interpreter, and friend and has been able to supply memories of shared experiences that far exceeded the usual mother-son relationship. Looking back together at our years of music and travel in the US, Cuba, Mexico, the Far East, and Europe, neither of us can believe that we were able to be in what often seemed like two places at once. He has been reading the manuscript and discussing it with me since I began. His approving reception has meant the world.

Barbara Stack is one of those multi-talents who come along just when you need them. As I thought about how one might start to write a book, the humbling idea came to me that if I didn't get some help, I would be stuck. Then I happened to open a book sitting on my coffee table, the autobiography of Alice Hamburg, another local activist woman. Right there in her acknowledgments, Alice wrote that she never could have done it without Stack. Yes! As it turned out, neither could I. Barbara taught me many big and small techniques, reading my copy and helping me distinguish the gold from the dross. She even drafted her friend Seth Rosenberg, who helped me apply for my FOIA files. And somewhere along the way she taught me to see myself as a writer.

Paul Slansky is an editor and writer with a clear political passion. He has worked closely with, among others, his friends Norman Lear and the late Carrie Fisher on their books, and I am happy to be able to say he worked with me on mine, mercifully helping me cut the manuscript in half to fit publishing standards.

And finally, my profound gratitude to the world champion bibliophile, Steve Wasserman, who from time to time put this irrefragable question to me: "So, how's the book coming along?"

DISCOGRAPHY, KEY LINKS, AND MORE

DISCOGRAPHY

Trouble in Mind (1957), LP, San Francisco Records M330, with Don Ewell, piano; Bob Mielke, trombone; P. T. Stanton, trumpet; Darnell Howard, clarinet; and Pops Foster, bass.

Livin' with the Blues (1959), LP, Dot DLP-3177, with Earl "Fatha" Hines, piano; Benny Carter, trumpet; Plas Johnson, sax; Herbie Harper or John Halliburton, trombone; Shelly Manne, drums; and Leroy Vinnegar, bass.

"I'm on My Way"/"Go away from My Window" (1960), 45 rpm, Trey 3012, produced by Lee Hazlewood.

When I Was a Young Girl (1960), LP, Horizon/World Pacific WP1603, with Tom Paley, banjo and guitar. Reissued on LP by Tradition/Everest as *Anthology of American Folk Songs* (1967), and on CD as *Anthology of American Folk Songs* by Tradition/Rycodisc (1997) and by Empire Music Works (2006).

On My Way (1961), LP, Capitol T-1758, with Kenny Whitson, piano and cornet; Wellman Braud, bass; Billy Strange, guitar; Earl Palmer or Jesse Sailes, drums; Ray Johnson, piano; Rocco Wilson, congas; and the Andrews Gospel Singers from Oakland.

Barbara Dane Sings the Blues with 6 & 12 String Guitar (1965), LP, Folkways FA2471.

Barbara Dane and the Chambers Brothers (1966), LP, Folkways FA2468.

FTA! Songs of the GI Resistance (1970), LP, Paredon/Smithsonian Folkways P-1003.

I Hate the Capitalist System (1973), LP, Paredon/Smithsonian Folkways P-1014, with Robby Merkin, Andy Pitt, and others.

When We Make It Through (1982), LP, Paredon/Smithsonian Folkways P-1046, with Pablo Menendez, Lucia Huergo, Jorge Aragón, Frank Padilla, Leopoldo Pons, and others.

"Gipper Gate Blues"/"Boulevard of Broken Dreams" (1986), 12-inch 45 rpm, Arhoolie 1600, Barbara Dane and the Good News Bonanza Band.

Sometimes I Believe She Loves Me: Barbara Dane & Lightnin' Hopkins (1996), Arhoolie CD 451.

What Are You Gonna Do When There Ain't No Jazz? (2002), GHB Records BCD240, with Butch Thompson, piano; Ray Skjelbred, piano; Richard Hadlock, sax; Bob Mielke, trombone; Clint Baker, guitar; Pete Allen, bass; Scott Black or Marc Caparone, trumpet; Les Muskutt, guitar; and Sven Stahlberg, drums.

Live at the Ash Grove, New Year's Eve 1961–62 (2003), CD, Dreadnaught Music 1604, with Kenny Whitson, piano and cornet; and Wellman Braud, bass.

Barbara Dane & Tammy Hall: Throw It Away (2016), CD, Dreadnaught Music 1701, with Tammy Hall, piano; Richard Hadlock, soprano sax; Pablo Menendez, harmonica; Ruth Davies, bass; and Bill Maginnis, drums.

Hot Jazz, Cool Blues and Hard-Hitting Songs (2018), two-CD retrospective, Smithsonian Folkways SFW40227.

APPEARS ON

Papa Bue's Viking Jazzband (1957), LP, Jazz Unlimited JU-1, with George Lewis, clarinet; P. T. Stanton, cornet; Dick Oxtot, banjo; Lelieas Sharpton, string bass; and Barbara Dane, vocals. Reissued on CD by Storyville (1991) as *George Lewis Jam Sessions*.

A Night at the Ash Grove (1958), LP, World Pacific Records WP-1254, various artists.

Folk Festival at Newport, Vol. 2. (1959), LP, Vanguard VSD 2054 (mono), VRS-9063 (stereo), various artists.

Blues over Bodega (1964), LP, Fantasy 5016, Lou Waters Jazz Band with Wally Rose and Barbara Dane.

Lightning Hopkins with His Brothers Joel and John Henry / with Barbara Dane (1966), LP, Arhoolie F1022.

Don Ewell Denver Concert with Barbara Dane (1966), LP, Pumpkin Records 120. Reissued as CD with more tracks (2004), Storyville 1018379. *Note:* vocal on both versions distorted due to recording speed.

Save the Children (1967), LP, Women Strike for Peace W-001, various artists.

L'American della Contestazione (1969), LP, Dischi del Sole DS-179/81.

The Firehouse Five Plus 2 Plus 1 (1976, recorded in 1958), LP, Calliope CAL-3017.

What Now People (Vol. 1) (1976), LP, Paredon Records P-2001, various artists.

What Now People (Vol. 2) (1977), LP, Paredon Records P-2002, various artists.

The Hot Club of San Francisco (1993), CD, Clarity Recordings CCD-1006.

Back to Bodega (1994), CD, Stomp Off Records CD1273, Down Home Jazz Band.

The Lady in Red (1999), CD, Clarity Recordings CCD-1019, the Hot Club of San Francisco.

They All Played for Us: Arhoolie Records 50th Anniversary Celebration (2012), Arhoolie Productions, CD/Book 540, various artists.

COMPILATIONS (selection)

Freedom Is a Constant Struggle: Songs of the Mississippi Civil Rights Movement (1994), CD, Folk Era FE1419CD

Protest: Songs of Struggle and Resistance from around the World (2004), CD, Ellipsis Arts CD1000

Hear Me Howling! Blues, Ballads & Beyond (2010), Arhoolie Productions, CD/Book 518, various artists

Classic Blues from Smithsonian Folkways, Vol. 2. (2003), CD, Smithsonian Folkways Recordings SFW40148-118

Classic Folk Music from Smithsonian Folkways (2004), CD, Smithsonian Folkways Recordings SFW40110-105

Classic Protest Songs from Smithsonian Folkways (2009), CD, Smithsonian Folkways Recordings SFW40197-117

The Age of Northern Soul (2012), CD, Outta Sight OSCD-032, various artists

Live at Caffè Lena: Music from America's Legendary Coffeehouse, 1967–2013 (2013), CD/book, Tompkins Square TSQ 2967

The Social Power of Music (2019), CD/book, Smithsonian Folkways Recordings SFW40231

APPEARS ON

Barbara Dane: A Life in Song (2003), narrated and produced by Dave Radlauer. Golden Reel Award winner, National Federation of Community Broadcasters. jazzhotbigstep.com/33901.html

A Wild Woman Sings the Blues: The Life and Music of Barbara Dane (2013), two-CD set, narrated by Holly Near and produced by Ian Ruskin. www.ruskinproductions.com

KEY LINKS

Barbara Dane official website: barbaradane.net
Barbara Dane documentary: barbaradane9lives.org
Paredon Records at Folkways Smithsonian: folkways.si.edu/paredon
Bandcamp: barbaradaneblue.bandcamp.com
Facebook: facebook.com/barbaradanelegacyproject
Twitter: twitter.com/BarbaraDaneBlue

THE BARBARA DANE LEGACY PROJECT

This book is a project of the Barbara Dane Legacy Project (BDLP), dedicated to celebrating Barbara Dane's lifelong dedication to music and social activism and to increasing public awareness of her work. The goals of the BDLP include the creation of the Barbara Dane multimedia collection, including thousands of archival photographs, clippings, audio tracks, video, contracts, correspondence, and memorabilia. This includes digitizing and cataloging more than 150 unreleased reel-to-reel tapes from Barbara Dane's jazz, blues, and folk collaborations, as well as her interviews and field recordings of activists and musicians from around the world. Another key project is the release of the upcoming documentary film *The Nine Lives of Barbara Dane*, directed by Maureen Gosling.

BDLP ADVISORY BOARD

David Amram
Ron Cohen
Judy Collins
James Early
Kristy Edmunds
Jane Fonda
Gary Giddins
Mark Hummel
Mike Kappus
Julie Lazar

Pablo Menendez
Carolyn Mugar
Ed Pearl
Jeff Place
Sandro Portelli
Bonnie Raitt
Silvio Rodríguez
Danny Scher
Dan Sheehy
Chris Strachwitz

INSTITUTIONAL PARTNERS

Arhoolie Foundation
Smithsonian Folkways Recordings

For inquiries: Nina Menendez, executive director, BDLP, danelegacyproject@gmail.com

INDEX

BD = Barbara Dane; bold page number = photo

3525 Club, 163

Acting in Concert for Peace, 358
activism
    antifascism, **42**, 345–46, 350–52, 372–75
    antiwar movements, 256, **256**, 281–83, 284, 288–91, 308–9, 316–18, 325, 333–39, 340–41, 345, 356–69, 371–75, 392. *See also countries by name*
    capital punishment, 189, 192
    civil rights movement, 40–42, **42**, 129–30, 206, 239–40, 256–57, 262–66, 285, 294–95, 308–9, 316–18
    Communist Party USA, 30, 32–33, 42–43, 60–61, 62–66, 77, 78–79, 127–29. *See also* Communist Party USA, expulsion from
    Free Speech Movement, 89–90, 272
    GI movement, 334–39, **336**, 341, 357, 358, 360, 362–69, 392
    labor movement, 43, 51–52, 76
    nuclear disarmament, 79–80, 129, 184–85, 240–41
    women's movement, 376–78
    See also singing/music as activism *and countries by name*

Adderley, Cannonball, 206
"Ain't Gonna Let Nobody Turn Me 'Round," 435
Alameda Naval Station, 362–63
Alarcón, Ricardo, 438
Albertson, Chris, 275
Adolfo y Justo, 300
Alfonso, Adolfo, 300
Alfonso, Carlos, 394
Alfonso, Ele, 394
Alfred Hitchcock Presents, 225–26
Allen, Pete, 112, 116, 408, 409
Allen, Steve, 184
Allison, Mose, 214–15
"All Too Soon," 429
Almanac Singers, 34, 51, 296
Alston, Chris, 64–65
alternate lyrics, BD's: "All Too Soon," 429; "Hey! Ba-Ba-Re-Bop," 46–47; "The Internationale," 306–7; *Romiosini*, 347–49, 373–74, 418; "The Coral Sea Shout," 363–64; "We Will Liberate the South," 344, 371; "On Your Way Down," 432
Álvarez, Lilian, 435–36
Álvarez, Santiago, 298
Amadeo Roldán Theatre, 300
American Indian Movement (AIM), 356
American Youth for Democracy (AYD), 30–31, 402
Amram, David, 384

Andrews Gospel Singers, 206–7, **207**, 418
Andrews, Ola, 418
"Another Man Done Gone," 432
Anthology of American Folk Songs, 209. See also *When I Was a Young Girl*
Anthony, Charlotte, 46
anti-communist movement, 60–61, 66, 104, 127–28
antifascism, **42**, 345–46, 350–52, 372–75
Anti-Imperialist Song Festival, 394
Antillano de Acero steel mill, 305–6, **305**
antiwar movements, 256, **256**, 281–83, 284, 288–91, 308–9, 316–18, 325, 333–39, 340–41, 345, 356–69, 371–75, 392. See also countries by name
Aragón, Jorge, 394
Arhoolie Records, 258–59, 409
Armstrong, Louis, 159–62, **162**, 163, 164–65, 169; European tour, 159–60, 163–66, 181, 349
Asbel, Bernie, 59
Asch, Moses (Moe), 237, 255, 285, 289, 397
Ash Grove, 110, 144–48, 150–51, **154**, 155–56, 174–75, 177, 184–85, 208, 235–36, 243, 285, 360, 362, 417
ASP (National Council of Arts, Sciences and Professions), 127
Aston, Norma, 194–96, 213–16
Atlantic Records, 188
Autie, Oscar, 429, 431
AYD (American Youth for Democracy), 30–31, 402

Baez, Joan, 238, 241, 243, 268, 289, 381, **382**
Baker, Clint, 409
Baker, Ella, 356
"Ballad of Richard Campos," 422
Bangert, Joe, 371, 421
Barbara Dane's Amerika, 398–405

Barbara's Blues, 199
Barden, Bill, 408
Barge, the, 216–17
Barlum Hotel, 40–42, 402
Barnet, Charlie, 181, 189
Barnet, Miguel, 301, 432, 435
Basie, Count (William James), 157–59
Basin Street West, 205
Bay Area, music scene/community, 111–16, 119–27, 193, 213, 426. See also Berkeley; Oakland; San Francisco
Bay Sound, 409
Bear's Lair, 112
Bearcats, Bob Mielke's, 112–13, 116, 426
Beat Generation, 89–91
Bechet, Sidney, 131
Bedell, Madeleine and Bob, 383
Beheiren, 359, 364
"Bella Ciao," 378
Bellcourt brothers, 356
Belski, Marvin, 373
"Be Reasonable," 441
Berkeley: move to Adeline and Ashby, 97; move to Dwight Way, 106–7; move to Berkeley Hills, 197; move to Josephine Street, 226–27. See also Bay Area, music scene/community
Berkeley Folk Music Festival, 235
Berzon, Melanie, 430–31
Bielawski, Gene, 74–75, 213
Bikel, Theodore, 144
Biltmore Pharmacy, 3–4, 6, 8, 13, 14–15
birthday concerts, BD's: seventy-fifth, 409, 418–19; ninetieth, 438–42
Black Diamond Band, 408
Black Panther Party, 342
Bligen, Benjamin and Ruth, 276
Blind Lemon, 112
"Blues over Bodega," 240–41
Blues over Bodega, 240
Blues, Miss (Dorothy Ellis), 417
Boudin, Leonard, 324
Boyle, Peter, 358, **359**

Brand, Oscar, 234
Braud, Wellman, 186, 189–90, 192, 194, 198–99, 203–4, 205, 206, 212–15, 417
Bravo, Ernesto, 296
Bravo, Estela, 296, 298–300, 302, 303, 305–9, 313
Brooklyn. *See* New York City
Broonzy, Big Bill, 20, 59–60, 218
"Brother Can You Spare a Dime?," 422
Brothers Four, 104, 231
Brown, Pat, 342–44
Brown, Pearly, 294
Brubeck, Dave, 165
Brubeck, Iola, 165
Bruce, Lenny, 143, 184–85, 218, 220–23, **221**
Buchholz, Horst, 230
Buck, George, 409
Burris, J. C., 198–99
Bushell, Garvin, 229
Butterfield, Paul, 286

Cabale, the, 255, 258, 271
Cadillac Square, 40, 42
Cafe Au Go Go, 286, **287**
Cafe Continental, 294
Cahn, Jesse, 417. *See also* Cahn, Nicky
Cahn, Nicholas (Nicky): birth, 71; childhood, 72, 73, 77, **77**, 82, 84, 85, 95, 97, 103, 107–8 116–17, **117**, 148; teenage years, 226–28, 257–58, 269–71, 313; adult years, 362, 414, 417; name change to Jesse, 417; music career, 417
Cahn, Rolf
personal life: childhood, 28; PTSD, 28, 44, 74, 85; college, 43; meeting and falling in love with BD, 27–30; marriage to and domestic life with BD, 37–39, 43–45, 57, 58, 65, 81, 84–85; move to and life in LA, 67, 69; divorce, 86–87, 90–100; as a father, **77**, 227–28, 257–58, 270–71
activism: 34, 40–41; activism for the Communist Party USA, 62, 77; expulsion from Communist Party USA, 81–82; as an FBI informant, 86–87; trip to Cuba in 1948, 62
jobs and business ventures: martial arts teacher, 39, 81, 82, 84; cement contractor and ditch digger, 69–70; sales and collections, 78; insurance sales, 84; Blind Lemon, 112; Cabale, the, 255
Call to Resist Illegitimate Authority, 336
Canada tour, 189–92, 194
Canter's Delicatessen, 151
Caparone, Marc, 409
capital punishment, 189, 192
Capitol Records, 188–89, 206–12, **208**, 286
Carawan, Guy, 276
Carnegie Hall, 288–90, **290**
Carter, Benny, 171
Carter, Bill, 202, 205
Casa de las Américas, 299, 319–20, 432, 436, **437**
Casner, Ambrose, 83, 376
Casner, Dorothy. *See* Spillman, Dorothy
Castro, Fidel, 300, 302, 308–10, **309**, 313, 321–22, 436, 437
Chambers Brothers, 264, 273, 285–86, **286**, 438–40, **439**
Chandler, Len, 262, 284, 294, 359

Index

Charters, Sam, 111
Checkerboard Lounge, 399–400
Checkmate, 225
Cherry, Don, 142
Chicago, performing in, 152, 166, 172–77
Chile, Roberto, 435
CIO (Congress of Industrial Organizations), 34
Citizens Committee of Inquiry, 357
City of Paris, 83, 84, 87, 94
civil rights movement, 40–42, **42**, 129–30, 206, 239–40, 256–57, 262–66, 285, 294–95, 308–9, 316–18
Clay, Francis, 175
Cloister Inn, 152, 166
Club Hangover, 131, 133, 170
Coast-to-Coast Hootenanny, 59. *See also* People's Songs
Coates, Mr. (BD's singing teacher), 21–22
coffeehouse culture, 106–7, 334. *See also* GI movement
coffeehouse movement. *See* GI movement
Cogan, Mike, 409
Cohen, Bob, 262
Cohen, Herbie, 134, 141, 144, 145
Coleman, Ornette, 142
Collette, Buddy, 142
Collins, Judy, 262, 263–64
Colorado, performing in, 184
Committee, the, 254
Communist Party USA, 30, 32–33, 42–43, 60–61, 62–66, 77, 78–79, 127–29; BD's expulsion from, 81–82, 85–87, 105, 393–94
Concerts, Inc., 212
Conn, Myrna and Andy, 257
Cooke, India, 418
Cooke, Maurie, 31–32
Cooney, Michael, **241**
Coral Sea, 362–64
"Coral Sea Shout, The," 363–64
Corey, "Professor" Irwin, 152

Cosmo Alley, 141–44
Cothron, Lonnie, 20–21
Cotton, James, 175
Covered Wagon project, 370
Cox, Ida, 115, 180
Creepy (bassist), 73
Cristall, Gary, 407
Crosby, David, 358
Crump, Tiny, 115
Cuba: tour in 1966, 296–310; trip to in 1967, 319–24; trip to in 1968, 329–32; later performances in, 394, 432–38
Cuban Missile Crisis, 227, 228
Cuban Union of Writers and Artists (UNEAC), 432, 433–35
"Cuba, que linda es Cuba," 302
Cultural Congress of Havana, 329–30
Cultural Council (Consejo de Cultura), 299, 301, 303, 305, 329, 331, 332
Cunningham, Sis, 34
Currie, Don, 198

D'Lugoff, Art, 289, 290
Dailey, Virginia "Dee Dee," 19, 68, 69–70, 72, 73
Daily Worker, 32, 62, 424
Dallas, performing in, 163
Damon and Dorian (Detroit friends), 29–30
Dane, Barbara
early life: birth of Barbara Brookfield Spillman, 3; southern roots, 4–5, 32, 403; early childhood and elementary school, 1–9; work at the pharmacy, 3, 6, 8, 13; teenage years and high school, 10–14, **12**, 17–23, **23**
young and middle adult life: college years, 24–28;

458

theater experience, 19, 22–23, 25, 27; odd jobs, 44–45, 64, 78, 99–100, *and see also* City of Paris; origin of stage name, 94. *See also* marriages to and domestic life with *husbands by name*; pregnancies; divorces
older adult life: health problems, 280, 348, 372–73, 394, 411, 416, 425. *See also* birthday concerts
career: early years: 14, 20–22, 105; foray into jazz/blues singing, 112–13, 119–22; blacklisted from music festivals, 183, 340, 406–7. *See also* activism; singing/ music as activism; guitars; radio appearances; television appearances; tours; travels; documentary biographies; *and albums by name*
photos of, **2, 12, 23, 33, 35, 42, 56, 77, 93, 102, 114, 117, 121, 129, 133, 154, 162, 168, 170, 172, 175, 176, 182, 203, 207, 208, 210, 219, 221, 232, 233, 241, 256, 259, 268, 275, 282, 286, 293, 295, 309, 318, 336, 338, 346, 349, 359, 380, 382, 395, 410, 424, 429, 430, 431, 434, 437, 439, 441**
See also fashion; sexism; sexual harassment/ assault; *relocation by name of city or house*
Davies, Ruth, 429, 433, 437, 438, **439**, 440
Davis, Miles, 235
Davis, Ossie, 393
Davis, Rennie, 337
Davis, "Reverend" Gary, 146
Dawn Club, 240
death penalty. *See* capital punishment
de Leon, Anna, 418
de Leuze, Jeanne, 121–22
Dellinger, Dave, 325, 356
Democracy Now!, 440, **441**
Den in the Duane, 157, 159
Denmark, 410
De Paris, Sidney, 229
De Paris, Wilbur, 229
De Patta, Margaret, 74–75, 213
Detroit: economy, 15, 18, 63; music community/scene, 17, 32–33; racism and discrimination in, 7–8, 16, 18, 32, 37, 40–42
Detroit College of Applied Science, 24
Detroit Institute of the Arts, 46
Detroit Unemployed Council, 43
Detrola, 44–45
Dickinson, Angie, 225–26
discrimination and racism, 7–9, 18, 22–23, 25, 32, 37, 40–42, 52–53, 343; in the music industry, 17, 32, 106, 180–81, 189–90. *See also* Detroit: racism and discrimination in
divorces, BD's: from Rolf Cahn, 86–87, 98–100; from Byron Menendez, 246
Dixie at the Bowl, 212–13
Dixieland jazz. *See* New Orleans jazz
Dixon, Willie, 174, **175**, 178, 180

Dizzy Gillespie Quintet, 160
Dobkin, Alix, 262
documentary biographies. See *Barbara Dane's Amerika* and *The Nine Lives of Barbara Dane*
Donahue, Tom "Big Daddy," 187–88
Dorian and Damon (Detroit friends), 29–30
Dot Records, 169, 211
Dougherty, Doc, 131
Douglas, K. C., 199
Du Bois, W. E. B., 127
Dukes of Dixieland, 160, 212
Duncan, Donald, 337, 357
Dusk 'Til Dawn Blues Festival, 417
Dylan, Bob, 231, 233–36, 238–39, 241, 242, 243, 268, 274, **275**, 284, 287, 289

Early, James, 396–97, 434, 435
Earthquake McGoon's, 163
East Berlin Political Song Festival, 372
Eastwood Gardens, 17
Easy Street, 163
Ebony magazine, 179–81
Edmunds, Kristy, 439
El Bordello, 194
El Cerrito Studio, 429–30
Eldridge, Roy, 160
Ellington, Duke (Edward Kennedy), 160, 161–62, 205
Elliott, Ramblin' Jack, 109
Elliott, June, 109
El Matador, 194, 214
Emilio, Frank, 300
ENA, La (Escuela Nacional de Arte; National School of Art), 310, 313–15, 322–23, 330
Encuentro de la Canción Protesta, 319–20, 353, 433
England, BD's popularity in, 188
Equal Accommodations Act (Michigan), 40–41
Erickson, Bill, 112, 120–21, **121**
Ertegun brothers, 188

Escuela Nacional de Arte (La ENA; National School of Art), 310, 313–15, 322–23, 330
Espín, Wilma, 310
Esteves, Sandra María, 381
Europe, performances in. *See countries and cities by name*
Ewell, Don, 132, 141, 168

Fallen Angel, 120
Fantasy Records, 126
Farantouri, Maria, 347–48, 374
Fariña, Dick, 284–85
Fariña, Mimi, 284
fashion, BD's, 11, 14, 28–29, 92, 155, 232
father, BD's. *See* Spillman, Gilbert
Faulk, John Henry, 231–32. See also *They Call It Folk Music* and *Folk Songs and More Folk Songs*
FBI files and surveillance, 38, 43, 45, 77, 86–87, 107, 127, 147, 298, 324, 335, 368
Fernández, Joseíto, 300
Fernández, Pablo Armando, 301
Festa dell'Unità (Festival of Unity), 345–48, **346**, 360
Festival Flamenco Gitano, 425
Festival of Unity (Festa dell'Unità), 345–48, **346**, 360
Finnish Peace Council, 411
Firehouse Five, 159, 161
Fireman's Ball, 13
Fitzgerald, Ella, 152–53
Fleming, Don, 419, 422
Fleming, George, 408
Folklore Center, 274
Folk Songs and More Folk Songs and *They Call It Folk Music*, 231–34, **232**, **233**
Folksville, USA, 94, 97, 104
Folkways Records, 112, 253, 255, 264, 285–86, 289, 294, 397, 440
Fonda, Jane, 337, 356–58, **359**, 365, 368
Ford, Henry, and factory; 5, 16–17,

Index

401–2, 414–15
Foster, George "Pops," 131–33
Fountain, Pete, 212
Fox, Mimi, 418
Franck, Peter, 272
Franco, Francisco, 350
Free Speech Movement, 89–90, 272
Freedom Schools, 256–57, 263, 285
Freedom Singers, 289, 335
Freight & Salvage, 409, 417, 418
Friedlander, Leo and Olga, 15–16
Frontline, 392
FTA! Show, The, 357, 358–59, **359**, 368
Fuller, Jesse "Lone Cat," 109–10, 185, 199, 273

Galli, Martha, **346**
Garay, Sindo, 303–4
Gardner, Fred, 333–36, 358
Gardner, Herb, 357
Garland, Jim, 403
Garson, Barbara, 343, 357
Gate of Horn, 172–77, **175**, 179, 180, 201, 218, 220, 221–22
Gateway Singers, 104–6
Gene and Francesca, 232–33
General Artists, 189
George Shearing Quintet, 160
Georgia Sea Island Singers, 234, 241
Gerdes Folk City, 273–74, 381
Germany, 372, 410, 417
Gerst, Harvey, 417
GHB label, 409
Gibbs, Terry, 184
Giddins, Gary, 164–65
Gilbert, Ronnie, 402, 418
Gillespie, Dizzy, 160
GI movement, 334–39, **336**, 341, 357, 358, 360, 362–69, 392
Ginsberg, Allen, 89, 107
"Gipper Gate Blues," 408–9
Gladstein, Richard, 215–16
Gladys's, 177
Glaser, Joe, 159–60, 163–65
Glaser, Tom, 46, 47

Gleason, Jackie, 160, 161, **162**
Glover, Danny, 434
Gomez, Yory, 433, 437, 440
González, Fernando, 435
González, Sara, 394, 437
"Goodbye, Daddy, Goodbye," 226
Good News Bonanza Band, 408–9
Goodman, Amy, 440, **441**
Goodman, Ernest, **33**
"Good Morning Blues," 437
"Good Old Wagon," 207
Goodrow, Gary, 358, **359**
Goodson & Vale, 59
Gosling, Maureen, 435, 437, 440, 442
"Go Tell It on the Mountain," 272, 377
Gottlieb, Carl, 357
Gottlieb, Lou, 92, 104–5
Gould, Josh, 337
"Go 'Way from My Window," 187
Granma, 301
Grant, Beverly, 422, 441
Greece, 346–49, 373–75
Green, Lil, 60
Greene, Debbie, 257
Greenwich Village, 51, 229, 274, 290
Gregory, Dick, 221–22, 337, 358, **359**
Grossman, Albert, 165, 172–74, 178, 182–83, 218, 235, 288–89
Grossman, Aubrey, 215–16
Guardian, The, 384
Guillén, Nicolás, 301
Güines, Tata, 300
guitars, BD's: first, 31–32, 45; skills on, 32, 121, 125–26; Martin, 58; Gibson, 255
Gunning, Sarah Ogan, 402–4, 405
Gus and Andy's, 279
Guthrie, Woody, 34, 59–60, 61–62
Guy, Buddy, 399–400
Guzman, Al, 406

Hackett, Bobby, 160
Hadlock, Richard, 408, 409, 429
Hall, Bill, 9
Hall, Tammy, 428–30, **429**, 433, 437,

461

438, 440
Hallinan, Vincent, 215–16
Hambone Kelly's, 240
Hamer, Fannie Lou, 264, 288, 289
Hamilton, Chico, 142
Hamilton, Frank, 178
Hare, Pat, 175
Harlem Globetrotters, 220
Harper, Herbie, 171
Harper, Johnny, 418
Havana Jazz Plaza Festivals, 394
Hawkins, Coleman, 160
Hayakawa, S. I., 204–5
Hayden, Tom, 337
Hayes, Lee, 104
Haymarket Square coffeehouse, 358
Hazlewood, Lee, 187–88
Healy, Mike and Joan, 416
Hefner, Hugh, 181–82, 221
Helfer, Erwin, 400
Henderson, Erma, 37, 40–41, 402
Hendrix, Jimi, 286
Hernández, Melba, 310
Herz, Alice, 281–82
Hester, Carolyn, 231
"Hey! Ba-Ba-Re-Bop," 46–47
Higbie, Barbara, 406
Higgins, Billy, 142
Hillery, Mable, **241**, 294, **346**
Hinchliffe, Roger, 411
Hines, Earl "Fatha," 133, 169–71, **170**, 181
Hitler, Adolf, and Henry Ford, 16–17
Hodes, Art, 115, 294
Hoffman, Abbie, 283
Hoffman, Ellen, 418
Hollywood Bowl, 212, 243
Hollywood Ten, 61
Holzman, Jac, 289
Honeydripper (Roosevelt Sykes), the, 218, **219**
Hootenanny, 237–39
Hopkins, Sam "Lightnin'," 146, 241, 258–59, **259**
Horizon Records, 208–9

Hot Jazz, Cool Blues and Hard-Hitting Songs, 440
House, Son, 292
House Un-American Activities Committee (HUAC), 60–61
Houston, Cisco, 34
Howard, Darnell, 132–33
Howard, Kid, 113–14
"How Long Blues," 399–400
Hoyt-Hughes, Kate, 145, 147
HUAC (House Un-American Activities Committee), 60–61
Hubert, Dave, 208
Huergo, Lucia, 394
Huerta, Dolores, 356
Hughes, Langston, 142
Hunter, Janie, 276
Hunters Point, 76, 82
Huỳnh Văn Ba, 307

"I Hate the Capitalist System," 402–3
I Hate the Capitalist System, 402, **441**
Il Piccolo, 106–7
"I'm on My Way," 187–88, 206, 225, 272, 418
India tour, 127, 165
Institute for Friendship with the Peoples (ICAP), 435
"Insubordination," 422
international performances. *See countries by name*
international antiwar activism. *See activism: antiwar movements and also countries by name*
International Women's Day, 418
"Internationale, The," 306–7
Irakere, 384
Iraq War, 419
Isla de la Juventud (Isle of Youth), 322
Isle of Youth (Isla de la Juventud), 322
Italy, 345–49, 360, 417
"It Hurts Me Too," 201
"It Isn't Nice," 263, 272

Jack's Record Cellar, 88–89

Jack's Waterfront Hangout, 120–22, 131
Jackson, Aunt Molly, 403
Jackson, Mahalia, 242, 347
James, Ashley, 442
James, Skip, 292
James, Thelma, 26–27
Japan, 359, 364–66
"Jarama Valley," 352
Jazz Camp West, 413
Jazz Workshop, 194, 198, 222
Jenkins, Esau, 276
Jet magazine, 203
jewelry business, Byron's, 96–97, 103, 106
Jewish community and culture, 15–16, 33, 70
Joe's Pub, 419–22, 440
Joe York Club, 43
Johnson, Daria, 438, 440
Johnson, Lonnie, 200–201
Johnson, Plas, 171
Johnson, Ray, 207
Jones, Bessie, 234–35, 241–42
Jones, Matt, 421
Jones, Sue, 11, 18, 19, 24
Jonesboro, Arkansas, 3, 15, 412–14
Joplin, Janis, 183, 242

Kabataang Makabayan (KM), 359, 366–67
Kaye, Lenny, 421
KCSM, 430–31
Kelly, Pearl, 148
Kennedy, Florynce, 337
Killeen, Texas, **336**, 337–38, **338**
King, Martin Luther, Jr., 240, 294, 316–17
King of Siam, 167, 169
Kingston Trio, 104
Kinoy, Arthur, 356
Kirkpatrick, Frederick Douglas, 345, 381
Kirpich, Billie, 53
KM (Kabataang Makabayan), 359, 366–67
Knotts, Don, 184

Knowling, Ransom, 20, 60, 218–19, **219**
KPFA, 89, 111–12, 216, 272, 275, 358, 409. *See also* Pacifica Foundation
Krupa, Gene, 160
KSAN, 187
Kunstadt, Len, 274–75
Kupferberg, Tuli, 421–22
Kweskin Jug Band, 284

labor movement, 43, 51–52, 76
Labor Youth League (LYL), 77
La Farge, Peter, 262
Lane, Mark, 254, 337, 357, 370, 423
Lark's Club, 112, 116
"Last Mile Blues," 192
La Strada, 279
Las Vegas: move to, 99
Lawyer's Guild, 356
Lazar, Julie, 439
Lead Belly (Huddie Ledbetter), 32, 104, 273
Leavitt, Al, 131–32
Ledbetter, Huddie "Lead Belly," 32, 104, 273
Lee, Bill, 178
Lee, Peggy, 211
Legere, Ben, 245
Lems, Kristin, 377
León, Julia, 350–51
Leventhal, Harold, 104, 237, 289
Levy, Howard, 334–35, 337, 357
Lewis, George, 113–14, 116, 132, 426
Lewis, Laurie, 406
Leyva, Barbara, 432, 433
Lieberman, Ernie, 59
Lightning Hopkins with His Brothers Joel and John Henry / with Barbara Dane, 258–59
Lima, Mickey, 86
Line of March, 392
Lipscomb, Mance, 146, 241
"Little Boxes," 224
Little Rock Nine, 129–30
Livin' with the Blues, 169–72, **172**

Lockard, Jay, 337
Lomax, Alan, 59–60, 61, 289, 419
Lönnbro, Anders, 398–99, 401–2, 404–5
Lopez, Orlando "Cachaíto," 300
Los Angeles: moves to, 67–70, 134–35, 141; buying a house in, 147–48; music community and scene, 73, 141–46, 150
Los Gallos, 315
Los Tradicionales, 321
Love-In for Peace, 338–39
Lowenthal Brown, Zoe, 209, 210
Lumumba, Patrice, 191–92
LYL (Labor Youth League), 77
Lynch, Karen, 384
Lyons, Jimmy, 241

MacDowell, Fred, 292
MacGinnis, Bill, 429
Mack, Tom, 169, 171
Mama Yancey Sings, Art Hodes Plays Blues, 294
Manhattan Center concert, 373–74
Manne, Shelly, 171
Manu-El:Bey, Noble I'm, 422
March Against the Vietnam War (1965), 282
Marchant, Don, 112
March on the Pentagon (1967), 325–27
March on Washington: March Against the Vietnam War (1965), 282; March on the Pentagon (1967), 325–27; Moratorium to End the War in Vietnam (1969), 345
Marine Flasher, 52–53
Marrero, Lawrence, 113
marriages to and domestic life with Rolf Cahn: 27–30, 37–39, 43–45, 57, 58, 65, 81, 84–85
Byron Menendez: 97–98, 100–101, **102**, 107, 108, **117**, 122–23, 124, 134–35, 141, 144, 147–49, 226–27, **241**, 245–46
Irwin Silber: 253–55, 257, 259–61, 267–71, **268**, 273, 276, 279–80, 382–84, 416, 422–24, 426–27
Martinson, Rita, 359
Mason, James, 225–26
Matador, the, 194, 214
Mathis, Johnny, 120
Matta, Roberto, 329
Maymudes, Vic, 145
McCarthy, Eugene, 66
McCarthyism. *See* anti-communist movement
McGhee, Brownie, 125–27, 145, 146, 165, 184, 199, 200–201, 204, 275
McGinnis, Bill, 408
McNichols Road, 3
Mediterraneum (the Med), the, 107
Melamed family, 360
Méndez, José Antonio, 300
Menendez Santana, Osamu: childhood, 344, 360–62, **361**; music career, 436, 437, 440, 441; children and in-laws, 433, 438
Menendez, Byron
personal life: childhood and young life, 96; meeting and falling in love with BD, 95–96; military service and PTSD, 96–97, 101, 107; marriage to and domestic life with BD, 97–98, 100–101, **102**, 107, 108, **117**, 122–23, 124, 134–35, 141, 144, 147–49, 226–27, **241**, 245–46; affairs, 149, 245; divorce,

246; life after divorce, 269, 271; older adult life, **424**, 425
jobs and business ventures: jewelry business, 96–97, 103, 106; in Las Vegas, 100; selling books in LA, 144–45; as a producer, 185; at Sugar Hill, 198, 214–15

Menendez, Nina
personal life: birth and childhood, 116–18, **117**, 129–30, **129**, 147, 211–12, 224, 228, **241**, **256**, 271, 276–77, 294, 313, 317–18, **318**, 326–27, 342–44; move to Oakland, 425
schooling and career: college in Cuba, 384; academic career, 424, 425, 434, 437; flamenco career, 313, 425–26
managing BD's career: 428, **430**, 431, 437, 438, 439, 440, 442

Menendez, Paul (Pablo)
personal life: birth and childhood, 101–2, 116–17, **117**, 118, 129–30, **129**, 168–69, 211–12, 224–25, 226–27, **241**, 254, **256**, 257, 271, 283; school in Cuba, 310, 313–15, 323; name change to Pablo, 314; marriage to Adria Santana, 323, 329, 330–32, **332**; marriage to Barbara Leyva, 432, 433
music talents and career: 168–69, 225, 283, 286, 310, **312**, 313–14; playing music with BD, 341–44, **346**, 351–52, 359, 360–69, **361**, **366**, 370–71, 394, **395**, 398–99, 404–5, 406, 410–11, **410**, 429, 437, **437**, 438, **439**, 440, 441. See also Mezcla

Menendez, Phyllis, 96
Mercer, Bessie, 108
Mercer, Michelle, 419–22
Mercouri, Melina, 373
Merriweather, Big Maceo, 201
Mexico City, 394
Meyers, Ann, 38
Mezcla, 406, 410–11, **410**, 438
Minas del Frío, Cuba, 304
Michel, Ed, 155
Mickleson, Donna, 334–35
Mielke, Bob, 112–13, 133, 169, 202, 408, 409, 426
Miles, Lizzie, 115–16, 180
Milordos, George, 418
misogyny. See sexism
Mississippi Caravan of Music, 256–57, 262–66
Mississippi Freedom Project, 262–66
Mississippi Freedom Singers, 394
Miss US Television pageant, 92–94, **93**
Mitchell, Ray, 187
Mitchnick, Marty, 38
Mobe, the (Mobilization Committee to End the War in Vietnam), 317, 325
Monterey Folk Festival, 241–42, **241**
Montgomery, Urreal "Little Brother," 146, 174, 177, 180, 218
Montgomery, Wes, 206

Moore, Thurston, 419, 421
Moratorium to End the War in Vietnam (1969), 345
Morton, Jelly Roll, 131
Moses, Bob, 262, 289
Moss, Al, 46
mother, BD's. *See* Spillman, Dorothy
moving, BD. *See locations by name of city or house*
Moving Star Hall singers, 276–78
Muddy Bottom Folk and Blues Society, 216
Mugar, Carolyn, 370, 423
Muldaur, Jenni, 419
Murphy, Turk, 114, 119, 163, 240
Murray, Bill, 68
Myerson, Alan, 357

NACLA (North American Committee on Latin America), 353–54
Napier, Bill, 113
Nash, Graham, 358
National Council of Arts, Sciences and Professions (NCASP or ASP), 127
National Maritime Music Hall, 51–52
National School of Art (Escuela Nacional de Arte, or La ENA), 310, 313–15, 322–23, 330
National Women's Music Festival, 377–78
NCASP (National Council of Arts, Sciences and Professions), 127
Near, Holly, 359, 402
Nelson, Barrett, 411
Netherlands, the, 417
New Christy Minstrels, 104
Newhart, Bob, and tour with, 189–92, 194
New Lost City Ramblers, 209, 231, 241
New New Orleans Jazz Band, 229
New Orleans jazz, 113–16
New Orleans Syncopators, 408
Newport Folk Festival: of 1959, 173, 178; of 1964, 267–68, 276; of 1965, 284–88; of 1966, 292–93, **293**; of 1969, 340
New York City: performing in, 157, 229–33, 286; move to, 86, 270–73, 280–81. *See also* State Street house; Strong Place house
Nicaragua, 394
Nichols, Red, 168
Night at the Ash Grove, A, 155
Nine Lives of Barbara Dane, The, 435, 437, 440, 442
Noblauch, George, 408
Noël (Barbara and Irwin's manager/assistant), 151–53, 155–56, 209, 297, 305
North American Committee on Latin America, 353–54
nuclear disarmament, 79–80, 129, 184–85, 240–41
Nye, Louis, 184

Oakland: performing in, 126, 431; move to, 392–94
Oak Publications, 253, 255, 269, **313**, 330
Obama, Barack, 66
Obenzinger, Hilton, 396
Ochoa, Amparo, 394
Ochs, Phil, 262, 264–65, 325, 289, 345, 358, 368, 381, **382**
October Crisis (Cuban Missile Crisis), 227, 228
Odetta, 151, 289, 417
Odza, Ted and Mimi, 197
"Oh Freedom," 418
Okinawa, 364–65
"Old Fashioned Love," 161
Oleo Strut, **336**, 337
Olsen, Jack Olshansky, 75–76, 82, 86, 213
Olsen, Tillie, 75–76, 82, 86, 213
On My Way, 206–8, 211–12
"On Your Way Down," 432
opera, 20
Orcas Island Jazz Festival, 407–8
Orchestra Hall, 59

Oregon, 342–44
O'Rourke, Jim, 419
Ortega, Manolo, 300
Ory, Kid, 114, 120, 212, 426
Otero, Lisandro, 301
Owl, The, 364
Oxtot, Dick, 112, 116, 120–21, **121**, 132

Pacifica Foundation, 111, 275, 358. *See also* KPFA
Pacific Coast tour, 189–92, 194
Pacific Counseling Service, 356, 364
Page, Stan, 126
Paley, Tom, 209
Palmer, Earl, 206
Papandreou, Andres, 373–74
Paredon Records, 353–55, **355**, 374–75, 382, 391, 392, 394–97, 402
parents, BD's. *See* Spillman, Dorothy; Spillman, Gilbert
Paris, 371–72
Parker, Francine, 359
Parra, Violeta, 347
Parras, Melinda, 366–68, **366**
Pasadena Jazz Festival, 158–59
Patri, Giacomo, 75
Paul Butterfield Blues Band, 286
Pavageau, Alcide "Slow Drag," 113
PCI (Communist Party of Italy), 345
peace movement. *See* antiwar movements
Peacock, Wazir, 394
Pearl, Ed, 144–47, 155, 174–75, 184, 185, 243
Peery, Carroll, 151, 258, 270–71
People on the Move, 111–12
People's Songs, 34, **35**, 46, 48, 51, 58 62, 73, 253
People's Songs Bulletin, 34, 59
Peraza, Armando, 95
Perea, Margarita, 438
Perenchio, Jerry, 189
Peter, Paul and Mary, 104, 241, 289, 325
Peterson, Steve, 384
Pham Tuyên, 341

Philadelphia Folk Festival, **295**
Philippines, 356, 359, 366–69
Pi de la Serra, Francesc, 350
Pierce, Norman, 88–89
Pietri, Pedro, 381
Pinckney, Mary, 276
Playboy's Penthouse, 181–82, **182**
PM East/PM West, 225, 231
Podolak, Mitch, 407
Polecats, the, 121, **121**
Porco, Mike, 274
Prado, Perez, 95
Prague, 48, 50, 54–55
pregnancies, BD's: with Nicky, 65–66, 67–71; with Paul, 97–101; with Nina, 116–18
presidential election of 1948, 63–66
Press Box Red, 423–24
Prieto, Abel, 434, 435–36
Progressive Party, campaigning for, 63–66
PSP (Puerto Rican Socialist Party), 354
PTSD: Rolf's, 28, 44, 74, 85; Byron's, 96–97, 101, 107
Puebla, Carlos, 300, 302, 321
Puerto Rican Socialist Party (PSP), 354
Purdy, Bob, 37
Purnell, Alton, 113

racism and discrimination, 7–9, 18, 22–23, 25, 32, 37, 40–42, 52–53, 343; in the music industry, 17, 32, 106, 180–81, 189–90. *See also* Detroit: racism and discrimination in
radio appearances, BD's, 111–12, 187–88, 199, 234, 275–76
Radnik, **56**, 57
"Railroad Bill" songs, 109
Rago, Jackie, 418
Raimon (Ramón Pelegero Sanchis), 350
Rainey, Ma, 141–42, 173, 180
Rancho Buri Buri, 82, 84, 87
Rancourt, Kim, 419, 422
Ranghelli, Lucy, Luigi, and Teresa, 360

Raskin, Francesca, 232–33
Reagan, Ronald, 408
Reagon, Bernice, 289, 294–95, **295**, 335
Reagon, Toshi, 294
Real Ambassadors, The, 165–66
Red Nichols and his Five Pennies, 168
Red Scare. *See* anti-communist movement
Red, Tampa, 177, 201
Reid, Clarence, 25
Reinhardt, Stephen, 155–56
Resist, 336–37
Retamar, Roberto Fernández, 301, 438
Rexroth, Kenneth, 89, 91
Rey, Alvino, 46
Reyes, Jorge, 394
Reynolds, Bud, 73, 213
Reynolds, Malvina, 73, 213, 224, 263–64
Reynolds, Nancy, 73
Ribback, Alan, 218
Riffe, Jed, 435, 442
Ritchie, Jean, 285
Ritsos, Yiannis, 347
Robeson, Paul, 19, 40, 102
Robichaux, Jim, 113
Robinson, Big Jim, 113
Robinson, Earl, 59, 61
Rochmes, Adam, 424
Rodney, Lester, 423–24
Rodríguez, Cuca, 323, 331–32, **332**
Rodríguez, Silvio, 298, 440
Romaine, Anne, 294
Romiosini, 347–49, 373–74, 418
Rose, Wally, 163, 240
Rosenberg, Julius and Ethel, 127
Rosmini, Dick, 190
Rossman, Devora, 334–35
Rubin, Jerry, 283
Rushing, Jimmy "Mr. Five by Five," 199–200
Rushton, Ken, 69
Rushton, Roselva, 69, 440

Sahl, Mort, 183–85
Sailes, Jesse, 206
Salán, Juan, 417
"Salvation Army Song, The," 181
Samuels, Louis (Lou), 74, 78, 83, 99, 100–101
Sánchez Manduley, Celia, 313
Sanders, Betty, 59
San Francisco: move to, Hunters Point, 74–76; move to Rancho Buri Buri, 82, 84. *See also* Bay Area music scene/community
San Francisco Folk Music Club, 95
San Francisco Labor School, 92, 105
San Francisco Mime Troupe, 358, 406, 411
San Francisco Records, 131
Santamaría, Haydée, 299, 310, 319
Santana, Adria, 315, **322**, 330–32, 332, 360–61, **361**, 432
Santana, Ivis, 331
Santana, Jimmy, 331
Santana, Rogerio, 323, 331–32, **332**
Santangelo, Michael, 231–33
Sarduy, Pedro Pérez, 301
Sausalito barge concerts, 216–17
Savio, Mario, 272
Schatz, Gert, 30–31
Schatz, Phil, 30–31, 34, 46, 51
Scheelar, Earl, 408
Schonebaum, Judy, **431**
Scobey, Bob, 115, 240
SDS (Students for a Democratic Society), 282
Sea Island Folk Festival, 276–77
Seeger, Anthony, 397
Seeger, Charles, 26
Seeger, Pete, 26, **33**, 34, 46, 51, 59–60, 62, 104, 178, 237–38, 262, 267, 273, 285, 289, 294, 296–97, 345, 381, **382**, 394, 397, 404, 405, 419–21, **420**, 423, **424**
Seeger, Toshi, 51, 267, 404, 423
segregation. *See* racism and discrimination
Sellers, Brother John, 231
sexism, 5, 46, 364, 376–77; in the Beat

community, 90–91
sexual harassment/assault, BD's, 1, 5–6, 12, 19, 67
Seyrig, Delphine, 372
SFJAZZ Center, 438–39, **439**
Shapiro, Ben, 141, 142, 185, 194–95, 235
Shapiro, Mickey, 142
Sharpton, Lee, 116
Shearing, George, 160
Sheer, Anita, 144
Shelter Half, 342, 343
Siegel, Barbara, 179
Silber, Ben, 383
Silber, Fred, 269
Silber, Irwin
  personal life: meeting BD, 51; relationship and domestic life with BD, 253–55, 257, 259–61, 267–71, **268**, 273, 276, 279–80, 382–84, 416, 422–24, 426–27; as a father and stepfather, 269–70, 273, 280–81, **332**; late life, 416, 422–27, **424**; death, 426–27. *See also* Silber, Sylvia
  career: as a director/producer, 59, 237, 273, 289; Folkways Records, 255; Oak Publications, 253, 255, 269, 313, 330; *Sing Out!* magazine, 229, 253, 265, 267, 269, 273, 274, 279, 287–88, 297, 313, 330; *Sing Out!* radio show, 275–76; *The Vietnam Songbook*, 340–41; *The Guardian*, 384; Paredon Records, 354, 391, 394–97; party-building, 391–94; *Frontline*, 392; books, 423–24
  travels: to Cuba, 297–305, 319–20; to Germany, 372; to Paris, 372; to Vietnam, 379–81. *See also countries and cities by name*
  activism, 317, 326, 391–92
Silber, Josh, 269, 313
Silber, Nina, 269
Silber, Sylvia, 230, 255, 260–61, 269, 273
Sill, Lester, 187–88
Simon, George, 161
Simone, Nina, 347, 383
Sims, Joe, 55
Sing-In for Peace in Vietnam, 288–90, **290**
singing/music as activism, 31–34, 42, 43, 51–52, 66, 127, 189, 256–57, 262–66, 282–83, **282**, 284, 319–24, 326, 335, 345, 347, 354–55, 358, 371–75
Sing Out! (magazine), 229, 253, 265, 267, 269, 273, 274, 279, 287–88, 297, 313, 330
Sing Out! (radio show), 275–76
Siqueiros, David Alfaro, 329–30
Skjelbred, Ray, 408, 418
Slim, Magic, 400
Slim, Memphis, 60, 173–74, **175**, 178, 180, 218
Slim, Watermelon, 421, 422
Small, Drink, 335
Smith, Bessie, 119, 134, 141–42, 166, 173, 180, 200, 275
Smith, Stephan, 421
Smithsonian Folkways, 397, 440. *See also* Folkways Records
Smitty's Corner, 174–76, **176**
Smock, Bob, 9

SNCC (Student Nonviolent Coordinating Committee), 262, 294
Socialism: What Went Wrong?, 424, 426–27
social justice. *See* civil rights movement
Songs of Protest: *The Vietnam Songbook*, 419–22
Sonic Youth, 419, 421
SOS (Support Our Soldiers), 337, 339
Southern Folk Cultural Revival, 294–95
Southern Students Organizing Committee (SSOC), 294
Spain, performing in, 350–52
Spann, Otis, 175
Spillman, Dorothy, **2**, 3–5, 15–16, 162, 376; divorce from Gil, 36; personal relationship with and support of BD, 13, 38, 50, 99, 271; marriage to Lou Samuels, 74, 83, 101; marriage to Ambrose Casner, 83; death, 412–14
Spillman, Dotty (Gil's second wife), 226
Spillman, Gilbert: work at the pharmacy, 3–4, 14–15; racism, 8–9, 37; divorce from Dorothy, 36–37; death of Sonny, 39–40; personal relationship with and support of BD, 8–9, 13–14, 25, 37–38, 58, 68–69, 82; divorce from Dotty (second wife), 226; health problems, 37, 226; death, 327–28
Spillman, Julia Anne (Julianne), **2**, 3–4, 39–40, 68, 226, 327–28, 401–2, 413–15
Spillman, Sonny, 3, 36, 39–40
Spivey, Victoria, 274–75
Spivey Records, 275
Spock, Benjamin, 72, 324, 325, 336
Spolestra, Mark, 284
Sproul Plaza, 272
SSOC (Southern Students Organizing Committee), 294
"St. James Infirmary," 407–8

Stallings, Mary, 206
Stanford, Sally, 120
Stanton, P. T., 112–13, 132
Staple Singers, 231, 234
Staples, Mavis, 234, 347
Stars of Jazz, 152, 161
State Department: and travel to Cuba, 296–98, 305; tours: Louis Armstrong European tour, 159–60, 163–66, 181, 349; McGhee/Terry India tour, 127, 165. *See also* World Youth Festival
State Street house (NYC), 381–82, 384, 392
Stecker, Jody, 418
steel mill concert in Cuba, 305–6, **305**
Steffens, Pete, 426–27
Stephenson, Andrew, 175
Stern, Gerd, 216
Stockholm Appeal, 79–80
Strachwitz, Chris, 258–59, 409
Stracke, Win, 59
Strange, Billy, 206
Strong Place house (NYC), 311, 381–82
Stryker, Fran, 26
Student Nonviolent Coordinating Committee (SNCC), 262, 294
Students for a Democratic Society (SDS), 282
Sugar Hill, Home of the Blues, 194–205, **197**, 211, 213–16, 374
"Su nombre es Pueblo," 437
Support Our Soldiers (SOS), 337, 339
Sutherland, Donald, 358, **359**
Sweden, performing in, 394, 411
Swedish Film Institute, 398. See also *Barbara Dane's Amerika*
Sweet Sixteen, 374
Sweet's Ballroom, 95
Sykes, Roosevelt (the Honeydripper), 218–19, **219**

Teagarden, Addie, 167
Teagarden, Jack "Big T," 167–69, **168**

television appearances, BD's: Miss US Television pageant, 92–94, **93**; *Folksville USA*, 94; *Stars of Jazz*, 152; *Timex All-Star Jazz Show*, 160–62, **162**; *Playboy's Penthouse*, 181–82, **182**; *Wake Up and Sing*, 224–25; *PM East/PM West*, 225; *Checkmate*, 225; *Alfred Hitchcock Presents*, 225–26; *The Tonight Show with Johnny Carson*, 230–31; *They Call It Folk Music* and *Folk Songs and More Folk Songs*, 231–34, **232**, **233**; *Hootenanny*, 237–38; in Cuba, 300–301; *Democracy Now!*, 440
Terkel, Studs, 59–60
Terry, Sonny, 125–26, 146, 165, 184, 199, 204, 275
Theodorakis, Mikis, 346–49, **349**, 373–75, 418
They Call It Folk Music and *Folk Songs and More Folk Songs*, 231–34, **232**, **233**
"This Little Light of Mine," 206
Thomas, Elmerlee, 106
Thompson, Butch, 409
Thompson, Era Bell, 179–80
Thornton, Willie Mae "Big Mama," 199
Throw It Away, 241, 428–32
Timex All-Star Jazz Show, 160–62, **162**
Tin Angel, 119–20
Tolk-Watkins, Peggy, 119–20
Tonight Show with Johnny Carson, The, 230–31
Toshiyuki, Tsurumi, 364
Totsie, Grandma, 361, 414
tours, BD's. *See* State Department tours and countries and cities by name
traditional jazz. *See* New Orleans Jazz
travels, BD's. *See* countries and cities by name; *see also* tours
Trey Records, 187–88

Troubadour, 185, 186
"Trouble in Mind," 230
Trouble in Mind, 132–34, **133**, 153, 168, 408
"Trouble Is a Man," 73
Troup, Bobby, 152, 161
Troutt, Rachel, 412–13
Turley, Hattie, 403
Turner, Gil, 262, 294

UAW (United Auto Workers), 43
UC Berkeley, 112, 272, **282**, 283
UCLA, 439–40
UFO (Unidentified Flying Object) coffeehouse, 335–36, 337
UNEAC (Cuban Union of Writers and Artists), 432, 433–35
unions. *See* labor movement
United Auto Workers (UAW), 43
United Hellenic Front, 373
United States Servicemen's Fund (USSF), 341, 356–57, 359
USSF (United States Servicemen's Fund), 341, 356–57, 359
USSR, performing in the, 308, 394, 411, 424

Valdez, Danny, 394
Vallejo, René, 308–9
Vancouver Folk Festival, 406–7
Vanessi's, 123
Vega, Justo, 300
Verve. *See* Folkways Records
Vesuvio, 95
Vietnam, trip to, 379–81
Vietnam Day, 283
Vietnam Songbook, The, 340–41, 379, 419–22, **420**
Vietnam Veterans Against the War (VVAW), 357–58
Vietnam War, 256, 282–83, 284, 290–91, 333, 357–58. *See also* antiwar movements
Viglietti, Daniel, 394
Village Gate, 290

Village Voice, **287**, 340
Vinnegar, Leroy, 171
Vinuesa, María Elena, 432–33
Voices of Liberation, 330
VVAW (Vietnam Veterans Against the War), 357–58

"Wake Up, Wake Up," 224
Wake Up and Sing, 224
Walden, Eleanor, 294
Walker, T-Bone, 199
Wallace, Henry, 63–66
Waller, Fats, 131
Walter, Kermit "Curly," 206–7, 211, 212
Ward, Clara, 180
Washington, DC. *See* March Against the Vietnam War (1965); March on the Pentagon (1967); Moratorium to End the War in Vietnam (1969)
Waters, Muddy, 175–77, **176**, 180
Watkins, Hollis, 394
Watkins, Joe, 113
Watson, Doc, 241
Watters, Lucius (Lu), 114–15, 240
Wayne University, 24–28
Weavers, the, 104, 241, 402
Webster, Ben, 205
Wein, George, 173, 199–200, 340, 384, 407
Weinberg, Jack, 272
Weiss, Max, 126
West, Hedy, 294
Westinghouse TV miniseries, 231–34, **232**, **233**
"We Will Liberate the South," 344, 371
When I Was a Young Girl, 208–11, **210**
When We Make It Through, 394
Whig, The, 356
Whitaker, Hudson "Tampa Red," 201
White, Bukka, 292
Whitson, Kenny, 150, 186, 189–90, 194, 198–99, 203–4, 206–7, 212–15, 417
Williams, Big Joe, 146, 177–78, 219–20

Williams, Jerry "Swamp Dogg," 358
Williams, Link, 266
Williams, Robert Pete, 292
Wilson, Rocco, 206
Wilson, Stan, 145
Winter Soldier Investigation, 357–58
Withers, Jane, 230–31
Witteborg, Lothar, 11
Wolf, Howlin', 292
Wolf, Lou, 356–57
"women's blues," 174, 180
women's movement, 376–78
Wood, Hally, 59
Wood, Jimmy, 263
World Assembly for Peace and Independence of the Peoples of Indochina, 372
World Federation of Democratic Youth, 52, 54, 55
World of Folk Music, 234
World Youth Festival, 48–57, 253

Yancey, Estella "Mama," 177, 180, 201–5, **203**, 293–94, 399–400, 405
Yancey, Jimmy, 177, 204, 294, 399, 400
Yarrow, Peter, **382**. *See also* Peter, Paul and Mary
Yerba Buena Jazz Band, 240
Yoshi's, 431, **431**
Young, Izzy, 265, 274

Zanes, Dan, 419
Zen Oakies, 417
Zinn, Jeff, 335
Zoraida (BD's home helper in Cuba), 433
Zubick, Bob, 11–12

ABOUT THE AUTHOR

BARBARA DANE was born in Detroit in 1927. Encouraged by Pete Seeger, she discovered the power of her voice to move people to action, singing at union functions and on civil-rights picket lines. Moving to San Francisco in 1949, she grew to national recognition as a blues, jazz, and folk singer in the 1950s and 1960s. An early and frequent performer at the legendary Ash Grove in Los Angeles, her swing and unique phrasing caught the ear of jazz aficionados across the country and she soon counted Langston Hughes and Lenny Bruce among her fans and friends. Dane was the first white woman featured in *Ebony* magazine, her work in jazz and blues inspired by Ma Rainey, Bessie Smith, and other Black women singers of the 1920s. Hearing her at the 1958 Pasadena Jazz Festival, Louis Armstrong commented, "Did you get that chick? She's a gasser!" and invited her to appear with him on the *Timex All-Star Jazz* TV special. In 1961, Dane opened her own blues club in San Francisco—Sugar Hill—where she presented Lightnin' Hopkins, Jimmy Rushing, Big Mama Thornton, Mose Allison, Tampa Red, and T-Bone Walker, among others.

Throughout the 1960s and '70s, Dane's presence at civil rights and peace demonstrations across the United States was obligatory. In 1966, she became the first American musician to tour post-revolutionary Cuba. She often sang internationally, including clandestine tours in Franco-era Spain, Marcos's Philippines under martial law, and North Vietnam under the threat of American bombs. In 1970, she cofounded Paredon, a record label dedicated to the voices of the '70s in their worldwide chorus of resistance. In 2022, she was honored with Cuba's national Medal of Friendship.